CAMBRIDGE TEXTS IN THE
HISTORY OF POLITICAL THOUGHT

BOSSUET
*Politics drawn from the Very Words of
Holy Scripture*

CAMBRIDGE TEXTS IN THE HISTORY OF POLITICAL THOUGHT

Series editors
RAYMOND GEUSS *Columbia University*
QUENTIN SKINNER *Christ's College, Cambridge*
RICHARD TUCK *Jesus College, Cambridge*

The series is intended to make available to students the most important texts required for an understanding of the history of political thought. The scholarship of the present generation has greatly expanded our sense of the range of authors indispensable for such an understanding, and the series will reflect those developments. It will also include a number of less well-known works, in particular those needed to establish the intellectual contexts that in turn help to make sense of the major texts. The principal aim, however, will be to produce new versions of the major texts themselves, based on the most up-to-date scholarship. The preference will always be for complete texts, and a special feature of the series will be to complement individual texts, within the compass of a single volume, with subsidiary contextual material. Each volume will contain an introduction on the historical identity and contemporary significance of the text concerned.

For a complete list of titles published in the series, see end of book

JACQUES-BENIGNE BOSSUET

Politics drawn from the Very Words of Holy Scripture

TRANSLATED AND EDITED BY
PATRICK RILEY
Michael Oakeshott Professor of
Political Philosophy,
University of Wisconsin, Madison

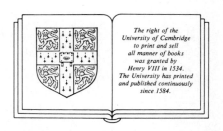

CAMBRIDGE UNIVERSITY PRESS
CAMBRIDGE
NEW YORK   PORT CHESTER
MELBOURNE   SYDNEY

Published by the Press Syndicate of the University of Cambridge
The Pitt Building, Trumpington Street, Cambridge CB2 1RP
40 West 20th Street, New York, NY 10011, USA
10 Stamford Road, Oakleigh, Melbourne 3166, Australia

© Cambridge University Press 1990

First published 1990

Printed in Great Britain at the Bath Press, Avon

British Library cataloguing in publication data
Bossuet, Jacques-Bénigne
Politics drawn from the very words of holy scripture –
(Cambridge texts in the history of political thought).
1. Monarchy. Theories
I. Title II. Riley, Patrick, *1941–* III. Politique tirée
des propres paroles de l'Escriture sainte. *English*
321.6'01

Library of congress cataloging in publication data
Bossuet, Jacques-Bénigne, 1627-1704.
[Politique tirée des propres paroles de l'Escriture sainte.
English]
Politics drawn from the very words of Holy Scripture / Jacques-Bénigne
Bossuet: translated and edited by Patrick Riley.
p. cm. – (Cambridge texts in the history of political
thought)
Translation of: Politique tirée des propres paroles de l'Escriture
sainte.
Includes bibliographical references.
ISBN 0 521 36237 7. –
1. Political science – Early works to 1800. 2. Political ethics.
3. Kings and rulers – Duties. 4. Monarchy. 5. Education of princes.
I. Riley, Patrick, 1941– . II. Title. III. Series.
JC155.B74513 1990
320 – dc20   89–25414   CIP
ISBN 0 521 36237 7 hardback

WV

In memoriam George Armstrong Kelly
1932–1987

Lux perpetua

Contents

Preface	*page* xi
Introduction	xiii
Chronology	lxix
Critical bibliography	lxxi
A note on the text	lxxiv
Biographical synopses	lxxvi

Politics drawn from the Very Words of Holy Scripture	1
Dedication	1

First Book. Of the principles of human society

First Article. Man is made to live in society	3
Article II. The society of mankind gives birth to civil society, that is to say, to states, peoples, and nations	8
Article III. To form nations and unite the people, it is necessary to have a government	14
Article IV. On laws	19
Article V. Consequences of the general principles of humanity	24
Article VI. On the love of country	27
Conclusion. To conclude this book, and to reduce it to an abstract	36

Second Book. On authority: that the royal and hereditary [type] is the most proper for government

First Article. By whom authority has been exercised since the beginning of the world ... 39
Article II [on the right of conquest] ... 52
Conclusion ... 54

Third Book. In which one begins to explain the nature and the properties of royal authority

First Article. Taking notice of the essential characteristics ... 57
Article II. Royal authority is sacred ... 57
Article III. Royal authority is paternal, and its proper character is goodness ... 62

Fourth Book. On the characteristics of royalty (continuation)

First Article. Royal authority is absolute ... 81
Second Article. On softness, irresolution and false firmness ... 96

Fifth Book. Fourth and final characteristic of royal authority

First Article. Royal authority is subject to reason ... 103
Article II. Means by which the prince can acquire necessary knowledge ... 129
Article III. On dangerous curiosities and kinds of knowledge: and on the confidence one must place in God ... 154
Article IV. Consequences of the preceding doctrine: concerning majesty and its adjuncts ... 160

Sixth Book. The duties of subjects toward the prince, based on the preceding doctrine

First Article. On the service one owes to the king 167
Article II. On the obedience due to the prince 173
Article III. Two difficulties drawn from Scripture: David and the Maccabees 184

Seventh Book. On the particular duties of royalty

First Article. General division of the prince's duties 191
Article II. On religion, inasmuch as it is the good of nations and of civil society 192
Article III. That the true religion is known through perceptible marks 196
Article IV. Errors of men of the world and statesmen concerning the affairs and practices of religion 211
Article V. What care great kings have taken for the worship of God 223
Article VI. Religious motives peculiar to kings 244

Eighth Book. The particular duties of royalty, continued: of justice

First Article. That justice is founded on religion 259
Article II. On government which is called arbitrary 263
Article III. On legislation and on judgments 268
Article IV. On the virtues which must accompany justice 273
Article V. Obstacles to justice 281

Ninth Book. The supports of royalty: arms, riches or finances, and counsels

Article I. On war and its just motives, general and particular 287
Article II. On unjust motives for war 293

Article III. On wars between citizens, together with their motives, and the rules which must be followed ... 302
Article IV. Though God made war for his people in an extraordinary and miraculous fashion, he wanted to harden them by giving them warlike kings and great captains ... 315
Article V. On military virtues, institutions, orders, and exercises ... 322
Article VI. On peace and war: various observations on both of them ... 333

Tenth and Final Book. Continuation of helps to royalty: Riches or finances; Counsel; the inconveniences and temptations which accompany royalty: and the remedies that one can bring to them

Article I. On riches or on finances. On commerce, and on taxes ... 345
Article II. On counsel ... 357
Article III. The prince is reminded of different characters of ministers or counselors: good, mixture of good and bad, and wicked ... 371
Article IV. To help the prince to know men well, one shows him, in a general way, some characters drawn by the Holy Spirit in the Books of Wisdom ... 383
Article V. On the conduct of the prince in his family, and on the care he must have for his health ... 389
Article VI and Last. The disadvantages and temptations which accompany royalty, and the remedies that one can bring to them ... 394
Conclusion. In what the true happiness of kings consists ... 409

Index ... 411

Preface

I have, as always, received constant support and excellent advice from two dear old friends: Judith Shklar and George Armstrong Kelly. The sudden death of the latter in December 1987 deprived the learned world of a great Enlightenment scholar, and me of a friend whose loss I regret every day. It is to him that I dedicate this edition of Bossuet's *Politique* – a work which fascinated him, and on which he could have written the definitive commentary. As consolation there are a few fine Bossuet pages in his *Mortal Politics in Eighteenth-Century France* – that extraordinary study of death and dying in French philosophy from Bossuet to Robespierre. If I miss the book he might have written, how much more do I miss the charming, generous, humane scholar who would have given it to us!

The best piece of practical advice I received in preparing this edition came, characteristically, from Judith Shklar – who urged me to view Bossuet not as a conventional Christian political philosopher in the Augustinian or Thomist mode, but as a "Judaizing Calvinist" who tried to "draw" a (not very Christian) politics from Kings and Chronicles. Not until I had finished my edition did I fully appreciate the exactness of her words: as usual, she saw the end when I could only see the beginning. To have such a friend, as generous as she is learned, is a constant joy.

The third person in my trinity of helpers was my wife, Joan A. Riley, whose excellent Catholic education enabled me to see at every turn the unorthodox nature of Bossuet's "orthodoxy." She also typed the entire manuscript and checked all of the Scriptural citations – a labor of love for which I can never be grateful enough.

Preface

My son, Patrick Riley Jr., of the Department of French, University of California, Berkeley, gave me a great deal of help with Book VII of the *Politique* – one of the most difficult, as well as the longest. For that kindness I am most grateful.

I would also like to thank my friend and colleague Theoharis Constantine Theoharis, of the Massachusetts Institute of Technology, who helped me to see the sheer oddity of Bossuet's reading of Judges and 1 Kings. His knowledge of Scripture provided me with many a suggestive hint.

Finally I would like to thank the Bibliothèque Nationale, Paris, which permitted me to see the original manuscript of the first six books of the *Politique* – the only surviving part in Bossuet's hand; and the British Museum – which supplied me with a photocopy of George Keating's 1826 translation of Book I of the *Politics*.

Patrick Riley

Cambridge, Massachusetts

Bastille Day
July 14, 1989

Introduction

I

Jacques-Bénigne Bossuet was born (1627) into a parliamentary family in Dijon which had been horrified by the Fronde, and by the weakening of monarchical authority during the minority of Louis XIV.[1] He was educated by the Jesuits, and had for his mentor Nicolas Cornet – the theologian who later "unmasked" Jansenism (and the "five propositions") as a form of demi-Calvinism in the Sorbonne.[2] After some years as a canon at Metz, his fame as a preacher began to grow: by 1662 he was preaching in Paris before Louis XIV ("On the Duties of Kings"), and in 1675 even served briefly as the King's spiritual counselor. He was named Bishop of Condom in 1669, and then (more importantly) tutor or preceptor to the Dauphin in 1670.[3] For this not

---

[1] For a good account of the life of Bossuet, see Thérèse Goyet, *L'Humanisme de Bossuet* (Paris: Librairie Klincksieck, 1965), Vol. I. One must make allowance for Goyet's claim that Bossuet was a classical humanist steeped in Plato and Aristotle, and for her insistence on his devotion to Descartes. Almost certainly she gives too much prominence to philosophy, ancient and modern, and too little to *l'Ecriture Sainte*. For a briefer but more judicious *vie de Bossuet*, see Jacques Truchet, *La Politique de Bossuet* (Paris: Armand Colin, 1966), pp. 7ff. (Truchet also offers the best-balanced assessment of Bossuet's political thought.)

[2] See the excellent notes to Bossuet's *Oraison funèbre de Nicolas Cornet* (1663), in Bossuet, *Œuvres*, ed. Abbé Velat (Paris: Pléiade, 1961), pp. 1198ff., particularly p. 1199: "Bossuet had been for twenty years the preferred student and the very dear friend of Nicholas Cornet." It was Cornet's unmasking of Jansenism which drove Antoine Arnauld from the Sorbonne, and (much later) from France itself.

[3] See Jacques Le Brun's Introduction to Bossuet, *Politique tirée des propres paroles de l'Ecriture Sainte* (Geneva: Librairie Droz, 1967), p. x. This introduction is valuable if one already knows the argument of the *Politique*.

Introduction

very scholarly youth Bossuet wrote the *Discourse on Universal History*, arguing that human affairs are shaped by divine *Providence particulière* (published in 1681), and the first six books of the *Politics drawn from the Very Words of Holy Scripture* – a *Politique* which he set aside by about 1679 (after describing the work in a long letter to Pope Innocent XI), and did not take up again until 1700.[4]

His tutorship came to an end in 1680, and in 1681 he was made Bishop of Meaux.[5] In the 1680s and 1690s Bossuet emerged as a great controversialist and defender of Catholic orthodoxy: against Luther and Calvin in the *Histoire des Variations*; against Fénelon's "quietism" or "disinterested love of God"; against Malebranche's neo-Cartesian assault on *Providence particulière*; against Richard Simon's "Spinozist" critique of the Old Testament; against Pierre Jurieu's contractarian and popular-sovereignty defenses of French Protestant *émigrés* against the French monarchy; against Leibniz' notion that the whole of Christendom should be charitably reunited while suspending final doctrinal decisions; against Hobbes' privileging of reason over revelation in arriving at monarchical conclusions.

But he was not merely a brilliant opponent and nay-sayer; in a positive vein he supported a moderate version of the "Gallican" thesis that monarchs derive their authority directly from God, not from the Church or the Pope;[6] and he crowned his mature writings with the brilliantly political *Oraisons funèbres* of Queen Marie-Thérèse of France, of Chancellor Le Tellier, of the great Condé, of Anne de Gonzague – his most glowing pages.

Beginning in 1700 he once again took up the *Politique*, little touched for twenty-two years; concurrently he worked on his last great theological statement, the *Défense de la tradition et des pères* – a final tribute to an Augustine saved from Calvinist and Jansenist rigorism. He died in the Spring of 1704, leaving the *Politics* without its closing summary; his nephew, the Abbé Bossuet, filled in the gap with a fragment of Augustine's *City of God*. After some publication difficulties (both political and theological), the posthumous *Politique* finally saw the light of day in 1709.[7]

---

[4] The text of this letter is given in Truchet, *La Politique de Bossuet*, pp. 118–19.
[5] Le Brun, Introduction to Bossuet's *Politique*, p. x.
[6] See A.-G. Martimort, *Le Gallicanisme de Bossuet* (Paris: Editions de Cerf, 1953), *passim*.
[7] These difficulties are recounted in Le Brun, Introduction to Bossuet's *Politique*, pp. xixff.

Introduction

The first six books of this work, finished by 1679, argue that a "general society" of the entire *genre humain*, governed by Christian charity, has given way (after the Fall) to the necessity of politics, law, and absolute hereditary monarchy; that monarchy – viewed as natural, paternal, universal, and divinely ordained (beginning with David and Solomon) – is then defended in Books II–VI.[8] Books VII–X, written in 1700–4, go on to take up the rights of the Church; the distinction between absolutism and arbitrariness; causes of just war; and finance and taxation (*inter alia*). The final section of the final book drives home the distinction between absolutism and arbitrariness with a harrowing account of the monarchical crimes of Saul, Belshazzar and Antiochus; the last words written by Bossuet himself place "the beautiful Psalms of David" in "the hands of pious kings."[9]

The break of twenty-two years in the composition of the *Politique* makes it a little repetitious and diffuse; and only Book V, which draws a parallel between monarchy and divinity (above all in the reign of David), contains a lyrical flight to match the best pages of the *Oraisons funèbres* and the *Histoire universelle*. Even so, the *Politique tirée des propres paroles de l'Ecriture sainte* remains the most extraordinary defense of divine-right absolute monarchy in the whole of French political thought.

II

It is always reasonable to ask: why is a work – such as Bossuet's *Politique* – exactly as it is? ("everything is what it is, and not another thing").[10] Thus Plato's *Republic* is as it is – with its huge middle section given over to education in mathematics and music – because for Plato "harmony" is mathematics (the eternal antidote to Heraclitean flux) made audible, and then an harmonious psyche is "writ large" in the harmonious *polis*, then larger (or largest) in the harmony of the spheres, the *kosmos*. So there is nothing "accidental" in the *Republic*, which views life (including political life) as a set of

---

[8] The original MS of these first six books is now in the Bibliothèque Nationale, Paris, where it bears the number fr. 1810. Le Brun prints (in an appendix) those passages from fr. 1810 which diverge from the published text of 1709.
[9] Bossuet, *Politique*, ed. Le Brun, p. 450.
[10] Bishop Butler's line is cited by G. E. Moore in *Principia ethica* (Cambridge: Cambridge University Press, 1903), facing page.

ever-expanding concentric harmonious spheres, "realizing" changeless mathematical eternity, as one moves from the *psyche* to the *polis* to the *kosmos*.[11] Bossuet's *Politique*, too, is as it is for a reason: but "reason" is not that reason.

Since Bossuet was an ecclesiastic, indeed a bishop, one would expect him to "ground" politics in religion, especially the Christian religion. But there are various ways of doing that; and in the eternal pull between reason and revelation, Bossuet comes down surprisingly firmly on the side of revelation and Scripture. "The constant frequenting of the Bible was the great originality of the Christian culture of Bossuet," writes Jacques Truchet, "for at this time the Catholics read it little enough."[12] Here the natural comparison is with St. Thomas Aquinas, who in the *Summa theologica* lets fragments of Scripture become mere "propositions" or "objections" to be evaluated on their rational merits, and on a footing of equality with other propositions drawn from "the Philosopher," or Cicero, or Roman lawyers such as Ulpian, or Justinian's *Institutes* and *Decretals*. In Thomism Scripture is not privileged; and often enough a saint or a prophet will be overridden by a philosopher or a jurisconsult.[13] One does not find St. Thomas speaking, with Bossuet, of *nôtre faible raison*.[14]

What weighs with Bossuet is reason's insufficiency to establish or reveal the highest things. It is not merely that human beings are ingenious rationalizers, that "reason can do nothing, because each calls reason the passion that transports him."[15] It is that St. Paul in 1 and 2 Corinthians – precisely in Scripture – has revealed reason's limitations; the word reveals the boundaries of the mind. "It is not at all in reasoning that one understands this mystery [of Christianity],"

---

[11] Plato, *Republic*, above all 444d–e: "Justice . . . means that a man must not suffer the principles in his soul to do each the work of some other . . . but that . . . having first attained to self-mastery and beautiful order within himself, and having harmonized these three principles . . . he should then and only then turn to practice." See also *Phaedo* 75d for the link between absolute justice and "absolute mathematical equality."

[12] Truchet, *La Politique de Bossuet*, pp. 15–16.

[13] See particularly the Questions on law in the *Summa* (90–97), in *The Political Ideas of St Thomas Aquinas*, ed. D. Bigongiari (New York: Hafner, 1953), pp. 3ff.

[14] Bossuet, *De la connaissance de Dieu et de soi-même*, in *Œuvres de Bossuet* (Paris: Didot Frères, 1841), vol. I, p. 85.

[15] Bossuet, *Cinquième avertissement aux protestants*, in *Œuvres* (1841 edn), Vol. IV, p. 403. One of the reasons that Bossuet put off finishing the *Politique* was that he had syphoned many of its central thoughts into the *Cinquième avertissement* (1690).

Introduction

Bossuet urges in the *Histoire universelle*; "it is in 'bringing into captivity every understanding unto the obedience of Christ,' it is 'in destroying human reasonings, and every height that exalteth itself against the knowledge of God.'"[16] And in the *Panégyrique de Saint François d'Assise* (1670), he offers a fuller reading of the anti-rationalism of 1 Corinthians: "God, then, indignant at human reason, which had not willed to know him through the works of his wisdom, willed that in future there would be no salvation for reason except through folly."[17]

For Bossuet, as for St. Paul in 1 Corinthians, it is especially Greek philosophy which gives unreasonable weight to *raisonnement*.

> There are errors into which we fall by reasoning, for man often entangles himself by dint of reasoning . . . What have the philosophers gained with their pompous discourses, with their sublime style, with their 'reasonings' so artfully arranged? Plato, with that eloquence which he believed divine – did he overturn a single altar at which monstrous divinities had been adored? . . . Is it not with reason that St Paul cries: "Where is the wise?"[18]

The problem of a "rational" ethics (and politics), however, for Bossuet, is not confined to Plato: in his notes on the *Nicomachean Ethics*, he complains of "the uncertainty of Aristotle's morality," adding that

> there is nothing, however, in which it is more essential to be certain than [on the question] of what ought to be done or not done. So that, if reason does not determine it, it is necessary that the law do so. Now human law cannot regulate the internal forum. Thus a divine law is necessary.[19]

Not that the unhappy effects of maladroit *raisonnement* are limited to antiquity; on the contrary, for Bossuet the great religious crisis of the 1690s – the fratricidal struggle with Fénelon over "quietism" and the "disinterested love of God" – was a clear case of reason's over-

---

[16] Bossuet, *Discours sur l'histoire universelle*, in *Œuvres* (1841 edn), Vol. I, p. 239.
[17] Bossuet, *Panégyrique de Saint François d'Assise*, in *Œuvres* (1961), p. 600. For a fine appreciation of this *panégyrique* (and others like it), see Jacques Truchet, *Bossuet panégyriste* (Paris: Editions du Cerf, 1962), pp. 50–51, 90–94, 118–20.
[18] Bossuet, *Histoire universelle*, in *Œuvres* (1841 edn), p. 239.
[19] Cited in Goyet, *L'Humanisme de Bossuet*, Vol. II, p. 417. For the full text of Bossuet's commentary on the *Ethics, Politics* and *Magna Moralia*, see Thérèse Goyet (ed.), *Platon et Aristote, notes de lectures* (Paris: Librairie Klincksieck, 1964).

Introduction

reaching itself in a way that had unfortunate political implications (since M. de Cambrai had been tutor to the new Dauphin). So obsessed with rationalizing Mme. de Guyon's mystical ecstasies has Fénelon become, Bossuet urges in *Relation sur le quiétisme* (1698/99), that, as at the birth of all such errors,

> cabals and factions stir up; passions and interests divide the world ... Eloquence dazzles the simple; dialectic hurls her lances at them; an exaggerated metaphysics flings minds into unknown lands; many no longer know what they believe, and holding everything in indifference, without understanding, without discerning, they join a party by whim. These are the times that I call those of temptation, if one is searching for obfuscation; and one must await with faith the later time in which truth will triumph and manifestly gain the upper hand.[20]

Here the efforts of reason are pitiable: "dialectic" merely hurls injurious weapons, and *une métaphysique outrée* literally "alienates" (by flinging minds into foreign terrains); but truth finally arrives, conveyed by a "faith" which passes safely through obscurity, cabals, factions, parties, passions, and interests. What is essential is that one avoid "the false philosophy which St. Paul has condemned."[21]

But the truth which post-Pauline reason cannot reveal – including "the truth of monarchy" (to anticipate Hegel's phrase)[22] – can be found in Holy Scripture, which is *un livre parfait*.[23] There is simply nothing to equal "a book as profound and as precise, not to mention as divine, as Scripture."[24] This is why the Preface to Bossuet's *Politique* is as it is, why it begins with a phrase from St. Paul's first letter to Timothy, then spins a world (including a political world) out of extra-rational Revelation.

> God is the King of kings: it is for him to instruct them and to rule

---

[20] Bossuet, *Relation sur le quiétisme*, in *Œuvres* (Pléiade 1961), pp. 1153–54. See also L. Cognet, *Le Crépuscule des mystiques: Le Conflit Fénelon–Bossuet* (Tournai: Desclée, 1958). To be avoided is Raymond Schmittlein's *L'aspect politique du différend Bossuet–Fénelon* (Mainz: Editions Art et Science Bade, 1954), which is merely abusive: Bossuet appears as "un serf ébloui par son souverain, un roturier avide de pouvoir" – unlike the aristocratic Fénelon (p. 25).
[21] Ibid., p. 1176.
[22] Hegel, *Encyclopaedia*, cited and treated in George Armstrong Kelly, *Hegel's Retreat from Eleusis* (Princeton: Princeton University Press, 1978).
[23] Bossuet, *Histoire universelle*, cited in Goyet, *L'Humanisme de Bossuet*, Vol. II, p. 298.
[24] Bossuet, *Cinquième avertissement*, in *Œuvres* (1841 edn), Vol. IV, p. 398.

Introduction

them as his ministers. Listen, then, Monseigneur [le Dauphin], to the lessons which he gives them in his Scripture, and learn from him the examples on which they must base their conduct.

Besides the other advantages of Scripture, it also enjoys this one, that it takes up the history of the world from its earliest origins, and shows us by this means, better than all other histories, the original principles which have formed empires. . . There one sees the government of a people whose legislator was God himself.[25]

In Bossuet's 1679 letter to Pope Innocent XI, describing the first six books of the *Politique*, *la raison* is totally eclipsed by *l'Ecriture*:

We shall uncover the secrets of politics, the maxims of government, and the sources of law, in the doctrine and in the examples of Holy Scripture . . . [which] surpasses, as much in prudence as in authority, all other books which give precepts for civil life, and and . . . one sees in no other place such certain maxims of government.[26]

If rightful politics must be drawn "from the very words of Holy Scripture," it is not surprising to find that the *Politique* gives a priority to Jewish law and institutions that had been much less prominent in the *Histoire universelle*. In the *History* Bossuet had urged that "just as Rome revered the laws of Romulus, of Numa and of the Twelve Tables; just as Athens turned to those of Solon; just as Sparta preserved and respected those of Lycurgus, the Hebrew nation ceaselessly put forward those of Moses."[27] Here four ancient cases are parallel ("just as") and apparently equal. But in the *Politique* one is told that "all that Sparta, all that Athens, all that Rome . . . had by way of wisdom, is nothing in comparison to the wisdom which is contained in the law of God, from which other laws have taken their best features . . . [in ancient Israel one sees] the finest and most just politics that ever was."[28] In the end, then, Greece, Rome, reason, and metaphysics yield to the philo-Judaic penchant which completely colors the *Politics*.

If reason alone – even Scholastic reasoning in the manner of St.

---

[25] Bossuet, *Politique*, ed. Le Brun, p. 1.
[26] Bossuet, *Correspondance*, ed. C. Urbain and E. Levesque (Paris: Hachette, 1909–25), Vol. II, pp. 135ff.
[27] Bossuet, *Histoire universelle*, cited in Goyet, *L'Humanisme de Bossuet*, Vol. II, p. 465.
[28] Bossuet, *Politique*, ed. Le Brun, pp. 1–2.

Introduction

Thomas – will not serve Bossuet's turn, falling back on Scriptural revelation has a double advantage. Positively, it gives a divine historical warrant to absolute monarchy in the style of David and Solomon ("the wisest of all kings"[29]); negatively it deprives Protestants of their principal foundation, individual interpretation of Scripture – if "true" Scripture must be that which is given by an authoritative Church tradition. In preferring revelation to reason, Bossuet defeats enemies on two fronts: he strikes down "rationalists" who will probably turn Cartesian doubt into Baylian Pyrrhonism, and he wrests the Bible back from Luther and Calvin. And a double triumph is doubly satisfying. "Qu'il est beau," Bossuet insists in the *Oraison funèbre d'Anne de Gonzague* (1685), "de méditer l'Ecriture Sainte !"[30] And in the great struggle with Fénelon in the 1690s, the harshest thing Bossuet can say is that M. de Cambrai finds none of his "inventions" in Scripture: "he cites no passages from it whatever to support his new dogmas," and falls back on *une vaine métaphysique*.[31]

It is not merely, however, that reason does not "yield" (out of itself) Israel, monarchy, David, and Solomon ("both excellent in the art of ruling"[32]), or that *raisonnement* can rationalize democracy or aristocracy. The problem is that, in its Cartesian-Malebranchian form, weighty in seventeenth-century France, reason often reduces Scripture to (so-called) "anthropologies," and denies God's *Providence particulière* in favor of "scientific" *généralité*: general laws of nature operating constantly and uniformly[33] – the deism of a physicist. The problem for Bossuet, then, is not undifferentiated "reason," but specifically "Cartesian" (more often Malebranchian) *rationalism*. Reason *à la* Descartes yields the wrong God: not the "King of kings," but the giver of universe-governing general physical laws. But that is not what Bossuet wants; with Pascal (at least on this point), he wants to be able to say: "God of Abraham, God of Isaac, God of Jacob – not of the philosophers and the theologians."[34]

---

[29] Ibid., p. 267.
[30] Bossuet, *Oraison funèbre d'Anne de Gonzague*, in *Œuvres* (1961 edn), p. 135. And reason is subordinated to revelation in a later passage from the same work: "Leur raison, qu'ils prennent pour guide, ne présente à leur esprit que des conjectures et des embarras" (p. 148).
[31] Bossuet, *Relation sur le quiétisme*, in *Œuvres* (1961 edn), p. 1176.
[32] Bossuet, *Politique*, ed. Le Brun, p. 2.
[33] On this point see my *The General Will before Rousseau: The Transformation of the Divine into the Civic* (Princeton: Princeton University Press, 1986), Chs. 1 and 2.
[34] Pascal, "Memorial," cited and treated in Jan Miel's superb *Pascal and Theology* (Baltimore: Johns Hopkins University Press, 1969).

Introduction

All of this becomes clear if one examines Bossuet's violently hostile reaction to Malebranche's *Traité de la nature et de la grâce* – a work that commanded M. de Meaux's attention throughout the 1680s, and which he combated publicly and privately as theologically and politically dangerous. For Malebranche seemed bent on the destruction of all of Bossuet's most cherished convictions – not least the providentialism that supported his politics.

III

In the *Traité de la nature et de la grâce* (1680), Malebranche argues that "God acts by general wills [*volontés générales*] when he acts as a consequence of general laws which he has established." And nature, he adds, "is nothing but the general laws which God has established in order to construct or to preserve his work by the simplest means, by an action [that is] always uniform, constant, perfectly worthy of an infinite wisdom and of a universal cause."[35] God, on this view, does not act by *volontés particulières*, by lawless *ad hoc* volitions, as do "limited intelligences" whose thought is not "infinite." Thus, for Malebranche, "to establish general laws, and to choose the simplest ones which are at the same time the most fruitful, is a way of acting worthy of him whose wisdom has no limits." On the other hand, "to act by *volontés particulières* shows a limited intelligence which cannot judge the consequences or the effects of less fruitful causes."[36]

Even at this point Malebranche's argument, though mainly a theological one, contains some points that could be read "politically" (and which Bossuet would soon see in that light): the general will manifests itself in general laws that are "fruitful" and worthy of an infinite wisdom, whereas particular will is "limited," comparatively unintelligent, and lawless. Malebranche himself, indeed, occasionally politicizes (or legalizes) his argument, particularly in his effort to justify God's acting (exclusively) through *volontés générales*. If "rain falls on certain lands, and if the sun roasts others . . . if a child comes into the world with a malformed and useless head . . . this is not at all because God wanted to produce those effects by *volontés particulières*; it is because he has established [general] laws for the communication of

---

[35] Malebranche, *Traité de la nature et de la grâce*, ed. Ginette Dreyfus, in *Œuvres complètes*, ed. A. Robinet (Paris: Vrin, 1958), Vol. v, pp. 147–48.
[36] Ibid., p. 166.

motion, whose effects are necessary consequences." Thus, according to Malebranche, "one cannot say that God acts through caprice or ignorance."[37] And those who claim that God ought, through special, *ad hoc volontés particulières*, to suspend general natural laws if their operation will harm the virtuous or the innocent, fail to understand that it is not worthy of an infinitely wise being to abandon general rules in order to find a suppositious perfect fit between the particular case of each finite being and a *volonté particulière* suited to that case alone. Those who want God to act, not through *les loix ou les volontés générales*, but through particular wills, simply "imagine that God at every moment is performing miracles in their favor."[38] This partisanship for the particular, Malebranche says, "flatters the self-love that relates everything to itself," and "accommodates itself quite well" to ignorance.[39]

For Malebranche's orthodox and conservative critics, most notably Bossuet, perhaps the most distressing aspect of the theory of divine *Providence générale* was the much-diminished weight and value given to literally read Scripture. In *Nature et grâce* Malebranche urges that "those who claim that God has particular plans and wills for all the particular effects which are produced in consequence of general laws" rely not on philosophy or reason but on the authority of Scripture to "shore up" their "feeling."[40] (The verb and the noun are sufficiently revealing.) But, Malebranche argues, "since Scripture was made for everybody, for the simple as well as for the learned, it is full of *anthropologies*" (italics in the original). Thus Scripture, Malebranche continues, endows God with "a body, a throne, a chariot, a retinue, the passions of joy, of sadness, of anger, of remorse, and the other emotions of the soul"; it even goes beyond this and attributes to him "ordinary human ways of acting, in order to speak to the simple in a more sensible way." St. Paul, in order to accommodate himself to everyone, speaks of sanctification and predestination "as if God acted ceaselessly" through *volontés particulières* to produce those particular effects; even Christ himself "speaks of his Father as if he applied himself, through comparable wills, to clothe the lilies of the field and to preserve the least hair on his disciples' heads." Despite all these "anthropologies" and "as ifs," introduced solely to make God lovable to "even the coarsest minds," Malebranche concludes, one

[37] Ibid., p. 32. [38] Ibid., p. 63.
[39] Ibid., pp. 87–88. [40] Ibid., pp. 61–62.

must use the idea of God (*qua* perfect being), coupled with those non-anthropological Scriptural passages that are in conformity to this "idea," in order to correct the sense of other passages that attribute "parts" to God, or "passions like our own."[41]

To make his own nonreliance on Scripture quite plain, Malebranche omitted any reference at all to the Bible in the original (1680) edition of *Nature et grâce*. (And it was as extraordinary for Malebranche to write a theological work without the Bible as it was for Bossuet to write a politics "drawn from Scripture": an exact inversion of usual expectations.) And when, later, out of prudence, he interpolated a number of Scriptural passages in the *Traité*, he took care to set them off from the 1680 text by labeling the new parts "additions" and having them set in a different type-face. Even in the Scripture-laden version of 1684, then, the authority of *l'Ecriture Sainte* is physically separated from the "idea" of an *être infiniment parfait*.[42]

Indeed, for Malebranche, it is precisely particular will, and not *volonté générale*, that "ruins" Providence. In his *Réponse à une dissertation de M. Arnauld* – and it should be noted that Antoine Arnauld had praised Bossuet's *Histoire universelle* for revealing the "hidden wills" of God, for throwing "light" on the divine *Providence particulière* always operating behind "the human causes of the establishment and decline of great empires"[43] – Malebranche argues that if an insistence on miracles and constant divine *volontés particulières* does not "overturn" Providence, it "at least degrades it, humanizes it, and makes it either blind, or perverse."

> Is there wisdom in creating monsters by *volontés particulières*? In making crops grow by rainfall, in order to ravage them by hail? In giving men a thousand impulses of grace which misfortunes render useless? . . . But all this is nothing. Is there wisdom and goodness in making impious princes reign, in suffering so great a number of heresies, in letting so many nations perish? Let M. Arnauld raise his head and discover all the evils which happen in the world, and let him justify Providence, on the supposition that God acts and must act through *volontés particulières*.[44]

---

[41] Ibid., pp. 61–62.
[42] If one examines the 1684 edition of *Nature et grâce* (Rotterdam: Chex Reinier Leers, 1684), one finds that all the Scriptural additions to the *Urtext* are set in italic type.
[43] Arnauld, *Réflexions philosophiques et théologiques*, in *Œuvres de Messire Antoine Arnauld* (Brussels: Culture et Civilisation, 1967), Vol. XXXIX, pp. 177, 313.
[44] Malebranche, *Réponse à une dissertation de M. Arnauld*, in *Œuvres complètes*, Vol. VI–VII, pp. 591–92.

The middle of that paragraph ("Is there wisdom?") might almost be an attack, *avant la lettre*, on Bossuet's *Politique*.

What distressed Malebranche's critics, but especially Bossuet, was the possibility that divine *généralité* had been extracted from a Cartesian notion of general laws of uniform motion (in physics), and simply grafted onto the idea of Providence. "Just as one has no right to be annoyed by the fact that rain falls in the sea, where it is useless," Malebranche argues, so too one has no right "to complain of the apparent irregularity according to which grace is given to men." Useless rain and useless grace both derive from "the regularity with which God acts"; thus God's grace is "a heavenly rain which sometimes falls on hardened hearts, as well as on prepared souls."[45] This horticultural language likening souls and soils did nothing to dispel the suspicions of traditionalists such as Bossuet that Cartesian "generality" and "uniformity" might be used in radical ways, to the detriment of orthodox teachings about grace and Providence based on Scripture and patristic writings. This kind of suspicion – best expressed by Bossuet himself when he says that he foresees "a great struggle within the Church being prepared in the name of Cartesian philosophy"[46] – was certainly not relieved by Malebranche's insistence that "what Moses tells us in *Genesis* is so obscure" that the world can be explained *à la* Descartes better than any other way.[47] "Obscurity" is no more welcome than "anthropology" or "as if" – particularly to the Bossuet who could open the *Politique* with the claim that Moses was "instructed by divine wisdom," indeed moved by divine "inspiration" to form "the wisest of all empires," to bring it to "the last degree of certainty and perfection."[48] And "instruction" and "inspiration" are divinely imparted *en particulier* to *un particulier*.

When Bossuet first read Malebranche's *Nature et grâce*, he is said to have written "pulchra, nova, falsa" on his published copy; and soon he was expressing his "horror" of Malebranchian *Providence générale*

---

[45] Malebranche, *Nature et grâce*, p. 50.
[46] Bossuet, letter to Marquis d'Allemans (May 1687), cited in Malebranche, *Œuvres complètes*, Vol. XVIII, p. 445.
[47] Malebranche, *Réponse au livre I*, in *Œuvres complètes*, Vol. VI–VII, XVIII, p. 780.
[48] Bossuet, *Politique*, ed. Le Brun, p. 2. For a good assessment of Moses' place in French political thought through Rousseau, see Bronislaw Baczko, "Moïse Législateur . . .," in *Reappraisals of Rousseau*, ed. S. Harvey et. al. (Manchester: Manchester University Press, 1980), pp. 111ff.

in a letter to a fellow bishop.[49] But the decisive, and very public, response came in September 1683 with the rhetorically superb *Oraison funèbre de Marie Thérèse d'Autriche*, pronounced by Bossuet during the funeral of the Queen of France at St. Denis, in the presence of the Dauphin and of the court. The central passage of this remarkable funeral oration (which was quickly published) is clearly and obviously aimed at Malebranche's "general" Providence.

> What contempt I have for those philosophers who, measuring the counsels of God by their own thoughts, make him the author of nothing more than a certain general order, from which the rest develops as it may! As if he had, after our fashion, only general and confused views, and as if the sovereign intelligence could not include in his plans particular things, which alone truly exist.[50]

Bossuet loses no time in drawing a political moral from this particularism: God has "ordained," in all nations, *les familles particulières* who ought to govern those nations, and, still more *en particulier*, he has ordained the precise persons within those families who will help a ruling house "to rise, to sustain itself, or to fall." Since "it is God who gives great births, great marriages, children, and posterity," it is certainly God who particularly gave Queen Marie-Thérèse to Louis XIV and France. Bossuet supports this claim with numerous Old Testament citations, particularly Genesis 17:6, where God tells Abraham that "kings will come out of thee."[51] (In the *Politique* Book VII, added to the manuscript in 1700, Bossuet generalizes all of this into the claim that "there is a *Providence particulière* in the government of human affairs," and that France benefits from *la protection particulière de Dieu sur ce royaume*.)[52]

He does not hesitate to use the language of grace to reinforce this political particularism. God, he argues, has "predestined" from all eternity the world's political "alliances and divisions"; by giving France a Habsburg queen through *une grâce particulière*, he has drawn together Austrian counsel and French courage (which are the *caractères particuliers* of those nations), much as he earlier gave the virtue of clemency to the kings of Israel. Theological notions are piled up to

---

[49] Bossuet, letter to Neercassel (June 1683), in Malebranche, *Œuvres complètes*, Vol. XVIII, pp. 248–49.
[50] Bossuet, *Oraison funèbre de Marie-Thérèse d'Autriche*, in *Œuvres* (1961 edn), p. 110.
[51] Ibid., pp. 110, 1238nn.
[52] Bossuet, *Politique*, ed. Le Brun, pp. 278, 59.

Introduction

particularly striking effect in a passage that begins by lamenting the "rarity" of purity in men, but more especially in "the great."

> And nonetheless it is true, Messieurs, that God, through a miracle of his grace, has been pleased to choose, among kings, some pure souls. Such was St Louis [IX], always pure and holy since childhood; and Marie-Thérèse, his daughter, [who] received this fine inheritance from him. Let us enter, Messieurs, into the plans of Providence, and let us admire the goodness of God . . . in the predestination of this princess.[53]

Here, of course, grace is a "miracle," and therefore precisely *not* something general; the queen is particularly "predestined" to rule.[54] (Why not turn to good political account a theological notion that Calvin had made problematical?) To be sure, such rule was not the queen's chief attribute; what really mattered was her piety. "She tells you," Bossuet insists, "through my mouth . . . that greatness is a dream, that joy is an error, that youth is a flower that withers, and that health is a deceiving name." Nonetheless he ends by admonishing the Dauphin, his old pupil, to ask God – "as Solomon did" – for the wisdom that will make him worthy of the throne of his ancestors.[55] And "asking," of course, supposes a *Providence particulière* that can intervene in human affairs to *give* what is asked for.

Bossuet actually sent a copy of the published version of this *Oraison funèbre* to Malebranche, who felt constrained to thank the bishop for his thoughtful gift.[56] Bossuet's criticism of "Cartesian" *Providence générale* was not always so public, however; indeed the fullest of his refutations is to be found in a 1687 letter to the Malebranchian Marquis d'Allemans. "I notice in you," Bossuet tells the Marquis, "nothing but an attachment which grows every day more blind to your patriarch" – though his "ridiculous" theory of nature and grace is "a perfect *galimatias*."[57]

To be more exact, in Bossuet's view, Malebranche does not really

---

[53] Bossuet, *Oraison funèbre de Marie-Thérèse*, pp. 109–11.
[54] Ibid., pp. 109–11. Bossuet's willingness to use theological notions for political ends can even now seem startling.
[55] Ibid., p. 133.
[56] Ginette Dreyfus, Introduction to Malebranche's *Nature et grâce* (1680 edn) (Paris: Vrin, 1958), pp. 127ff. ("l'opposition commune de Bossuet et de Fénelon").
[57] Bossuet, Letter to d'Allemans, p. 444.

Introduction

offer nature *and* grace at all: he offers just nature, and grace vanishes. It is bad enough, M. de Meaux complains, that Malebranche prides himself on having "explained Noah's Flood through the operation of natural causes": but if d'Allemans continues to follow this "infallible doctor" he will "lead you to find, in these same causes," the Israelites' passage through the Red Sea, as well as all other Scriptural "marvels of this kind." If one means by natural causality the "effects which happen through the force of the first laws of movement," then Malebranchian generality will finally "render everything natural, even to the resurrection of the dead and the healing of those born blind."[58]

Much of this "heresy" (as Bossuet does not hesitate to call it) arises from misunderstanding the Cartesian method of doubt:

> For on the pretext that one should admit only what one clearly understands – which, within certain limits, is quite true – each person gives himself freedom to say: I understand this, I do not understand that; and on this sole foundation, one approves or rejects whatever one likes . . . Thus is introduced, under this pretext, a liberty of judging which involves advancing with temerity whatever one thinks, without regard for tradition.[59]

This clearly refers to Malebranche's notion that one must conceive God through the idea of an *être parfait*, and not through Scriptural "anthropologies." But this preference for "ideas" given by reason, this contempt for authoritative tradition, leaves Bossuet "terrified" and fearful of "great scandal": heretics, he says, always "begin with novelty," move on to "stubbornness," and end with "open revolt."[60]

Bossuet concludes his letter to d'Allemans – spoken, he says "as one does to a friend" – with a final, chilling remark about thinking that one can do theology because reason provides knowledge of "physics and algebra"; and he reminds Malebranche's disciple that one cannot favor both Malebranchian *Providence générale* and Bossuet's own *Histoire universelle* (which d'Allemans had praised).

> It is easy for me to show you that the principles on which I reason are directly opposed to those of your system . . . There is a great difference in saying, as I do, that God leads each thing to the end which he proposes for it by the means which he [actually] follows, and in saying that he contents himself with giving some general

---

[58] Ibid., p. 444.   [59] Ibid., p. 445.   [60] Ibid., p. 446.

Introduction

laws, from which result many things which enter only indirectly into his plans . . I turn away from your ideas of general laws.[61]

Bossuet was perfectly right, of course, in characterizing his own *Histoire universelle* as a work built on *Providence particulière*, not on general laws. "Remember, Monseigneur," Bossuet admonishes the Dauphin at the end of the *Histoire*, "that this long chain of particular causes, which make and unmake empires, depends on the secret decrees of divine Providence." It is God who "holds the reins of every kingdom and holds every heart in his hands." His action, moreover, in shaping universal history, is completely particular: "Should he wish to see a conqueror, he will spread terror before him . . . should he wish to see legislators, he will send them his spirits of wisdom and foresight."[62] Bossuet – after virtually anticipating Hegel's "cunning of history" by urging that, thanks to secret Providence, rulers "achieve either more or less than they plan," and that "their intentions have always led to unforeseen consequences"[63] – concludes with an apotheosis of *Providence particulière* that Montesquieu must have had in mind (if only to oppose it through Malebranchian *généralité*) when he wrote *Considerations on the Greatness and Decline of the Romans* fifty years later.[64]

> Thus God reigns over every nation. Let us no longer speak of coincidence or fortune; or let us use those words only to cover our ignorance. What is coincidence to our uncertain foresight is concerted design to a higher foresight, that is, to the eternal foresight which encompasses all causes and all effects in a single plan. Thus all things concur to the same end; and it is only because we fail to understand the whole design that we see coincidence or strangeness in particular events.[65]

Since Bossuet wants to argue in the *Politique* that modern France

---

[61] Bossuet, letter to d'Allemans, p. 447.
[62] Bossuet, *Discours sur l'histoire universelle*, in *Œuvres de Bossuet* (Versailles: J. A. Lebel, 1818), Vol. xxxv, p. 556.
[63] Ibid., p. 556.
[64] Montesquieu, *Considerations on the Causes of the Greatness of the Romans and their Decline*, Ch. 18: "It is not chance that rules the world . . . There are general causes, moral and physical, which act in every monarchy, elevating it, maintaining it, or hurling it to the ground . . . the main trend draws with it all particular accidents" (trans. D. Lowenthal [Ithica: Cornell University Press, 1968], p. 169.
[65] Bossuet, *Histoire universelle*, in *Œuvres* (1818 edn), p. 557.

Introduction

enjoys "*la protection particulière de Dieu*,"[66] it is essential to be able to show that the Fronde – *the* great political trauma of Bossuet's lifetime – rose and fell not through natural *généralité* but through supernatural *Providence particulière*. In the *Oraison funèbre d'Anne de Gonzague* (1685), Bossuet begins with a vivid sketch of the Fronde period:

> What do I see during this time? What trouble! What a horrifying spectacle presents itself to my eyes – the monarchy shaken to its very foundations, civil war, foreign war, fire within and without; the remedies on every side more dangerous than the evils themselves; princes arrested with great danger, and set free with a still greater danger; a prince [Condé] who was regarded as the hero of his age, made useless to his country.[67]

Is all of this to be explained through "Cartesian" general natural laws? By no means. "What shall I say? Was all of this one of those tempests that heaven must sometimes discharge, and did the profound calm of our times have to be preceded by such storms?"[68] A Malebranchian might be struck by such "naturalism," but not Bossuet (who does not find lightning enlightening). Nor will other facets of nature do: "Was this like France in labor, ready to give birth to the miraculous reign of Louis?"[69] Even that does not suffice; the real truth is that, through *Providence particulière*, "God . . . wanted to show that he brings death, and that he brings resurrection; that he plunges all the way to hell, and then withdraws; that he saves the earth and breaks it, and that he heals in a moment all these wounds."[70] "Tempests" and labor-pains are only natural phenomena; since Louis's reign is precisely "miraculous," it is a particular exception to mere general laws. What God "graciously" does is not a mere echo of "Cartesian" physics.

Despite Bossuet's self-representation as a traditionalist, it is fair to note that his *particularisme* is, in its own way, as radical as "Cartesian" *généralité* – radical with respect to charity as the heart of the Christian *ethos*. "Though I speak with the tongues of men and of angels, and have not charity, I am become as sounding brass or a tinkling cym-

---

[66] Bossuet, *Politique*, ed. Le Brun, p. 59.
[67] Bossuet, *Oraison funèbre d'Anne de Gonzague*, cited in Truchet, *Politique de Bossuet*, p. 203.
[68] Ibid., p. 204.   [69] Ibid., p. 204.   [70] Ibid., p. 204.

Introduction

bal," St. Paul had said. "Faith, hope, charity, these three: but the greatest of these is charity."[71] But Bossuet's particularism is even permitted to modify (what one might call) the "generality" of charity, as something owed universally to "all men."

In an unpublished part of the original manuscript of the *Politique*, Book I article v – written at the very time that Bossuet was becoming familiar with Malebranchism – he begins by saying that "to have a true idea of human society one must first think that the whole human race *en général* is a great family," indeed that "the common society and the love that all men owe each other exists always," despite the formation of particular "nations"; but he moves quickly to the notion that "the distance between places and other reasons not permitting that this love be practiced towards all, each [person] must practice it towards those who are conjoined to him by particular ties [*par des liens particuliers*]."[72] Charity, then, both begins and ends at home:

> There is the true spirit of charity, which, embracing all men, and ready to extend itself to all of them, attaches itself . . . with a more particular care to those who are presented to it by particular connections and occasions [*par des liaisons et des occasions particulières*].[73]

The title of the very next section (article 6) of Book I, revealingly, is: "On the love of the fatherland."[74] Here love has become very *particulière* indeed. And it is worth noticing that the *Politique*, nearly half of whose five hundred pages are devoted to *verbatim* citation of Scripture, never quotes, even once, or even refers to I Corinthians 13 – "but the greatest of these is charity."[75] Indeed it is no accident that, in connection with "drawing" divine-right absolute monarchy "from the very words of Holy Scripture," Bossuet should have found the Old Testament (with its stress on monarchy and law) much more usable than the New (with its insistence on universal charity).

It is with good reason, then, that Jacques Truchet – the best and most balanced commentator on Bossuet's politics – correctly says that

---

[71] St. Paul, I Corinthians 13.
[72] Bossuet, *Politique*, excerpts from the original MS of 1679, pub. in Le Brun edn, p. 455.
[73] Ibid., p. 455.
[74] Ibid., p. 33.
[75] Le Brun's table of Scriptural citations, an appendix to his edition of the *Politique*, shows no reference whatever to I Corinthians 13.

it has not been sufficiently noticed [that] this politics "drawn from the very words of holy Scripture" is drawn essentially from [the books] of the Old Testament. Not that the author wanted to limit himself to it; but the Old Testament presents a series of historical books, as well as a mass of precepts touching on institutions, justice, government, war, etc., while the New offers only a few such texts to be considered. From this results the fact that the perusing of Scripture from a political viewpoint necessarily yields a book whose tone is scarcely evangelical.[76]

Bossuet, Truchet urges, felt this imbalance; and it led him to undertake "correctives" to propositions which were too harsh. For example, Bossuet first cites – under the heading, "there are ways of securing vanquished peoples" – several particularly horrifying examples of these "ways" used by the Jewish nation ("David . . . wanted to make an example [of the Ammonites] which would leave on this people an eternal impression of terror that would take away their courage for fighting: and he passed over their bodies, in all their cities, chariots armed with knives"). He then adds: "One can subtract from this severity that which the spirit of gentleness and of clemency inspires in the new law, for fear that we will be told, as were [Christ's] disciples who wanted to strike down everything: 'You do not know the spirit of which you are made.' A Christian conqueror must spare blood, and the spirit of the Gospel on this point is quite different from that of the law."[77] But why, then, as Truchet reasonably asks, "begin by elaborating so much on the severity of the law? A too-literal exegesis is at the root of it."[78] And the result is that, in Bossuet, the "new" law of love merely *modifies* harsh or murderous examples "drawn" from Judges and Kings.

To be sure, in the published version of the *Politique* one is told that there is (or more accurately once was) a charity-governed *société générale du genre humain* – before the Fall and the advent of the "passions"; after the Fall, the stress is on *des états particuliers*.[79] On this point, not astonishingly, Bossuet's theology is politically repli-

---

[76] Truchet, *Politique de Bossuet*, pp. 29–30. Truchet achieves more in fifty pages than most book-length studies.
[77] Ibid., pp. 29–30.
[78] Ibid., p. 30.
[79] Bossuet, *Politique*, ed. Le Brun, Book I.

Introduction

cated. In his magisterial *Défense de la tradition et des pères* we learn that before the Fall God willed generally to save "all men," but that in the post-lapsarian period he willed *en particulier* to save the Christian few.[80] For Bossuet both God and society move, in tandem, from the *générale* to the *particulière*: from *volonté générale* (in God) and *société générale* (in men) to *Providence particulière* and particular monarchies. In both of these parallel operations, love pitches her tent in an ever-smaller area.

Here a comparison with Leibniz may be instructive. If Leibniz – Bossuet's great contemporary and correspondent – could define justice as *caritas sapientis*, the "charity of the wise" ("charity must prevail over all other considerations in the world"[81]), Bossuet was too fearful of ordinary human post-lapsarian motivation to let justice be so defined. If, indeed, for Bossuet, charity and wisdom were fully in place, no politics would be necessary. But the chasm between charity and *l'esprit du monde* is what strikes Bossuet: "the character of the Christian is to love all men, and not to fear being hated by them; thus the spirit of fraternal charity forms the particular character of the Christians." Lamentably enough, however, "the spirit of the world, quite different from that of the Christian, encloses four kinds of spirits which are diametrically opposed to charity: the spirit of resentment, the spirit of aversion, the spirit of jealousy, the spirit of indifference. There is the progress of evil."[82] And monarchies ("Christian" as they may be) are in, and of, *le monde*. Bossuet seems (as it were) to push charity back, before the Fall: it has little present weight in politics. He cannot deny St. Paul's "the greatest of these is charity," or Christ's "a new law I give unto you." But he can diminish charity by locating it principally in a pre-lapsarian Eden. It still, of course, has a present *regulative* role: Bossuet eloquently denounces the uncharitable *mauvais riche* in a sermon delivered at the Louvre

---

[80] Bossuet, *Défense de la tradition et des pères*, in *Œuvres complètes de Bossuet* (Bar-le-Duc: Louis Guérin, 1870), Vol. v, p. 324. Following St. Augustine, Bossuet urges that, if all men are not saved, the obstacle comes not at all "from the *volonté* of God, which is *générale*," but from the refractory will of man. See also Theodore Delmont, *Bossuet et les Saints-Pères* (Geneva: Slatkine, 1970 [reprint]), pp. 590ff.

[81] Leibniz, letter to Mme. de Brinon (1694), in *Die Werke von Leibniz*, ed. Onno Klopp (Hanover: Klindworth Verlag, 1864–84), Vol. vii, p. 296. For a full treatment of Leibniz' *caritas sapientis*, see my *Leibniz: Political Writings*, 2nd edn (Cambridge: Cambridge University Press, 1988), pp. 3ff.

[82] Bossuet, "La charité fraternelle," in *Pensées chrétiennes et morales*, in *Œuvres* (1841 edn), Vol. iv, p. 769.

Introduction

before the King himself, thereby reminding us of his admiration for St. Vincent de Paul.

> Know that the oppression of the weak and the innocent is not the whole crime of those who are cruel. The evil rich man brings us to recognize that in addition to that furious ardor which stretches out its hand to do violence, cruelty also enjoys that hardness which closes the ears to pleas, the entrails to compassion, and the hands to lending aid. It is, Messieurs, this harshness that creates thieves who take away nothing, and murderers who spill no drop of blood . . . Yes, Messieurs, there are some who are dying of hunger on your lands, in your castles, in your cities, in the countryside, at the gate or in the vicinity of your palaces: no one runs to their aid. Alas! They ask of you only what is superfluous, some scraps from your table, some remains of your great outlay.[83]

To be sure, Bossuet softens this boldness by carefully saying that "in the sight of so just a king, such inhumanities would never dare to appear"[84] – since he wants to balance charity and monarchy, St. Paul and St. Louis; but he has described their actual appearance with his usual eloquence. What he never does, however, in the manner of Leibniz, is to suggest the "institutionalizing" of charity through the foundation of academies and universities, schemes for the improvement of agriculture and commerce – plans that Leibniz drew up by the dozen.[85] Bossuet's method is to shame the great, through overwhelming oratorical power, into doing . . . what in fact they never did.

Bossuet, then, on the whole, finds the Old Testament *ethos* of monarchy and law more politically useful than the "new law" of love. Sometimes, nonetheless, for all the fact that Book I of the *Politique* opens with the phrase, "Ecoute, Israël," Bossuet can be ferociously hard on the ancient Jews. In Book II of the *Histoire des variations* he says, apparently approvingly:

> St Augustine establishes, following St Paul, that one of the differences between Christian justice and that of the [Jewish] law, is that the justice of the law is based on the spirit of fear and terror,

---

[83] Bossuet, *Sermon du mauvais riche*, cited in Truchet, *Politique de Bossuet*, pp. 216–18. See also Jacques Truchet, *La prédication de Bossuet* (Paris: Editions de Cerf, 1960), Vol. I, pp. 281ff.
[84] *Sermon du mauvais riche*, p. 216.
[85] See the editor's Introduction to *Leibniz: Political Writings*, pp. 24–26.

Introduction

instead of which Christian justice is inspired by a spirit of joy and of love.[86]

And he says something still less charitable in the *Histoire universelle*. After urging that the seventy-year Babylonian Captivity was only a "shadow" of Titus' permanent ruin of the Jews, he goes on to say that

> Titus, enlightened enough to recognize that Judaea was perishing by a manifest effect of God's justice, did not know what crime God had willed to punish so terribly. It was the greatest of all crimes, a crime unheard of till then, that is to say, that of deicide – which also gave rise to a vengeance of which the world had not seen such an example... There is the story of the Jews. They persecuted their Messiah, in his own person and in that of his followers; they stirred up the world against his disciples; they did not leave them at rest in any city; they armed the Romans and the emperors against the nascent Church; they stoned St Stephen, killed the two Jameses (whose holiness made them venerable even among them); they immolated St Peter and St Paul by the sword and by the hands of the Gentiles. It was necessary that they perish. So much blood, mixed with that of the prophets whom they massacred, cried out for vengeance before God.[87]

But more often, and more characteristically, Bossuet wants to establish *continuity*: to stress, in Christ's case, not his "new" insistence on charity, but his royal descent from the house of David. In this vein Bossuet wants to urge that the Church is the successor to the synagogue ("Jesus Christ . . . had begun, in the womb of the synagogue, to build his Church, which was to last eternally"[88]), that there is an unbroken line from St. Peter to Christ to David to Moses to Abraham to Adam to God – all of them (in some sense) "kings." "It is in Jesus Christ, son of David and of Abraham, that all the nations were to be blessed and sanctified."[89]

In this more typical vein stressing unbroken continuity – and Protestantism represents (*inter alia*) discontinuity, a new "division" like that of Roboam in the Old Testament – Bossuet argues in the *Histoire universelle* that the Church is a "perpetual miracle" which goes back

---

[86] Bossuet, *Histoire des variations des églises protestantes*, in *Œuvres* (1841 edn), Vol. IV, p. 47. This is sometimes viewed as Bossuet's finest single work.
[87] Bossuet, *Histoire universelle*, in *Œuvres* (1841 edn), Vol. I, p. 227.
[88] Bossuet, *Conférence avec M. Claude*, in *Œuvres* (1841 edn), Vol. I, p. 550.
[89] Bossuet, *Histoire universelle*, in *Œuvres* (1841 edn), Vol. I, p. 238. The shift in tone from ten pages earlier is astonishing.

Introduction

to Jesus Christ, "in whom she brought together the succession of the ancient peoples, and found herself reunited with the prophets and the patriarchs." And he goes on in this more conciliatory tone to say that

> the books of the Old Testament [are] . . . the most ancient books there are in the world . . . are the sole ancient ones in which knowledge of the true God was taught, and his worship ordained . . . the books which the Jewish people have always so religiously guarded, and of which they are still today the inviolable bearers throughout the world.[90]

The sacred books of the Egyptians and the Romans, the mysteries of Numa, have "perished," Bossuet adds, but "the Jews are the only ones whose sacred Scriptures" have been preserved. Stressing continuity again (by urging that "Christ was sent by his Father to fulfil the promise of the law"), Bossuet finally says:

> It was thus that the body of Holy Scripture was formed – the Old as much as the New Testament: Scriptures which have been regarded, since their beginning, as true in everything, as given by God himself, and which have been preserved with so much religiousness that no one thought himself able, without impiety, to alter a single letter.
>
> It is thus that they have come down to us, always holy, always sacred, always inviolable; some preserved by the steadfast tradition of the Jewish people, the others by the tradition of the Christian people.[91]

In this remarkable passage, unbroken continuity matters more than the difference between the "old" and the "new" law – even if Bossuet himself has followed Augustine in drawing a line between "fear and terror" and "joy and love." This is undoubtedly why Bossuet cites St. Paul's letter to the Romans 13 – "let every soul be subject unto the higher powers" – no fewer than twenty-two times in the *Politique*, but 1 Corinthians 13 not once.[92] (If Bossuet privileges revelation over reason, it is nonetheless his reason that reveals the parts of Scripture that are to have decisive weight.) And his search for "royal" continuity between the parts of Scripture, at the expense of "new" law, sacrifices charity to monarchy in a way that is at least as radical as anything conceived by the "Cartesian" Malebranche.

[90] Ibid., pp. 248–49.   [91] Ibid., pp. 248–49.   [92] See n. 75, above.

Introduction

IV

It is worth stressing the fact that Bossuet's providentialist particularism flows logically out of his theology – unless one inverts this and holds that the theology is an *ex post facto* rationalization or "reflection" of the politics. Bossuet's providentialism, then, isn't there just to "justify" Louis XIV *en particulier*; his providentialism does this in effect, but was not (apparently) designed for this purpose.

Above all, for Bossuet, a "Cartesian" *Providence générale* cannot explain what God does in particular, in virtue of *une Souveraineté aussi universelle et aussi absolue* – as the *Traité du libre arbitre* makes clear.

> It is useless, in explaining [divine] prescience, to place in God a general concourse whose action and effect are determined by our liberty. For neither a concourse so understood, nor the will to establish it, have determined anything, and in consequence do not serve at all in explaining how God knows particular things [*les choses particulières*]; such that, to establish the universal prescience of God, he must be given means which are certain, by which he can turn our will to all the particular effects which it may please him to ordain... For he, whose knowledge and will always yield the ultimate precision in all things, does not content himself with willing that they be *en général*, but he descends... to that which is most particular.[93]

For Bossuet, providentialist particularism must not (mistakenly) take the form of Protestant fatalism: human freedom must be made congruent with divine Providence (in the more-or-less Thomistic way suggested by Bossuet's *Traité de libre arbitre*). One must somehow avoid both "Pelagianism" – which only lets God "concur" in radically free human actions – and Calvinism.

> Let us recognize, then, in the Reformation – I say in the two parts, and as much in Calvinism as in Lutheranism – that false and dangerous science which, to show that it understands the highest mysteries of God, has found in his immutable decrees the ruin of human free will, and at the same time the extinction of the regrets of conscience.[94]

---

[93] Bossuet, *Traité du libre arbitre*, in *Œuvres* (1841 edn), Vol. I, p. 108.
[94] Bossuet, *Deuxième avertissement aux protestants*, in *Œuvres* (1841 edn), Vol. IV, p. 326.

Introduction

One must beware "the shipwreck of the Calvinist, who, to maintain the prescience and the Providence of God, takes from man the liberty of choice, and makes God the necessary author of all human events . . . [Calvinism] breaks against the rocks."[95]

All of these considerations lead to what Bossuet takes to be the only coherent reconciliation of particular Providence and human freedom; and in the *Traité du libre arbitre* he insists that

> we conceive God as a being who knows all, who previews all, who provides for everything, who governs everything, who makes what he will of his creatures, [a being] to whom all the world's events must be related. If free creatures are not included in this order of divine Providence, one deprives him of the conduct of what is most excellent in the universe, that is, intelligent creatures. There is nothing more absurd than saying that he does not interfere with the governance of nations, the establishment or the ruin of states, how they are governed, and by which laws.[96]

The link (or a link) between Bossuet's providentialist particularism and the (politically correct) reading of Scripture is this: if one sees that the case of the Maccabees (for example) is *tout particulier* (to recall Bossuet's phrase from the *Cinquième avertissement aux protestants* [1690])[97] – then Pierre Jurieu, as Protestant mouthpiece, cannot get away with "finding" a precedent for Protestant revolt against Catholic authority "in" the Old Testament. If God really does everything radically *en particulier*, then nothing is a "general" precedent which can be used later in a "parallel" case. For precedent supposes subsuming a new particular case under an old general rule.

In the *Cinquième avertissement*, Bossuet says that

> I maintain that the action of the Maccabees, and of the Jews who followed them, being extraordinary and coming from a special order of God in a particular case and state of affairs, cannot be used consequentially for other cases and other conditions [e.g. the revolt of the Protestant Netherlands against Catholic Spain]. In a word, there is nothing comparable between the Jews of that time and our reformed ones . . . For in the Christian religion

---

[95] Ibid., p. 326.
[96] Bossuet, *Traité du libre arbitre*, pp. 117ff.
[97] Bossuet, *Cinquième avertissement aux protestants*, in *Œuvres* (1841 edn), Vol. IV, pp. 388–90.

there is not the slightest place or race that one is obliged to preserve, on pain of letting religion and the covenant perish.[98]

After describing the particular case of the Maccabees in great detail, Bossuet goes on to urge that "it was too clear that this example was extraordinary, a case and a condition which was *tout particulier*, manifestly divine in its effects and in its causes: such that, to make [present] use of this example, one would have to be able to say and show that one was manifestly and particularly inspired by God." As for "generalizing" and updating this highly particular case, Bossuet will not have it: "however devoted to the House of Orange one may be, no one will ever seriously say that William I, prince of Orange, was a man manifestly inspired, a Phineas, a Mathathias, a Judas Maccabeus."[99]

And in this same connection, indeed on the same page, Bossuet adds that, since the Maccabees were ordered by God, *en particulier*, to preserve themselves – but no one else is so ordered, so there is no general rule – "the Church, persecuted by infidel or heretical princes, was never inspired by the example of the Maccabees to animate itself to resistance."[100] And what the Church never did *en général*, the Protestants cannot now do *en particulier*. On the contrary, for Bossuet, the "spirit" of Christianity is that of passive obedience to public power; and this passivity he claims to find in St. Augustine. According to this greatest Church Father, Bossuet urges, Christ left to his disciples "no power and no force whatever against the public power, when they were oppressed with as much injustice and violence as was Jesus Christ himself."[101]

From all of these particularities, a general conclusion emerges: in Bossuet, as in Jurieu and others, the ostensible subject of an argument is not always the real one; there is (what one might call) a "method of indirection," in which one seems to be talking directly about (say) the post-Solomonic division of the tribes of Israel, the breaking up of greater Israel into Judah and Israel beginning with Roboam, and so forth – but one is really talking (indirectly) about the Protestant "division" within the Church.

The Maccabees stand in for the Dutch, revolting against Catholic Spain; David *contra* Saul is "really" Protestant resistance against

---

[98] Ibid., p. 389.   [99] Ibid., p. 389.   [100] Ibid., p. 389.
[101] Bossuet, *Défense de l'histoire des variations*, in *Œuvres* (1841 edn), Vol. IV, p. 418.

Introduction

Louis XIV. More is at stake than mere Scriptural exegesis (not that Bossuet was unconcerned with that); political controversy is masked as Scriptural "interpretation." The whole business becomes astonishingly oblique: but the heat and the anger are supplied by the "real" subject.[102]

For Bossuet, Jurieu's "prodigious abuse" of Scripture shows how important it is that the Word be correctly – traditionally and authoritatively – interpreted; otherwise the particular case of the Maccabees will be made into a general rule, a dangerous precedent. As Bossuet asks in the *Conférence avec M. Claude*,

> Does the Church give us Scripture only on paper, the outer bark of the Word, the body of the letter? Doubtless, no: she gives us the spirit, that is to say the sense, of Scripture; for to give us Scripture without the sense is to give us a body without a soul, and a letter that kills. Scripture without its legitimate interpretation, Scripture destitute of its natural sense, is a knife to cut our throats. The Arian has cut his own throat through ill-understood Scripture; the Nestorian has cut his; the Pelagian has cut his. God forbid that the Church give us Scripture alone, without giving us its sense![103]

The problem, however, in the seventeenth century, is plainly not the Nestorian or the Arian, but the Lutheran or the Calvinist; and that is why Bossuet insists that the Catholics reproached Luther "for inspiring so much contempt for the authority of the Church," and for having placed the decision of religious matters "in the hands of individuals, and for having given them Scripture as if it were so clear that one need only read it to understand it, without consulting the Church or tradition."[104]

But one must not, at the opposite extreme, fall into the mistake of letting Church tradition replace Scripture, viewed as something partly defective: if Protestants wrongly jettison tradition in favor of *l'Ecriture même*, Catholic Biblical scholars such as Richard Simon (in his *Histoire critique du Vieux Testament*) use and abuse that tradition to raise skeptical or even "Spinozist" doubts about the literal truth and accuracy of Scripture. Simon had urged that "the Catholics who are

---

[102] As is still the case in Israeli political debates which try to "draw" arguments from Scripture.
[103] Bossuet, *Conférence avec M. Claude*, in *Œuvres* (1841 edn), Vol. IV, p. 557.
[104] Bossuet, *Histoire des variations*, in *Œuvres* (1841 edn), Vol. IV, p. 24.

Introduction

persuaded that their religion does not depend solely on the text of Scripture, but also on the tradition of the Church, are not at all scandalized to see that the ravages of time and the negligence of copyists" have introduced changes into these sacred books, as well as into "profane" ones. "It is only preoccupied or ignorant Protestants," Simon insists, "who can be scandalized over this."[105] But Bossuet was profoundly scandalized: and he could not countenance Simon's driving a wedge between the text and its authoritative interpretation. Bossuet wants to affirm, simultaneously, the literal truth of Scripture (siding on that point with Jurieu) and the necessity of an authoritative reading of it – to steer between the reefs of "Calvinistic" literalism and "Spinozistic" textual criticism.

For Bossuet a terrible example of what happens if one does not read Scripture literally, traditionally and *en particulier* is to be found in Jurieu's *Babylonian Captivity*; M. de Meaux is outraged by Jurieu's suggestion that early Christians offered passive obedience to the Roman monarchy only because of weakness, not conviction – that the martyrs were really cowards who miscalculated.[106] In this spirit Bossuet revises Christ's "render to Caesar" and Paul's "obey the powers that be" – two of his favorite texts in the *Politique* – in an effective satire.

> You, Jews, who suffer the yoke of the Romans with so much pain, render to Caesar that which is due him: that is to say, be careful not to irritate him, until you feel yourself in a condition to defend yourself better. Yes, my brothers, a St Peter or a St Paul will say, let us say that one must obey the powers established by God, and that their authority is inviolable; but this is only because we are so few in number: in this condition and in this state boast of your obedience despite any ordeal. Increase, however; and when you shall be stronger, then you will begin to interpret our precepts, saying that we accommodated them to the times; as if obeying and submitting were only a waiting for new powers and for a more favorable conjunction, or as if submission were only a policy.[107]

And Bossuet's final thrust against Jurieu – whom he suspects of

---

[105] Cited in Orest Ranum, Introduction to Bossuet's *Discourse on Universal History* (Chicago: University of Chicago Press, 1976), p. xxxv n. 36.
[106] Bossuet, *Cinquième avertissement*, in *Œuvres* (1841 edn), Vol. IV, p. 379.
[107] Ibid., p. 379.

Introduction

"finding" old Biblical warrants for new Protestant rebelliousness – is as amusing as it is uncharitable.

> Let him confuse everything, let him mix heaven and earth; let him change . . . the perpetual rules based on the order of God and the tranquillity of states into precepts accommodated to the times; let him even change the patience of the first Christians into weakness, let him make their obedience forced; let him search on all sides for pretexts for rebellion in his ancestors: he is overwhelmed from every quarter by Scripture, by the tradition, by the examples of the ancient Church.[108]

If "render to Caesar" is to be understood very literally, not as cowardly or calculating accommodation, then there is a "new" divine warrant for monarchy: God the Father established such government in Israel, and now the Son authorizes its "successor" in Rome. For one can "draw" the right politics "from" Scripture ("the very words") only if those words are read literally, in the light of Church authority.

V Divine-right absolute monarchy

For Bossuet, who has insisted that it is "absurd" to claim that God "does not interfere with the govenance of nations," or determine "by which princes" those nations will be ruled, the principal evidence of this salutary divine "interference" is of course Scripture – now rescued from Jurieu's imaginative interpretations. For Bossuet the sheer "pastness" of Old Testament events scarcely matters; the monarchical efforts of David and Solomon enjoy a kind of timeless, exemplary validity.

> When Solomon said, "The king speaks with authority, and none can say to him: Why do you do that?," he explained not only the form of government among the Hebrews, but still more the constitution of the kingdom then known, and, so to speak, the common law of monarchies.[109]

Bossuet, nonetheless, has his problems with Scripture viewed as a fountain of divine-right absolute monarchy; and these emerge most

[108] Ibid., p. 385.   [109] Ibid., p. 401.

Introduction

clearly in connection with the end of the book of Judges (which scarcely serves his turn) and in connection with Samuel (1 Kings) – in which the "ungrateful" Israelites, forsaking God and Samuel, demand a king in a "sinful" way. Plainly it taxed Bossuet's ingenuity to "draw" unequivocal monarchism from these problematical passages of Scripture.

It is not surprising that Judges Ch. 21 should be passed over in silence: no amount of exegetical inventiveness could coax monarchy out of the words, "in those days there was no king in Israel: but every one did that which seemed right to himself."[110] (Bossuet's total silence on this final verse from Judges is the more striking, since the *Politique* contains no fewer than seventy-three references to the rest of that book.[111])

The latest chapter of Judges which Bossuet treats, indeed, is 19, in which "all the tribes [of Israel] assembled" to punish some members of the tribe of Benjamin who had raped and murdered the wife of a Levite; and Bossuet briefly grants that "in some parts of Scripture, authority resides in a community." But he hastily retreats from that sentence, finally urging that, before the advent of King Saul, Israel "was in effect a kind of republic, but which had God for its king."[112] So anxious is he to "find" monarchy universally in place – but in the "people of God" *en particulier* – that he winds up weakening his claim that "histories show us a great number of republics, of which some govern themselves through the whole people (and which are called democracy), and the others by the great (which are called aristocracy)."[113] The notion of a Jewish *demos*, and of Jerusalem fitted up with an *agora*, was anathema to Bossuet – even if the Greeks were "charmed" by republicanism, preferring "the inconveniences of liberty to those of legitimate subjection."[114]

In his reading of 1 Kings 8, Bossuet turns potential ruin to his advantage: and the art with which he does so is consummate. He begins with what looks like an intractable text. When the Israelites say to Samuel, "make us a king," he is "displeased," and prays to the

---

[110] Judges 21:24. Bossuet notices this passage momentarily in *Politique* Book 1, but does not connect it with his general reading of Judges.
[111] See Le Brun's index to Bossuet's citation of Scripture in his edition of the *Politique*.
[112] Bossuet, *Politique*, ed. Le Brun, pp. 51–52.
[113] Ibid., p. 51.
[114] Bossuet, *Histoire universelle*, cited in Truchet, *Politique de Bossuet*, p. 100.

Introduction

Lord – who in his turn complains that the people have "rejected" and forsaken him, have "served strange gods"; he then urges Samuel to "foretell" the people that the king they want will be arbitrary and high-handed.

> Then Samuel told all the words of the Lord to the people that had desired a king of him,
> And said: This will be the right of the king, that shall reign over you: He will take your sons and put them in his chariots, and will make them his horsemen...
> Your daughters also he will take to make him ointments, and to be his cooks, and bakers.
> And he will take your fields, and your vineyards, and your best olive-yards, to... give his eunuchs and servants...
> Your flocks also he will tithe, and you shall be his servants.
> And you shall cry out in that day from the face of the king... and the Lord will not hear you in that day, because you desired unto yourselves a king.[115]

This looks unpromising; but in the *Politique* Book IV, Bossuet actually manages to wring unquestionable monarchical sovereignty from this text. "Will kings have the right to do all of this licitly? God forbid. For God does not give such powers: but they will have the right to do it with impunity with respect to human justice. This is why David said [following the murder of Uriah]: 'to thee only have I sinned, O Lord; have pity on me!' For he was king, says St Jerome of this passage, and had God alone to fear."[116]

With an unobtrusive skill which would pass unnoticed by someone not familiar with 1 Kings 8, Bossuet manages to transform God's rather petulant forecast of kingly high-handedness into a sovereignty beyond human control. Another reading of Kings might view the divine prediction as a grim portent of terrible things to come; Bossuet draws from the text the suggestion that only bad kings will fulfil the prediction, but that even they will be beyond all terrestrial jurisdiction. This is an exegetical *tour de force* – though precisely a "forced" reading of Scripture. (Sometimes, as in the *Cinquième avertissement aux protestants*, Bossuet urges that 1 Kings 8 describes what kings will indeed have a *right* to do – but only in desperate times: "in the case of certain extreme necessities, in which the individual good must be

---

[115] 1 Kings 8:11ff.   [116] Bossuet, *Politique*, ed. Le Brun, p. 95.

Introduction

sacrificed to the good of the state."[117] And this draws further unquestionable sovereignty out of a passage that had seemed to block Bossuet's passage.)

It is with visible relief that Bossuet arrives at Saul, David and Solomon – all divinely "authorized" and "anointed"; and much of the *Politique* is taken up with a minutely detailed examination of their reigns. But Bossuet does not content himself with Saul as "first" king: in Book I of the *Politique* he quietly makes the "succession" from Moses to Joshua into a royal succession ("after the death of Moses, the whole people recognized Joshua... the prince dies, but authority is immortal").[118] And in the *Cinquième avertissement*, he speaks of "the supreme authority, not only in the person of Moses, but also in that of Joshua," and reglosses 1 Kings 8 by insisting that "the Hebrew people had in Samuel a sovereign magistrate."[119] (That monarchy should begin, *ex nihilo*, from a popular request, was more than Bossuet could bear.)

In Book X of the *Politique*, added to the manuscript in 1703, when Bossuet had a year to live, Samuel has become fully a king: he is now a "sovereign" (the term is used four times in two pages) whom the people depose – in effect – in asking for a king. In this final, bold reading of 1 Kings 8, Bossuet's reasoning seems to be roughly this: kings do not really arise through popular will or demand; Samuel was already in place as *juge souverain*; the people were too ignorant to see that they had a sovereign and therefore "asked" for one; but since they had effectively deposed Samuel, they got Saul as a kind of royal punishment – and then had to be rescued, as it were, by David.[120] This "reading" would serve two Bossuetian ends at a stroke: it would show, first, that monarchy does not really arise through popular demand, since Samuel was already *souverain*; and secondly, that when the people do choose they do badly and pitch upon Saul (much as another populace elected Barabbas over Christ). This would show further continuity between Abraham and Moses, viewed as "kings," and David, Solomon, Judas Maccabeus, and Christ; Samuel as *souverain* would fit into the royal "line," so that there would be no "republican" *interregnum* in early Jewish history.

---

[117] Bossuet, *Cinquième avertissement*, in *Œuvres* (1841 edn), Vol. IV, p. 400.
[118] Bossuet, *Politique*, ed. Le Brun, p. 22.
[119] Bossuet, *Cinquième avertissement*, in *Œuvres* (1841 edn), p. 396.
[120] Bossuet, *Politique*, ed. Le Brun, pp. 409ff.

Introduction

Nothing, of course, could shore up divine-right monarchy better than God's own monarchy: it is no accident that the first words of the *Politique* are, "God is the King of kings,"[121] and that Bossuet should go astonishingly far in establishing what he calls *la généalogie royale de Jesus-Christ* (in the *Elévations sur les mystères*):

> It was truly necessary that Jesus Christ have for ancestors all the kings of Judah who had issued from David, in order to show the people that, true king of the Jews, this title was as if hereditary with him.[122]

And in the *Politique* Bossuet cites no fewer than five times Christ's "render to Caesar": not only was he himself an (hereditary) king, descended from David, but he was respectful of the kingship of others – even when that "other" was Tiberius: "It was under Tiberius, not merely an infidel, but actually evil, that our Lord said to the Jews, 'render to Caesar that which is Caesar's.' "[123]

If one considers what Bossuet has done just to Judges 21, 1 Kings 8 and Matthew 22:21, one finds that he has wrung unquestionable sovereignty, divinely ordained, from questionable texts; that Moses, Joshua, Samuel, and Christ were (almost) as fully "kings" as Saul, David, and Solomon. It is impressive, if less than persuasive.

Perhaps Bossuet sensed that even the Old Testament itself is somewhat equivocal on the subject of monarchy: for, temporarily abandoning Scriptural citation, he devoted his finest sheerly rhetorical effort in the whole of the *Politique* to making monarchy soar and sing. Can it be accidental, indeed, that the only sustained lyrical flight in that book, the only passage fully the equal of the greatest pages in the *Oraisons funèbres*, is the one likening the monarch to God? Here, briefly, the "geometric" method of the *Politique* – which is morcelized into articles and propositions, buttressed with fragments of Scripture – is set aside, and one sees briefly why Bossuet was viewed as the greatest Catholic preacher of the seventeenth century.

I do not call majesty that pomp which surrounds kings, or that

---

[121] Ibid., p. 1.
[122] Bossuet, *Elévations sur les mystères*, in *Œuvres* (1841 edn), Vol. IV, p. 702. See also Bossuet, *Oraison funèbre de Henri de Gornay* (1658), cited in Truchet, *Politique de Bossuet*, pp. 200–201.
[123] Bossuet, *Politique*, ed. Le Brun, p. 199.

Introduction

external show which dazzles the vulgar. That is the reflection of majesty, but not its true self.

Majesty is the image of the greatness of God in a prince.

God is infinite, God is all. The prince, in his quality of prince, is not considered as an individual; he is a public personage, all the state is comprised in him: the will of all the people is included in his own. Just as all virtue and excellence are united in God, so the strength of every individual is comprehended in the person of the prince. What greatness this is, for one man to contain so much!

The power of God can be felt in a moment from one end of the world to the other: the royal power acts simultaneously throughout the kingdom. It holds the whole kingdom in position just as God holds the whole world.

If God were to withdraw his hand, the entire world would return to nothing: if authority ceases in the kingdom, all lapses into confusion . . .

"What is done solely at the emperor's bidding?," asks St Augustine. "He has only to move his lips, the least of all movements, and the whole empire stirs. It is he who does all things by his command, in the image of God. He spoke, and it was done; he commanded, and all was created."[124]

So magnificent is this passage from Book v of the *Politique* – the authentic voice of Bossuet – that one can (briefly) forget that Augustine was far from being the unequivocal monarchist who is presented here. So moving are Bossuet's powers that one does not (instantly) remember that Augustine – in his dark passage on "the judge" (who innocently tortures the innocent to death) – had called social life "miserable,"[125] and had insisted that Romulus, founder of the Roman *imperium*, in effect relived Scripture by murdering Remus, as Cain had murdered Abel ("the city's walls stained with a brother's blood"[126]). To convert the Augustine who saw the sack of Rome (A.D.410) prefigured in a fratricidal founding into a straightforward monarchist by divine right – that is a conversion to rival that of Saul on the road to Damascus.

But Bossuet, finding as much monarchism in *De civitate Dei* as in Judges and Kings, goes on to say:

---

[124] Ibid., pp. 177–78.
[125] St. Augustine, *The City of God*, Book XIX, cited in *The Political Writings of St Augustine*, ed. H. Paolucci (Chicago: Gateway, 1962), pp. 135–37.
[126] Ibid., Book XV.

Introduction

Finally, gather together all that we have said, so great and so august, about royal authority. You have seen a great nation united under one man: you have seen his sacred power, paternal and absolute: you have seen that secret reason which directs the body politic, enclosed in one head: you have seen the image of God in kings, and you will have the idea of the majesty of kingship.

God is holiness itself, goodness itself, power itself, reason itself. In these things consists the divine majesty. In their reflection consists the majesty of the prince ...

An indefinable element of divinity is possessed by the prince, and inspires fear in his subjects. The king himself would do well to remember this. "I have said, Ye are gods: and all of you are children of the most high ..." But, O gods of flesh and blood, of mud and dust, you will die like other men, you will fall like the greatest. Greatness divides men for a little while; a common fall levels them in the end.[127]

"O kings," Bossuet finally says, "be bold therefore in the exercise of your power: for it is divine and beneficial to the human race; but wield it with humility." For "it is conferred on you from without. In the end it leaves you weak, it leaves you mortal, it leaves you still sinners: and it lays upon you a heavier charge to render to God."[128]

The language is glorious, even if the doctrine has lost its hold. And in the end these pages, which rival the *Oraisons funèbres*, do amount to a kind of funeral oration – this time for King David, whose life and reign are lovingly recounted in the remaining pages of Book v: "all the actions and all the words of David breathed forth something so great, and in consequence so royal, that one need only read his life and hear his speeches to have an idea of magnanimity."[129]

Not content with Scriptural authority and rhetorical power in his magnification of monarchy, Bossuet actually appealed to "profane" history and to the Homeric epics to shore up the assertion that even the most celebrated republics had "at first lived under kings." In Book II of the *Politique*, republicanism is reduced to a shadowy demi-existence.

> Rome began in that way [with monarchy], and finally came back to it, as to its natural state.
>
> It was only late, and little by little, that the Greek cities

---

[127] Bossuet, *Politique*, ed. Le Brun, pp. 178–79.
[128] Ibid., p. 179. [129] Ibid., pp. 180ff.

Introduction

formed their republics. The ancient opinion of Greece was that expressed by Homer in that celebrated sentence from the *Iliad*: "Several princes are not a good thing; let there be only one prince and one king." . . . All the world thus began with monarchies; and almost the whole world has remained [in that state] as its most natural condition.

We have seen, too, that its basis and its model is in the paternal empire, that is to say in nature itself.[130]

In the end, Bossuet's monarchism is supported by God, Scripture, nature, paternity, rhetoric, universal practice, and Homer: an exhaustive and impressive catalogue.

One should hasten to add that Bossuet was by no means unaware of the terrible faults of monarchs: to see that, one has only to look at his appalling description of Herod in the *Elévations sur les mystères*, where the King is the quintessence of *les politiques du monde* – steeped in *leurs vains ombrages, leurs fausses délicatesses, leur hypocrisie, leur cruauté*. Indeed the main thing which shows him to be an *habile politique* is that, fearing Jesus Christ as a "new king," Herod "dreamt only of pushing a dagger into his entrails," while pretending to follow the Magi and adore him.[131] And Bossuet's long account of Saul's murderous assaults on David, in several of the books of the *Politique*, would give pause to a James I or Charles I.

For Bossuet, however, it is not that monarchy is (usually) so good – the "image" of God that it ought to be — but that all other political forms are (usually) still worse. Even the "people of God," the beneficiaries of David, Solomon, Josaphat, and Judas Maccabeus, knew this: "It was not that they had not seen the disadvantages of the independence of the prince – since they had seen so many bad kings, so many intolerable tyrants; it was rather that they saw less disadvantage in enduring them as they were, than in leaving the slightest power to the multitude."[132]

All of this comes out most clearly, for Bossuet, in the case of Pilate's judgment of Christ – a case in which Pilate's feebleness is outweighed by the mob's screaming for Barabbas; monarchy may be bad, but democracy is worse. The most memorable passage in Book IV

---

[130] Ibid., pp. 52–53.
[131] Bossuet, *Elévations sur les mystères*, in *Œuvres* (1841 edn), Vol. IV, p. 723.
[132] Bossuet, *Cinquième avertissement*, in *Œuvres* (1841 edn), Vol. IV, p. 402.

of the *Politique* is the one in which Bossuet shows that "it is a pitiable thing to see Pilate in the story of the Passion," since he "spilled innocent blood from not having been able to resist the great men of the kingdom."

> He had said to them that "he saw no cause [justifying execution] in this man ... He said to them once again: You accuse him of having incited the people to sedition: and behold I, having examined him before you, find no cause in this man, in those things wherein you accuse him. No, nor Herod either. For I sent you to him, and behold nothing worthy of death is done to him ... But the whole multitude together cried out, saying: Let him be crucified, and set at liberty Barabbas, who had been arrested for sedition and murder ... they were instant with loud voices, requiring that he might be crucified: and their voices prevailed. And Pilate gave sentence that it should be as they required. And he released unto them the murderer and the seditious one, and abandoned Jesus to their will."[133]

Why should Pilate "struggle so much," Bossuet wonders, "only to abandon justice in the end? All his excuses condemn him: 'Take him yourselves, and crucify him.' As if a magistrate could be innocent, by permitting a crime that he could stop." Pilate "feared the reaction of the people," when in fact "he ought to have feared only doing evil."[134]

In these remarkable passages, *vox populi* is a *vox contra Deos* – Father and Son. But the "great" of the realm are no better: it is they who brought unjust charges; and "if the prince himself, who is the judge of judges, fears the great, what will be secure in the state?"[135] Since neither the Barabbas-loving many nor the Christ-hating few can be relied on, one must put one's faith in monarchy, and hope for the charity of a Solomon. Faith, hope, charity, these three – but the greatest of these is (monarchical) faith.

This fear that one will get Pilate, even as one hopes for Solomon, had afflicted Bossuet since his days as a brilliant court preacher: as early as 1662, indeed, Pilate haunted him. And what was particularly distressing was that Pilate knew better; one can "enlighten" a ruler (as Bossuet strove to enlighten the Dauphin) and he may still yield to popular pressure or aristocratic hate.

[133] Bossuet, *Politique*, ed. Le Brun, pp. 103–104.
[134] Ibid., pp. 103–104.
[135] Ibid., p. 104.

Introduction

> I cannot omit in this place what our divine Savior suffered through ambition and worldly politics, in order to expiate the sins that politics commits.
>
> Always, if one does not take care, politics condemns the truth, and enfeebles and miserably corrupts the best intentions. Pilate lets us see this quite well, by letting himself be easily surprised by the traps which the Jews threw before his trembling ambition . . . Let us wonder, Christians, in the case of Pilate, at the shameful and miserable weakness of a worldly and political virtue. Pilate had some probity and some justice; he even had some power and vigor: he was capable of resisting the persuasions of the pontiffs and the cries of a mutinous people . . . [But] his weakness had the same effect that malice would have had: it made him flagellate, it made him condemn, it made him crucify innocence itself; fear made him carry out, against a man who seemed just, that which a declared iniquity could not have done worse.[136]

"God preserve from such sins," Bossuet concludes, "the most just of all kings" – Louis XIV. If one examines the gulf between Bossuet's ideal monarch in Book v of the *Politique*, and his account of what most monarchs turn out to be and do – crowned by a litany of royal crimes performed by Saul, Belshazzar and Antiochus (in the final pages of *Politique* x) – one can only conclude that Bossuet's monarchism rested on a rather desperate hope.

To be sure, one can indeed hope that a God-reflecting monarch will be neither as murderous as Saul and Herod nor as feeble as Pilate; for one of Bossuet's great points is that monarchs must be absolute but not arbitrary. Unquestionable sovereignty must unquestionably be regular, lawful, respectful of property and personal rights – and not degenerate into the *gouvernement à l'Ottomane* which was soon to be described in the final pages of Montesquieu's *Lettres persanes*.

> There is among men a kind of government which is called arbitrary, but which is not found among us in well-ordered states.
>
> Four attributes accompany these kinds of government.
>
> Firstly: subject peoples are born slaves, that is to say truly serfs; and among them there are no free persons.
>
> Secondly: no one possesses private property: all the sources of wealth belong to the prince, and there is no right of inheritance, even from father to son.

---

[136] Bossuet, *Sermon pour le Vendredi saint* (1662), in Truchet, *Politique de Bossuet*, p. 240.

Introduction

Thirdly: the prince has the right to dispose as he wishes, not only of the goods, but also of the lives of his subjects, as one would do with slaves.

And finally, in the fourth place, there is no law but his will.[137]

Declining to ask whether arbitrary power is "permissible or illicit," Bossuet contents himself with noticing that "there are nations and great empires which are content with it; and it is not for us to awaken doubts in them about the form of their government." Nonetheless such power is "barbarous and odious," and is "quite far from our own *moeurs*," so that in France "there is no arbitrary government."[138]

> It is one thing for a government to be absolute, and another for it to be arbitrary. It is absolute with respect to constraint – there being no power capable of forcing the sovereign, who in this sense is independent of all human authority. But it does not follow from this that the government is arbitrary, for besides the fact that everything is subject to the judgment of God . . . there are also [constitutional] laws in empires, so that whatever is done against them is null in a legal sense: and there is always an opportunity for redress, either on other occasions or in other times.[139]

Arbitrariness, then, is excluded; but absolutism must be clung to. For "government is established to free all men from all oppression and from all violence . . . This constitutes the state of perfect liberty: there being fundamentally nothing less free than anarchy, which takes away all legitimate claims among men, and knows no law other than force."[140]

Even if, however, a ruler is "arbitrary," or tyrannical, or impious, for Bossuet, nothing can justify active resistance to his sovereignty – save a king's directly ordaining the violation of divine law, and even then one must passively accept punishment for having resisted. Book IV of the *Politique* makes it clear that "there is no co-active power against the prince," and Book VI adds that "declared impiety and even persecution do not exempt subjects from the obedience they owe to princes."[141] This last proposition he shores up through the words of Christ and St. Paul, adding in Plato's *Crito* for good (classical) measure.

In the *Cinquième avertissement aux protestants*, which amplifies

---

[137] Bossuet, *Politique*, ed. Le Brun, pp. 291ff. [138] Ibid., pp. 291ff.
[139] Ibid., pp. 291ff. [140] Ibid., pp. 291ff. [141] Ibid., pp. 94, 198.

Politique IV and VI, Bossuet urges that Christ himself said, "render to Caesar that which is Caesar's, and to God that which is God's: by which he placed on the same footing, so to speak, what one owes to the prince and what one owes to God himself." Christ knew, Bossuet insists, that "his disciples would be persecuted by princes, since he had so often predicted it"; but this did not lead him to "deduct" anything from "the strict obedience which he prescribed to them." As for Christ's own case, Bossuet goes on, his "doctrine" was that "persecution does not take away from persecuted saints the quality of subjects . . . [or] arm subjects against the public power." That is why Christ "recognized in Pilate, minister of the emperor, 'a power given him from above.' "[142] And in one of the most striking paragraphs of the *Cinquième avertissement*, Bossuet fuses Christ's passive obedience to the Romans with that of Socrates to the Athenians in the *Crito* – marshaling the whole of Mediterranean antiquity against all resistance.

> Socrates, a pagan, knew well that one is obliged to obey the laws and the magistrates of one's country, even if they condemn you unjustly . . . By these solid principles this philosopher consented to perish, rather than destroy public judgments by his resistance, and would not have wanted to escape from prison against the authority of the laws, for fear of falling, after this life, into the hands of the eternal laws, when they take up the defense of their sisters the civil laws (it was thus that he spoke).[143]

"And will Jesus Christ," Bossuet asks, "be less just and less patient than a philosopher, or want to show his disciples that self-defense against the public power is legitimate?" No, Bossuet answers; this would be "a manifest profanation of the words of Jesus Christ."[144]

If, however, it was Bossuet's view that one should passively submit even to the cowardly agent (Pilate) of an infidel and evil ruler (Tiberius) – for even they are divinely appointed, *en particulier* – he plainly preferred submission to a monarch of pious orthodoxy. (And was not Louis XIV at least called *Rex Christianissimus*?) All this is for an obvious reason: one of the monarch's main functions is to maintain – "gently" if possible, by force if necessary – orthodox religion

---

[142] Bossuet, *Cinquième avertissement*, in *Œuvres* (1841 edn), Vol. IV, pp. 377–78.
[143] Ibid., p. 386.   [144] Ibid., p. 387.

Introduction

(Roman Catholicism).[145] One of the central arguments of Book VII of the *Politique* – added to the manuscript in 1700, fifteen years after the revocation of the Edict of Nantes – is that "division" and "schism" in the Church are as terrible now as when Roboam "divided" Israel after the death of Solomon: for Bossuet's usual method is to show that Scriptural history is being (as it were) relived by the Protestants. But it is also being relived, in a happy form, by Louis XIV: that is why Bossuet (in a passage that now seems extravagant) treats the King as a new Constantine – and in a "high" tone borrowed directly from Scripture.

> Let us not, then, fail to publish this miracle of our times [the revocation of the Edict]; let us pass on an account of it to future centuries. Take up your sacred pens, you who compose the annals of the Church: agile instruments of a prompt writer and a diligent hand, hasten to place Louis with the Constantines and the Theodosiuses.[146]

After describing the suppression of ancient heterodoxies by the Christian emperors ("thus heresy fell with its venom, and discord retreated into hell, whence it had come"), Bossuet goes on to say that modernity (for once) enjoys an advantage over antiquity:

> But our Fathers had not seen, like us, an inveterate heresy fall at a stroke; the misled flocks coming back *en masse*, and our churches too small to receive them; their false pastors abandoning them, without even waiting for the order, happy to be able to allege their banishment as an excuse; everything calm in so great a movement; the universe astonished to see in so new an event the most certain mark and the finest employment of authority – and the merit of the prince recognized and revered more than his authority itself.[147]

Touched by so many "marvels," Bossuet concludes, "let us open our hearts to the piety of Louis."

> Let us push our acclamations to heaven itself, and let us say to this new Constantine, to this new Theodosius, to this new Marcian, to this new Charlemagne, that which the six hundred

---

[145] Bossuet, *Politique*, ed. Le Brun, op. cit, Book VII (entire).
[146] Bossuet, *Oraison funèbre de Michel Le Tellier* (1686), in Truchet, *Politique de Bossuet*, pp. 183–84.
[147] Ibid., pp. 183–84.

Fathers once said at the Council of Chalcedon: "You have affirmed the faith, you have banished the heretics: this is the worthiest work of your reign, its true character. Thanks to you, heresy is no more: God alone could have brought about this marvel. King of heaven, preserve the king of earth: this is the plea of the Church, the plea of the bishops."[148]

It was no doubt such a passage that led to Lamartine's contemptuous characterization of M. de Meaux in *Raphaël*: "Bossuet, golden tongue, adulating soul, gathering into himself, in his conduct and in his words before Louis XIV, the despotism of a theocrat and the obligingness of a courtier."[149]

Not the smallest reason for Bossuet's virtual obsession with King David in the *Politique*, incidentally, is that he finds in him a kind of "ancestor" of Louis XIV: just as Louis (and not only the Pope) is the guardian of Christianity – and this is proved by the "miracle" of the revocation of the Edict of Nantes by the new Constantine-Theodosius – so too David (and not merely a pontiff) was the guardian of the law. One is not meant to be thinking only of David when Bossuet says that

> the great kings of the house of David made their reign celebrated by the great care which they took to maintain the order of the ministry and of all the functions of the priests and Levites, according to the law of Moses. David himself had given them the example . . . being himself a prophet and ranked in Scripture among the number of men inspired by God.
>
> With this counsel and by a particular inspiration [*une inspiration particulière*], he regulated the hours of the divine service . . . [and] established the necessary subordination in this great body of ministers consecrated to God.[150]

Despite the fulsomeness of his praise of Louis XIV as religion-saver in the *Oraison funèbre de Michel Le Tellier*,[151] what is more usual with Bossuet is a careful balancing of the claims of the Church and those of the state. As a moderate Gallican,[152] Bossuet was a co-author of the 1682 declaration "that kings and sovereigns are not subject in

---

[148] Ibid., p. 184.
[149] Lamartine, *Raphaël*, ch. XCIV, cited in Truchet, *Politique de Bossuet*, p. 9.
[150] Bossuet, *Politique*, ed. Le Brun, p. 251.
[151] See Truchet, *Politique de Bossuet*, pp. 181–82.
[152] As De Maistre resented Bossuet's Gallicanism, saying (in *Du Pape* II, xii) that M. de Meaux "laisse bien loin derrière lui tous les adorateurs de Louis XIV."

temporal matters to any ecclesiastical power by the order of God . . . that their subjects cannot, in the name of this authority, be dispensed from the submission and the obedience which they owe them."[153] And in this vein he urges – finding an early Christian *Provenance* for modern Gallicanism – that the ruler who was most nearly Antichrist, Julian the Apostate, lost nothing of his *auctoritas* through his lack of *caritas*.

> One sees clearly that the stronger the Church became the more brightly shone her submission and her modesty. This is what was clear, more than ever, under Julian the Apostate, when the number of Christians had so grown and the Church had become so powerful . . . The Church was attacked [by Julian] in so formidable a way, that everyone agreed that she had never been in so much danger. Nonetheless the Church was as submissive in her condition of powerfulness as she had been under Nero and Domitian, when she had just been born. Let us conclude, then, that the submission of Christians was an effect of the principles of their religion – without which they would have been able to oblige the Severuses, the Valerians, the Diocletians, to treat them considerately, and Julian to the point of fearing them as enemies more redoubtable than the Persians.[154]

If even "the Apostate" would benefit from Gallicanism *avant la lettre*, what Bossuet plainly hopes for is a Charlemagne who will uphold the rights of the Church, and consult with it when "schism" and "division" threaten orthodox unity. Book VII of the *Politique* reminds the reader that when Charlemagne was called on to stamp out a resuscitated version of Nestorian heresy in Spain, he "consulted the Holy See, and at the same time the other bishops," informed the neo-Nestorians that their innovations were inconsistent with the tenets of the *Eglise universelle*, and demanded that they relent. "That was how this prince decided," Bossuet concludes, "and his decision was nothing else than an absolute submission to the decisions of the Church." And that is because Charlemagne knew that "the priesthood and the empire are two powers which are independent, but united."[155] Distantly echoing Dante's *De monarchia*, Bossuet insists that

> the sacerdotal authority in the spiritual [realm], and the empire in

---

[153] Ibid., p. 170.
[154] Bossuet, *Cinquième avertissement*, in *Œuvres* (1841 edn), Vol. IV, p. 381.
[155] Bossuet, *Politique*, ed. Le Brun, pp. 258–59.

Introduction

the temporal, arise only through God. But the ecclesiastical order recognizes the empire in the temporal [sphere], as kings in the spiritual [realm] acknowledge themselves to be humble children of the Church. The state of the world turns on these two powers. That is why they owe each other mutual help.[156]

As a final facet of Bossuet's monarchism, it is worth remembering that M. de Meaux – who had grown up with the civil wars of the Fronde and spent his maturity witnessing Louis XIV's endless foreign wars – took care in Book IX of the *Politique* to magnify "pacific" rulers and to diminish "bellicose" ones. And he made this the more striking by sacrificing his much-loved favorite, King David, on this particular moral altar. After showing, indeed, that God had ordained certain wars that David executed, Bossuet suddenly says that "God, after all, nonetheless, does not love war, and prefers the pacific to the warriors." The proof, of course, is scriptural: God forbad David to build the Temple because "he did not want to receive" that edifice "from a bloody hand."

> David was a holy king, and the model of princes: so pleasing to God that he had deigned to call him a man after his own heart. He had never spilt any but infidel blood, in wars which were called the Lord's wars ... But it sufficed that this was human blood, to cause him to be judged unworthy to present a Temple to the Lord, the author and protector of human life.[157]

Only the hands of Solomon, "so free from blood," were judged "worthy to raise the sanctuary to him." And God "made of this peaceful one one of the most excellent pre-figurings of his incarnate Son."[158]

Given Bossuet's constant "parallels" between David and Louis XIV, the inescapable conclusion of Book IX is that the King of France would do better to imitate Solomon than David. For if God finally spurned the David who had executed divinely ordained wars, what must he make of Louis's seizure of Strasbourg or his invasion of Holland – which led Leibniz to call the *Rex Christianissimus* by the name of *Mars Christianissimus*?[159] In the *Politique* Book IX, Bossuet

---

[156] Ibid., pp. 259–60.   [157] Ibid., p. 353.   [158] Ibid., p. 353.
[159] Leibniz, *Mars Christianissimus*, in *Leibniz: Political Writings*, pp. 121ff. The whole work is a parody of Bossuet's Scripturalism, and is a defense of the "new" law of charity against the Old Testament *ethos*.

speaks of David, but thinks of Louis; the "method of indirection" holds sovereign sway.

VI

One would not expect a partisan of divine-right absolute monarchy to favor social contract theory, which views government as the product of human "will and artifice" (Oakeshott),[160] set up between equals in a state of nature – that is, in the absence of any natural (especially paternal) authority. Certainly there is no trace of contractarianism in Bossuet's claim that "there never was a finer state constitution than that which one sees in the people of God," which was "formed" by Moses, who was instructed by "the whole of divine wisdom" and inspired to construct a polity *vraiment divine* – a divine politics then sustained by "two great kings of this people, David and Solomon . . . both excellent in the art of ruling."[161]

Soon one begins to see that Bossuet opposed contractarianism not just *en général* but *en particulier*; for Pierre Jurieu, speaking for French Protestant *émigrés*, had used contract theory to urge that the Edict of Nantes was a contract between the Huguenots and the French monarchy (which made Louis XIV guilty of breach of contract, *inter alia*), and tried to find a Scriptural provenance for this modern contractarianism by "locating" a contract in Jewish antiquity: more precisely in David's "waiting" for popular approval before reassuming the throne (after the revolt of Absalom). Jurieu had argued in his *Pastoral Letters to the Faithful of France who Groan under the Babylonian Captivity* (1686–89) that David "did not want to remount the throne, except by the same [popular] authority by which he had first ascended it," and that "David wanted to show, by this conduct, that peoples are the masters of their crowns, and that they take them from, and give them to, whom they will."[162]

This use of contractarianism – which at once avows popular

---

[160] Michael Oakeshott, Introduction to Hobbes' *Leviathan* (Oxford: Basil Blackwell, 1957), p. xii. For a fuller reading of Hobbes in this light, see my *Will and Political Legitimacy: A Critical Exposition of Social Contract Theory in Hobbes, Locke, Rousseau, Kant and Hegel* (Cambridge, Mass.: Harvard University Press, 1982), Ch. 2.
[161] Bossuet, *Politique*, ed. Le Brun, p. 2.
[162] Jurieu, *Lettre* XVII, cited by Bossuet in *Cinquième avertissement*, in *Œuvres* (1841 edn), Vol. IV, p. 392.

Introduction

sovereignty and denies the divine ordination of David in particular and of kings in general – was more than Bossuet could endure.

> What! Even rebellious peoples have so much power, and under a legitimate king? And in a plot as strange as that of a son against his father, must one still adore the right of the people? . . . The minister [Jurieu] does not blush at such an excess . . . Did David have need of the authority of a rebel people to place himself on his throne and to re-enter his palace? No, without doubt.[163]

On Jurieu's view, Bossuet suggests, "a prince chased from power, but in the end victorious, will not dare to use his right except with the consent and the authority of the rebels; and instead of punishing them, he must demand their pardon for his victory. See, my brothers, the maxims which are preached to you; see how Holy Scripture is abused." Jurieu is " a strange theologian" who will have it that "a man whom God had made king still had need of the people to bear this title."[164]

And if David – as the Dauphin is told in the Preface of the *Politique* – can still give seventeenth century monarchs "not only examples from [his] life, but even more precepts,"[165] then Jurieu must be wrong in thinking (say) that the Edict of Nantes was a "contract" which binds and limits the monarchy through popular authority. For if David could wait to resume a rightful throne out of kingly prudence, after all, might not Louis XIV, a cautious Constantine-Theodosius, wait to "restore" a rightful Church out of similar prudence?

Bossuet needs to be able to say that Jurieu "makes a prodigious abuse of Scripture"[166] because the Bishop and the pastor agree that Scripture is indeed the definitive authority in politics: Bossuet would not dispute Jurieu's claim that Scripture offers "the most certain rule" because "it is only divine authorities that can make any impression on minds."[167] All the more important, then, that Scripture be read literally and authoritatively, that one should not "find" Biblical "contracts" which still resound in seventeenth-century palaces.

But Bossuet, anxious as he was to find a permanent model of perfect government in Hebrew monarchy, and to overturn any

---

[163] Ibid., p. 392.
[164] Ibid., p. 397.
[165] Bossuet, *Politique*, ed. Le Brun, p. 2.
[166] Bossuet, *Cinquième avertissement*, in *Œuvres* (1841 edn), pp. 393–94.
[167] Ibid., pp. 393–94 (Bossuet quoting Jurieu).

Introduction

suggestion that the throne of David and Solomon arose out of popular concession or "will," also offered "secular" objections to contractarianism which show an appreciation of Hobbes' writing and turns of phrase, if not of his conclusions. Beginning with an attack on Jurieu, Bossuet soon broadens the argument of the *Cinquième avertissement aux protestants* to take in the whole contract tradition.

> He [Jurieu] has imagined that the people are naturally sovereign; or, to speak as he does, that they naturally possess sovereignty, since they give it to whom they please. Now this is to err in principle, and not to understand terms. For, to consider men as they naturally are, and before all established government, one finds only anarchy, that is to say a savage and wild liberty in all men where each one can claim everything, and at the same time contest everything; where all are on guard, and in consequence in a continual war against all; where reason can do nothing, since each calls reason the passion that transports him; where even natural law itself remains without force, since reason has none; where in consequence there is neither property, nor domain, nor good, nor secure repose – nor, to speak truly, any right whatsoever, except that of the strongest (and again one never knows who that is, because each can become such by turns, according as the passions conspire to throw more or fewer people together.)[168]

To know whether "the human race in its entirety" has ever been in such a state of nature, "or whether some peoples have been in it in some places," to know "how and by what degrees they left it" – to know this, Bossuet goes on, "it would be necessary to count to infinity, and understand all the thoughts which can arise in the human heart."[169]

Hobbes, then, has at least seen the predicament clearly in *Leviathan* XIII – even if his contractarianism will not provide the right deliverance. That is more than one can say for Jurieu:

> To imagine now, with M. Jurieu, in the people considered to be in this condition, a sovereignty, which is already a species of government, is to insist on a government before all government,

---

[168] Ibid., pp. 403–404. For a brief but excellent account of Bossuet's criticism of Jurieu, see Nannerl O. Keohane, *Philosophy and the State in France* (Princeton: Princeton University Press, 1980), pp. 254–55.
[169] Bossuet, *Cinquième avertissement*, in *Œuvres* (1841 edn), pp. 403–404.

Introduction

and to contradict oneself. Far from the people being sovereign in this condition, there is not even a people in this state. There may well be families, as ill-governed as they are ill-secured; there may well be a troop, a mass of people, a confused multitude; but there can be no people, because a people supposes something which already brings together some regulated conduct and some established law – something which happens only to those who have already begun to leave this unhappy condition, that is to say, that of anarchy.[170]

Not to see the diametrical opposition of sovereignty and anarchy, for Bossuet, is like the failure to distinguish between day and night; but Jurieu's failure is of just that kind.

If it pleases M. Jurieu to call sovereignty this unruly liberty which ought to yield to law and to the magistrate, he can do so; but this is to confuse everything – it is to confuse the independence of each man in a state of anarchy with sovereignty . . . Here, then, is the sovereign of M. Jurieu: whoever is strongest in a condition of anarchy; that is to say, the multitude and the greater number against the smaller. There is the people that he makes the master and the sovereign over all kings and over every legitimate power.[171]

Not only, in Bossuet's view, has Jurieu mistaken anarchy for "popular sovereignty"; he has made the still worse mistake of imagining "that it is against reason for a people to deliver itself up to a sovereign without some pact, and that such an agreement must be null and against nature."[172] Here Bossuet's sarcastic fury can barely contain itself:

"It is," he says, "against nature to deliver oneself without some pact," that is to say, to deliver oneself without reserving the right of sovereignty to oneself . . . It is as if he said: It is against nature to risk something to pull oneself out of the most hideous of all conditions, which is that of anarchy; it is against nature to do that which so many peoples have done.[173]

If Hobbes is right, then, that the state of nature is a state of war – here "charity" seems to be as vestigial for Bossuet as it had been for the sage of Malmesbury – that does not mean that a "social contract"

[170] Ibid., p. 404. [171] Ibid., p. 404.
[172] Ibid., p. 404. [173] Ibid., p. 404.

is the means of peace and felicity; and here some broader comparisons of Bossuet and Hobbes may be instructive.

Of course both Bossuet and Hobbes give prominence to the notion of *covenant*. But for Bossuet the covenant is "there," on the opening page of the *Politique* ("Ecoute, Israël"), and is (or rather historically was) a pact between God and Abraham – from whom "kings" then issue in an anointed patriarchal succession. By contrast Hobbes brings in "covenant" in a fully religious sense too late for Bossuet: *Leviathan* is half over before Book III arrives, and Abraham's covenant finally materializes in Chapter XL. For Hobbes, moreover, "wills . . . make the essence of all covenants,"[174] and it is covenants expressive of everyone's will which endow sovereigns with legitimate authority (*Leviathan* XIV); if there is not a Jurieuean popular "sovereignty" in Hobbes, there is at least a transfer of popular natural right to a sovereign beneficiary by an act of will ("when a man hath . . . granted away his rights, then he is said to be obliged, or bound, not to hinder those, to whom such right is granted . . . from the benefit of it: and that he *ought*, and it is his DUTY not to make void that voluntary act of his own").[175] For Bossuet there is one permanent covenant – in Genesis – which provides the world with monarchs for all time ("kings shall come out of you"); for Hobbes a covenant can arise – with the "will" of all as its "essence" – whenever the state of nature needs escaping from. The will of Abraham is replaced by the wills "of every one of those that are to be governed" (*Leviathan* XLII).[176]

So Hobbes, while in some sense an "absolute monarchist," is usually no believer in such monarchy by "divine right" or paternal succession (through "descent" from Abraham): for Hobbes monarchy is mainly an antidote to the vainglorious pride which aristocracy and democracy aggravate.[177] And Hobbes, moreover, argues all of this (in the first half of *Leviathan*) on the basis of reason alone: revelation enters the work mainly in Book III, as a kind of support for what has already been established. As George Kelly says in *Mortal Politics in Eighteenth-Century France*, "Bossuet's king had God close by his side in his mystical process of natural selection, coronation and election. Hobbes began with purely rational principles, keeping his *Dieu abscons* completely at bay, and always on

---

[174] Hobbes, *Leviathan*, ed. Oakeshott, Ch. XL, p. 307.
[175] Ibid., Ch. XIV, p. 86.   [176] Ibid., Ch. XLII, p. 377.
[177] Ibid., Ch. XIX (entire).

Introduction

an Erastian leash, until an extra and mysterious might was needed to wield the heavy sword."[178]

To be sure, the frontispiece of *Leviathan* quotes the Book of Job: "non est potestas super terram qui comparetur ei"; but the rest of Scripture makes a much-delayed appearance – as Hobbes himself explains at the beginning of Book III.

> I have derived the rights of sovereign power, and the duty of subjects hitherto, from the principles of nature only; such as experience has found true, or consent (concerning the use of words) has made so: that is to say, from the nature of men, known to us by experience, and from definitions (of such words as are essential to all political reasoning) universally agreed on. But in that I am next to handle, which is the nature and rights of a Christian commonwealth, whereof there dependeth much upon supernatural revelations of the Will of God; the ground of my discourse must be, not only the natural word of God, but also the prophetical.[179]

Hobbes, moreover, given his principles, had to give primacy to reason over revelation, because Scripture (for him) has no "intrinsic" meaning at all: the Bible must be made "canonical" by legitimate sovereign authority; therefore politics must come first (established on rational grounds alone), and then an existing sovereign can declare Scripture canonical (or not). Inverting Bossuet, what Hobbes offers is a "Holy Scripture drawn from the very words of politics." This is immediately visible in Hobbes' attack on Bishop Bramhall in *Liberty, Necessity and Chance*:

> The Bible is a law. To whom? To all the world? He knows it is not. How came it then to be a law to us? Did God speak it *viva voce* to us? Have we any other warrant for it than the word of the prophets? Have we seen the miracles? Have we any other assurance of their certainty than the authority of the Church? And is the authority of the Church any other than the authority of the Commonwealth, or that of the Commonwealth any other than that of the head of the Commonwealth, or hath the head of the

---

[178] George Armstrong Kelly, *Mortal Politics in Eighteenth-Century France*, special book-length number of *Historical Reflexions* (Waterloo, Canada), Vol. 13, No. 1 (Spring 1986), 9. Kelly's splendid few pages on Bossuet show what a wonderful full-length study of M. de Meaux he might have written – had not death intervened in December 1987.

[179] Hobbes, *Leviathan*, ed. Oakeshott, Ch. XXXII, p. 242.

Introduction

Commonwealth any other than that which hath been given him by the members? . . . They that have the sovereign power make nothing canon which they make not law, nor law, which they make not canon. And because the legislative power is from the assent of subjects, the Bible is made law by the assent of the subjects.[180]

For Hobbes, then, popular "assent," which creates sovereignty, also "creates" the Bible – as something "canonical." Scripture may give an account of the Creation; but Scripture is itself the creation of the will of finite beings. Scripture thus has no "natural" or inherent authority – Hobbes cannot say, with Bossuet, that *l'Ecriture Sainte* is knowably *un livre parfait*. It is, till made canonical, simply *un livre*.

A reading of *Liberty, Necessity and Chance* would only have confirmed Bossuet's belief that contractarianism is impious and dangerous – whether one tries to make King David into a Lockian *avant la lettre*, or uses the idea of "contract" in modern times. For what, Bossuets asks triumphantly in the *Cinquième avertissement*, is the most striking recent result of contractarian and popular sovereignty thinking? Nothing less than the judicial murder (as he takes it to be) of Charles I by Cromwell.

Let us come to the true authors of the crime. It was Cromwell and the fanatics, I grant. But what principles did they use to get the people to enter into their sentiments? What principles does one still see in their apologies – in that of a Milton, and in a hundred other libels with which the Cromwellites inundated all Europe? Of what are these books full . . . if not the absolute sovereignty of peoples over their kings, and all the other principles which M. Jurieu, following Buchanan, still maintains?[181]

The *reductio ad Cromwellum*: always effective, even for a liberal constitutionalist such as Kant a century later.[182]

---

[180] Hobbes, *Liberty, Necessity and Chance*, in *Hobbes' English Works*, ed. W. Molesworth (London: John Bohn, 1841), Vol. 5, p. 179.
[181] Bossuet, *Cinquième avertissement*, in *Œuvres* (1841 edn), p. 410.
[182] Kant, *Rechtslehre*, in *Kant's Political Writings*, ed. H. Reiss (Cambridge: Cambridge University Press, 1970), pp. 145–46n. For a fuller treatment of Kant's views on the overthrow of monarchs, see my *Kant's Political Philosophy* (Totowa NJ: Rowman and Littlefield, 1983), pp. 105ff.

Introduction

VII A brief conclusion

One can throw some final light on Bossuet's politics "from Scripture" through a comparison of M. de Meaux with three of his greatest contemporaries: Malebranche, Bayle, and Leibniz – all of whom knew, or corresponded with Bossuet.

Bossuet–Malebranche

Does not Bossuet himself, in his defense of *Providence particulière*, sometimes use equivocal phrases which show that he worries – as he should – about Malebranche's central question

> Is there [divine] wisdom and goodness in making impious princes reign, in suffering so great a number of heresies, in letting so many nations perish? . . . let him justify Providence, on the supposition that God acts and must act through *volontés particulières*.[183]

Here one can note that in Book x of the *Politique* – the last to be written, when Bossuet was near death – M. de Meaux uses equivocal language which reveals doubt and hesitation: "God *seemed* to want to authorize" the monarchy of Jeroboam, though it arose through rebellion and murder; Jeroboam himself "*seemed* to become a legitimate king."[184] Does the use of the verb *paraître* show some weakening of Bossuet's *particularisme* – at the very time (post-1700) that he began to countenance and use the term *volonté générale* in reference to God (in the *Défense de la tradition et des pères*)?[185] After all, one should remember that Bossuet's main objection to the preface to the Benedictine edition of the works of St. Augustine (which he examined and revised in c. 1700) was that the editors had insufficiently distanced the Bishop of Hippo from Jansenism and Calvinism, had diminished the gulf between Africa and Geneva, by under-stressing the general will of God to save all men before the Fall: "Saint Augustin même contre les

---

[183] Malebranche, *Réponse à une dissertation de M. Arnauld*, in *Œuvres complètes*, Vol. VI–VII, pp. 591–92.
[184] Bossuet, *Politique*, ed. Le Brun, p. 388. There is further hesitation in Bossuet's saying that "Dieu sembla vouloir ensuite autoriser le nouveau royaume," etc. (p. 388).
[185] Bossuet, *Défense de la tradition et des pères* in *Œuvres complètes* (1870 edn), Vol. V, p. 324.

Introduction

Pélagiens a reconnu une volonté générale antécédente."[186] If *particularisme* might seem to shade into Calvinist "election" of a few *en particulier*, might not Bossuet have had some reason to tilt a little toward *généralité* in theology and in theological politics ("from Scripture") at the end of his life? Might there not be a parallel between the resurrection of theological *généralité* and the birth of doubts about political *particularité* after about 1700? (One says "doubts," merely: Bossuet was never to be, in the manner of Malebranche, a precursor of Rousseau's "la volonté générale est toujours droite."[187])

Bossuet–Bayle

Does not Bayle have a point when he says (in the *Dictionnaire*) that we should judge Abraham and David not merely through the "literal sense" of Scripture, but through *lumière naturelle* and "general ideas" of equity, that over-literal Scripturalism might lead to the countenancing of "crimes"?[188]

The part of Bayle's thought which is most opposed to Bossuet's particularism is the very rough treatment meted out to King David, and then to Abraham, in the *Dictionnaire* – in the Malebranchian language of *généralité* and *particularité*. Following a vivid description of some of David's crimes, including several massacres and the killing of Uriah, Bayle observes that "the profound respect that one ought to have for this great king" should not blind one to the "blemishes" that disfigured his life; otherwise some will fancy that "it suffices, in order for an action to be just, that it have been done by certain people whom we venerate." Nothing could be "more fatal . . . to Christian morality" than this countenancing of crimes carried out by great men: "It is important for true religion that the life of the orthodox be judged by general ideas of rightness and of order [*par les idées générales de la droiture et de l'ordre*]." Bayle concludes with virtually the same words that he went on to apply to Abraham's adultery and Sarah's connivance: "There is no middle ground: either these actions [of

---

[186] Bossuet, Notes on the Benedictine edition of the *Œuvres de S. Augustin*, c. 1700, first published in *Revue Bossuet*, Vol. I, 159ff., partic. p. 175: "One must beware of imitating Jansénius too much, by striving to render useless that place in [Augustine's] *De spiritu et littera*, which is clearly for the general will . . ."
[187] Rousseau, *Du contrat social*, Book II, Ch. 6.
[188] Bayle, *Dictionnaire historique et critique* and *Commentaire philosophique*, treated fully in my *The General Will before Rousseau*, pp. 79ff.

Introduction

David's] are worthless, or actions similar to them are not evil. Now, since one must choose one or the other of these two possibilities, is it not better to place the interests of morality above the glory of an individual [*la gloire d'un particulier*]?"[189] From "Sarah" one will learn that the "interest of morality" is precisely *générale*; one must not try to derive *la morale naturelle* from the (frequently bad) conduct of someone who "does great wrong to the eternal laws."[190]

To show more plainly that morality is a "general" interest, while an individual reputation in Scripture is only particular, Bayle remarks that even the Patriarch Abraham, yielding to lust, was as susceptible to "the snares of Satan" as are "manifestly criminal persons,"[191] and that St. Augustine's justificatory efforts involve a morality more lax than that of the Jesuits Bauni and Escobar – those accommodating latitudinarians so ferociously attacked by Pascal in the *Lettres provinciales*. (It was surely no accident that Bayle pitched upon the very figures that Pascal – justly or not – had saddled with permanently horrible reputations.[192]) In Bayle's "Sarah," then, the *interêt général de la moralité* is pitted against Satanic snares, manifest criminality, and Jesuitical laxity; and these should not be admitted, accordingly to Bayle, just to justify a hero of Scripture, even one who happened to be a prophet.[193] (All of this would horrify Bossuet, who views Abraham as the fountain of all later monarchy; for the father of kings to be an adulterer is particularly inconvenient.)

Bossuet–Leibniz

Finally, does not Bossuet – a bishop, after all – subordinate charity (as the first of the Christian virtues) too much to the exigencies of *l'esprit du monde*? And when he does turn to religion, does he not cling too much to the Old Testament law that he (often enough) describes as "harsh" and "hard," resting excessively on "fear" and "terror"? Does not Leibniz do better to urge that justice is the "charity of the wise" – thereby fusing 1 Corinthians 13 and a Platonic rule of the wise?[194]

---

[189] Bayle, *Dictionnaire historique et critique*, "David," cited in Elisabeth Labrousse, *Pierre Bayle* (Paris: Editions Seghers, 1965), Vol. II, pp. 136–37.
[190] Ibid., pp. 136–37.
[191] Bayle, *Dictionnaire historique et critique* (Rotterdam: 1720), Vol. III, "Sarah."
[192] Pascal, *Les [Lettres] Provinciales*, ed. Louis Cognet (Paris: Garnier Frères, 1965), pp. 72ff.
[193] Bayle, *Dictionnaire historique et critique*, Vol. III.
[194] On this point see my *Leibniz: Political Writings*, pp. 3ff.

Introduction

Even if Victor Hugo was unjust and uncharitable in his view of Bossuet –

> Judas buvant le sang que Jésus-Christ suait,
> La ruse, Loyola, la haine, Bossuet
> L'autodafé, l'effroi, le cachot, la Bastille
> C'est nous[195] –

should not Bossuet have done better? Is not his "realism" a little too complacent and convenient – given the Christian standards that were (after all) his own? He does say, in the *Histoire universelle*, that "Jesus Christ propounded new ideas of virtue, practices that were more perfect and more purified. The end of religion, the soul of virtue, and the summary of the law, is charity . . . On this foundation of charity, he perfected all the conditions of human life."[196] But human life includes politics and justice. To be sure, Bossuet eloquently condemns Herod, Pilate, the *mauvais riche*; but his politics does nothing to exclude or avoid them. To reconcile Hobbesian sovereignty and Pauline charity may be as hard as Leibniz thought it was.

An example will make this plainer. In Book X of the *Politique*, speaking about the regulation of marriage and of sexual practices, Bossuet cites with apparent approval (or at least without contradiction) the law of Deuteronomy that sexually debauched sons be turned over to magistrates by their parents and then stoned to death.[197] Despite his admission in the *Histoire universelle* that "for Jesus Christ the summary of the law is charity," Bossuet appears to have forgotten Christ's repudiation of Deuteronomy in the Gospel according to St. John – where Christ, defending the woman taken in adultery, says, "let him who is without sin cast the first stone."[198] Sometimes Bossuet's Scriptural literalism is either horrifying or thoughtless: the charitable Christ of St. John's Gospel is minimized (or spends his time rendering to Caesar), but the David driving chariots armed with knives over prostrate enemy bodies is recounted twice in detail.

A perfectly just assessment of Bossuet's political thought is difficult, given that his central notions are either dead (divine-right absolute monarchy) or moribund (*Providence particulière*): the latter still has a

---

[195] Victor Hugo, *La Légende des siècles, Voix basses dans les ténèbres*, cited in Truchet, *Politique de Bossuet*, p. 9.
[196] Bossuet, *Histoire universelle*, cited in Goyet, *L'Humanisme de Bossuet*, Vol. II, pp. 300–301.
[197] Bossuet, *Politique*, ed. Le Brun, p. 392.
[198] John Ch. 8.

Introduction

few defenders; the former, none. At least, however, one can attempt a judgment which will steer between the adulation of La Bruyère ("let us speak in advance the language of posterity: a Father of the Church"[199]) and the violent antipathy of Raymond Schmittlein – for whom Bossuet is "a serf dazzled by his sovereign, a commoner avid for power" who "did nothing but legitimize the monstrous egoism and the indecent pride of Louis XIV."[200] Those extremes are so extreme that the truth can hardly fail to lie between them.

What is certain is that, within the Christian tradition that was his own, Bossuet did not preserve the balance of an Augustine – acknowledging political necessity but shrinking from the deification of the profane. What is equally certain is that the objections of Malebranche, Bayle, and Leibniz have a force that Bossuet could not counteract. If a Christian political philosopher must strive for the best available balance of *caritas* and *potestas*, one can say that Bossuet threw off the equilibrium in favor of the latter – even if one can understand his fear of *frondeurs* and "anarchists."

But what is most certain is that Bossuet's notion of God is unacceptable. In Book VIII of the *Politique* he insists that "under a just God there is no purely arbitrary power" – but *within* God that power is frighteningly arbitrary. Book X of the *Politique* reveals that, for the "crime" of enumerating the people, David was given his choice of war, famine, or plague – to be visited upon a people which had merely let itself be counted. A non-crime in a ruler leads to the "punishment" of an innocent populace – and Bossuet has not a word to say about this conception of an *être parfait*. A reading of Bossuet makes one appreciate with ever greater force the words of Rousseau from *La Nouvelle Héloïse*: "I would rather believe the Bible falsified or unintelligible, than God unjust or evil-doing."[201]

And what is finally certain is that the sheer magnificence of Bossuet's prose, always of a marmoreal splendor, could occasionally sustain worthy causes – such as Solomon's pacifism over David's bellicosity – in a way that makes one wish that he had consistently turned such wonderful gifts in happier directions.

---

[199] Cited in Truchet, *Politique de Bossuet*, p. 7.
[200] Schmittlein, *L'Aspect politique du différend Bossuet–Fénelon*, pp. 25, 13.
[201] Rousseau, *La Nouvelle Heloîse*, ed. R. Pomeau (Paris: Garnier Frères, 1960), p. 671.

Chronology

1627	Born at Dijon, of a family of magistrates.
1642	Arrives in Paris for studies at the Collège de Navarre; his mentor is Nicolas Cornet, the Jesuit theologian who "exposed" Jansenism as a form of demi-Calvinism.
1652	Ordained a priest; receives his doctorate in theology; installs himself at Metz.
1657	Preaches at Metz before Anne of Austria; receives honorific title of "Counselor and Preacher to the King."
1662	Preaches before Louis XIV at the Louvre "On the Duties of Kings."
1669	Named Bishop of Condom; delivers the funeral oration of Henrietta of England, widow of Charles I.
1670	Made tutor to the Dauphin, for whom he will write the *Discourse on Universal History* and *Politics drawn from the Very Words of Holy Scripture*. Delivers the funeral oration of Henrietta of England, widow of Charles I.
1671	Elected to the Académie Française.
1677–79	Writes Books I–VI of the *Politics*; gives a long account of the work in a letter to Pope Innocent XI.
1681	Publishes the *Universal History*; named Bishop of Meaux.
1683	Delivers the funeral oration of Marie-Thérèse of Austria, wife of Louis XIV, before the Dauphin and the court: the decisive public blow against Malebranche's theory of *Providence générale*.
1685–87	Three great funeral orations: Anne de Gonzague, Michel Le Tellier, Prince de Condé.

Chronology

1688	Publishes the *Histoire des variations des Eglises protestantes* – his main attack on Calvinism and Lutheranism.
1690	Publishes the *Cinquième Avertissement aux Protestants*, an attack on Jurieu's theory of popular sovereignty and the social contract.
1690s	Correspondence with Leibniz over the restoration of a universal *Respublica Christiana*.
1698	Publishes the *Relation sur le quiétisme*, against Fénelon's "disinterested love of God."
1700	Begins writing the last four books of the *Politics*, as well as the *Défense de la tradition et des pères* – rescuing St. Augustine from the Jansenists and Calvinists.
1704	Death of Bossuet, at Paris.
1709	Posthumous publication of the *Politics*.

Critical bibliography

Principal editions of Bossuet's works cited in this edition
Œuvres de Bossuet (Versailles: J. A. Lebel, 1818).
Œuvres de Bossuet (Paris: Didot Frères, 1841). (This was the version most used in the present edition.)
Œuvres complètes de Bossuet (Bar-le-Duc: Louis Guérin, 1870).
Œuvres, ed. Abbé Velat (Paris: Pléiade, 1961).

Correspondance, ed. C. Urbain and E. Levesque (Paris: Hachette, 1909–26).
Politique tirée des propres paroles de l'Ecriture Sainte, ed. Abbé Bossuet (Paris: Pierre Cot, 1709).
Politique tirée des propres paroles de l'Ecriture Sainte, critical edn with Introduction by Jacques Le Brun (Geneva: Droz, 1967).
"Examen d'un nouvelle éxplication du mystère de l'euchariste" (c. 1670) and "Notes" on the Benedictine edition of the works of St. Augustine (c. 1700), in *Révue Bossuet* (Paris: 1900–1904), Vol. I.
Platon et Aristote: Notes de lectures, ed. Thérèse Goyet (Paris: Librairie Klincksieck, 1964).
Discourse on Universal History, ed. Orest Ranum (Chicago: University of Chicago Press, 1976). Contains an excellent Introduction.
The Political Science [i.e. Book 1 of the *Politique*], trans. George Keating (London: The Catholic Spectator, 1826), reprinted as a booklet in 1842. Accurate, and captures much of the grandeur of Bossuet's style; but the substantial abridgements are nowhere indicated.
Politics drawn from the Scriptures [i.e. fragments from the *Politique*], in *Sources in Western Civilization: The Seventeenth Century*, ed. A. Lossky (New York: Free Press, 1967). Excellent, if slightly free, renderings of a few parts of the *Politique*.

Studies of Bossuet
Delmont, Theodore. *Bossuet et les Saints-Pères* (Geneva: Slatkine, 1970). Excellent on Bossuet's devotion to Augustine, and on his use of the writings of Ambrose and Jerome.

[Les] Dernières Années de Bossuet: Journal de Ledieu, ed. C. Urbain and R. Levesque (Paris: Desclée de Brouwer, 1928), Vol. I, Appendix II, "La Politique et la lettre à Innocent XI." A detailed account, by Bossuet's private secretary, of M. de Meaux's reworking of the *Politique* in 1700–1704, and of publication difficulties between Bossuet's death (1704) and the publication of the *Politics* (1709).

Dreyfus, Ginette. Introduction to Malebranche's *Traité de la nature et de la grâce* (Paris: Vrin, 1958), pp. 127ff., "l'opposition commune de Bossuet et de Fénelon." Valuable on Bossuet's providentialist *particularisme* and his hostility to Malebranchian *Providence générale*.

Floquet, Pierre A. *Bossuet précepteur du Dauphin* (Paris: Didot Frères, 1864). Full of useful information, but adulatory in tone: the "transcendent capacity of the master" (Bossuet) was bent on "forming for France a sovereign worthy of her."

Gouhier, Henri. *Fénelon philosophe* (Paris: Vrin, 1977). Begins with a short but superb account of philosophy in seventeenth-century France, then moves on to the Fénelonian "quietism" that so distressed Bossuet.

Goyet, Thérèse. *L'Humanisme de Bossuet*, 2 vols. (Paris: Librairie Klincksieck, 1965). An invaluable account of Bossuet's education. But one must make allowance for her claim that Bossuet was a classical humanist steeped in Plato and Aristotle, and for her insistence on his devotion to Descartes. She gives too much prominence to philosophy, ancient and modern, and too little to *L'Ecriture Sainte*.

Hugo, Victor. *La Légende des siècles: Voix basses dans les ténèbres*. The classic account of Bossuet as enemy of the human race, lumped with Judas and Torquemada.

Kelly, George Armstrong. *Mortal Politics in Eighteenth-Century France*, double number of *Historical Reflexions* (Waterloo, Canada), Vol. 13, No. 1 (Spring, 1986). The few superb pages on Bossuet make one wish that Kelly had written the full-length Bossuet study which he had in mind.

Keohane, Nannerl O. *Philosophy and the State in France* (Princeton: Princeton University Press, 1980). Contains a brief but fine chapter on Bossuet's politics.

Lacour-Goyet, Georges. *L'Education politique de Louis XIV* (Paris: Librairie Hachette, 1923). Particularly good on Gallicanism, and on Hobbesian elements in Bossuet's thought.

Lanson, Gustave. *Bossuet* (Paris: Lecène, Oudin et Cie., 1891). Claims that much of Bossuet's *Politique* is Hobbism – but with Hobbes' *système aride et sans pitié* improved by Bossuet's addition of *la moralité* and *la charité*.

Le Brun, Jacques. *La Spiritualité de Bossuet* (Paris: Librairie Klincksieck, 1972). Good on Bossuet's religious education, on the struggle with Fénelon, and on Bossuet's old age and death.

Martimort, Aimé-Georges. *Le Gallicanisme de Bossuet* (Paris: Editions du Cerf, 1953). Treats Bossuet as an "excellent moralist," but complains that Gallicanism arises from French provincialism and damages the universality of the Church.

Critical bibliography

Nourrisson, Jean-Félix. *La Politique de Bossuet* (Paris: Didier, 1867). Calls Bossuet "the most imperturbable intelligence" of the seventeenth century, but views the *Politique* as undermined by "essential vices": *odieuse doctrine, théorie subversive,* and *déraisonnables maximes.*

Oakeshott, Michael. *On Human Conduct* (Oxford: Clarendon Press, 1975). Brief but valuable remarks on Bossuet's debt to Thomism.

Ranum, Orest. Introduction to Bossuet's *Discourse on Universal History* (Chicago: University of Chicago Press, 1976). An excellent account of Bossuet's historical thought, with incidental illumination of the politics.

Rébelliau, Alfred. *Bossuet* (Paris: Librairie Hachette, 1900). Balanced, fair-minded, judicious – neither adulatory nor tendentious. Good on Bossuet's *rapports* with Malebranche and Fénelon.

Reynolds, E. E. *Bossuet* (Garden City, NY: Doubleday, 1963). Bossuet *contra* a set of "personalities": Fénelon, Mme. Guyon, etc. Not philosophically or theologically serious.

Rosso, Corrado. "Demiurgia e parabola delle élites nelle *Considérations* di Montesquieu," in *Storia e ragione,* ed. A. Postigliola (Naples: Liguori Editore, 1987). Fine comparative study of the philosophies of history of Montesquieu and Bossuet.

Sanders, E. K. *Jacques-Bénigne Bossuet* (London: Society for Promoting Christian Knowledge, 1921). Even-handed; views Bossuet's sincere Christianity as constantly compromised – by himself and by events.

Schmittlein, Raymond. *L'Aspect politique du différend Bossuet–Fénelon* (Mainz: Editions Art et Science Bade, 1954). Violently hostile. Urges that under a "thin crust" of Scripture one finds pure Hobbism. Calls Bossuet "a serf dazzled by his sovereign" who wanted only "to legitimize the monstrous egoism and the indecent pride of Louis XIV." By contrast Fénelon is virtually a saint.

Skinner, Quentin. *The Foundations of Modern Political Thought: The Age of Reformation* (Cambridge: Cambridge University Press, 1978). Sees more clearly than any other study Bossuet's debt to Protestantism – to viewing Scripture as the basis of politics. Contains a brilliant page on Bossuet and Luther.

Tavénaux, R. *Jansénisme et politique* (Paris: Colin, 1965). "Places" Bossuet – in the middle – in the controversy over Jansenism.

Truchet, Jacques. *Bossuet panégyriste* (Paris: Editions du Cerf, 1962). The only full and adequate study of this branch of Bossuet's literary activity.

La Politique de Bossuet (Paris: Armand Colin, 1966). The most valuable single book on Bossuet's political thought. A balanced, judicious and thorough introduction is followed by well-chosen texts of Bossuet – parts of the *Politique* and *Histoire universelle,* excerpts from the main *Oraisons funèbres* and sermons, etc. Indispensable to any serious study of Bossuet.

La Prédication de Bossuet, 2 vols. (Paris: Editions du Cerf, 1960). Excellent on moral and political themes in Bossuet's sermons.

A note on the text

"Sir, nobody reads him." Dr. Johnson's remark to Boswell (during their tour of the Hebrides) has certainly applied with full force to Bossuet's *Politique tirée des propres paroles de l'Ecriture Sainte* – for until now only a few fragments have been translated into English. George Keating's version of Book 1 of the *Politics*, published in *The Catholic Spectator* (London) in 1826, is accurate and useful – but contains substantial cuts of which one is not warned. Fragments drawn from various books of the *Politique* are to be found in *Sources in Western Civilization: The Seventeenth Century* (New York: Free Press, 1967) and in *Heritage of Western Civilization* (Englewood Cliffs, New Jersey: Anchor, 1958); but these (good) translations substantially overlap, and together offer less than a twentieth of the whole work.

A great deal of Bossuet's *Politique* consists of Scriptural citations – from which divine-right absolute monarchy is "drawn." Bossuet used St. Jerome's Vulgate, and whenever possible I have used the English version called the Douay Bible – that late sixteenth-century rendering of the Vulgate whose near-Shakespearian splendor most nearly matches the elevated, oratorical tone used by Bossuet in his *Politics*. Sometimes Bossuet abridges Scripture, without notice; sometimes he freely reduces whole passages to an (accurate enough) quintessence. So it is very much his version of Scripture, as well as his reading of it.

The Vulgate, of course, contains books omitted from the King James Bible – such as the two books of Maccabees; moreover in Jerome's Bible there are four books of Kings rather than two, etc. But all of this is indicated in the Scriptural citations, which are placed at the end of each book.

A note on the text

The marmoreal splendor of Bossuet's tone – high, lofty, grand, rhetorical – is beyond capturing in modern English; his great, rolling periods have a cumulative effect (in French) which is dissipated by the unavoidable breaking up of some of his more gigantic structures. But I have tried to match my Anglicizing of his French to the early-modern English rendering of the Douay Bible; at least consistency is achieved, if not perfect adequacy. But then those who want Bossuet unvarnished will rightly turn to the *propres paroles* of M. de Meaux himself.

Biographical synopses

Ancient and Scriptural figures

AUGUSTINE, St. (Augustinus Aurelius) (345–430), Bishop of Hippo, the greatest of the Fathers of the Church. For Bossuet in the *Politics*, Augustine is mainly a defender of Roman Imperial power and an advocate of passive obedience to that power. The dark side of *The City of God*, calling social life "miserable" (and treating Romulus as a fratricide comparable to Cain) is radically downplayed by Bossuet.

CHRIST, Jesus. For Bossuet, Christ is not so much the giver of the "new law" of charity (Gospel according to St. John) as the advocate of passive acceptance of established authority. Bossuet stresses Christ's saying "render to Caesar," and his recognition of Pilate's (and Tiberius') authority over him.

DAVID, second King of Israel. For Bossuet, David is *the* king *par excellence*; Book v of the *Politics* is a long eulogy for him. On Bossuet's view, David made terrible mistakes – such as indulging Absalom to a nearly fatal degree – but always recovered his footing through prudence and fortitude. Above all Bossuet stresses David's loyalty to Saul, despite the latter's treachery. The *Politics* ends with praise of "the beautiful Psalms of David."

JULIAN ("the Apostate"), Roman Emperor 361–63. For Bossuet, Julian illustrates how seriously Christians took the doctrine of passive obedience to impious rulers: even Julian was faithfully obeyed.

Biographical synopses

MACCABEES. For Bossuet, the Maccabees rightly rebelled, by the "particular will" of God, against Antiochus of Syria (who intended the destruction of the Jews). But their divinely ordained rebellion should not be seen as a general "precedent" for later attacks on established authority.

MOSES. For Bossuet, Moses is the divinely instructed "founder" of a Jewish polity which remains a permanent model of good government. Bossuet views Moses, and his successor Joshua, as a king in everything but name.

PAUL, St. On Bossuet's reading, Paul is mainly the author of Romans 13 ("obey the powers that be"), not of 1 Corinthians 13 ("but the greatest of these is charity"). 1 Corinthians 13, indeed, is not mentioned even once in Bossuet's *Politics*.

PILATE, Pontius, Roman governor of Judaea under Tiberius (A.D. 14–37). For Bossuet, Pilate is the perfect example of an intelligent man who had some sense of justice, but whose fear of unpopularity led him to sacrifice an innocent victim (Jesus). Bossuet uses Pilate to illustrate the importance of resisting both popular demands and aristocratic cabals. By contrast Bossuet says nothing about Judas' betrayal – because Judas had no authority to exercise.

ROBOAM, son and successor of Solomon as King of Israel. For Bossuet, Roboam's spurning of wise counsel in favor of the bad advice of rash youth led to division and schism within Israel. Bossuet views Roboam as a kind of forerunner of Protestant "schism" centuries later.

SAMUEL. On Bossuet's view, Samuel was a "sovereign pontiff" whom the Jewish people spurned in asking for a king (1 *Kings* 8). In Bossuet's interpretation, Samuel nobly endured popular ingratitude and did everything possible to shore up Saul's authority.

SAUL, first King of Israel. For Bossuet, Saul's genuine courage and original simplicity were corrupted by envious hatred of David. On Bossuet's view, God finally let Saul be destroyed for refusing to follow divine orders *à la lettre*.

Biographical synopses

SOLOMON, son and successor of David, and third king of Israel. For Bossuet Solomon was magnificent without ostentation. Above all he is praised as "pacific," and Bossuet stresses that Solomon was permitted to build the Temple in Jerusalem which David (the warrior) had only been allowed to plan. God, Bossuet urges, did not want to receive the edifice "from a bloody hand."

Modern figures

ARNAULD, Antoine (1612–1694), the most intrepid French defender of Jansenism, finally driven into exile for his convictions. Bossuet was heartened by his anti-Malebranchian insistence that God operates in human affairs through "particular wills," not just general laws.

BAYLE, Pierre (1647–1706), Calvinist theologian and man of letters, driven into exile in Rotterdam just before the revocation of the Edict of Nantes. In his *Historical and Critical Dictionary* (1696), Bayle opposes "equity" and "natural light" to Bossuet's Scriptural literalism, and criticizes David and Abraham as violators of the "general interest of morality."

DESCARTES, René (1596–1650), commonly viewed as the founder of modern philosophy. For Bossuet the Cartesian "method of doubt" is dangerous to authority and tradition.

FÉNELON, François de Salignac de la Motte (1651-1715), disciple and then principal theological opponent of Bossuet. Bossuet opposed Fénelon's "quietism" and "disinterested love of God" as depriving Christians of legitimate hope of salvation, and saw to it that Fénelon's *Maximes des saints* was officially condemned at Rome.

HOBBES, Thomas (1588–1679), English political philosopher. For Bossuet Hobbes is right about "appetitive" human nature, and about the state of nature as a state of war; but he is wrong in thinking that sovereignty established by will and consent is the appropriate remedy. To Hobbesian consent Bossuet opposes divine-right monarchy, descended from David and Solomon.

JURIEU, Pierre (1637-1713), Calvinist minister and theologian, later exiled to Holland. Author of the *Letters to the Faithful of France who*

Biographical synopses

Groan under the Babylonian Captivity (1686), arguing that Louis XIV has broken his "contract" with the French people by revoking the Edict of Nantes. Bossuet specially resisted Jurieu's effort to "find" social contracts in Scripture and his claim that David ruled by popular "consent."

LEIBNIZ, Gottfried Wilhelm (1646–1716), the greatest German philosopher of the early Enlightenment, and author of the *Monadology* and *Theodicy*. Bossuet opposed his notion of reunifying the *Respublica christiana* by "suspending" doctrinal differences between Catholics and Protestants. Above all, Leibniz' definition of justice as the "charity of the wise" was (ironically) too Christian for Bossuet.

MALEBRANCHE, Nicolas (1638–1715), French philosopher who fused Cartesianism and Augustinian theology. For Malebranche in *Nature and Grace* (1680), God operates through general, simple, uniform laws, not through a "particular Providence" intervening in human affairs. Bossuet publicly rebuked Malebranche in his funeral oration for Queen Marie-Thérèse (1683).

PASCAL, Blaise (1623–1662), author of the anti-Jesuit *Lettres provinciales* and of the posthumously published *Pensées* – the greatest French theological work of the seventeenth century. Pascal's anti-rationalist and anti-Cartesian stress on the God of Abraham, Isaac and Jacob, "not of the philosophers and the theologians," must have struck a sympathetic chord in Bossuet.

Politics drawn from the Very Words of Holy Scripture
To Monseigneur the Dauphin

God is the King of kings: it is for him to instruct them and to rule them as his ministers. Listen, then, Monseigneur, to the lessons which he gives them in his Scripture, and learn from him the examples on which they must base their conduct.

Besides the other advantages of Scripture, it also enjoys this one, that it takes up the history of the world from its earliest origins, and shows us by this means, better than all other histories, the original principles which have formed empires.

No history reveals better the goodness and the badness of the human heart, what sustains and what overturns kingdoms; what religion can do to establish them, and impiety to destroy them.

The other virtues and the other vices are also shown in their natural characters in Scripture, and nowhere else does one see such clear evidence of their true effects.

There one sees the government of a people whose legislator was God himself; the abuses which he reprimanded and the laws which he established – which comprise the finest and justest polity that ever was.

All that Sparta, all that Athens, all that Rome – or, to go back to the beginning, all that Egypt and the best-governed states – had by way of wisdom, is nothing in comparison to the wisdom which is contained in the law of God, from which other laws have taken their best features.

To Monseigneur the Dauphin

Moreover, there was never a finer state constitution, than that under which you will see the people of God.

Moses, who formed it, was instructed in all the divine and human wisdom with which a great and noble genius can be embellished; and this inspiration only brought to the last degree of certainty and perfection, what had been only sketched in the usages and the knowledge of the wisest of all the empires and their greatest ministers – such as the patriarch Joseph, like him inspired by God.

Two great kings of this people, David and Solomon, the one a warrior, the other pacific, both excellent in the art of governing, will give you examples of it not only in their lives, but also in their precepts: the one in his divine poetry, the other in the lessons which eternal wisdom dictated to him.

Jesus Christ will teach you, by himself and by his apostles, all that can make states happy; his Gospel renders men more fit to be good citizens on earth, as it teaches them by that means to render themselves worthy of becoming citizens of heaven.

God, in fine, by whom kings reign, forgets nothing that may teach them to reign well. The ministers of princes, and those who have a part under their authority in the government of states and in the administration of justice, will find in his word lessons which only God could give them. It is a part of Christian morality to form the magistrature by his laws: God wills to decide everything, that is to say, to give decisions for all states; and more especially for that on which all others depend.

This, Monseigneur, is the greatest of all objects that can be proposed to men, and they cannot be too attentive to the rules upon which they will be judged by an eternal and irrevocable sentence. Those who believe that piety enfeebles politics will be confounded; and that which you shall behold is truly divine.

FIRST BOOK

Of the principles of human society

First Article

Man is made to live in society

1st Proposition
Men have but one and the same end and one and the same object, which is God

"Hear, O Israel, the Lord our God is one Lord. Thou shalt love the Lord thy God with thy whole heart, and with thy whole soul, and with thy whole strength."[1]

2nd Proposition
The love of God obliges men to love one another

A doctor of the law asked Jesus:[2] "Master, which is the first commandment? Jesus answered him: The first commandment of all is: Hear, O Israel, the Lord thy God is one God: and thou shalt love the Lord thy God with thy whole heart, and with thy whole soul, and with thy whole mind, and with thy whole strength. This is the first commandment, and the second is like to it: Thou shalt love thy neighbor as thyself."[3]

"On these two commandments dependeth the whole law and the prophets."[4]

We must then love one another, because we must all love the same God, who is our common father, and his unity is our bond. "There is but one God, says St. Paul; if there are others who reckon many gods,

---

[1] Deut. 6:4–5. [2] Matt. 23:35. [3] Mark 12:28–31. [4] Matt. 23:40.

there is but one God for us, the father; of whom are all things, and we unto him."[5]

If there are nations that do not know God, he is not less their creator, and he has not the less made them after his own image and likeness. For he said, in creating man, "Let us make man to our own image and likeness":[6] and, in the next verse, "God created man to his own image, to the image of God he created him."[7]

He repeats it frequently, so that we should learn upon what model we are formed, and that we should love in each other the image of God. For which reason our Lord said that the precept of loving our neighbor, is like that of loving God, because it is natural that he who loves God, loves also for the love of him, all that is made after his image; and these two obligations are alike.

We see also that when God forbids an attempt on the life of man, he gives this reason: "I will require the blood of your lives at the hand of every beast, and at the hand of man: whosoever shall shed man's blood, his blood shall be shed: for man was made to the image of God."[8]

The very beasts are, as it were, called in this passage to the judgment of God, to give account of the human blood they have shed. God speaks thus to cause sanguinary men to tremble; and it is true, in one sense, that God will redemand, even of the animals, the men they have devoured, when, despite their cruelty, they shall rise again on the last day.

3rd Proposition
All men are brothers

Firstly, they are all children of the same God. "One is your master, and all you are brethren. And call none your father upon earth: for one is your father who is in heaven."[9]

Those whom we call fathers, and from whom we come according to the flesh, do not know who we are; God alone knew us from all eternity, and it is for this reason that Isaiah said, "For thou art our father, and Abraham hath not known us, and Israel hath been ignorant of us: thou O Lord, art our Father, our protector; from everlasting is thy name."[10]

[5] 1 Cor. 8:46.   [6] Gen. 1:26.   [7] Ibid., 1:27.
[8] Ibid., 9:5–6.   [9] Matt. 23:8–9.   [10] Isa. 43:16.

Secondly, God has established the fraternity of men, in making them all descend from one, who is, therefore, the common father, and carries in himself the image of the paternity of God. We do not read that God made the other animals all descend from one common stock: "God made the beasts of the earth according to their kinds: and saw that it was good; and he said, Let us make man to our image and likeness."[11]

God speaks of man in the singular number, and marks distinctly that he would make but one only, from whom all others should be born, as it is said in the Acts: "And hath made of one, all mankind, to dwell upon the whole face of the earth."[12] The Greek says, "that God made him of the same blood."[13] He even willed that the woman whom he gave to the first man should be drawn from him, to the end that all should be one in the human race.[14] "The Lord built the rib which he took from Adam, into a woman: and brought her to Adam. And Adam said, this now is bone of my bone, and flesh of my flesh: she shall be called woman, because she was taken out of man. Wherefore a man shall leave father and mother, and shall cleave to his wife, and they shall be two in one flesh."[15]

Thus the character of friendship is perfect in the human race; and men, who have all but one common father, ought to love each other as brothers. God forbid that kings should believe themselves exempt from this law, or that they should imagine that it diminishes the respect which is due to them. God distinctly declares that the kings whom he will give to his people, "shall be taken from the number of their brethren,"[16] and adds, that "they shall not be puffed up with pride," and that on this condition, their reign shall be long.[17]

Men having forgotten their fraternity, and murders having multiplied upon the earth, God resolved to destroy mankind, with the exception of Noah and his family,[18] by whom he restored the human race, and willed that in this renovation of the world, we shall all still have one common father.

Soon afterwards, he forbad murder, reminding men that they are all brothers, descended from the same Adam, and subsequently, from the same Noah: "I will require the blood of the lives of man, at the hand of every man, and of his brother."[19]

---

[11] Gen. 1:25–26. [12] Acts 17:26. [13] Ibid., 17:26.
[14] Gen. 2:22–24. [15] Ibid., 2:22–24. [16] Deut. 17:15.
[17] Ibid., 17:20. [18] Gen 6. [19] Ibid., 9:5.

4th Proposition
No man is a stranger to another man

Our Lord, after having established the precept of loving our neighbor, interrogated by a doctor of the law [concerning] whom we are to regard as our neighbor, condemned the error of the Jews, who regarded as such only those of their nation. He showed them, by the parable of the Samaritan, who assists the traveler who was despised by a priest and by a Levite, that it is not on our nation, but upon humanity in general, that the union of men must be founded. "A priest saw a traveler wounded, and passed by, and a Levite near him, continued his road. But a Samaritan seeing him, was touched with compassion." He relates with what care he assisted him, and then he says to the scribe: "Which of these three, in thy opinion, was neighbor to him that fell among robbers: and the scribe said: he that showed mercy to him: and Jesus said to him, Go, and do thou in like manner."[20]

This parable teaches us that no man is foreign to another man, were he even of a nation as hated by our own, as was that of the Samaritans by the Jews.

5th Proposition
Each man ought to take care of other men

If we are all brethren, all made after the image of God and equally his children, all one race and one blood, we ought to take care of each other; and it is not without reason that it is written, "God has charged every one to have compassion towards his neighbor."[21] If they do not do it in good faith, God will avenge it; for, as Ecclesiasticus adds: "Our ways are always before him, and they cannot be hidden from his eyes."[22] We must then succor our neighbor, as having to render account to God, who sees us.

There are none but parricides and the enemies of the human race, who say, like Cain, "I know not where is my brother: am I my brother's keeper?"[23] "Have we not all one father? Hath not one God created us? Why then doth every one of us despise our brother, violating the covenant of our fathers?"[24]

---

[20] Luke 10:29–37. [21] Ecclus. 17:12. [22] Ecclus. 13.
[23] Gen. 4:9. [24] Mal. 2:10.

6th Proposition
Interest itself unites us

"A brother, that is helped by his brother, is like a strong city."[25] Remark how strength is multiplied by society, and by mutual assistance.

"It is better, therefore, that two should be together, than one: for they have the advantage of their society: If one fall, he shall be supported by the other: woe to him that is alone, for when he falleth he has none to lift him up. And if two men lie together, they shall warm one another: how shall one alone be warmed? And if a man prevail against one, two shall withstand him: a three-fold cord is not easily broken."[26]

They console, they assist, they fortify each other. God, having willed to establish society, has established that each one shall find in it his well-being, and remain attached to it through that interest.

For which reason, he has given to men different talents. One proper for one thing, and another for another, to the end that they must act together as the members of one body, and that their union be cemented by mutual wants. "For as in one body we have many members, but all the members have not the same office; so we, being many, are one body in Christ, and each one members of each other."[27] Each of us has his gift, and his special grace.

"For the body also is not one member, but many. If the foot should say, because I am not the hand, I am not of the body: is it therefore not of the body? And if the ear should say, because I am not the eye, I am not of the body: is it therefore not of the body? If the whole body were the eye, where would be the hearing? If the whole were hearing, where would be the smelling? But now God hath set the members, every one of them in the body, as it hath pleased him. And if they all were one member, where would be the body? But now there are many members, indeed, yet one body. And the eye cannot say to the hand: I need not thy help: nor again the head to the feet: I have no need of you. Yea much more those that seem to be the more feeble members of the body, are more necessary: And such as we think to be the less honorable members of the body, upon these we bestow more abundant honor: and those that are our uncomely parts, have more

---

[25] Prov. 18:19.   [26] Eccles. 4:9–12.   [27] Rom. 12:4–5.

abundant comeliness. But our comely parts have no need: but God hath tempered the body together, giving the more abundant honor to that which he wanted. That there might be no schism in the body, but the members might be mutually careful one for another."[28]

Thus, by different talents, the strong have need of the weak, the great of the little, each one of him who appears the most remote from him; because mutual wants attract all, and render all necessary.

Jesus Christ, in forming his Church, established unity on this foundation, and shows us what are the principles of human society.

The world subsists by this law. "All things live, and remain forever, and for every use all things obey him. All things are double, one against another, and he hath made nothing defective."[29]

We see, then, human society supported upon these irreversible foundations; one same God, one same object, one same end, one common origin, one same blood, one same interest, one mutual want,[30] alike for the affairs, as for the enjoyments of life.

Article II

The society of mankind gives birth to civil society, that is to say, to states, peoples, and nations

1st Proposition
Human society has been destroyed and violated by the passions

God was the bond of human society. The first man having separated himself from God, by a just punishment division was cast in his family, and Cain killed his brother Abel.[1]

The whole of the human race was divided. The children of Seth were called the children of God; and the children of Cain were called the children of men.[2]

---

[28] 1 Cor. 12:14–25.   [29] Ecclus. 42:24–26.   [30] Paraphrase of Eph. 4:3–6.
[1] Gen. 4:8.   [2] Ibid., 6:2.

These two races, by their alliances, only augmented corruption. The giants were the offspring of their union, men known in Scripture,[3] and in all the traditions of the human race,[4] by their injustice and their violence.

"All the thoughts of men turned at all times to evil, and God repented of having made them. Noah alone found grace before him," so general was the corruption.[5]

It is easy to comprehend that this perversity renders men unsociable. Man governed by his passions, thinks only of satisfying them without considering others. "I am, said the proud man in Isaiah, and there is none also besides me upon earth."[6]

The language of Cain resounds everywhere. "Am I my brother's keeper?"[7] that is to say, I have nothing to do with him, nor do I trouble myself about him.

All the passions are insatiable. "The cruel man is not appeased by blood;[8] the avaricious man is not satisfied with money."[9]

Thus each one desires all for himself. "You join, said Isaiah, house to house, and lay field to field. Shall you alone dwell in the midst of the earth?"[10]

Jealousy, so universal among men, exposes the profound malignity of their hearts. Our brother does us no injury, he takes nothing from us; nevertheless, he becomes to us an object of hatred, only because we see him more happy, or more industrious, or more virtuous than ourselves. "Abel pleased God by innocent means, and Cain could not bear it. The Lord had respect to Abel, and to his offerings. But to Cain and his offerings he had no respect, and Cain was exceeding angry, and his countenance fell."[11] Thence arise treasons and murder. "And Cain said to Abel his brother: Let us go forth abroad; and when they were in the field, Cain rose up against his brother and slew him."[12]

A similar passion exposed Joseph to the fury of his brothers, when, far from hurting them, he went in search of them for their father, who was uneasy about them.[13] "His brethren, seeing he was beloved by his father, more than all his sons, hated him, and could not speak peaceably to him."[14] Their rage made them resolve upon killing him; and

---

[3] Ibid., 6:4. [4] Ibid., 6:4. [5] Ibid., 6:5,6,8,11.
[6] Isa. 47:8. [7] Gen. 4:9. [8] Ecclus. 12:16.
[9] Eccles. 5:9. [10] Isa. 5:8. [11] Gen. 4:4–5.
[12] Ibid., 4:8. [13] Ibid., 37:12ff. [14] Ibid., 4.

there was no other means of dissuading them from that tragic plan but in the proposal to sell him.[15]

From so many insensate passions, and so many different interests arising from them, results that there is no faith to be reposed, or safety to be found among men. 'Believe not a friend, and trust not a prince: keep the doors of thy mouth from her, that sleepeth in thy bosom. For the son dishonoreth the father, and the daughter riseth up against her mother, the daughter-in-law against her mother-in-law: and a man's enemies are they of his own household."[16] From thence arise those cruelties so frequent in mankind. There is nothing so brutal or so sanguinary as man. "All lie in wait for blood; every one hunteth his brother to death."[17]

"Cursing, and lying, and killing, and theft, and adultery have overflowed, and blood hath touched blood,"[18] that is to say, that one murder draws on another.

Thus human society, established by so many sacred bonds, is violated by the passions, and as St. Augustine says: "There is nothing more sociable than man by nature, or more unsociable than man by corruption."[19]

2nd Proposition
Human society, from the beginning of things, was divided into many branches by the different nations that have been formed

Besides that division which was made among men by their passions, there was another, which necessarily arose from the multiplication of the human race.

Moses points it out to us when, after having named the first descendants of Noah, he thereby shows the origin of nations and of people. "By these, he says, were divided the islands of the Gentiles in their lands, every one according to his tongue, and their families in their nations."[20]

From whence it appears that two things divided human society into many branches. The one, the diversity and distance of countries in which the children of Noah were spread and multiplied; the other, the diversity of languages.

[15] Ibid., 19–28.   [16] Micah 7:5–6.   [17] Ibid., 2.
[18] Hos. 4:2.   [19] St. Augustine, *De civitate Dei* I. XII. xxv.   [20] Gen. 10:5.

This confusion of language happened before the separation, and was sent to men in punishment of their pride. It disposed men to separate from one another, to extend themselves throughout the earth which God had given them to inhabit.[21] "Come ye, therefore, said the Lord, let us go down, and there confound their tongue, that they may not understand one another's speech. And so the Lord scattered them from that place into all lands."[22]

Speech is the bond of society among men, by the communication which it gives of their thoughts. In proportion as they do not understand one another, they are strangers to each other. "If I know not the power of the voice, I shall be to him to whom I speak a barbarian, and he that speaketh a barbarian to me."[23] And St. Augustine remarks that that diversity of languages makes a man better pleased with his dog than with man his equal.[24]

Behold then the human race divided by tongues and by countries: and thence it has happened that inhabiting the same country, and having the same language, has been a motive to men to unite more strictly together.

There is even some appearance that, in the confusion of tongues at Babel, those who were found to have most conformity in language were thereby disposed to choose the same vicinity: to which parentage contributed much; and Scripture seems to remark these two causes which began to form around Babel the different bodies of nations, when it says, that men composed them, "in dividing themselves each one according to his language and family."[25]

3rd Proposition
The earth they inhabit together, serves as a bond amongst men, and forms the unity of nations

When God promised to Abraham, that he would make of his children a great people, he at the same time promised them a land which they should inhabit in common. "And I will make of thee a great nation."[26] And shortly after, "And to thy seed will I give this land."[27]

When he introduced the Israelites into that land promised to their fathers, he praised it before them, that they might love it. He con-

[21] Gen. 11:9. [22] Ibid., 7–8. [23] 1 Cor. 14:11.
[24] St. Augustine, *De civitate Dei* I. XIX. vii. [25] Gen. 10:5.
[26] Gen. 12:2. [27] Ibid., 7.

stantly called it "A good and spacious land, flowing with milk and honey."[28]

Those who made the people disgusted with this land which was to nourish them so abundantly were punished with death, as seditious men and enemies of their country. "The men whom Moses sent to reconnoitre the land, and who at their return had made the whole multitude to murmur against him, speaking ill of the land, that it was naught, were struck with death in the sight of the Lord."[29]

Those among the people who had viewed this land with contempt were excluded from it and died in the desert. "You shall not enter into the land which I swore to your fathers I would give them. Your children, who are innocent and take no part in your unjust disgust, will enter into the land which displeased you; as for you, your dead bodies will rot in the desert."[30]

Thus human society demands that we should love the land on which we dwell together; regarding it as one mother, and one common nurse; being attached to, and united by it. This is what the Latins call *caritas patrii soli*,[31] the love of one's country: and they regarded it as a bond among men.

Men, in effect, feel themselves bound by something strong, when they think that the same earth which bore them, and nourished them during life, will receive them into its bosom when they are dead. "Where you shall dwell, I also will dwell; your people shall be my people, said Ruth, to her mother-in-law Naomi – the land that shall receive thee dying, in the same will I die: and there will I lie buried."[32]

Joseph dying said to his brothers, "God will visit you after my death, and will make you go out of this land to the land which he swore to our fathers: carry my bones with you out of this place."[33] These were his last words. It was a consolation to him in dying, to hope to follow his brethren to the land which God had given to them for their country; and where his bones would repose more peaceably in the midst of his fellow citizens.

This is a sentiment natural to all people. Themistocles, the Athenian, was banished from his country as a traitor: he planned its ruin with the king of Persia, to whom he had surrendered himself; and nevertheless, in dying he forgot Magnesia, which the king had

---

[28] Exod. 3:8.   [29] Num. 14:36–37.   [30] Ibid., 30–32.
[31] Cicero, *De officiis* III. XXVII. 100; *De legibus* I. XV. 43.
[32] Ruth 1:16–17.   [33] Gen. 50:23–24.

given him, and, although he had been so well treated, ordered his friends to bear his bones to Attica, to be buried privately; since the rigor of the public decrees would not permit it to be done otherwise. At the approach of death, when reason returned, and when his revenge ceased, the love of his country awoke in him: he believed he had satisfied his country: he believed he would be recalled from his exile after his death: and, as they then said, that the land would be more kind, and more easy to his bones.[34]

This is why good citizens are fond of their native land. "And it came to pass that Nehemias took up wine and gave it to the king, and I was as one languishing away before his face. And the king said to me: Why is thy countenance sad, seeing thou dost not appear to be sick? . . . And I said to the king: king, live forever: why should not my countenance be sorrowful, seeing the city of the place of the sepulchre of my fathers is desolate, and the gates thereof are burnt with fire? . . . If it seem good to the king, and if thy servant hath found favor in thy sight, that thou would send me into Judaea, to the city of the sepulchre of my father, and I will re-build it."[35]

Being arrived in Judaea, he summoned his fellow citizens, whom the love of their common country had united together, "You know, he said, the affliction wherein we are, because Jerusalem is desolate, and the gates thereof are consumed with fire: come and let us build up the walls of Jersualem."[36]

While the Jews remained in a strange land, and so remote from their own country, they ceased not to mourn and to swell, if we may say so, with their tears, the waters of Babylon, in thinking of Zion.[37] They could not resolve to sing their favorite songs, which were the canticles of the Lord, in a foreign land. Their instruments of music, formerly their consolation and their joy, remained suspended on the willows planted on the banks, and they had forgotten how to use them. "O Jerusalem, they said, if ever I forget thee, let my right hand be forgotten."[38] Those whom the conquerors had left in their native land esteemed themselves happy, and they said to the Lord, in the Psalms which they sang during their captivity, "Thou shalt arise and have mercy on Zion, for it is time, O Lord, to have mercy on it, for the stones thereof have pleased thy servants, and they shall have pity on the earth thereof."[39]

[34] Thucydides, *Peloponnesian War* I. 138. [35] Neh. 2:1,3–5. [36] Ibid., 17.
[37] Ps. 136:1. [38] Ibid., 136:5. [39] Ps. 101:14–15.

Article III

To form nations and unite the people, it is necessary to have a government

1st Proposition
Everything divides itself, and becomes partial among men

It was not enough that men inhabited the same country, or spoke the same language, because having become untractable by the violence of their passions, and incompatible by their different humors, they could not be united, at least to submit altogether to one government, which regulates all.

Through that defect, Abraham and Lot could not go on well together, and were constrained to separate. "Neither was the land able to bear them, that they might dwell together: for their substance was great, and they could not dwell together. Whereupon also there arose a strife between the herdsmen of Abraham and Lot . . . Abraham, therefore, said to Lot: let there be no quarrel . . . If thou wilt go to the left hand, I will take to the right."[1]

If Abraham and Lot, two just men, and moreover near relations, could not agree together on account of their servants, what disorder must not have arisen among the wicked?

2nd Proposition
Only the authority of government puts a bridle on the passions, and to the violence become natural to men

"If thou shalt see the oppressions of the poor, and violent judgments, and justice perverted in the province, wonder not at this matter: for he that is high hath another higher, and there are others still higher than these. Moreover, there is the king that reigneth over all the land subject to him."[2] Justice has only to sustain the authority and subordination of the powers.

---

[1] Gen. 13:6,7,9.   [2] Eccles. 5:7,8.

It is necessary to have a government

This order is the bridle of licentiousness. When every one does what he wills, and has no other rule than his desires, all runs into confusion. A Levite violates all that is most holy in the law of God. In Scripture, the cause is given for this. "In those days there was no king in Israel, but every one did that which seemed right to himself."[3]

This is why, when the children of Israel are ready to enter into the land in which they ought to form a body of the state, and a regulated people, Moses says to them: "You shall not do there the things we do here this day, every man that which seemeth good to himself. For until this present time you are not come to rest, and to the possession the Lord your God will give you."[4]

3rd Proposition
It is by the sole authority of government that union is established among men

This effect of legitimate command is marked to us by these words, so often repeated in the Scriptures: at the command of Saul, and of the legitimate authority, "all Israel went out as one man.[5] All the multitudes as one man, were forty-two thousand three hundred and sixty."[6] Behold, such is the unity of a people, when each one renouncing his own will, transfers and reunites it to that of the prince and the magistrate. Otherwise there is no union; the people become wanderers, like a flock dispersed. "May the Lord, the God of the spirits of all flesh, provide a man that may be over this multitude, and may go out and in before them, and may lead them out, or bring them in: lest the people of the Lord be as sheep without a shepherd."[7]

4th Proposition
In a regulated government, each individual renounces the right of occupying by force what he finds suitable

Take away the government, the earth and all its goods are as common among men, as the air and the light. God said to all men: "Increase and multiply, and fill the earth."[8] He gave to them all, indiscrimately, "every herb bearing seed upon the earth, and all trees that have in themselves seed of their own kind."[9] According to this right of nature,

[3] Judg. 17:6.   [4] Deut. 12:8,9.   [5] 1 Kings 11:7.   [6] Esd. 2:64.
[7] Num. 27:16,17.   [8] Gen. 1:28; 9:7.   [9] Ibid., 1:29.

no one has a particular right to any thing whatever, and every thing is the prey of all.[10]

In a regulated government no individual has a right to occupy any thing. Abraham being in Palestine, asked of the Lords of that country, even the land in which he buried his wife Sarah: "Give me the right of a burying place with you."[11]

Moses ordained, after the conquest of the land of Canaan, that it should be distributed to the people by the authority of the sovereign magistrate: "Joshua shall go before thee."[12] And he afterwards said to Joshua himself, "Thou shalt bring this people into the land which the Lord swore he would give to their fathers, and thou shalt divide it by lot."[13]

The matter was thus accomplished. Joshua made the partition among the tribes and among the individuals, according to the project and the orders of Moses.[14]

From thence arose the right of property; and in general all rights should come from the public authority, without its being permitted to invade anything, or to attempt anything by force.

5th Proposition
By the government each individual becomes stronger

The reason is that each one is secured. All the powers of the nation center in one, and the sovereign magistrate has the right to combine them. "What, shall your brethren go fight and will you sit here? . . . We ourselves will go armed and ready for battle, before the children of Israel . . . We will not return into our houses until the children of Israel possess their inheritance."[15]

Thus the sovereign magistrate has in his hands all the strength of the nation, which submits to, and obeys him. "And they made answer to Joshua, and said: All that thou hast commanded us we will do: and whithersoever thou shalt send us we will go. He that shall gainsay thy mouth, and not obey all thy words, that thou shalt command him, let him die: only take thou courage, and do manfully."[16]

All strength is transferred to the sovereign magistrate: every one strengthens him to the prejudice of his own, and renounces his own

---

[10] For Bossuet's (limited) Hobbesianism, see editor's Intro., sec. VI.
[11] Gen. 23:4.   [12] Deut. 31:3.   [13] Ibid., 7.
[14] Josh. 13, 14.   [15] Num. 32:6,14,17,18.   [16] Josh. 1:16,18.

life in case of disobedience. The people gain by this; for they recover in the person of the supreme magistrate more strength than they yielded for his authority, since they recover in him all the strength of the nation reunited to assist them.

Thus an individual is at ease from oppression and violence, because in the person of the prince he has an invincible defender, and much stronger beyond comparison than all those who may undertake to oppress them.

The sovereign magistrate has an interest in guaranteeing by force every individual, because if any other force than his own prevails among the people his authority and his life are in danger.

Proud and violent men are enemies to authority, and their natural language is, "Who is Lord over us?"[17]

"In the multitude of people is the dignity of the king":[18] if he suffers it to be dissipated and overpowered by violent men he does injury to himself.

Thus the sovereign magistrate is the natural enemy of all violence. "They that act wickedly are abominable to the king: for his throne is established by justice."[19]

The prince is then by his charge, to each individual, "as then one is hid from the wind, and hideth himself from a storm, as rivers of waters in drought, and the shadow of a rock that standeth out in a desert land . . . And the work of justice shall be peace . . . and my people shall sit in the beauty of peace, and in the tabernacles of confidence and of wealthy rest."[20] Such are the natural fruits of a regulated government.

In willing to give everything to force, each one finds himself weak in his justest claims, by the multitude of concurrences against which he has to be prepared. But under a legitimate power, each one finds himself strong, in placing all strength in the magistrate, who has an interest in keeping all in peace, that he may himself be in safety.

In a regulated government, widows, orphans, wards, even infants in the cradle are strong. Their property is preserved for them; the public takes care of their education; their rights are defended, and their cause is the cause of the magistrate. The whole of the Scripture charges them to do justice to the poor, to the weak, to the widow, the orphan, and to the ward.[21]

---

[17] Ps. 11:5. [18] Prov. 14:28. [19] Ibid., 16:12.
[20] Isa. 32:2,17,18. [21] Deut. 10:18, Ps. 61:3.

It is then with reason that St. Paul desires, that "supplications, prayers, intercessions, and thanksgivings be made . . . for kings and all who are in high stations, that we may lead a quiet and a peaceful life, in all piety and chastity."[22]

From all this it results that there is no state worse than that of anarchy, that is to say, a state in which every one would do all that he wills; no one will do that which he wills; where there is no master, every one is master; where every one is master, every one is a slave.

6th Proposition
The government perpetuates itself, and renders states immortal

When God told Moses that he was about to die, Moses then said to him: "May the Lord, the God of the spirits of all flesh, provide a man that may be over this multitude."[23] Then by the order of God, Moses appointed Joshua his successor, "And he set him before Eleazar the priest, and all the assembly of the people, and laying his hands on his head, he repeated all things that the Lord had commanded,"[24] as a sign that power was continued from the one to the other.

After the death of Moses, all the people acknowledged Joshua. "As we obeyed Moses in all things, so will we obey thee also."[25] The prince dies, but authority is immortal, and the state subsists for ever. For which reason, the same designs are pursued: the war begins, is continued, and Moses revives in Joshua. "And he said to the Rubenites . . . remember the word which Moses, the servant of the Lord, commanded you"; and a little after, "and so you shall return into the land of your possession, and you shall dwell in it, which Moses, the servant of the Lord, gave you."[26]

Princes must necessarily change, since men are mortal: but the government ought not to change; authority remains firm, counsels are continued and are eternal.

After the death of Saul, David said to the men of Jabes Galaad, who had well served that prince, "Let your hands be strengthened, and be ye men of valor, for although your master, Saul, be dead, yet the house of Judah hath anointed me to be their king."[27]

---

[22] 1 Tim. 2:102.
[23] Num. 27:16–17.
[24] Ibid., 22, 23.
[25] Josh. 1:17.
[26] Ibid., 13, 14.
[27] 2 Kings 2:7.

Article IV

On laws

1st Proposition
The laws must be joined to the government to give it perfection

That is to say, it is not sufficient that the prince or the sovereign magistrate should regulate cases as they occur, according to circumstances; but it is necessary that they should establish general rules of conduct, in order that the government may be constant and uniform: and that is what is called law.

2nd Proposition
The first principles of all the laws are fixed

All the laws are founded upon the first of all laws, which is the law of nature; that is to say, on right reason and on natural equity. The laws ought to regulate all things human and divine, public and private; and are begun by nature, according to St. Paul. "For when the Gentiles, who have not the law, do by nature those things that are of the law, these having not the law, are a law to themselves: who show the work of the law written in their hearts, their conscience bearing witness to them, and their thoughts within themselves accusing them, or else defending them."[1]

The laws ought to establish the sacred and profane right, the public and private right, in a word, the just observance of divine and human things among citizens, together with rewards and punishments.

One must then, before all things, regulate the worship of God. It was thus Moses began: thus, that he laid down the foundation of society among the Israelites. At the head of the Decalogue we see this fundamental precept: "I am the Lord, thy God; thou shalt not have any strange gods before me, etc."[2]

Next follow the precepts which regard society. "Thou shalt not kill;

---

[1] Rom. 2:14–15. [2] Exod. 20:2–3.

thou shalt not steal,"[3] and the rest. Such is the general order of legislation.

3rd Proposition
There is an order in the laws

The first principle of the laws is to acknowledge a divinity, from whence is derived all that is good and existence itself. "Fear God and keep his commandments; for this is the whole duty of man."[4] And the other is, "to do to others, as we would be done unto."[5]

4th Proposition
A great king explains the character of the laws

Interest and passion corrupt men. The law is without interest and without passion. "The law of the Lord is unspotted, converting souls: the testimony of the Lord is faithful, giving wisdom to little ones."[6] It precedes experience and supplies them from infancy with good maxims. "The justices of the Lord are right rejoicing hearts."[7] One is delighted to observe how equal they are to every one, and how, in the midst of corruption, they preserve their integrity. "They are lightsome."[8] In the laws are collected the purest lights of reason. "They are true, and justified in themselves,"[9] for they follow the first principle of natural equity, with which no person can disagree, but such as are completely blind. "They are more to be desired than gold and many precious stones; and sweeter than honey and the honeycomb."[10] From them proceed abundance and repose.

David remarks in the law of God these excellent properties, without which there is no true law.

5th Proposition
The law rewards and punishes

This is why the law of Moses is everywhere found accompanied by punishments: it is this principle which renders them equally just and necessary. The first of all laws, as we have remarked, is that we should

---

[3] Ibid., 13ff. [4] Eccles. 12:13. [5] Matt. 7:12; Luke. 6:31.
[6] Ps. 18:18. [7] Ibid., 9. [8] Ibid., 9.
[9] Ibid., 10. [10] Ibid., 11.

not do to others that which we would not be done unto. Those who depart from this original law, so just and so equitable, thereby deserve that that should be done unto them, which they would not have done to themselves; since they have made others suffer, what they do not wish to suffer. This is the just foundation of punishments, conformable to that sentence pronounced against Babylon. "Take vengeance upon her: as she has done to others, so do to her."[11] She has spared nobody, spare her not: she has made others suffer, let her suffer.

On the same principle rewards are founded. Whoever serves the public or individuals, the public and individuals ought to serve him.

6th Proposition
The law is sacred and inviolable

To understand perfectly the nature of the law, it must be remarked that all those who have spoken well about it have regarded it, in its origin, as a covenant and a solemn treaty, by which men agree together, by the authority of princes, upon what is necessary to form their society.

We do not mean by this that the authority of the laws depends upon the consent and acquiescence of the people: but only that the prince who by his character has no other interest than that of the public, is assisted by the experience of past heads of the nation, and supported by the experience of past centuries.

This truth, constant amongst all men, is admirably explained in the Scripture. God assembles his people, and causes the law to be proposed to them, by which he established the sacred and profane, the public and private law of the nation, and makes all agree to it in his presence. "Moses called all Israel, and as he had recited to them all the articles of this law, he said to them: Keep therefore, the words of this covenant, and fulfil them, that you may understand all that you do. You all stand this day before the Lord your God. Your princes and tribes, and ancients and doctors, all the people of Israel, your children, and your wives, and the stranger that abideth with thee in the camp; that you may pass in the covenant of the Lord thy God, and in the oath which the Lord thy God maketh with thee. And that he may raise thee up a people to himself, and he may be thy God.

[11] Jer. 50:15.

Neither with you only, do I make this covenant, but with all that are present, and all that are absent."[12]

Moses receives this covenant in the name of all the people who had given him their consent. "I was the mediator, and stood between the Lord and you, to show you the words he gave to you, and you gave to him."[13]

All the people expressly consent to the covenant. "The Levites shall say, with a loud voice: Cursed be he that abideth not in the words of the law, and fulfilleth them not: and all the people shall say Amen."[14]

We must remark that God had no need of the consent of men to authorize his law, because he is their creator, and can oblige them to whatever he pleases; nevertheless, to render the thing more solemn, and more firm, he obliges them to the law, by an express and voluntary covenant.

7th Proposition
The law is reputed to be of divine origin

The covenant, which we have just read, has a double effect: it unites the people to God, and it unites the people in themselves. The people could not unite amongst themselves by an inviolable society, if the covenant had not been originally made in the presence of a superior power, such as that of God, the natural protector of human society, and the inevitable avenger of every contravention of the law.

But when men bind themselves to God, promising him to observe, as well in his regard as among themselves, all the articles of the law which he proposes to them, then the treaty is inviolable, authorized by a power to whom all are subject.

This is why all nations have been desirous to give to their laws a divine origin; and those which did not have it, pretended to have it.

Minos boasted of having learned from Jupiter the laws which he gave to the Cretans; Lycurgus, and Numa,[15] and all other legislators, have wished that the convention by which the people bound themselves to keep the law should be strengthened by the divine authority, in order that no one should speak against them.

Plato, in his *Republic*, and in his book of *Laws*, proposes none but

---
[12] Deut. 29:2,9–15.
[13] Ibid., 5:5.
[14] Ibid., 27:14,26.
[15] Livy, *History* I.19–21.

such as he wishes should be confirmed by the oracle, before they are received;[16] and it is thus that the laws become sacred and inviolable.

8th Proposition
There are fundamental laws that cannot be changed; it is even dangerous to change, without necessity, those which are not fundamental

It is principally of these fundamental laws that it is written, that in violating them, "The foundations of the earth shall be moved."[17] After which, there shall remain only the fall of empires.

In general the laws are not laws, if they have not something inviolable in them. To mark their solidity and firmness, Moses ordained, "Thou shalt write upon the stones, all the words of this law, plainly and clearly."[18] Joshua accomplished this commandment.[19]

The other civilized nations agree to this maxim, "Let there be an edict, and let it be written according to the law of the Persians and the Medes, said to Ahasuerus the wise men of his council, who were always near his person, who knew the laws and judgments of their fathers."[20] This attachment to the laws, and to ancient maxims, strengthens society, and renders states immortal.

We lose a veneration for the laws when we see them often changing. It is then that nations seem to stagger, as if they were troubled, and had taken wine, as the prophets express themselves.[21] A vertiginous spirit possesses them, and their fall is inevitable: "because they have transgressed the laws, they have changed the ordinance, they have broken the everlasting covenant."[22] It is the state of a sick and restless man, who knows not what position to find rest in. "There are two nations, says the Son of Sirach, which my soul abhorreth, and the third is no nation, which I hate, and the foolish people who dwell in Sichem,"[23] namely, the people of Samaria, who, having overset order, forgot the law, established a religion, and an arbitrary law, did not merit the name of a people.

We fall into this state when the laws are variable and without consistency, that is to say, when they cease to be laws.

---

[16] Plato, *Republic* v.461e; *Laws* 1.634e.
[17] Ps. 81:5.
[18] Deut. 27:8.
[19] Josh. 8:32.
[20] Esther 1:13,19.
[21] Isa. 19:14.
[22] Ibid., 24:5.
[23] Ecclus. 50:27–28.

Article v

Consequences of the general principles of humanity

Sole Proposition
The division of property among men, and the division of men even into peoples and nations, ought not to alter the general society of mankind

"If any one of thy brethren that dwelleth within the gates of thy city, in the land which the Lord thy God will give thee, come to property: thou shalt not harden thy heart, nor close thy hand, but shall open it to the poor man, thou shalt lend him that which thou perceivest he hath need of. Beware lest perhaps a wicked thought steal in upon thee; and thou shalt say in thy heart: The seventh year of remission draweth nigh; and thou turn away thy eyes from thy poor brother, denying to lend him that which he asketh: lest he cry against thee to the Lord, and it become a sin unto thee. But thou shalt give to him: neither shalt thou do any thing craftily in relieving his necessities: that the Lord thy God may bless thee at all times, and in all things to which thou shalt put thy hand."[1]

The law would be too inhuman if, in the division of property, it did not give to the poor some resource in the rich. It ordains in that spirit that they should demand their debts with great moderation.[2] "Thou shalt not take the nether, nor the upper millstone to pledge: for he hath pledged his life to thee . . . When thou shalt demand of thy neighbor any thing that he oweth thee, thou shalt not go into his house to take away a pledge: but thou shalt stand without, and he shall bring out to thee what he hath. But if he be poor, the pledge shall not lodge with thee that night, but thou shalt restore it to him presently before the going down of the sun: that he may sleep in his own raiment, and bless thee, and thou mayest have justice before the Lord thy God."[3]

---

[1] Deut. 15:7–10.   [2] Ibid., 24:6,10–13.   [3] Ibid., 24:6,10–13.

Consequences of the principles of humanity

The law studies in everything to preserve among citizens this spirit of mutual assistance. "Thou shalt not pass by if thou seest thy brother's ox or his sheep go astray: but thou shalt bring them back to thy brother. And if thy brother be not nigh, or thou know him not, thou shalt bring them to thy house, and they shalt be with thee until thy brother seek them, and receive them. Thou shalt do in like manner with his ass, and with his raiment, and with every thing that is thy brother's, which is lost: if thou find it, neglect it not as appertaining to another."[4] That is to say, take care of it as if it were your own, to restore it carefully to him who lost it.

By these laws there is no division which hinders us from taking care of that which belongs to another, as if it were our own, and that we should not give a part to another of what we possess, as if it really belonged to us.

It is thus that the law places, as it were in common, the property that has been divided for the public and private convenience.

It leaves, even in the lands so justly divided, some mark of the ancient community, but reduced to certain limits for the sake of public order. "Going into thy neighbor's vineyard, thou mayest eat as many grapes as thou pleasest: but must carry none with thee. If thou go into thy friend's corn, thou mayest break the ears, and rub them in thy hand: but not reap them with a sickle."[5]

"When thou hast reaped the corn in thy field, and hast forgot and left a sheaf, thou shalt not return to take it away: but thou shalt suffer the stranger, and the fatherless, and the widow, to take it away, that the Lord thy God may bless thee in all the works of thy hands."[6] He ordains the same thing of olives, and of grapes, in the vintage.[7]

Moses, by this means, recalls to the memory of the possessors, that they should always regard the earth as a common mother and the nurse of all men, and does not will that the division which has been made of it should make them forget the original right of nature [*le droit primitif de la nature*].

He includes strangers in this right. "Leave, he said, those forgotten olives, and grapes, and sheafs, for the stranger, for the fatherless, and the widow."[8]

He recommends particularly, in judgments, the stranger and the fatherless, honoring in all the society of mankind. "Thou shalt not

---

[4] Ibid., 22:1–3. [5] Ibid., 23:24–25. [6] Ibid., 24:19.
[7] Ibid., 20–21. [8] Ibid., 19, 20, 21.

pervert the judgment of the stranger nor of the fatherless . . . Remember that thou also wast a stranger and a slave in Egypt."[9]

So far is he from desiring that we should fail in humanity to strangers, that he even extends, in some measure, this humanity to animals. When you find a bird sitting, the legislator forbids you to take both the mother and its young: "Thou shalt let her go, keeping the young which thou hast caught."[10] As if he had said, she loses enough in losing them, without losing her liberty.

In the same spirit of mildness, the law forbids to "boil a kid in the milk of its dam"[11] and to "muzzle the ox that treadeth out thy corn on the floor."[12]

"Doth God take care for oxen?"[13] as St. Paul asks. Has he made the law for them and for goats, and for beasts; and is it not evident that he would inspire men with mildness and humanity in all things; in order that, being kind to animals, they should feel the better what they owe to their like?

We must not then imagine that the limits which separate the lands of individuals, and states, are made to cause division in mankind; but only that they should not attempt anything against each other, and that each one should respect the peace of the other. It is for this end that it is said: "Thou shalt not take nor remove thy neighbor's landmark, which thy predecessors have set in thy possession, which the Lord thy God will give thee in the land."[14] And again: "Cursed be he that removeth his neighbor's landmarks."[15]

Still more must we respect the limits which separate states, than those which separate individuals; and we ought to preserve the society which God has established among all men.

There are only certain cursed and abominable people, from whom all society is interdicted on account of that frightful corruption they would not fail to spread amongst their allies. "Thou shalt make no league with them, neither shalt thou make marriages with them. Thou shalt not give thy daughter to his son, nor take his daughter for thy son: for she will turn away thy son from following me, that he may rather serve strange gods."[16]

Except in such cases, God forbids the aversions which nations have for each other; and on the contrary, he makes them value all the bonds of society which exist between them. "Thou shalt not abhor the

---

[9] Ibid., 17–18.   [10] Deut. 22:6–7.   [11] Ibid., 14:21.   [12] Ibid., 25:4.
[13] 1 Cor. 9:9.   [14] Deut. 19:14.   [15] Ibid., 27:17.   [16] Ibid., 7:2–4.

Edomite, because he is thy brother; nor the Egyptian, because thou wast a stranger in his land."[17]

Thus have been preserved, among all peoples, certain common principles of society and concord. Nations the most remote from each other are united by commerce, and agree to preserve faith and treaties. There are amongst all civilized nations certain persons, to whom all mankind appear to have given a security for the preservation of commerce between them. Even war does not prevent this commerce; the persons of ambassadors are regarded as sacred: whoever violates their character, is held in horror; and David took, with reason, a terrible vengeance on the Ammonites and their king, who had maltreated his ambassadors.[18]

Nations that do not know these laws of society are inhuman and barbarous, enemies of all justice and of mankind; to them Scripture applies this odious charge, "without affection, without fidelity."[19]

Here is a fine rule of St. Augustine's for the application of charity. "Where reason is equal, lot should decide. The obligation of loving each other, is equal amongst all men, and for all men. But as we cannot equally serve all men, we ought to attach ourselves principally to serve those whom place, time, and other similar circumstances unite to us in a particular manner, as by a sort of destiny."[20]

Article VI

On the love of country

1st Proposition

We must be good citizens, ready to sacrifice to our country, in case of need, all that we possess, even our very lives, when there is question of war

If we are obliged to love all men, and as it is true to say that to a Christian there is no such thing as a stranger, it is more reasonable

---

[17] Ibid., 23:7. [18] 2 Kings 10:2–7; 13:30–31.
[19] Rom. 1:31. [20] St. Augustine, *De doctrina Christiana* I. I.xxviii.

that we should love our fellow citizens. All the love we have for ourselves, for our family, and for our friends is reunited in the love we have for our country, where our happiness, and that of our family and of our friends is included.

This is why the seditious, who do not love their country and bring division into it, are the execration of mankind. The earth cannot bear with them, but opens to swallow them up. It is thus that Core, Dathan, and Abiron perished. "If these men die the common death of men, said Moses, and if they be visited with the plague, wherewith others also are wont to be visited, the Lord did not send me: but if the Lord do a new thing, and the earth opening her mouth, swallow them down, and all things that belong to them, and they go down alive into hell, you shall know that they have blasphemed the Lord. And immediately as he had made an end of speaking, the earth broke asunder under their feet: and opening her mouth, devoured them with their tents and all their substance."[1]

Thus do they merit to be cut off, who cast division among the people. We must not associate with them; in approaching them, we approach the plague. "Depart, said Moses to the multitude, from the tents of these wicked men, and touch nothing of theirs, lest you be involved in their sins."[2]

We must not spare our goods when there is question of serving our country. "And Gideon said to the men of Soccoth: Give, I beseech you, bread to the people that is with me, for they are faint, that we may pursue Zebee, and Salmana, the Kings of Median." They refused, and Gideon justly chastised them.[3] Whoever serves the public, serves each individual. We must even without hesitation expose our lives for our country. This sentiment is common to all nations, and above all it is apparent in the people of God.

When the wants of the state required it, everybody without exception was obliged to go to war; and it is for this reason that their armies were so numerous.

The city of Jabes Galaad, besieged and reduced to extremity by Naas, King of the Ammonites, sends to expose the extremity of its peril to Saul, who "taking both the oxen, cut them in pieces, and sent them into all the coasts of Israel, by messengers, saying: Whosoever shall not come forth, and follow Saul and Samuel, so shall it be done

---

[1] Num. 16:28–32.   [2] Ibid., 26.   [3] Judg. 8:5,15–17.

to his oxen. And the fear of the Lord fell upon the people, and they went out as one man. And he numbered them in Bezec: and there were of the children of Israel three hundred thousand: and of the men of Judah, thirty thousand. And they said to the messengers that came: thus shall you say to the men of Jabes Galaad: tomorrow, when the sun shall be hot, you shall have relief."[4]

These convocations were common; we must transcribe the whole of the history of the people of God, to relate every example.

It was a subject of complaint for those who were not called, and they took it as an affront. "And the men of Ephraim said to Gideon: What is this that thou meanest to do, that thou wouldst not call us when thou wentest to fight against Madian? And they chid him sharply, and almost offered violence. And he appeased them by praising their valor."[5]

They made the same complaint to Jephtha; and the matter arose even to a sedition;[6] so much did they pride themselves on the honor of being convoked on these occasions. Each one exposed his life, not only for the people, but for his single tribe. "I and my people, said Jephtha, were at great strife with the children of Ammon: and I called you to assist me, and you would not do it. And when I saw this, I put my life in my own hands (a noble mode of speaking, which signifies that he exposed his life) and passed over against the children of Ammon."[7]

It is shameful to remain in repose at home, whilst our fellow citizens are in labor and peril for our common country. David sent Uriah to repose at home, and that good subject replied: "The ark of God, and Israel and Judah dwell in tents, and my Lord Joab, and the servants of my Lord abide upon the face of the earth: and shall I go into my house, to eat and to drink, and to sleep with my wife? By thy welfare, and by the welfare of thy soul, I will not do this thing."[8]

There is no more joy for a good citizen, when his country is ruined. Whence this discourse of Mathathias, chief of the house of the Asmonites, to the Maccabees. "Woe is me, wherefore I was born to see the ruin of my people, and the ruin of the holy city, and to dwell there, when it is given into the hands of the enemies? The holy places are come into the hands of strangers, her temple is become as a man without honor. The vessels of her glory are carried away captive; her

---

[4] 1 Kings 11:7–9.   [5] Judg. 8:1–3.   [6] Ibid., 12:1.
[7] Ibid., 2–3.   [8] 2 Kings 11:10–11.

old men are murdered in the streets, and her young men are fallen by the sword of the enemies. What nation hath not inherited her kingdom, and gotten of her spoils? All her ornaments are taken away. She that was free is made a slave. And behold our sanctuary, and our beauty, and our glory is laid waste, and the Gentiles have defiled them. To what end then should we live any longer?"[9]

We see here everything that unites citizens amongst themselves and with their country: their altars and sacrifices, glory, goods, repose, and safety of life, in a word, the society of things divine and human. Mathathias, touched by all these things, declared that he could no longer live seeing his citizens suffer, and his country desolated. "On saying these words, he and his sons rent their garments, and they covered themselves with haircloth, and made great lamentation."[10]

Thus did Jeremiah "when, his people being led into captivity, and the holy city desolated, full of bitter sadness, he groaningly pronounced his lamentations,"[11] which still move those who hear them.

The same prophet said to Baruch, who in the midst of his country's ruin still thought to himself and of his fortune: "Thus saith the Lord God of Israel to thee, Baruch: . . . Behold them whom I have built, I do destroy; and them whom I have planted, I do pluck up, and all this land. And dost thou seek great things for thyself? Seek not: be content that I save thy life."[12]

It is not enough to weep for the ills of one's citizens; one must risk his life in their service. It is to this that Mathathias, dying, incited his family: "Now hath pride and chastisement gotten strength, and the time of destruction, and the wrath of indignation. Now therefore, O my sons, be ye zealous for the law, and give your lives for the covenant of your fathers."[13]

This sentiment remained engraved on the hearts of his children; nothing was more ordinary on the lips of Judas, Jonathan and Simon than these words: let us die for our notion and for our brothers. "Gird yourselves, said Judas, and be valiant men, that you may fight with these nations that are assembled against us to destroy us. For it is better for us to die in battle, than to see the evils of our nation and of our sanctuary."[14] And again: "God forbid we should flee away from the enemy: if our time be come, let us die manfully for our brethren, and let us not stain our glory."[15]

---

[9] 1 Macc. 2:7–13. [10] Ibid., 14. [11] Lam. 70. [12] Jer. 45:2,4,5.
[13] 1 Macc. 2:49–50. [14] 1 Macc. 3:58–59. [15] 1 Macc. 9:10.

On the love of country

Scripture is full of examples which teach us what we owe to our country; but the finest of all these examples is that of Jesus Christ himself.

2nd Proposition
Jesus Christ established, by his doctrine and by his example, the love that citizens ought to have for their country.

The son of God made man not only fulfilled all the duties that human society demands of a man, charitable to all and the savior of all, and those of a good son towards his parents, to whom he was subject:[16] but also those of a good citizen, recognizing himself "sent to the sheep that are lost of the house of Israel."[17] He withdrew into Judaea, that he might "go about doing good, and healing all that were oppressed by the devil, for God was with him."[18]

He was recognized as a good citizen, and served as a strong recommendation around himself to love the Jewish nation. The senators of the Jewish people, in order to oblige him to help "the servant of a centurion who was dear to him, being sick . . . came to Jesus and besought him earnestly, saying to him: He is worthy that thou shouldst do this for him: for he loveth our nation; and he hath built us a synagogue. And Jesus went with them, and healed the servant."[19]

When he thought about the misfortunes which so nearly threatened Jerusalem and the Jewish people, he could not hold back his tears. "And when he drew near, seeing the city, he wept over it, saying: If thou also hadst known, he said, and that in this thy day, the things that are to thy peace; but now they are hidden from thy eyes."[20] He said these words while entering Jerusalem, in the midst of the acclamations of the people.

This care which pressed on him during his triumph, did not leave him during this Passion. As he was being led to the torture, "there followed him a great multitude of people, and of women, who bewailed and lamented him. But Jesus, turning to them, said: Daughters of Jerusalem, weep not over me; but weep for yourselves, and for your children. For behold, the days shall come, wherein they will say: Blessed are the barren, and the wombs that have not borne

---

[16] Luke 2:51. [17] Matt. 15:24. [18] Acts 10:38.
[19] Luke 7:3–6,10. [20] Ibid., 19:41–42.

Of the principles of human society

fruit, and the breasts that have not given suck."[21] He did not complain of the evils which were being unjustly visited on him, but of those which so iniquitous a proceeding would draw on his people.

He forgot nothing that might prevent them. "Jerusalem, Jerusalem, thou that killest the prophets, and stonest them that are sent unto thee, how often would I have gathered together thy children, as the hen doth gather her chickens under her wings, and thou wouldst not? Behold, your house shall be left to you, desolate."[22]

He was, both during his life and at his death, an exact observer of the laws and praiseworthy customs of his country – even those from which he knew himself to be most exempt.

It was complained against St. Peter that he was not paying the regular tribute to the Temple, and this apostle maintained that indeed he owed nothing. "But Jesus warned him by saying: The kings of the earth, of whom do they receive tribute or custom? of their own children? or of strangers? And he said: Of strangers. Jesus said to him: Then the children are free. But that we may not scandalize them, go to the sea, and cast in a hook: and that fish that shall first come up to thee, take: and when thou hast opened its mouth, thou shalt find a stater: take that, and give it to them for thee and me."[23] He ordered a tribute to be paid which he owed not, as a son, for fear of causing the least trouble to public order.

Thus, in the desire which the Pharisees had to find him acting contrary to the law, they could never reproach him but with mere nihilities, or with miracles performed on the Sabbath day, as if the Sabbath ought to stop the works of God as well as man.[24]

He was submissive in all things to public order, causing that to be "given to Caesar, which was Caesar's: and to God, what was God's."[25]

Never did he undertake anything that interfered with the authority of the magistrates. "And one of the multitude said to him: Master, speak to my brother that he divide the inheritance with me. But he said to him: Man, who hath made me a judge or a divider over you?"[26]

Moreover, the omnipotence he possessed did not keep him from suffering himself to be taken without resistance. He reproved St.

[21] Luke 23:27–29. [22] Matt. 23:37–38. [23] Ibid., 17:24–26.
[24] Luke 13:14; John 5:9,16; 10:14. [25] Matt. 23:21.
[26] Luke 12:13–14.

32

Peter who had struck with his sword, and cured the wound that apostle had made.[27]

He appeared before the High Priests, before Pilate, and before Herod, replying precisely to the fact proposed to him, by those who had a right to interrogate him. "And the High Priest said to him: I adjure thee by the living God, that thou tell us if thou be the Christ, the Son of God. Jesus saith to him: Thou hast said it."[28] He satisfied Pilate on his royalty, in which consisted all his imputed crime; assuring him at the same time, "that it was not of this world."[29] He said not a word to Herod, who had no command in Jerusalem, to whom also they sent him through ceremony: and who only desired to see him from mere curiosity, and after having satisfied the lawful interrogatory. Moreover, he condemned only, by his silence, the manifestly iniquitous procedure they employed against him, without complaint, without murmur, "delivering himself to him that judged him unjustly."[30]

Thus was he faithful and affectionate, to the end, to his ungrateful country, and to his cruel fellow citizens, who thought only of satiating themselves with his blood, with so blind a fury, that they preferred to him a rebel and a murderer.

He knew that his death would have been the salvation of those ungrateful citizens, if they had done penance: for which reason he prayed for them in particular, even on the cross to which they had nailed him.

Caiaphas having pronounced that it was necessary Jesus should die, "that the whole nation might not perish," the Evangelist remarks: "And this he spoke not of himself: but being the High Priest of that year, he prophesied that Jesus should die for the nation. And not only for the nation, but to gather together in one the children of God, that were dispersed."[31]

Thus he shed his blood with a particular regard for his nation; and in offering up the great sacrifice, which was to effect the expiation of all the universe, he willed that the love of country should find a place in it.

---

[27] Ibid., 22:50–51; John 18:10–11.   [28] Matt. 26:63–64; Luke 22:70.
[29] John 18:36.   [30] 1 Peter 2:23.   [31] John 11:52–53.

3rd Proposition
The apostles and the first faithful, were always good citizens

Their master had inspired them with this sentiment. He had foretold them, that they would be persecuted by the whole earth, and said to them, at the same time: "Behold, I send you as sheep in the midst of wolves."[32] That is to say, that they had only to suffer without murmuring, and without resistance.

While the Jews persecuted St. Paul, with an implacable hatred, this great man takes Jesus Christ, who is the truth itself, and his conscience to witness, that, affected with an extreme and continual grief for the blindness of his brethren, "he wishes to be an anathema for them. I speak the truth in Christ; I lie not, my conscience bearing me witness in the Holy Ghost, etc."[33]

In an extreme famine he made a collection for those of his nation, and brought himself, to Jerusalem, the alms he had collected for them in all Greece. "I came to bring alms to my nation."[34]

Neither he nor his companions ever excited sedition, nor assembled the people tumultuously.[35]

Constrained by the violence of his fellow citizens to appeal to the Emperor, he assembled the Jews of Rome, to declare to them: "I was constrained to appeal unto Caesar, not that I had anything to accuse my nation of."[36] He did not accuse them; but he complained of them, and never spoke but with compassion for their obstinacy. In effect, accused before Felix, governor of Judaea, he simply defended himself against the Jews, without making any reproach to such violent persecutors.[37]

During three hundred years of pitiless persecution, the Christians always followed the same conduct.

Never were there better citizens, nor any more useful to their country, nor who served more willingly in their armies, provided they were not obliged to become idolaters. Listen to the testimony of Tertullian: "You say that the Christians are useless. We navigate with you, we carry arms with you, we cultivate the earth, we exercise

---

[32] Matt. 10:16. [33] Rom. 9:1–3. [34] Acts 24:17; Rom. 15:25–26.
[35] Ibid. 12, 18. [36] Acts 28:19. [37] Ibid., 24:10ff.

merchandise."[38] That is to say, we live like others, in all that regards society.

The Empire had not better soldiers; besides having fought valiantly, they obtained, by their prayers, what they could not effect by their arms. Witness the rain obtained by the letters of Marcus Aurelius.[39]

To them it was forbidden to cause trouble, to upset idols, to do any violence, the laws of the Church permitting them only to await the stroke with patience.

The Church did not rank those as martyrs who drew death upon themselves by their own violence or by their false zeal. There might have been sometimes extraordinary inspirations; but these examples were not followed, as being above order.

We even see, in the acts of some martyrs, that they made a scruple at cursing the gods; they knew how to repress error, without angry words. St. Paul and his companions acted thus, which caused the secretary of the community of Ephesus to say: "Ye men of Ephesus . . . you ought to be quiet, and to do nothing rashly, for you have brought hither these men, who are neither guilty of sacrilege nor of blasphemy against your goddess."[40] They gave no scandal, and preached the truth without, as much as was in their power, disturbing the public repose.

How submissive and peaceable the persecuted Christians were the following words of Tertullian admirably express. "Beside the public orders by which we are pursued, how often do the people cast stones at us, and set fire to our houses, in their bacchanalian fury? They spare not the Christians even after death: they tear them from the repose of the sepulchre, and, as it were, from the asylum of death. And yet, what vengeance do you receive from people so cruelly treated? Could we not with a few torches set fire to the city, if amongst us it were permitted to do evil for evil? And if we would act as declared enemies, should we want troops or armies? The Moors, or the Marcomani, and the Parthians even, who are confined in their limits, do they find themselves in greater number than we who fill all the earth? It is but a short time since we first appeared in the world; and already we fill your cities, your isles, your castles, your assemblies,

---

[38] Tertullian, *Apologeticus*, Ch. 42.   [39] Ibid., Ch. 45.   [40] Acts 19:37.

your camps, your tribes, your decurii; the palace, the senate, the bar, the public places. We leave you nothing but the temples. To what war would we not be disposed, were we even in number unequal to you, we who so resolutely endure death, if it were not that our doctrine disposes us rather to be killed than to kill? We could even, without taking arms, and without rebellion, punish you in abandoning you: your solitude and the silence of the world, would fill you with horror; the cities would appear to you dead; and you would be reduced in the midst of your empire, to seek whom to command. There would remain to you more of enemies than of citizens; for you have now fewer enemies, on account of the prodigious multitude of Christians."[41]

"You lose, he continues, in losing us. You have by our means an infinite number of people, I say not who pray for you, for you do not believe it, but from whom you have nothing to fear."[42]

He gloried, and with reason, that amongst so many attempts against the sacred persons of the Emperors, there never was found a single Christian, notwithstanding the inhumanity that was practised against them all. "And in truth, he said, we have no occasion for precautions against attempting anything against them. Those whose manners God regulates, ought not only to spare the Emperors, but also all men. We are for the Emperors, such as we are for our neighbors. For it is equally forbidden for us to say, or to do, or to will evil to any one. That which is not permitted against the Emperor, is not permitted against anybody: that which is not permitted against anybody is still less, without doubt, against him whom God has made so great."[43]

Behold! Such were the Christians who were so unworthily treated.

Conclusion

To conclude this book, and to reduce it to an abstract

Human society may be considered in two manners: either as it comprises all mankind in one great family; or as it is reduced into nations,

[41] Tertullian, *Apologeticus*, Ch. 37.   [42] Ibid., Ch. 43.   [43] Ibid., Ch. 36.

To conclude this book

or into peoples composed of many particular families, having each their rights.

Society, considered in the latter sense, is called civil society. It may be defined, according to what has been said, a society of men united together under the same government, and under the same laws.

By this government and these laws, the peace and the life of all men are put, as much as may be, in safety.

Whoever, then, does not love the civil society of which he forms a part, that is to say, the state in which he was born, is an enemy to himself and to all mankind.

SECOND BOOK

On authority: that the royal and hereditary [type] is the most proper for government

First Article

By whom authority has been exercised since the beginning of the world

1st Proposition
God is the true king

A great king recognized this, when he spoke thus in the presence of his whole people: "Blessed be thou, Lord God of Israel our father, for ever and ever. Thine, O Lord, is the greatness, and the power, and the glory, and the victory, and the majesty: for all that is in the heaven and in the earth is thine; thine is the kingdom, O Lord, and thou art exalted as head above all. Both riches and honor come of thee, and thou reignest over all; and in thine hand is power and might; and in thine hand it is to make great, and to give strength unto all."[1]

The empire of God is eternal, and from that comes the fact that he is called the king of the centuries.[2]

The empire of God is absolute: "Who will dare to say to you, O Lord: Why do you act thus? Or who will stand against your judgment?"[3]

This absolute empire of God has, for its original title and foundation, the Creation. He has drawn everything out of nothingness, and that is why everything is in his hand: "The word which came to

---

[1] 1 Par. 29:10–12.   [2] Apoc. 15:3.   [3] Wisd. 12:12.

On authority

Jeremiah from the Lord, saying: Arise, and go down to the potter's house, and there I will cause thee to hear my words. Then I went down to the potter's house, and, behold, he wrought a work on the wheels. And the vessel that he made of clay was marred in the hands of the potter: so that he made it again another vessel, as seemed good to the potter to make it. Then the word of the Lord came to me, saying, O house of Israel, cannot I do with you as this potter? saith the Lord. Behold, as the clay is in the potter's hand, so are ye in mine, O house of Israel."[4]

2nd Proposition
God has visibly exercised a personal empire and authority over men

Thus has he acted since the beginning of the world. At that time he was the sole king of men, and governed them visibly.

He gave to Adam the precept that pleased him, and told him by what penalty he obliged him to follow it.[5] He banished him; he told him that he had incurred the penalty of death.

He declared himself visibly in favor of the sacrifice of Abel against that of Cain. He reproved Cain for his jealousy: after this wretch had killed his brother, he called him to judgment, he interrogated him, he convicted him of his crime, he reserved vengeance for himself and forbad it to any other;[6] he gave to Cain a kind of safeguard, a mark to keep any other man from harming him.[7] All [of these were] functions of public power.

Thereafter he gave laws to Noah and to his children: he forbad blood-letting and murder to them, and ordered them to populate the earth.[8]

In the same way he led Abraham, Isaac and Jacob.

He publicly exercised a sovereign empire over his people in the desert. He was their king, their legislator, their leader. He visibly gave the signal to camp and to decamp, and the orders of war as much as of peace.

This reign continued visibly under Joshua and under the Judges: God sent them; he established them; from this comes [the fact that] the people were saying to Gideon: "Rule thou over us, both thou, and

[4] Jer. 18:1–6.   [5] Gen. 2:17.   [6] Ibid., 4:4–6,9,10.
[7] Ibid., 15.   [8] Ibid., 9:5–7.

thy son, and thy son's son also . . . And Gideon said unto them, I will not rule over you, neither shall my son rule over you: the Lord shall rule over you."[9]

It is he who establishes kings. He sanctified Saul and David through Samuel; he established royalty in the house of David, and ordered him to make his son Solomon reign in his place.[10]

This is why the throne of the kings of Israel is called the throne of God. "Then Solomon sat on the throne of the Lord as king instead of David his father, and prospered; and all Israel obeyed him."[11] And again: "Blessed be the Lord thy God, said the Queen of Sheba to Solomon, which delighted in thee to set thee on his throne, to be king for the Lord thy God."[12]

3rd Proposition
The first empire among men is the paternal empire

Jesus Christ, who always goes to the bottom of things, seems to have indicated it by these words: "Every kingdom divided against itself is brought to desolation; and every city or house divided against itself shall not stand."[13] From kingdoms he passes to cities, from which kingdoms arise; and from cities he goes back to families – as to the model and principle of cities and of the whole of human society.

At the beginning of the world God said to Eve, and through her to all women: "You will be under the power of the man, and he will command you."[14]

To the first child that Adam had, who was Cain, Eve said, "I have gotten a man from the Lord."[15] See then, too, children under paternal power. For this child was even more in the possession of Adam, to whom the mother herself was subject by the order of God. Both [Adam and Eve] held this child, and their empire over him, from God. "I have gotten a man, Eve said, but by the grace of God."

God having placed in our parents, as being in some fashion the authors of our life, an image of the power by which he made everything, he also transmitted to them an image of the power which he has over his works. That is why we see in the Decalogue that after having said, "Thou shalt adore the Lord thy God, and serve only him," he adds as well: "Honor thy father and thy mother, that thy days may be

---

[9] Judg. 8:22–23. [10] 1–4 Kings. [11] 1 Par. 29:23. [12] 2 Par. 9:8.
[13] Matt. 12:25. [14] Gen. 3:16. [15] Ibid., 4:1.

long upon the land which the Lord thy God giveth thee."[16] This precept is a kind of consequence of the obedience which must be rendered to God, who is the true father.

From this we can judge that the first idea of command and of human authority, has come to men from paternal authority.

Men lived for a long time at the beginning of the world, as not only Scripture but all the ancient traditions attest: and human life began to decline only after the deluge, where such a great change was made in the whole of nature. A large number of families found themselves united under the authority of a single grandfather by this means; and this union of so many families had the look of a kingdom.

Assuredly during the time that Adam lived Seth, whom God gave him in place of Abel, rendered him (together with his whole family) an entire obedience.

Cain, who first violated human fraternity by a murder, was also the first to withdraw himself from the paternal empire: hated by all men and constrained to establish a refuge for himself, he built the first city, to which he gave the name of his son, Enoch.[17]

All other men lived in the countryside in this first simplicity, having for law the will of their parents and the ancient customs.

Such, after the deluge, was the conduct of several families, above all among the children of Shem, who preserved for a long time the ancient traditions of the human race – in both the worship of God and in the manner of government.

Thus Abraham, Isaac and Jacob persisted in the observance of a simple and pastoral life. They, with their families, were free and independent, and treated as equals with kings. Abimelech, King of Gerar, came to find Abraham; "and both of them made a covenant."[18]

There was made a similar covenant between another Abimelech, son of the former, and Isaac the son of Abraham. "We saw certainly, said Abimelech, that the Lord was with thee; and we said, Let there be now an oath betwixt us, betwixt us and thee, and let us make a covenant with thee."[19]

Abraham himself personally made war on the kings who had pillaged Sodom, defeated them, and offered a tenth of the spoils to Melchisedech, King of Salem, most high priest of God.[20]

This is why the children of Heth, with whom he made an agree-

---

[16] Exod. 20:12. [17] Gen. 4:17. [18] Ibid., 21:23–32.
[19] Ibid., 26:28. [20] Ibid., 14:18–20.

ment, called him lord, and treated him as a prince. "Hear us, my lord: thou art a mighty prince among us – that is to say they stood up again only through him.

He [Abraham] also passed for a king in profane histories. Nicholas Damascene, careful observer of ancient things, calls him a king; and his reputation in the whole East caused him to give his all to his country. But at bottom the life of Abraham was pastoral; his kingdom was his family, and he alone exercised a domestic and paternal empire, after the example of the first men.[21]

4th Proposition
Nonetheless kings were established early, either by the consent of peoples, or by arms (where one speaks of the right of conquest)

These two ways of establishing kings are known in ancient histories. It is thus that Gideon, son of Abimelech, made the people of Shechem take him for their sovereign. "Whether is better for you, he said to them, either that all the sons of Jerubbaal, which are threescore and ten persons, reign over you, or that one reign over you? Remember also that I am your bone and your flesh . . . And their hearts inclined to follow Abimelech."[22]

It is thus that the people of God itself asked for a king to judge it.[23]

The same people transmitted the whole authority of the nation to Simon and to his posterity. The act is drawn up in the name of the priests, of the whole people, of the great and of the senators, who consented to make him prince.[24]

We see in Herodotus that Dejoces was made King of the Medes in the same way.[25]

As for kings by conquest, everyone knows the examples.

Moreover it is certain that there were kings very early in the world. One sees in the times of Abraham, that is to say about four hundred years after the flood, kingdoms already formed and long established. One sees first four kings make war against five others.[26] One sees Melchisedech, King of Salem, most high priest of God, to whom Abraham gave tithes.[27] One sees Pharaoh, King of Egypt,[28] and

[21] Ibid., 23:6.　[22] Judg. 9:2–3.　[23] 1 Kings 8:5.
[24] 1 Macc. 14:28–41.　[25] Herodotus I. 96.　[26] Gen. 14:1–9.
[27] Ibid., 18–20.　[28] Ibid., 12:15.

On authority

Abimelech, King of Gerar.[29] Another Abimelech, also King of Gerar, appeared at the time of Isaac:[30] and this name was apparently common to the kings of that country, as was that of Pharaoh to the kings of Egypt.

All of these kings seemed to be well authorized; one sees them surrounded by well-ordered officials, a court, the great, an army and a military leader to command them,[31] a consolidated power. "He that toucheth this man or his wife, said Abimelech, shall surely be put to death."[32]

Men who, as has been said, saw the image of a kingdom in the union of several families under the leadership of a common father, and who had found gentleness in that life, brought themselves easily to create societies of families under kings who took the place of fathers.

It is apparently for that reason that the ancient peoples of Palestine called their kings Abimelech, that is to say: my father the king. Subjects took themselves to be children of the prince: and, each one calling him, My father the king, this name came to be shared by all the kings of the country.

But in addition to this innocent way of making kings, ambition invented another. Ambition made conquerors, of whom Nimrod, grandson of Ham, was the first. "This man, violent and a warrior, began to be powerful on earth, and soon conquered four cities from which he formed his kingdom."[33]

Thus kingdoms formed by conquests are ancient, since one finds them so soon after the flood, under Nimrod, grandson of Ham.

This ambitious and violent disposition soon spread rapidly among men. We see Chedorlaomer, King of the Elamites (that is to say the Persians and the Medes) extend his conquests very far in the neighboring lands of Palestine.[34]

These empires, while at first violent, unjust and tyrannical, can in the course of time and by the consent of peoples, become legitimate; this is why men have recognized a right which is called that of conquest – of which we shall have to speak at greater length before leaving this matter.

---

[29] Ibid., 20:2. [30] Ibid., 26:1. [31] Ibid., 12:15; 21:22.
[32] Ibid., 26:11. [33] Ibid., 10:8–10. [34] Ibid., 14:4–7.

5th Proposition
In the beginning there was an infinity of kingdoms, all of them small

It appears in Scripture that almost every city and each small country had its king.[35]

There were thirty-three kings just in the small country that the Jews conquered.[36]

The same thing appears in all the ancient authors, for example in Homer and in others as well.

The common tradition of the human race on this point is faithfully reported by Justin, who remarks that in the beginning there were only minor kings, each content to live within his limits, peaceably, with the people in his care. "Ninus, he says, was the first to break with this concord of the nations."[37]

It does not matter whether this Ninus was Nimrod, or whether Justin erroneously made him the first of the conquerors. It suffices that one see that the first kings were established with gentleness, after the example of paternal government.

6th Proposition
There have been forms of government other than royalty

Histories show us a great number of republics, of which some were governed by the whole people and were called *democracy*, while others [were ruled] by the great and were called *aristocracy*.

The forms of government have mingled in various ways, and have composed several mixed states, of which there is no need to speak here.

We see in several places in Scripture that authority can be located in a community.

Abraham asked the right of burial from the whole assembled people, and it was this assembly that granted it.[38]

It seems that in the beginning the Israelites lived in a kind of republic. On some subject of complaint which came up in the time of Joshua against the people of Reuben and of Gad, "the children of Israel gathered themselves together at Shiloh, to go to war against

---

[35] Gen. 14.   [36] Josh. 12:2,4,7–24.
[37] Justin I. 1.   [38] Gen. 23:3–5.

them . . . but first they sent ten ambassadors to hear their reasons: they gave satisfaction, and the whole people was appeased."[39]

A Levite whose wife had been raped and killed by some from the tribe of Benjamin, without any justice being done, all the tribes assembled in order to punish this assassination, and said to each other in this assembly: "There was no such deed done nor seen from the day that the children of Israel came up out of the land of Egypt unto this day: consider of it, take advice, and speak your minds."[40]

Indeed it was a kind of republic, but one which had God for its king.

7th Proposition
Monarchy is the most common, the most ancient, and also the most natural form of government

The people of Israel on its own reduced itself to a monarchy, as being the universally received [form of] government. "Now make us a king, to judge us like all the nations."[41]

If God was angered, that is because up till then he had governed this people by himself, and was its true king. That is why he said to Samuel, "they have not rejected thee, but they have rejected me, that I should not reign over them."[42]

This government, moreover, was incomparably the most natural which was first seen among all the peoples.

This we have seen in sacred history: but here a slight recourse to profane histories will show us that polities with a republican form lived at first under kings.

Rome began in this way, and finally came back to it, as if to her natural condition.

It was only late, and little by little, that the Greek cities formed their republics. The ancient opinion of Greece was that expressed by Homer in this celebrated sentence from the *Iliad*: "To have several princes is not a good thing; let there be only one prince and one king.[43]

At present there is not a single republic which was not subject to monarchs in other times. The Swiss were the subjects of the princes of the house of Austria. The United Provinces simply got out from

---

[39] Josh. 22:11–14,33.   [40] Judg. 19:30.   [41] 1 Kings 8:5.
[42] Ibid., 7.   [43] Homer, *Iliad* II. 204–205.

under the domination of Spain and that of the house of Burgundy. The free cities of Germany had their individual lords, in addition to the Emperor who was the common leader of the whole Germanic body. The cities of Italy which made themselves into republics at the time of the Emperor Rudolph, bought their liberty from him. Even Venice, which prides itself on having been a republic since its origin, was still subject to the emperors during the reign of Charlemagne and long thereafter; then she transformed herself into a popular state, from which she has arrived, rather late, at the condition in which we see her.

Thus the whole world began with monarchies; and almost the whole world has preserved itself in that state, as being the most natural.

We have also seen that it [monarchy] has its foundation and its model in the paternal empire, that is in nature herself.

Men are all born subjects: and the paternal empire, which accustoms them to obey, accustoms them at the same time to have only one leader.

8th Proposition
Monarchical government is the best

If it is the most natural, it is consequently the most durable, and from this the strongest as well.

It is also the most opposed to division, which is the essential evil in states, and the most certain cause of their ruin; in accordance with these already-related words: "Every kingdom divided against itself shall be made desolate: and every city or house divided against itself shall not stand."[44]

We have seen that in this sentence our Lord has traced the natural progression of government, and seems to have wished to point out to kingdoms and to cities the same means of uniting which nature has established in families.

Indeed it is natural that when families have to unite to form a state-body, they range themselves under the government which is proper to them.

When states are formed, one seeks for unity, and one is never so

---

[44] Matt. 2:25.

On authority

unified as under a single leader. In addition one is never stronger, because everything happens in concert.

Armies, in which human power appears most clearly, naturally want a single chief; everything is in peril when the command is divided. "After the death of Joshua the children of Israel consulted the Lord, saying: Who shall go up before us against the Canaanites, and shall be the leader of the war? And the Lord said: Judah shall go up: behold I have delivered the land into his hands."[45] The tribes, equal between themselves, wanted one of them to command. Besides it was not a matter of giving a leader to each tribe, since each tribe had its own. "And there shall be with you the princes of the tribes, and of the houses in their kindreds, whose names are these,"[46] etc.

Since military government naturally needs to be exercised by one person alone, it follows that this form of government is the most fitting to all those states which are weak and imperilled, if they are not shaped for war.

And this form of government must in the end prevail, because military government, which holds the power, naturally pulls the state after itself.

This happens above all in warrior-states, which transform themselves easily into monarchy, as did the Roman republic, and several others of the same nature.

It is better that this be established early and gently, because it is too violent when it gets the upper hand by open force.

9th Proposition
Of all monarchies the best is the successive or hereditary, above all when it passes from male to male and from eldest to eldest

It is this [kind of monarchy] that God established among his people. "For he has chosen the princes from the tribes of Judah, and within the tribe of Judah he has chosen me (it is David who is speaking), and he has chosen me among all my brothers. And among my sons . . . he hath chosen Solomon my son, to sit upon the throne of the kingdom of the Lord over Israel. And he said to me . . . : I will establish his

---

[45] Judg. I. 1–2.   [46] Num. I. 4–5ff.

[Solomon's] kingdom for ever, if he continues to keep my commandments and my judgments."[47]

See, then, royalty by succession attached to the house of David and of Solomon. "And the throne of David shall be firm for ever."[48]

In virtue of this law the eldest was to succeed to the prejudice of his brothers. That is why Adonias, who was the eldest son of David, said to Bethsabee, mother of Solomon: "Thou knowest that the kingdom was mine, and all Israel had preferred me to be their king; but the kingdom is transferred, and is become my brother's; for it was appointed him by the Lord."[49]

He spoke truly, and Solomon was in agreement with him when he replied to his mother (who was asking for Adonias a favor of extreme consequence according to the *moeurs* of these peoples): "Ask for him also the kingdom; for he is my elder brother, and hath Abiathar the priest and Joab supporting his interests."[50] He meant to say that one must not strengthen a prince who has a natural title, and a great party within the state.

At least, then, if something extraordinary does not happen, the eldest ought to succeed: and one will scarcely find two contrary examples in the house of David, except at the beginning.

10th Proposition
Hereditary monarchy has three principal advantages

Three reasons show us that this government is the best.

The first is that it is the most natural, and that it perpetuates itself by itself. Nothing is more durable than a state which lasts and perpetuates itself by the same causes which cause the universe to last, and which perpetuate the human race.

David touched on this reason when he spoke in this way: "It would have been little for you, o Lord, to have raised me to royalty; you have also established my house for a long time to come: for this is the law of Adam, o Lord God."[51] He meant that it is the natural order that the son succeed his father.

The people, by themselves, have grown accustomed to this. "I saw

[47] 1 Par. 28:4–7.   [48] 2 Kings 7:16.   [49] 3 Kings 2:15.
[50] Ibid., 22.   [51] 2 Kings 7:19.

On authority

all men living, that walk under the sun with the second young man, who shall rise up in his place."[52]

There are no intrigues, no cabals in a state, with a view to making oneself king, where nature has already made one: death, we say, seizes the living and the king never dies.

The government is best, which is the farthest from anarchy. In something as necessary as government among men, one must provide the easiest principles, and the order which best rolls on by itself.

The second reason which favors this government, is that it makes the authorities who guide the state the ones who are most interested in its preservation. The prince who works for the state works for his children; and the love he bears his kingdom, mixed with that he has for his family, becomes natural to him.

It is natural and sweet to show a prince no other successor than his son: that is to say another self, as nearly as may be. Thus he sees without envy the passing of his kingdom into other hands; and David heard with joy this acclamation of his people: "May God make the name of Solomon greater than thy name, and make his throne greater than thy throne."[53]

Here one need not worry about the disorders caused in a state by the ill-humor of a prince or a magistrate who is angry about working for his successor. David, kept from building the Temple – a work so glorious, and so necessary to the monarchy as much as to religion – rejoiced to see this great work reserved for his son Solomon, and made the preparations for it with as much care, as if he himself were to have the honor of it. "Solomon, my son, whom alone God hath chosen to do this great work, is to build a house prepared not for man, but for God. And I with all my ability have prepared the expenses for the house of my God."[54]

He here received a double joy: the first to prepare at least the edifice of the Lord his God which he was not permitted to build; the second to give his son the means to construct it soon.

The third reason [favoring hereditary monarchy] is drawn from the dignity of [ruling] houses, in which kingdoms are hereditary.

"It would have been little for you, o Lord, to have raised me to royalty; you have also established my house for a long time to come,

[52] Eccles. 4:15.   [53] 3 Kings 1:47.   [54] 1 Par. 29:1–2.

and you have made me remarkable above all men ... What can David add more, seeing thou hast thus glorified thy servant, ... [and] hast shown all this magnificence?"[55]

This dignity of the house of David increased as kings were born into it; the throne of David and the princes of the house of David became the most natural object of public veneration. The people became attached to this house; and one of the means that God used to make the Messiah respected was to have him born of this house. He was acclaimed with love under the name, "son of David."[56]

Thus it is that peoples become attached to royal houses. The jealousy that one naturally feels against those whom one sees above him here turns into love and respect; the great themselves obey without repugnance a house which has always looked masterly, and which one knows will never be equaled by any other house.

Nothing is stronger to extinguish partialities, and to hold in duty those equals whose ambition and jealousy make them incompatible.

11th Proposition
It is a novel advantage to exclude women from the succession

For the three reasons alleged, it is clear that hereditary kingdoms are the most firm. The people of God, moreover, did not admit to the succession that sex which is born to obey; and the dignity of reigning houses seems to be insufficiently sustained in the person of a woman, who after all is obliged to recognize a master when she marries.

Where women succeed, kingdoms pass not only out of reigning houses, but out of the whole nation. Now it is much more suitable that the head of state not be a foreigner; and that is why Moses established this law: "Thou mayst not make a man of another nation king, that is not thy brother."[57]

Thus France, where the succession is regulated according to these maxims, can glory in having the best state-constitution that is possible, and the most in conformity to that which God himself has established. All of which taken together shows both the wisdom of our ancestors, and the particular protection of God over this kingdom.

---

[55] 1 Par. 17:17–18.   [56] Matt. 20:31; 21:9.   [57] Deut. 17:15.

12th Proposition
One must keep to the form of government which he finds established in his country

"Let every soul be subject to higher powers: for there is no power but from God: and those that are, are ordained by God. Therefore he that resisteth the power, resisteth the ordinance of God."[58]

There is no form of government whatsoever, nor any human institution, which does not have its disadvantages; such that it is necessary to remain in the condition to which a length of time has accustomed the people. That is why God takes under his protection all legitimate governments, in whatever form they are established: whoever undertakes to overthrow them is not only a public enemy, but also the enemy of God.

Article II

1st Proposition
There is a very old right of conquest, attested by Scripture

As far back as the time of Jephtha, the King of the Ammonites complained that the people of Israel, in leaving Egypt, had taken many lands from his predecessors, and demanded them back.[1] Jephtha established the right of the Israelites through two incontestable titles: the first was legitimate conquest, and the other a peaceable possession of three hundred years.

He put forward the right of conquest; and to show that this conquest was legitimate, he posed as the fundamental point "that Israel took nothing by force from the Moabites or the Ammonites: that on the contrary she made a great detour in order not to trespass on their lands."[2]

He showed afterwards that the contested places no longer belonged to either the Ammonites or the Moabites, when the Israelites took

---
[58] Rom. 13:1–2. [1] Judg. 11:13. [2] Ibid., 15–17.

them, but [that they belonged to] Sihon King of the Amorites, whom they had vanquished in a just war. For he had first marched against them, and God had delivered him into their hands.[3]

Here one must apply the right of conquest established by the law of nations and recognized by the Ammonites, who possessed many lands by this title alone.[4]

From this he [Jephtha] moved on to the [right of] possession: and he showed first that the Moabites did not complain at all of the Israelites when they conquered these places – where, indeed, the Moabites had no further claim.

"Art thou better than Balac the son of Sephor king of Moab: or canst show that he strove against Israel and fought against him?"[5]

It is clear from history, indeed, that Balac had never made war at all, though he may have had some such plan.[6]

And not only the Moabites refrained from complaining: but the Ammonites themselves had left the Israelites in peaceful possession for three hundred years. "Why, Jephtha said, have you for so long a time attempted nothing about this claim?"[7]

Finally he concluded in this way: "I do not trespass against thee, but thou wrongest me by declaring an unjust war against me. The Lord be judge and decide this day between the children of Israel and the children of Ammon."[8]

To go back farther, one sees Jacob using this right [of conquest] in the gift which he made to Joseph, in this way: "I give thee a portion above thy brethren, which I took out of the hand of the Amorites with my sword and bow."[9]

There is no need to examine what this was, and how Jacob had taken it from the Amorites: it suffices to see that Jacob claimed it by right of conquest, as the fruit of a just war.

The memory of this gift of Jacob to Joseph was preserved among the people of God as something holy and legitimate down to the time of Our Savior, of whom it is written that "he came near the land which Jacob gave to his son Joseph."[10]

Thus one sees a domain acquired by the right of arms over those who used to possess it.

---

[3] Ibid., 20–21.   [4] Ibid., 23–24.   [5] Ibid., 25.
[6] Num. 24:25.   [7] Judg. 11:26.   [8] Ibid., 27.
[9] Gen. 48:22.   [10] John 4:5.

2nd Proposition
To make the right of conquest incontestable, peaceable possession must be added

One must, however, notice two things in this right of conquest: first, that one must link it to peaceable possession, as was seen in the discussion of Jephtha; second, that in order to make this right incontestable one must confirm it by offering a friendly coming to terms.

Thus the wise Simon the Maccabee, warred on by the King of Asia over the cities of Joppe and Gazara, responded: "As for these two cities, they ravaged our country; yet for these we will give a hundred talents."[11]

Though the conquest was legitimate, and Joppe and Gazara were unjust aggressors, and had been taken in a good war, Simon offered a hundred talents in order to have peace, and to make his right incontestable.

Thus one sees that this right of conquest, which begins with force, transforms itself as it were into common and natural right by the consent of peoples, and by peaceable possession. And one supposes that conquest has been followed by the tacit acquiescence of subject peoples, whom one accustoms to obedience by honorable treatment – or that some kind of agreement intervened, like that which was reported between Simon the Maccabee and the kings of Asia.

Conclusion

Thus we have established by the Scriptures, that royalty has its origin in Divinity itself;

That God too exercised it visibly over men from the beginning of the world;

That he continued this supernatural and miraculous exercise over the people of Israel, until the time of the establishment of the kings;

That he then chose a monarchical and hereditary state, as the most natural and the most durable;

That the exclusion of the sex born to obey, was natural to sovereign power.

Thus we have found that by the order of divine Providence, the

---

[11] 1 Macc. 15:35.

Conclusion

constitution of this kingdom was from its origin most in conformity to the will of God, as it is declared in the Scriptures.

We have not, however, forgotten that in antiquity other forms of government appeared, concerning which God prescribed nothing to the human race: such that each people must follow, as if divinely ordained, the government established in its country, for God is a God of peace who wants tranquillity in human affairs.

But since we are writing in a monarchical state, and for a prince touched by the succession to so great a kingdom, we shall henceforth turn all of the instruction which we draw from Scripture toward the kind of government under which we live: though from the things said about this kind of state, it will be easy to determine about other kinds.

THIRD BOOK

In which one begins to explain the nature and the properties of royal authority

First Article

Taking notice of the essential characteristics

Sole Proposition
There are four characteristics or qualities essential to royal authority

First, royal authority is sacred;
Secondly, it is paternal;
Thirdly, it is absolute;
Fourthly, it is subject to reason.
All of this must be established, in order, in the following articles.

Article II

Royal authority is sacred

1st Proposition
God establishes kings as his ministers, and reigns through them over the peoples

We have already seen that all power comes from God.[1]
"The prince, St. Paul adds, is God's minister to thee for good. But

---
[1] Rom. 13:1–2.

The nature of royal authority

if thou do that which is evil, fear: for he beareth not the sword in vain. For he is God's minister: an avenger to execute wrath upon him that doth evil."[2]

Thus princes act as ministers of God, and his lieutenants on earth. It is through them that he exercises his Empire. "And now say you that you are able to withstand the kingdom of the Lord, which he possesseth by the sons of David?"[3]

It is in this way that we have seen that the royal throne is not the throne of a man, but the throne of God himself. "God hath chosen Solomon my son, to sit upon the throne of the kingdom of the Lord over Israel."[4] And again: "Solomon sat on the throne of the Lord."[5]

And in order that no one believe that it was peculiar to the Israelites to have kings established by God, here is what Ecclesiasticus says: "Over every nation he set a ruler. And Israel was made the manifest portion of God."[6]

Thus he governs all peoples, and gives them, all of them, their kings; though he governs Israel in a more particular and announced fashion.

2nd Proposition
The person of kings is sacred

It appears from all this that the person of kings is sacred, and that to attempt anything against them is a sacrilege.

God anoints them through his prophets, with a sacred unction,[7] as he anoints the pontiffs and their altars.

But even without the external application of this unction, they are sacred through their charge, as being the representatives of divine majesty, deputized by his providence for the execution of his plans. It is thus that God calls Cyrus his anointed. "Thus saith the Lord to my anointed Cyrus, whose right hand I have taken hold of, to subdue all the nations."[8]

The title of "Christ" is given to kings; and everywhere one sees them called Christs or the Lord's anointed.

Under this venerable name, the prophets themselves revered them, and viewed them as associates in the sovereign empire of God, whose authority they exercised over the people. "Speak of me before the

---

[2] Ibid., 4. [3] 2 Par. 13:8. [4] 1 Par. 28:5. [5] Ibid., 29:23.
[6] Ecclus. 17:14–15. [7] 1 Kings 9:16; 16:3. [8] Isa. 45:1.

Lord, and before his anointed, whether I have taken any man's ox, or ass; if I have wronged any man, if I have oppressed any man, if I have taken a bribe at any man's hand. And they said: never; and Samuel said: the Lord and his anointed are witness this day, that you have no complaint to make against me."[9]

It is thus that Samuel, after having judged the people for twenty-one years with absolute power on behalf of God, rendered an account of his conduct before God and before Saul, whom he jointly called as witness, and established his innocence through their testimony.

One must protect kings as sacred things; and whoever neglects to guard them is worthy of death. "As the Lord liveth, said David to Saul's captains, you are the sons of death, who have not kept your master, the Lord's anointed."[10]

Whoever guards the life of the prince places his own in the guardianship of God himself. "As thy life hath been much set by this day in my eyes, David said to king Saul, so let my life be much set by in the eyes of the Lord, and let him deliver me from all distress."[11]

God placed him twice in Saul's hands, who moved heaven and earth to ruin him; David's people pressed him to get rid of this unjust and impious prince; but this proposal horrified him. "The Lord, he said to them, be merciful to me, and let it never happen that I lay my hand upon my master, because he is the Lord's anointed."[12]

Far from attempting anything against Saul's person, he was actually seized with fright for having cut the end of his coat, even though he did that solely to show him how religiously he had spared him. "David's heart struck him, because he had cut off the hem of Saul's robe":[13] so far was the person of the prince sacred to him, and so far he feared having violated the respect due him by the slightest irreverence.

3rd Proposition
One must obey the prince by reason of religion and conscience

St. Paul, after having said that the prince is the minister of God, concludes thus: "wherefore be subject of necessity, not only for wrath, but also for conscience' sake."[14]

---

[9] 1 Kings 12:3–5.   [10] Ibid., 26:16.   [11] Ibid., 24.
[12] Ibid., 24:7, 11; 26:23.   [13] Ibid., 24:6.   [14] Rom. 13:5.

This is why "one must serve, not to the eye, as it were pleasing men, but, as the servants of Christ doing the will of God, from the heart."[15]

And again: "Servants, obey in all things your temporal masters, not serving to the eye, as pleasing men, but in simplicity of heart, fearing God. Whatsoever you do, do it from the heart, as to the Lord, and not to men; knowing that you shall receive of the Lord the reward of inheritance. Serve ye the Lord Christ."[16]

If the apostle speaks thus of slavery, a condition contrary to nature, what must we think of legitimate subjection to princes and to magistrates, the protectors of public liberty?

This is why St. Peter says: "Be ye subject therefore to every human creature for God's sake: whether it be to the king as excelling; Or to governors as sent by him for the punishment of evildoers, and for the praise of the good."[17]

Even if rulers do not acquit themselves of this duty, one must respect in them their charge and their ministry. "Servants, be subject to your masters with all fear, not only to the good and gentle, but also to the angry and unjust."[18]

There is thus something religious in the respect one gives to the prince. The service of God and respect for kings are inseparable things, and St. Peter places these two duties together: "Fear God, Honor the King."[19]

God, moreover, has put something divine into kings. "I have said: You are Gods, and all of you the sons of the most High."[20] It is God himself whom David makes speak in this way.

This accounts for the fact that the servants of God swear by the life and health of the king, as by a divine and sacred thing. Uriah spoke to David: "By thy welfare and by the welfare of thy soul I will not do this thing."[21]

Even if the king should be an infidel [does this hold true], from the respect one should have for the ordination of God. "By the health of Pharaoh, you shall not depart hence."[22]

Here one must listen to the first Christians, and to Tertullian, who speaks as follows in the name of all of them: "We shall swear, not by the genius of the Caesars, but by their life and by their health, which

[15] Eph. 6:5–6. [16] Col. 3:22–24. [17] 1 Peter 2:13–14.
[18] Ibid., 18. [19] Ibid., 17. [20] Ps. 81:6.
[21] 2 Kings 11:11; 14:19. [22] Gen. 42:15–16.

is the most august of all geniuses. Do you not know that geniuses are demons? But we, who see in the emperors the choice and judgment of God, who gave them the command over all peoples, respect in them what God has placed there, and we uphold that through a great oath."[23]

He adds: "What more can I say about our religion and about our piety for the emperor, whom we must respect as he whom our God has chosen: such that I can say that Caesar is more to us than to you, because it is our God who has established him?"[24]

Thus it is the spirit of Christianity to make kings respected in a kind of religious way – which Tertullian (again) calls very well "the religion of the second majesty."[25]

This second majesty simply flows out of the first, that is to say the divine, which, for the good of human affairs, has lent some of its brilliance to kings.

4th Proposition
Kings should respect their own power, and use it only for the public good

Their power coming from on high, as has been said, they must not believe that they are the owners of it, to use it as they please; rather must they use it with fear and restraint, as something which comes to them from God, and for which God will ask an accounting of them. "Hear, therefore, ye kings, and understand: learn ye that are judges of the ends of the earth. Give ear, you that rule the people, and that please yourselves in multitudes of nations: For power is given you by the Lord, and strength by the most High, who will examine your works, and search out your thoughts: Because being ministers of his kingdom, you have not judged rightly, nor kept the law of justice, nor walked according to the will of God. Horribly and speedily will he appear to you; for a most severe judgment shall be for them that bear rule. For to him that is little, mercy is granted: but the mighty shall be mightily tormented. For God will not except any man's person, neither will he stand in awe of any man's greatness, for he made the little and the great, and he hath equally care of all. But a greater punishment is ready for the more mighty. To you, therefore, O kings,

---

[23] Tertullian, *Apologeticus*, Ch. 32.
[24] Ibid., Ch. 33.   [25] Ibid., Ch. 35.

are these my words, that you may learn wisdom, and not fall from it."[26]

Kings must tremble, then, in using the power that God gives them, and consider how horrible is the sacrilege of using for evil a power that comes from God.

We have seen kings seated on the throne of the Lord, holding in their hand the sword that [God] himself has placed there. What a profanation, what audacity, on the part of unjust kings, to be seated on the throne of God in order to give judgments contrary to his laws, and to use the sword he has placed in their hand, to do acts of violence and to cut the throats of children!

Let them respect their power, then, because it is not their power, but the power of God, which must be used in a holy and religious way. St. Gregory of Nazianze spoke thus to the emperors: "Respect the purple: recognize the great mystery of God in your persons: He governs by himself the celestial things: He divides those of the earth with you. Be gods, then, to your subjects."[27] That is to say, govern them as God governs, in a way that is noble, disinterested, beneficent – in a word divine.

Article III

Royal authority is paternal, and its proper character is goodness

After the things which have been said, this truth has no further need of proofs.

We have seen that kings hold the place of God, who is the true Father of the human race.

We have also seen that the first idea of power that there was among men, is that of paternal power; and that kings were fashioned on the model of fathers.

Moreover, all the world agrees that obedience, which is due to public power, is only found (in the Decalogue) in the precept which obliges one to honor his parents.

[26] Wisd. 6:2–10.   [27] St. Gregory, *Discourse* XXXV. 11.

From all of this it appears that the name "king" is a father's name, and that goodness is the most natural quality in kings.

Let us, nonetheless, reflect particularly on so important a truth.

1st Proposition
Goodness is a royal quality, and the true prerogative of greatness

"The Lord your God is the God of gods, and the Lord of lords, a great and mighty and terrible, who accepteth no person nor taketh bribes.[1] He doth judgment to the fatherless, and the widow, loveth the stranger, and giveth him food and raiment."[2]

Because God is great and self-sufficient, he turns (as it were) entirely to do good to men, in conformity to this word: "For according to his greatness, also is his mercy with him."[3]

He places an image of his greatness in kings, in order to oblige them to imitate his goodness.

He raises them to a condition in which they have nothing more to desire for themselves. We have heard David saying: "What can David add more, seeing thou hast thus glorified thy servant, and known him?"[4]

And at the same time he declares to them that he gives them this greatness for love of the nations. "Because the Lord hath loved his people, therefore, he hath made thee king over them."[5] And again: "God, whom thou hast pleased, . . . hath set thee upon the throne of Israel, because the Lord hath loved Israel for ever, and hath appointed thee king, to do judgment and justice."[6]

That is why, in those passages where we read that the kingdom of David was raised over the people, the Hebrew and the Greek [text] use [the phrase] *for* the people. This shows that greatness has for its object the good of subject peoples.

Indeed God, who has made all men from the same earth, bodily, and has placed equally in their souls his image and resemblance, has not established between them so many distinctions as to make (on one side) the proud and (on the other) slaves and wretches. He made the great only to protect the small; he gave his power to kings only to procure the public good, and for the support of the people.

---

[1] Deut. 10:17. [2] Ibid., 18. [3] Ecclus. 2:23.
[4] 2 Kings 7:20; 1 Par. 17:18. [5] 2 Par. 2:11. [6] 3 Kings 10:9.

2nd Proposition
The prince is not born for himself, but for the public

This is a consequence of the preceding proposition; and God confirms this truth by the example of Moses.

He gave him his people to lead, and at the same time he made him forget himself.

After a great deal of effort, and after he had endured the ingratitude of the people for forty years to lead them to the promised land, he was excluded from it: God declared to him that this honor was reserved for Joshua.[7]

As for Moses, he said to him: "You shall not bring these people into the land, which I will give them."[8] It is as if he said: You will do the work, and another will have the fruit of it.

God announced his approaching death to him; Moses, without surprise and without thinking of himself, begged him only to provide for the people. "May the Lord the God of the spirits of all flesh provide a man, that may be over this multitude: And may go out and in before them, and may lead them out, or bring them in: lest the people of the Lord be as sheep without a shepherd."[9]

He ordained a great war from him in these terms: "Revenge first the children of Israel on the Madianites, and so thou shalt be gathered to thy people."[10] He wanted to make him know that he did not work for himself, that he was made for others. Immediately and without saying one word about his approaching death, he gave his orders for the war, and completed it quietly.[11]

He spent the little life remaining to him in teaching the people, and in giving them the instructions which comprise the book of Deuteronomy. And then he died without the slightest earthly reward, at a time when God was giving them so liberally. Aaron had the priesthood for himself and his posterity; Caleb and his family were magnificently provided for; others received other gifts; Moses nothing; one does not know what became of his family. He was a public person born for the good of the universe; but that is also true greatness.

May princes understand that their true glory is not to exist for themselves; and that the public good which they obtain is a worthy

---

[7] Deut. 31:7.   [8] Num. 20:12.   [9] Ibid., 27:16–17.
[10] Ibid., 31:2.   [11] Ibid., 3–8.

enough reward on earth, while waiting for the eternal goods which God reserves for them.

3rd Proposition
The prince must provide for the needs of the people

"The Lord said to David: thou shalt feed my people Israel, and thou shalt be prince over Israel."[12]

"God has chosen David, and took him from the flocks of sheep . . . to feed Jacob his servant, and Israel his inheritance."[13] He merely changed the flock: instead of grazing sheep, he grazed men. "To graze" [*paître*] in the language of Scripture is "to govern," and the name "pastor" signifies the prince – so much are these things united.

"I said to Cyrus, the Lord says, Thou art my shepherd."[14] That is to say: you are the prince whom I have established.

It is not only Homer, then, who calls princes the shepherds of nations; it is the Holy Ghost. This name sufficiently warns them to provide for the need of the whole flock, that is to say the whole people.

When sovereign power was given to Simon the Maccabee, the decree was conceived in these terms: "The whole people made him prince, that he should have the charge of the holy"[15] – that is, of the Jewish people, which was also called the holy people.

It is a royal right [*droit*] to provide for the needs of the people. Whoever undertakes it to the prejudice of the prince, undertakes against royalty. It is for this that royalty is established, and the obligation to take care of the people is the basis of all the rights that sovereigns have over their subjects.

This is why, in times of great need, the people has a right to appeal to its prince. "In an extreme famine, the people cried to Pharaoh for food."[16] The famished people asked for bread from their king, as from a shepherd, or rather as from their father. And the foresight of Joseph had placed Pharaoh in a position to provide.[17]

Concerning the obligations of the prince, here is a fine sentence from the Wise Man: "Have care of them, and so sit down and when thou hast acquitted thyself of all thy charge, take thy place."[18]

[12] 2 Kings 5:2. [13] Ps. 77:70–71. [14] Isa. 44:28.
[15] 1 Macc. 14:42. [16] Gen. 41:55. [17] Ibid., 56.
[18] Ecclus. 32:1–2.

The nature of royal authority

That sentence contains two precepts:

First precept: "Be among them as one of them" Do not be proud; make yourself accessible and familiar: do not believe yourself (as they say) made of other metal than your subjects. Put yourself in their place, and be towards them as you would have them be if they were in your place.

Second precept: "Have care of them, and sit down when thou hast acquitted thyself of all thy charge." Then you are permitted to rest: the prince is a public person, who must believe that something is lacking in him, if something is lacking to the people of the state.

4th Proposition
Among the people, those for whom the prince must provide most are the weak

For they have greater need of him who is, by his charge, the father and protector of all.

It is for this reason that God commends principally to judges and to magistrates, widows and the fatherless.

Job, who was a great prince, also said: "The eye that saw me gave witness to me: Because I had delivered the poor man that cried out; and the fatherless, that had no helper. The blessing of him that was ready to perish came upon me, and I comforted the heart of the widow."[19] And again: "I was an eye to the blind, and a foot to the lame. I was the father of the poor."[20] And again: "I sat first, and when I sat as a king, with his army standing about him, yet I was a comforter of them that mourned."[21]

His tenderness for the poor passes explanation. "If I have denied to the poor what they desired, and have made the eyes of the widow wait: If I have eaten my morsel alone, and the fatherless hath not eaten thereof: (For from my infancy mercy grew up with me: and it came out with me from my mother's womb:) If I have despised him that was perishing for want of clothing, and the poor man that had no covering: If his sides have not blessed me, and if he were not warmed with the fleece of my sheep . . . may my shoulder fall from its joint, and let my arm with its bones be broken."[22] To be pitiless to one's people, is to

---

[19] Job 29:11–13. [20] Ibid., 15–16.
[21] Ibid., 25. [22] Ibid., 31:16–22.

Royal authority is paternal

separate oneself from his own members, and one [thereby] merits the loss of those [members] of his body.

He gave liberally; he gave, penetrated by compassion; he gave without making people wait. What could be more paternal and more royal?

In the vows which David made for Solomon on the day of his coronation, he spoke only of the care he should have for the poor, and located in this point the happiness of his reign. "He will judge thy people with justice, and thy poor with judgment." He did not grow weary of praising this goodness to the poor. "He shall judge the poor of the people, and he shall save the children of the poor: and he shall humble the oppressor." And again: "All kings of the earth shall adore him: all nations shall serve him. For he shall deliver the poor from the mighty: and the needy that have no helper. He shall spare the poor and needy: and he shall save the souls of the poor. He shall redeem their souls from usuries and iniquity: and their names shall be honorable in his sight." His favors to the poor will bring him, together with great riches, the prolongation of his days and the blessing of all the nations. "And he shall live, and to him shall be given of the gold of Arabia, for him they shall always adore: they shall bless him all the day."[23] There is a marvelous reign, worthy of prefiguring that of the Messiah.

David had well realized that nothing is so royal as to be the help of him who has none; and this is all he wished for his son the king.

Those who command the nations, be they princes, be they governors, should (following the example of Nehemias) relieve a burdened people. "The former governors that had been before me were chargeable to the people ... and their officers also oppressed the people. But I did not so for the fear of God. On the contrary I contributed to the rebuilding of the walls, and I bought no land," being more concerned to give than to enrich myself, "and all my servants were gathered together to the work. I held a great dinner, to which came the magistrates and the leading men of the city, without taking my yearly allowance as governor: for the people were very much impoverished."[24]

It was thus that Nehemias rejoiced at having relieved an

---

[23] Ps. 71.   [24] Neh. 5:15–18.

impoverished people; and he afterwards said, full of confidence: "Remember me, O my God, for good according to all that I have done for this people."[25]

5th Proposition
The true character of the prince is to provide for the needs of the people: while that of the tyrant is to think only of himself

Aristotle has said this, but Sacred Scripture has pronounced it with more force.[26]

It represents in a word the character of a proud and tyrannical soul, making it say: "I am, and besides me there is no other."[27]

It curses princes who think only of themselves, in these terrible words: "And the word of the Lord came to me, saying: "Son of man, prophesy concerning the shepherds of Israel: prophesy, and say to the shepherds: Thus saith the Lord God: Woe to the shepherds of Israel, that fed themselves: should not the flocks be fed by the shepherds? You ate the milk, and you clothed yourselves with the wool, and you killed that which was fat: but my flock you did not feed. The weak you have not strengthened, and that which was sick you have not healed, that which was broken you have not bound again, neither have you sought that which was lost: but you ruled over them with rigor, and with a high hand. And my sheep were scattered, because there was no shepherd: and they became the prey of all the beasts of the field, and were scattered. My sheep have wandered in every mountain, and in every high hill; and my flocks were scattered upon the face of the earth, and there was none that sought them . . . Therefore, ye shepherds, hear the words of the Lord: As I live, saith the Lord God, forasmuch as my flocks have been made a spoil, and my sheep are become a prey to all the beasts of the field, because there was no shepherd: for my shepherds did not seek after my flock, but the shepherds fed themselves, and fed not my flocks: Therefore, ye shepherds, hear the words of the Lord: Thus saith the Lord God: Behold I myself come upon the shepherds, I will require my flock at their hands, and I will cause them to cease from feeding the flock any more, neither shall the shepherds feed themselves any more: and I

---

[25] Ibid., 19. [26] Aristotle, *Eudemian Ethics* IV. 1134b. [27] Isa. 47:10.

will deliver my flock from their mouth, and it shall be no more meat for them."[28]

Here one sees firstly, that the character of the bad prince is to feed himself, and never to consider the flock.

Secondly, that the Holy Spirit demands an accounting from him, not only of the evil he has done, but of him he has failed to heal.

Thirdly, that all the evil which the ravishers do to their people, when they abandon them and think only of their pleasure, falls back on them.

6th Proposition
The prince who is useless for the people's good is punished, as well as the evil [ruler] who tyrannizes

It is the rule of divine justice to punish not only those violent servants who abuse the power that he has given them, but also those useless servants who do not make the most of the talent he has placed in their hand. "The unprofitable servant cast ye out into the exterior darkness" – that is, in the deep and dark prison which is without the house of God – "[where] there shall be weeping and gnashing of teeth."[29]

This is why we have just heard that he reproached those shepherds, not only for devouring his flock, but for not healing them, for neglecting them and letting them be devoured.

Mordochai sent word to Queen Esther, during the extreme peril of the people of God: "Think not that thou mayest save thy life only, because thou art in the king's house, more than all the Jews. For if thou wilt now hold thy peace, and the Jews will be delivered by some other occasion: and thou, and thy father's house shall perish."[30]

7th Proposition
The bounty of the prince must not be altered by the ingratitude of the people

No one was ever so ungrateful to Moses as the Jewish people. No one was ever so good to the Jewish people as Moses. Throughout Exodus and Numbers one hears only the insolent murmurings of this people against him: all their complaints are seditious, and never does he hear

---

[28] Ezra 34:2–10.   [29] Matt. 25:30.   [30] Esther 4:13–14.

from their mouths any quiet remonstrances. From threats they passed on to actions. "All the multitude cried out, and would have stoned him."[31] But during this fury he pleaded their cause before God, who wanted to abandon them. "I will strike them therefore with pestilence, and will consume them: but thee I will make a ruler over a great nation, and a mightier than this is. Yes, Lord, Moses answered, so that the Egyptians can blaspheme against you. Rather let the strength of the Lord be magnified, O God patient and full of mercy . . . and forgive, I beseech thee, the sins of his people, according to the greatness of thy mercy."[32]

He did not merely respond to the promises that God made him, occupied with the perilous state of this ungrateful people, and always forgetting himself.

Much more importantly, he sacrificed himself for them. "Lord, either forgive them this sin, or strike me out of the book that thou hast written."[33] Which is to say: take away my life.

David imitated Moses. Despite all his bounties, his people had followed the revolt of Absalom, and afterwards that of Seba.[34] He was not less good to them for that reason, and indeed did not fail to devote himself and his family to this so often rebellious people: "It is I; I am he that have sinned, I have done wickedly: these that are the sheep, what have they done? Let thy hand . . . be turned against me, and against my father's house."[35]

8th Proposition
The prince should yield nothing to his resentment or his ill-humor

"God forbid, said Job, that I should have been glad at the downfall of him that hated me, and have rejoiced that evil had found him. For I have not given my mouth to sin, by wishing a curse to his soul."[36]

Saul's beginnings were admirable, before fortune had perverted the good dispositions which had made him worthy of royalty. A part of the people had refused to obey him: "Shall this fellow be able to save us? And they despised him, and brought him no presents."[37] But when he had just won a glorious victory, "the whole people said to Samuel: Who is he that said: Shall Saul reign over us? Bring the men

---

[31] Num. 14:10. [32] Ibid., 12–19. [33] Exod. 32:32. [34] 2 Kings 15; 20.
[35] 2 Kings 24:17. [36] Job 31:29–30. [37] 1 Kings 10:27.

and we will kill them. And Saul said: No man shall be killed this day, because the Lord this day hath wrought salvation in Israel."[38]

On this day of triumph and salvation, he could not offer to God a worthier sacrifice than that of clemency.

Here is yet another example of this virtue in the person of David. While Saul was persecuting him, he was with his troops in Carmel, where there was an extraordinarily rich man named Nabal. David treated him with all possible goodness: he not only did not permit his soldiers to do him the slightest wrong – a thing which is difficult in the lawlessness of war, among troops tumultuously gathered without regular pay (as David's were) – but Nabal's own people themselves admitted that he protected them in all things. "These men were very good to us, and gave us no trouble; neither did we ever lose any thing all the time that we conversed with them . . . [on the contrary] they were a wall unto us both by night and day, all the while we were with them keeping the sheep."[39] This is the true use of power: what good is it to be the strongest, if it is not to sustain the weak?

It is thus that David used it: and nonetheless when his soldiers (on a feast day) went to ask Nabal, with all possible politeness, for as little as he wanted to give them, this fierce man not only refused them, but flew into a rage against David in an outrageous way, without the slightest respect for so great a man, destined for royalty by the order of God, and without being moved by the persecution that David was unjustly suffering, calling him rather a rebellious servant who wanted to play the master.[40]

After this blow the gentleness of David was pushed to the limit: he rushed to vengeance: but God sent to him Abigail the wife of Nabal, as prudent as she was beautiful, who spoke to him in these terms: "Let not my lord the king, I pray, regard this naughty man Nabal . . . The Lord liveth, and thy soul liveth, who hath withholden thee from coming to blood, and hath saved thy hand to thee . . . The Lord will surely make for my lord a faithful house, because thou, my Lord, fightest the battles of the Lord: let not evil therefore be found in thee, all the days of thy life . . . When the Lord shall have done to thee, my lord, all the good that he hath spoken concerning thee, and shall have made thee prince over Israel, this shall not be an occasion of grief to thee, and a scruple of heart to my lord, that thou hast shed innocent

---

[38] 1 Kings 11:12–13.   [39] 1 Kings 25:15–16.   [40] Ibid., 8ff.

blood, or hast revenged thyself; and when the Lord shall have done well by my lord, thou shalt remember thy handmaid."[41]

She spoke to David as if assured of his goodness, and touched him indeed in a way that he could feel, making him see that greatness is only given to men for well-doing, as he had always done; that, moreover, his whole power would have no further charm for him, if he could reproach himself for using it with violence.

David, penetrated by this speech, cried out: "Blessed be the Lord the God of Israel, who sent thee this day to meet me, and blessed be thy speech, which has calmed my anger; and blessed be thou, who hast kept me today, from coming to blood, and revenging me with my own hand."[42]

How he enjoyed the sweetness of taming his anger: and what horror he felt over the action he was going to undertake!

He recognized, indeed, that power must be odious, even to him who had it in his hand, when it brings him to sacrifice innocent blood to his private resentment. One is not powerful, if he cannot resist the temptation of power; and when one has abused it, he always feels within himself that he has not deserved it.

Such was David: and nothing makes us deplore more what love and pleasure can do to men, than to see so good a prince pushed to the very murder of Uriah by this blind passion.

If the prince should not yield anything to his private resentments, for an even stronger reason he should not let himself be mastered by his temper, nor by aversions or irregular inclinations: rather he must always act reasonably, as will be shown in what follows.

9th Proposition
A good prince spares human blood

"O that some man, David had said, would get me a drink of the water out of the cistern, that is in Bethlehem, by the gate. And the three valiant men broke through the camp of the Philistines, and drew water out of the cistern . . . and brought it to David; but he would not drink, but offered it to the Lord, saying: The Lord be merciful to me, that I may not do this: shall I drink the blood of these men that went, and the peril of their lives?"[43]

---

[41] Ibid., 25–31.   [42] Ibid., 32–33.   [43] 2 Kings 23:15–17.

"He felt, St. Ambrose says, his conscience wounded by the peril undergone by these valiant men to satisfy him; and this water, which he saw as purchased at the price of blood, caused him only feelings of horror."[44]

10th Proposition
A good prince detests bloody acts

"Ye men of blood, depart from me,"[45] said David. There is nothing that agrees less with the protector of the life and well-being of the whole people, than cruel and violent men.

After the murder of Uriah this same David, who had been thrown into this bloody act by a blind love against his nature, always believed that he was swimming in blood; and having a horror of himself, he cried out: "Deliver me from blood, O God."[46]

Acts of violence and cruelties, which are always detestable, are still more so in princes, who are established to stop and punish them. God, who had patiently endured the impieties of Achab and of Jezebel, pronounced the final and irrevocable sentence, after they spilled the blood of Naboth. Thus Elias was sent to say to this cruel king: "Thou hast slain, moreover also thou hast taken possession of the goods of Naboth, and art still adding to thy crimes . . . Thus saith the Lord: in this place wherein thy dogs have licked the blood of Naboth, they shall lick thy blood also . . . and I will cut down thy posterity, and I will kill of Achab him that pisseth against the wall . . . And the dogs shall eat Jezebel in the field of Jezrahel . . . If Achab die in the city, the dogs shall eat him: but if he die in the field, the birds of the air shall eat him."[47]

Antiochus called the Great, King of Syria, perished in a way that was apparently less violent, but not less terrible. God punished him by abandoning him to the reproaches of his conscience and to furious grief, which finally turned into an incurable illness.

His avarice had led him to pillage the Temple at Jerusalem, and then to persecute the people of God. He undertook great murders, and spoke with great pride.[48] But then suddenly, while he was listening to talk of the victories of the Jews, whom he was persecuting to the extreme, "he was struck with fear, and exceedingly moved: and he

---

[44] St. Ambrose, *Apol. David* VII. 34.
[45] Ps. 138:19.
[46] Ps. 50:16. [47] 3 Kings 31:19,23,24. [48] 1 Macc. 1:23–25.

laid himself down upon his bed, and felt sick for grief, because it had not fallen out to him as he had imagined. And he remained there many days: for great grief came more and more upon him, and he made account that he should die. And he called for all his friends and said to them: Sleep is gone away from my eyes, and I am fallen away, and my heart is cast down from anxiety. And I said in my heart: into how much tribulation am I come, and into what floods of sorrow, wherein now I am: I that was pleasant and beloved in my power! But now I remember the evils that I have done in Jerusalem . . . and I sent to destroy the inhabitants of Judah without cause. I know therefore that for this cause these evils have found me: and behold I perish with great grief in a strange land."[49]

Added to this grief were pains in his entrails and ulcers all over his body: he became intolerable to himself, as well as to others, from the smell exhaled by his rotten members. In vain did he recognize divine power in these words: "It is just to be subject to God, and that a mortal man should not equal himself to God." God rejected these forced submissions. "Then this wicked man prayed to the Lord, of whom he was not like to obtain mercy."[50]

"Thus the murderer and blasphemer, being grievously struck, as himself had treated others, died a miserable death."[51] That is to say, he found God pitiless, as he himself had been.

This is what happens to violent and bloody kings. Those who oppress the people and exhaust them with cruel vexations, ought to expect the same vengeance: for it is written: "The bread of the needy, is the life of the poor; he that defraudeth them thereof is a man of blood."[52]

11th Proposition
Good princes risk their life for the safety of their people, and also preserve it for love of them

Both [truths] are clear in these two examples.

During the revolt of Absalom, David sent his army into battle, and wanted to march with it, as was usual with him. "But the people said to him: Thou shalt not go forth; for if . . . half of us should fall, they will not greatly care. For thou alone art accounted for ten thousand: it

---

[49] Ibid., 6:8–13.   [50] 2 Macc. 9:5,9,12,13.   [51] Ibid., 28.   [52] Ecclus. 34:25.

is better therefore that thou shouldest be in the city to succor us. And the king said to them: What seemeth good to you, that will I do."[53]

He gave way without resistance; he made no show of withdrawing regretfully. He did not play at being valiant, for he really was.

"In a combat of the Philistines against David, when he was growing faint, a Philistine was going to run him through. Abisai the son of Sarvia rescued him, and striking the Philistine killed him. Then David's men swore unto him, saying: Thou shalt go no more out with us to battle, lest thou put out the lamp of Israel."[54]

The valor of David made itself felt among the Philistines, to the proud giant Goliath, and even to the bears and lions, whom he tore apart like lambs.[55] We do not read, however, that he engaged in combat during this time. One should not under-value the self-restraint of a king so valiant that he preserved himself for his state, [any more than one should under-estimate] the piety of his subjects.

For the rest the history of [the Jewish] kings, and that of the Maccabees, are full of famous examples of princes who risked their lives for the people; it is useless to report them.

Pagan antiquity admired those who devoted themselves to the fatherland. Saul at the beginning of his reign, and David at the end of his, sacrificed themselves to divine vengeance to save their people.

We have already recounted the example of David: let us look at that of Saul.

Saul, victorious, who had resolved to pursue his enemies to the end, according to the ancient customs (of which one sees examples among all the nations), "adjured the people, saying: Cursed be the man that shall eat food till evening, till I be revenged of my enemies"[56] – that is, the Philistines who were enemies to the state. Jonathan, who had not heard this oath of his father's, ate from extreme need,[57] against this command; and God, who wanted to show either how formidable was the sacredness of an oath, or how prompt everyone must be in knowing public orders, showed his anger toward the whole people.[58] At this, what did Saul do? "As the Lord liveth who is the savior of Israel, he said, if it was done by Jonathan my son, he shall surely die . . . Be you [Israel] on one side, and I with Jonathan my son will be on the other side . . . O Lord God of Israel, give a sign, by which we may know in whom lies the sin which has angered you

---

[53] 2 Kings 18:3–4.   [54] 2 Kings 21:15–17.   [55] 1 Kings 17:36.
[56] 1 Kings 14:24.   [57] Ibid., 27.   [58] Ibid., 37.

against your people. If this iniquity be in me, or in my son Jonathan, give a proof."[59] Immediately the die was cast: God ruled, the whole people was delivered; only Saul and Jonathan remained. Saul followed up without hesitating: "Cast lots between me, and Jonathan my son. And Jonathan was taken."[60] This young prince admitted what he had done; his father persisted invincibly in wanting to execute him; the whole people had to unite to stop the execution;[61] but on Saul's side the vow was fulfilled, and Jonathan was sacrificed to death without resistance.

12th Proposition
Government ought to be mild

"Be not as a lion in thy house . . . oppressing thy subjects and thy servants."[62]

The prince should be fearsome only to the evil. For, as the apostle says, "princes are not a terror to the good work, but to the evil. Wilt thou then not be afraid of the power? Do that which is good, and thou shalt have praise from the same. For he is God's minister to thee, for good. But if thou do that which is evil, fear: for he beareth not the sword in vain."[63]

Thus government is mild by its nature; and the prince should be harsh only when forced to be so by crimes.

Apart from that, it is fitting for him to be good, affable, indulgent, in such a way that one scarcely feels that he is master. "Have they made thee ruler? be not lifted up: be among them as one of them."[64]

It is up to the prince to practise this precept from Ecclesiasticus: "Bow down thy ear cheerfully to the poor, and pay what thou owest, and answer him peaceable words with mildness."[65]

Mildness helps in understanding, and in responding well. "Be meek to hear the word, that thou mayest understand: and return a true answer with wisdom."[66]

By mildness one better expedites matters, and one acquires great glory. "My son, do thy works in meekness, and thou shalt be beloved above the glory of men."[67]

Moses was the gentlest of all men,[68] and thereby the most worthy of

[59] 1 Kings 14:39–41. [60] Ibid., 42. [61] Ibid., 45. [62] Ecclus. 4:35.
[63] Rom. 13:3–4. [64] Ecclus. 32:1. [65] Ecclus. 4:8. [66] Ibid., 5:13.
[67] Ibid., 3:19. [68] Num. 12:3.

command under a God who is goodness itself. "He sanctified him in his faith, and meekness, and chose him out of all flesh to be the leader of his people."[69]

We have seen the goodness and gentleness of Job who, "seated in the midst of the people like a king surrounded by his court, was the comforter of the afflicted."[70]

Moses never failed to listen to the people, ungrateful as this people was for his bounty: "And the people stood by Moses from morning until night."[71]

David was loving and good. Nathan moved him through pity, and began in this way (the most readily felt) to make David understand his crime. "A poor man, he said, had nothing at all but one little ewe lamb; ... it slept in his bosom, and it was unto him as a daughter: and a rich man despoiled him of it and killed it," etc.[72]

The woman of Thecua, who came to persuade him to recall Absalom, reached him by the same path. "Alas! I a widow woman: for my husband is dead; one of my sons has killed his brother; and my assembled relatives want to take from me that which remains, and quench the spark which is left to me: And the king said to her: Go, and I will give charge concerning thee."[73]

She managed to move him, by reminding him of the good of the people as the thing most dear to him. "Why hast thou thought such a thing against the people of God, and why hath the king spoken this word, to sin, and not recalled your banished son, as all the people desire?"[74]

One can see, from the things that have been said, that the whole life of this prince was full of goodness and mildness. Thus it is not without reason that we read in a Psalm which is apparently by Solomon: "O Lord, remember David, and all his meekness."[75]

Thus, among the many fine qualities of David, his son found none more memorable, nor more pleasing to God, than his great meekness.

There is nothing, moreover, which the nations celebrate so much. "We have heard that the kings of the house of Israel are mild and merciful."[76] The Syrians spoke in this way to their king Benadad, who was the prisoner of a king of Israel. A fine reputation of these kings among foreign peoples, a truly royal quality!

[69] Ecclus. 45:4. [70] Job 29:25. [71] Exod. 18:13.
[72] 2 Kings 12:3–4. [73] 2 Kings 14:5–8. [74] 2 Kings 14:13.
[75] Ps. 131:1. [76] 3 Kings 20:31.

13th Proposition
Princes are made to be loved

We have already related these words: "Solomon sat on the throne of the Lord . . . and he pleased all: and all Israel obeyed him."[77]

This young prince was not yet known: he showed himself, and won all hearts just by being seen. The throne of the Lord, on which he was seated, brought him to be loved naturally, and made obedience pleasant.

From this natural attraction of peoples toward their princes arose the memorable dispute between the people of Judah and the other Israelites over who would best serve the King. "All the men of Israel running together to the king, said to him: Why have our brethren the men of Judah stolen thee away, and brought the king and his household over the Jordan, as if it were for them alone to serve him? And the men of Judah answered: Because the king is nearer to me: why art thou angry for this matter? Have we eaten any thing of the king's, or have any gifts been given us? And the men of Israel answered: I have ten parts in the king more than thou, and David belongeth to me more than to thee: why hast thou done me a wrong, and why was it not told me first, that I might bring back my king? And the men of Judah answered more harshly than the men of Israel."[78]

Each [side] wanted to have the King: each, passionate for him, envied others the glory of possessing him. Sedition would have come about if the prince – who is indeed a public good – had not given himself equally to all.

There is a charm for all peoples in the sight of the prince: and nothing is easier than for him to make himself loved passionately. "In the cheerfulness of the king's countenance is life: and his clemency is like the latter rain."[79] The rain, which comes to refresh an earth dried out by the heat of the day or the summer, is no more agreeable than a prince who tempers his authority with mildness; and his face delights everyone when it is serene.

Job explains admirably this secret charm of the prince. "They waited for me as for rain, and they opened their mouth as for a later shower. If at any time I laughed on them, they believed not, and the light of my countenance fell not on earth."[80] After the great heat of

---

[77] 1 Par. 29:23.   [78] 2 Kings 19:41–43.
[79] Prov. 16:15.   [80] Job 29:23–24.

the day or of the summer, that is to say after trouble and affliction, these words were consoling; the people were delighted to see him pass by, and, happy to receive a glance, preserved it as something precious.

Let the prince, then, be easy in distributing mild looks, and in saying obliging words. "Shall not the dew assuage the heat, so also the good word is better than the gift."[81]

And again: "A sweet word multiplieth friends, and appeaseth enemies, and a gracious tongue in a good man aboundeth."[82]

One must, nonetheless, join actions to words. "As clouds, and wind, when no rain followeth, so is the man that boasteth, and doth not fulfil his promises."[83]

A prince who does good is adored by his people. "All the land . . . was at rest all the days of Simon, and he sought the good of his nation; and his power and his glory pleased them well all his days."[84]

How power is strengthened, when it is thus cherished by the nations! And how much reason had Solomon to say: "Mercy and truth preserve the king, and his throne is strengthened by clemency."[85]

See, then, a fine protection for the King, and a worthy support for his throne.

14th Proposition
A prince who makes himself hated by his acts of violence is always close to perishing

He is viewed not as a man, but as a ferocious beast. "As a roaring lion, and a hungry bear, so is a wicked prince over the poor people."[86]

He can be sure that he is living in the midst of enemies. Since he loves no one, no one loves him. "He says in his heart: I am, and besides me there is no other. Evil shall come upon him, and he shall not know the rising thereof: and calamity shall fall violently upon him, which he cannot keep off: misery shall come upon him suddenly, which he shall not know."[87]

"Crush the head of the princes of the enemies that say: There is no other beside us."[88] It is not, as we shall see, that it is permitted to violate them; God forbid! But the Holy Spirit teaches us that they do

---

[81] Ecclus. 18:16.   [82] Ecclus. 6:5.   [83] Prov. 25:14.   [84] 1 Macc. 14:4.
[85] Prov. 20:28.   [86] Prov. 28:15. [87] Isa. 47:10–11. [88] Ecclus. 36:12.

The nature of royal authority

not deserve to live, and that they have everything to fear – as much from their peoples, pushed to the limit by their acts of violence, as from God, who has announced that "bloody and deceitful men shall not live out half their days."[89]

15th Proposition
The prince must keep himself from rude and mocking words

We have seen that the prince must keep his hands free of blood and violence: but he must also restrain his language, whose wounds are often no less dangerous; according to this saying of David: "Their tongue is a sharp sword."[90] And again: "They have sharpened their tongues like a serpent: the venom of asps is under their lips."[91]

The anger of the prince, declared through his words, causes murders, and verifies the saying of the wise: "The wrath of a king is as messengers of death."[92]

His speech, far from being raging and violent, should not even be harsh. Such language alienates every mind. "A mild answer breaketh wrath, but a harsh word stirreth up fury."[93]

Above all, mocking speech is insupportable in his mouth. "Hurt not the servant that worketh faithfully, nor the hired man that giveth thee his life."[94] And again: "Laugh no man to scorn in the bitterness of his soul: for there is one that humbleth and exalteth, God who seeth all."[95]

Do not take pride, then, in your power; and do not let it carry you to insolent mockeries. There is nothing more odious. What can one expect from a prince from whom one doesn't even receive honorable words?

On the contrary, it is part of the prince's goodness to reprimand scandal-mongering and outrageous raillery. The means are easy: a severe look suffices. "The north wind driveth away rain, as doth a sad countenance a backbiting tongue."[96]

Scandal-mongering is never more insolent, than when it dares to show itself to the prince's face; and it is there, in consequence, that it must be reprimanded.

[89] Ps. 54:24. [90] Ibid., 5. [91] Ps. 139:4. [92] Prov. 16:14.
[93] Prov. 15:1. [94] Ecclus. 7:22. [95] Ibid., 12. [96] Prov. 25:23.

FOURTH BOOK

On the characteristics of royalty (continuation)

First Article

Royal authority is absolute

In order to make this term [absolute] odious and insupportable, many [writers] pretend to confuse absolute government and arbitrary government. But nothing is more distinct, as we shall make clear when we speak of justice.

1st Proposition
The prince need account to no one for what he ordains

"Observe the mouth of the king, and the commandments of the oath of God. Be not hasty to depart from his face, and do not continue in an evil work: for he will do all that pleaseth him. And his word is full of power: neither can any man say to him: Why dost thou so? He that keepeth the commandment, shall find no evil."[1]

Without this absolute authority, he can neither do good nor suppress evil: his power must be such that no one can hope to escape him; and, in fine, the sole defense of individuals against the public power, must be their innocence.

This doctrine is in conformity with the saying of St. Paul: "Wilt thou then not be afraid of the power? Do that which is good."[2]

---

[1] Eccles. 8:2–5.   [2] Rom. 13:3.

2nd Proposition
When the prince has decided, there can be no other decision

The judgments of sovereigns are attributed to God himself. When Josaphat established judges to judge the people, he said: "It is not in the name of man that you judge, but in the name of God."[3]

This is what Ecclesiasticus is made to say: "Judge not against a judge."[4] For still stronger reasons [one must not judge] against the sovereign judge who is the king. And the reason which is given [by Ecclesiasticus] is that, "he judgeth according to that which is just." It is not that he is always so judging, but that he is assumed to be so judging; and that no one has the right to judge or to review after him.

One must, then, obey princes as if they were justice itself, without which there is neither order nor justice in affairs.

They are gods, and share in some way in divine independence. "I have said: You are gods, and all of you the sons of the most High."[5]

Only God can judge their judgments and their persons. "God hath stood in the congregation of gods, and being in the midst of them he judgeth gods."[6]

It is for that reason that St. Gregory, Bishop of Tours, said to King Chilperic in a council: "We speak to you, but you listen to us only if you want to. If you do not want to, who will condemn you other than he who has said that he was justice itself?"[7]

It follows from this that he who does not want to obey the prince, is not sent to another tribunal; but he is condemned irremissibly to death as an enemy of public peace and of human society. "Whoever will be proud and will not obey the command of the pontiff and the ordinance of the judge will die, and you will thus eradicate the evil from among you."[8] And again: "Whosoever shall refuse to obey all your orders, may he die."[9] It is the people who speak thus to Joshua.

The prince can correct himself when he knows that he has done badly; but against his authority there can be no remedy except his authority.

This is why he must take care of what he orders. "Take heed what

---

[3] 2 Par. 19:6. [4] Ecclus. 8:17. [5] Ps. 81:6.
[6] Ibid., 1. [7] Gregory of Tours, *Historia Francorum*, I. v. 19.
[8] Deut. 17:12. [9] Josh. 1:18.

you do; and whatsoever you judge, it shall rebound to you. Let the fear of the Lord be with you, and do all things with great care."[10]

It is thus that Joseph instructed the judges, to whom he was entrusting his authority: how much of this he recollected when he himself had to judge!

3rd Proposition
There is no co-active force against the prince

One calls co-active [coercive] force a power to constrain and to execute what is legitimately ordained. To the prince alone belongs legitimate command; to him alone belongs co-active force as well.

It is for that reason also that St. Paul gives the sword to him alone. "If thou do that which is evil, fear; for he beareth not the sword in vain."[11]

In the state only the prince should be armed: otherwise everything is in confusion, and the state falls back into anarchy.

He who creates a sovereign prince puts everything together into his hands, both the sovereign authority to judge and all the power of the state. "Our king shall judge us, and go out before us, and fight our battles for us."[12] This is what the Jewish people said when they asked for a king. Samuel declares to them upon this basis that the power of their prince will be absolute, incapable of being restrained by any other power. "This will be the right of the king, that shall reign over you, saith the Lord: He will take your children, and put them in his service: he will seize your lands and the best of that which you have in order to give it to his servants," and so forth.[13]

Will they have the right to do all of that legally? God forbid! For God gives no such powers: but they will have the right to do it with impunity with respect to human justice. That is why David said: "To thee only have I sinned, and have done evil before thee. O Lord, have pity on me!"[14] Because he was the king, said St. Jerome of this passage, he had God alone to fear.[15]

And St. Ambrose says of these same words, *to thee only have I sinned*: "He was king, he was subject to no laws, because kings are free of the punishments which bind criminals. For the authority of

---

[10] 2 Par. 19:6–7. [11] Rom. 13:4. [12] 1 Kings 8:20.
[13] Ibid., 11–15. [14] Ps. 50:6. [15] St. Jerome, *In Psalmos* L.

Characteristics of royalty (continuation)

command will not permit the laws to condemn them to the gallows. Thus David sinned not at all against him who had no power to punish him."[16]

When sovereign power was given to Simon the Maccabee, the power which was given to him was expressed in these terms: "That he should be prince, and captain-general of the whole people, and that he should have charge of the saints (as the Jews were called), and that he should appoint rulers over their public works, and over the country, and over the armor, and over the strongholds. And that he should take care of the people, and that he should be obeyed by all, and that all the public acts and decrees should be written in his name, and that he should be clothed with purple, or wear a buckle of gold. And that it should not be lawful for any of the people, or of the priests, to disannul any of these things, or to gainsay his words, or to call together an assembly in the country without his permission: or to be clothed with purple, or to wear a buckle of gold, which is the mark of a prince: and that whosoever shall do otherwise, shall be a criminal. The people consented to this decree, and Simon accepted the sovereign power on these terms. And it was said that this ordinance should be graven in brass, and set up within the compass of the sanctuary, in a conspicuous place; and that the original would remain in the public archives, in the hands of Simon and his children."[17]

There is what one can call the royal law of the Jews, in which all the power of the kings is excellently explicated. To the prince alone belongs the general care of the people: that is the first article and the foundation of all the others. To him belong public works, to him strongholds and arms, to him decrees and ordinances, to him marks of distinction: no power which does not depend on his, no assembly except by his authority.

It is thus that, for the good of the state, one places all force in one alone. Place any power outside, and you divide the state, ruin the public peace, and create two masters, contrary to this oracle of Scripture: "No man can serve two masters."[18]

The prince is, by his charge, the father of the people: by his greatness he is above small interests: still more, all his greatness and his natural interest, is that the people be preserved – for if a people is lacking, he is no longer prince. Thus there is nothing better than to

---
[16] St. Ambrose, *In Psalmos, Apol. David.* x. 51.
[17] 1 Macc. 14:42–49.   [18] Matt. 6:24.

4th Proposition
Nonetheless kings are not freed from the laws

"When he is made king, he shall not multiply horses to himself ... he shall not have many wives, that may allure his mind, nor immense sums of silver and gold. But after he is raised to the throne of his kingdom, he shall copy out to himself the Deuteronomy of this law in a volume, taking the copy of the priests of the Levitical tribe. And he shall have it with him, and shall read it all the days of his life, that he may learn to fear the Lord his God, and keep his words and ceremonies. Let his heart not be lifted up with pride over his brethren, nor decline to the right or to the left, that he and his sons may reign a long time ..."[19]

It must be remarked that this law comprehends not only religion, but also the law of the kingdom, to which the prince is subject as much as anyone else – or rather more than the others, through the rightness [*droiture*] of his will.

This is what princes find it painful to hear. "What prince can you show me," says St. Ambrose, "who believes that that which is not good is not permitted; who holds himself obligated by his own laws; who believes that power should not permit itself what is forbidden by justice? For power does not destroy the obligations of justice: on the contrary, it is by observing what justice prescribes that power avoids crime. And the king is not freed from the laws; but if he sins he destroys the laws by his example." He adds: "Can he who judges others escape his own judgment, and should he do that which he condemns?"[20]

Hence that fine law of a Roman emperor: "It is a saying worthy of the majesty of the prince, to recognize oneself as subject to the laws."[21]

Thus kings are subject, like the others, to the equity of the laws; both because they must be just, and because they owe to the people the example of justice-keeping; but they are not subject to the penalties of the laws. Or, as theology puts it, they are subject to the

---

[19] Deut. 17:16–20. [20] St. Ambrose, *In Psalmos, Apol. David. altera* III, 8.
[21] Justinian's *Codex* 1. I, title XIV, law 4.

laws, not with respect to coercive power, but with respect to directive power.[22]

5th Proposition
The people must keep itself in a condition of repose under the authority of the prince

So it appears in the tale in which the trees choose a king.[23] They speak to the olive-tree, to the fig-tree, and to the vine. These delightful trees, content with their natural abundance, did not want to weigh themselves down with the cares of government. "And all the trees said to the bramble-bush: Come thou and reign over us."[24] The bramble-bush is accustomed to thorns and to cares. It is the only one that is born armed; it has its natural protection in its thorns. Thereby it could seem worthy of reigning. Thus it is made to speak in a way befitting a king. "It answered the trees which had chosen it: If you truly make me your king, come ye and rest under my shadow; but if you mean it not, let fire come out from the bramble-bush and devour the cedars of Lebanon."[25]

As soon as there is a king, the people has only to remain at rest under his authority. If an impatient people stirs, and does not want to keep itself tranquil under royal authority, the fire of division will flare up in the state, and consume the bramble-bush together with all the other trees, that is to say the King and the nations. The cedars of Lebanon will be burned: in addition to the great power, which is the royal one, the other powers will be overturned, and the whole state will no longer be anything but a single cinder.

When a king is authorized, "each remains at rest, without any fear, every one under his vine, and under his fig-tree, from one end of the kingdom to the other."[26]

Such was the condition of the Jewish people under Solomon, and the same under Simon the Maccabee. 'And every man tilled his land with peace; . . . the ancient men sat all in the streets, and spoke together of the public good; and the young men put on them glory, and the robes of war . . . And every man sat under his vine, and under his fig-tree, and lived without fear."[27]

[22] St. Thomas Aquinas, *Summa theologica* Ia IIae, q. XCVI, a.5.
[23] Judg. 9:8–13.   [24] Ibid., 14.   [25] Ibid., 15.
[26] 3 Kings 4:25.   [27] 1 Macc. 14:8,9,12.

To enjoy this repose one needs not just external peace: one needs internal peace as well, under the authority of an absolute prince.

6th Proposition
The people must fear the prince; but the prince must only fear doing evil

"He that will be proud, and refuse to obey the commandment of the priest ... and the decree of the judge, that man shall die, and thou shalt take away the evil from Israel: and all the people hearing it shall fear, that no one afterwards swell with pride."[28]

Fear is a bridle necessary to men because of their pride and their natural indocility.

The people must thus fear the prince; but if the prince fears the people, all is lost. The weakness of Aaron, to whom Moses had left the command while he was on the mountain, was the cause of the adoration of the golden calf. "What have these people done to you?" Moses said to him, "and why have you led them to so great an evil?"[29] He imputes the people's crime to Aaron, who had not repressed it, though it was within his power to do so.

Note these terms: "What have these people done to you for you to lead them to so great an evil?" One is the enemy of the people, by not resisting them on such occasions.

Aaron answered him: "Let not my Lord be offended: for thou knowest this people, that they are inclined to evil. They said to me: make us gods, that may go before us; for we do not know what has become of Moses, who brought us out of Egypt."[30]

What an excuse for a sovereign magistrate, to fear angering the people! God did not accept it, "and he was exceeding angry against Aaron also, and wanted to destroy him; but Moses prayed for him."[31]

Saul attempted to place the blame on the people, for not having executed the orders of God. [It is a] vain excuse, which God rejects; for he [Saul] was established to resist the people whenever they drifted into evil. "Listen," Samuel said to him, "to what the Lord has pronounced against you. You have rejected his word; he has also rejected you, and you shall not be king." Saul said to Samuel: "I have

---

[28] Deut. 17:12–13. [29] Exod. 32:21.
[30] Ibid., 22–23. [31] Deut. 9:20.

sinned because I have transgressed the commandment of the Lord, and thy words, fearing the people, and obeying their words."[32]

The prince must firmly repulse importunate persons who ask unjust things of him. The fear of angering, pushed too far, degenerates into criminal weakness. "There are those who lose their souls through shame-facedness; the imprudent one whom they dare not refuse causes them to perish."[33]

7th Proposition
The prince must make himself feared by great and small alike

Solomon, from the beginning of his reign, spoke firmly to his brother Adonias. As soon as Solomon had been crowned, Adonias sent word to him: "Let King Solomon swear to me this day, that he will not kill his servant. And Solomon said: If he be a good man, there shall not so much as one hair of his head fall to the ground: but if not, he shall die."[34]

Subsequently Adonias conspired [*cabala*] to make himself king, and Solomon had him killed.[35]

He said to the High Priest Abiathar, who had followed Adonias' cause: "Retire to the countryside in your house: for indeed thou art worthy of death, but I pardon you, because thou didst carry the ark of the Lord God before David my father, and because you served him faithfully."[36]

His dignity and his past services saved his life; but he lost his sovereign right to sacrifice, and was banished from Jerusalem.

Joab, the greatest captain of his time, and the most powerful man of the realm, was also of the same party. Having learned that Solomon had found out, he took refuge in the corner of the altar, where Solomon ordered Banaias to kill him. "Thus," Solomon said, "thou shalt remove the innocent blood which hath been shed by Joab, from me, and from the house of my father ... because he murdered two just men, better than himself, Abner the son of Ner, and Amasa the son of Jether ... and their blood shall return upon his head."[37]

The altar is not made to serve as the refuge of assassins; and the

---

[32] 1 Kings 15:16,23,24. [33] Ecclus. 20:24.
[34] 3 Kings 1:51–52.   [35] 3 Kings 2:22–25.
[36] Ibid., 26.   [37] Ibid., 28, 31–33.

royal authority must make itself felt by the wicked, howsoever great they be.

In the New Testament, and among more humane people, one has less need of these bloody executions than under the ancient law and among the Jews – a hard people, and inclined to revolt. But, in the end, the public peace obliges kings to keep everyone in a state of fear – the great still more than ordinary individuals, because it is from the side of the great that the greatest troubles can come.

8th Proposition
Royal authority must be invincible

If there is in the state an authority capable of stopping the course of public power, or of hampering its exercise, no one is safe. Jeremiah executed the orders of God, by declaring that the city would be delivered up to the King of Babylonia in punishment of its crimes. "And the princes said to the king: We beseech thee that this man may be put to death: for on purpose he weakeneth the hands of the men of war . . . and the hands of the people . . . for this man seeketh not peace to this people, but evil. And king Sedecias said: Behold he is in your hands: for it is not lawful for the king to deny you anything."[38] The government was weak, and the royal authority was no longer a refuge for a persecuted innocent.

The King wanted to save Jeremiah, because he knew that God had commanded him to speak as he did. "He had Jeremiah brought particularly before him, and said to him: You shall not die; but let no man know these words. But if the princes shall hear that I have spoken with thee, and shall come to thee, and say to thee: Tell us what thou hast said to the king, answer [in this way]: I presented my supplication before the king, in order that he not send me back to prison, to die there."[39] A feeble prince, who feared the great, and who soon lost his kingdom, not daring to follow the advice which Jeremiah gave him by the order of God.

Evilmerodach, King of Babylonia, was one of those weak princes who let themselves be led by force. By his order Daniel had discovered the deceit of the priests of Baal, and had burst the sacred dragon which the Babylonians worshiped. "And when the Babylonian

---

[38] Jer. 38:4–5.   [39] Ibid., 14, 24–26.

Characteristics of royalty (continuation)

lords had heard this, they took great indignation: and being gathered together against the king, they said: The king is become a Jew. He hath destroyed Baal, he hath killed the dragon, and he hath put the priests to death. And having said these things among themselves, they came to the king: Deliver us Daniel, or else we will destroy thee and thy house."[40]

He granted their demand; and if God delivered Daniel from the wild beasts, this king was no less guilty of his death, to which he had given his consent.

It is easy to undertake [plots] against a weak prince. Evilmerodach, who let himself be intimidated by threats to destroy himself and his house, was killed on another occasion because of his debauches and injustices: for every weak prince is unjust, and his house will lose its royalty.

Thus these weaknesses are pernicious to individuals, to the state, and to the prince himself, against whom one dares everything once he lets it start.

The prophet Daniel was again exposed to wild beasts, through the weakness of Darius the Mede. "And Daniel excelled all the princes, and governors, because a greater spirit of God was in him. And the king thought to set him over all the kingdom: whereupon the princes, jealous of his greatness, looked for an occasion to ruin him, and surprised the king. King Darius, live for ever: All the princes of the kingdom, the magistrates, and governors, the senators, and judges have consulted together that an imperial decree, and an edict be published: That whosoever shall ask any petition of any god, or man, for thirty days, but of thee, O king, shall be cast into the den of lions."[41]

The King made this law, as tyrannical as it was impious, according to the most authentic forms, which rendered it irrevocable among the Medes and the Persians.[42] One owes no obedience at all to kings, against God. "Thus Daniel prayed in his usual way three times a day, his windows open and turned toward Jerusalem. Those who had suggested the law entered *en masse*, and found him at his prayers."[43]

They carried their complaint to the King; and to press him further, they insisted on both the customs of the Medes and Persians, and his own authority. "Know thou, O king, that the law of the Medes and

---

[40] Dan 14:27–28.   [41] Dan. 6:3,4,6,7.   [42] Ibid., 8–9.   [43] Ibid., 10, 11.

Persians is, that no decree which the king hath made, may be altered."[44]

Darius abandoned Daniel, who had served him so well, and contented himself with giving evidence of a deep-felt sorrow.[45] God delivered this prophet once again; but the King had sacrificed him, so far as it was in his power, to the fury of the lions, and to the jealousy of the great, who were more ferocious than the lions themselves.

A king is truly weak, who spills innocent blood from not having been able to resist the great men to his kingdom, nor able to revoke an unjust law made when he had been taken by surprise. Assuerus, king of the same nation, revoked the law published against the Jews,[46] when he learned of its injustice, though it had been made in the most authentic manner.

It is a pitiable thing to see Pilate, in the story of the Passion. "For he knew that by envy the Jews had delivered him."[47]

He had said to them that "he saw no cause [justifying death] in this man . . ."[48] He said to them once again: You accuse him of having incited the people to sedition; and behold I, having examined him before you, find no cause in this man, in those things wherein you accuse him. No, nor Herod either. For I sent you to him, and behold, nothing worthy of death is done to him . . . But the whole multitude together cried out, saying: Let him be crucified, and set at liberty Barabbas, who had been arrested for sedition and murder. And Pilate spoke to them again, desiring to release Jesus. But they cried again, saying: Crucify him, crucify him. And he said to them the third time: Why, what evil hath this man done? I find no cause of death in him. I will chastise him, therefore, and let him go. But they were instant with loud voices, requiring that he might be crucified; and their voices prevailed. And Pilate gave sentence that it should be as they required. And he released unto them the murderer and the seditious one, and abandoned Jesus to their will."[49]

Why struggle so much, only to abandon justice in the end? All his excuses condemn him. "Take him yourselves, and judge him according to your law."[50] And again: "Take him yourselves, and crucify him." As if a magistrate could be innocent, by permitting a crime that he could stop.

---

[44] Ibid., 15.   [45] Ibid., 16–18.   [46] Esther 8:5–8.
[47] Matt. 27:18; Mark 15:10.   [48] Luke 23:4.
[49] Ibid., 14–25.   [50] John 18:31; 19:6.

Reason of state is alleged on his behalf: "If thou release this man, thou art not Caesar's friend. For whosoever maketh himself a king, speaketh against Caesar."[51] But Pilate knew well, and Jesus had declared, that "his kingdom is not of this world."[52] He feared the reaction of the people, and the threats they made to complain of him to Caesar. He ought to have feared only doing evil.

It was in vain "that he washed his hands in front of the whole people, saying: I am innocent of the blood of this just man; look you to it."[53] Ecclesiasticus condemns him: "Seek not to be made a judge, unless thou have strength to extirpate iniquities: lest thou fear the person of the powerful, and lay a stumbling-block for thy integrity."[54]

This weakness in judges is deplored by the prophet. "The great solicit, and the judge can refuse them nothing."[55]

If the prince himself, who is the judge of judges, fears the great, what will be solid in the state? Thus it is necessary that authority be invincible, and that nothing can overwhelm the ramparts, under whose shelter the public repose and the safety of individuals are protected.

9th Proposition
Firmness is an essential characteristic in royalty

When God established Joshua to be prince and captain general, he said to Moses: "Command Joshua, and encourage and strengthen him: for he shall go before this people, and shall divide unto them the land which thou shalt see."[56]

When he had been designated successor to Moses, who was going to die, "God himself said to him: Take courage and be valiant, for thou shalt bring the children of Israel into the land which I have promised, and I will be with thee."[57]

When, after the death of Moses, he placed himself at the head of the people, God said to him again: "Moses my servant is dead: arise, and pass over this Jordan . . . take courage and be strong." And again: "Be firm and strong, and keep the law which Moses my servant gave to you." And again: "Behold I command thee, take courage, and be strong. Fear not and be not dismayed: because the Lord thy God is with thee in all things."[58] It is as if he had said: if you tremble,

---

[51] Ibid., 19:12. [52] John 18:36. [53] Matt. 27:24. [54] Ecclus. 7:6.
[55] Mic. 7:3. [56] Deut. 3:28. [57] Ibid., 31:23. [58] Josh. 1:2,6,7,9.

everything trembles with you. When the head is shaken, the whole body totters: the prince must be strong, because he is the foundation of public tranquillity in peace and in war.

Immediately Joshua commanded with firmness. "And Joshua commanded the princes of the people, saying: Pass through the midst of the camp, and command the people, and say: Prepare you victuals, for after the third day you shall pass over the Jordan . . . And he said to the Rubenites, and the Gadites, and the half tribe of Manasses: Remember the word, which Moses gave you . . . and march before your brethren with your arms, and fight valiantly."[59]

He hesitated in nothing, he spoke firmly, and for its own safety the people asked of him: "Whoever will not obey thee, let him die; only be firm and act the man."[60]

The means of strengthening the prince, is to establish authority, and to let him see that everything flows from him. Assured of obedience, he is pained only by himself; in strengthening himself he has done everything, and everyone follows: otherwise he hesitates, he gropes his way along and everything is done sluggishly. The leader trembles when he lacks confidence in his members.

This is how God installs princes: he strengthens their power, and orders them to use it with firmness.

David followed this example, and spoke thus to Solomon: "Now, then my son, the Lord be with thee . . . the Lord also give thee wisdom and understanding, that thou mayest be able to rule thy people . . . For then thou shalt be able to prosper, if thou keep the commandments, and judgments, which the Lord commanded Moses to teach Israel: take courage and act manfully, fear not, nor be dismayed."[61]

In dying he reiterated the same thing: and here are the last words of this great king to his son: "I am going the way of all flesh: take thou courage, and show thyself a man. And keep the charge of the Lord thy God."[62] Always firmness and courage: nothing is more necessary to sustain authority; but always [one must have] the law of God before his eyes: one is firm only when he follows it.

Nehemias knew well that the public power ought to be managed with firmness. "All these men thought to frighten us, thinking that our hands would cease from the work . . . wherefore I strengthened

---

[59] Ibid., 10–14. [60] Ibid., 18.
[61] 1 Par. 22:11–13. [62] 3 Kings 2:2–3.

my hands the more. Samaia said to me: Let us shut ourselves up in the house of God in the middle of the temple, for they will come tonight to kill thee . . . And I said: Should such a man as I am flee? I knew that these false prophets were not sent by God, and that they had been hired to terrify me, so that I might sin, and they might have some evil to upbraid me with."[63]

Those who intimidate the prince and keep him from acting with vigor, are confounded by God. "Remember me, O Lord, and deal with Tobias and Sanaballat, who wanted to terrify me, according to their works."[64]

10th Proposition
The prince must be firm against his own council and his favorites, when they want to make him serve their individual interests

Besides firmness against dangers, there is another sort of firmness which is no less necessary to the prince: that is firmness against the artifices of his favorites and against the ascendancy that they gain over him.

The weakness of Assuerus, King of Persia, is pitiful in the Book of Esther. Aman, irritated against the Jews because of the private quarrel which he had with Mardochai, undertook to destroy him together with his whole nation. He wanted to make the King the instrument of his vengeance, and, playing the zealot for the good of the state, he spoke thus: "There is a people scattered through all the provinces of thy kingdom . . . that use new laws and ceremonies, and moreover despise the king's ordinances: and thou knowest very well that it is not expedient for thy kingdom that they should grow insolent by impunity. If it please thee, decree that they may be destroyed, and I will pay ten thousand talents to thy treasurers. And the king took the ring that he used, from his own hand, and gave it to Aman . . . and he said to him: As to the money which thou promisest, keep it for thyself, and as to the people, do with them as seemeth good to thee."[65] Instantly the orders were dispatched, the couriers were sent throughout the king-

---

[63] Neh. 6:9–13. [64] Ibid., 14.
[65] Esther 3:8–11. [66] Ibid., 12–15.

Royal authority is absolute

dom,[66] and the King's accommodativeness caused a hundred million men to perish in a moment.

Let princes take care not to comply so easily! In other people the difficulty of executing [a project] gives rise to better counsels; in the prince, for whom speaking is acting,[67] one can scarcely say how detestable accommodativeness is.

It cost Assuerus only three words, and the pain of removing his ring from his finger: through this tiny movement, a hundred million innocents had their throats cut, and their enemy enriched himself on their spoils.

Hold yourself firm, then, O prince! The easier it is for you to execute your plans, the more difficult must you make it for anyone to shake you.

It is to you principally that this word of the wise man is addressed: "Winnow not with every wind, and go not into every way."[68] The prince who is easily led, and too prompt in deciding, loses everything.

Assuerus was too happy to be able to change his mind, and to have been capable of revoking his orders before their execution. Princely action is ordinarily too prompt, and leaves you only regret at having done an irreparable evil.

11th Proposition
One should not lightly change his view after a mature deliberation

As much as one should be slow in resolving oneself to action, just as much should one be firm when one has determined himself with full knowledge. "Go not into every way," the wise man has told you;[69] and he adds: "For so is every sinner proved by a double tongue." That is to say, he pronounces and retracts, without ever arriving at anything. He adds: "Be steadfast in the truth of thy judgment, and let your discourse be one."[70] That is (according to the Greek text), let it not change easily.

---

[67] Ps. 32:9. [68] Ecclus. 5:11.
[69] Ibid., 11. [70] Ibid., 12.

Second Article

On softness, irresolution and false firmness

1st Proposition
Softness is the enemy of government: on the character of the lazy, who have indecisive minds

"The hand of the strong shall bear rule: but that which is slothful, shall be under tribute."[1] A great king says so: it is Solomon. In place of [the word] "strong," the Hebrew [text] says: [the hand] of those who are industrious and attentive:[2] for attention is the power of the soul.

"The sluggard willeth and willeth not: but the soul of them that work shall be made fat."[3] The Hebrew says once again: men who are attentive and industrious.

He who wants weakly, wants without willing: nothing is less proper to the exercise of command, which is only a firm and resolute will.

He wills nothing; he has only languishing desires. "Desires kill the slothful: for his hands have refused to work at all. He merely longeth and desireth all the day."[4] He always would, he never wills.

Thus nothing succeeds for him, he fails in everything. "He that is loose and slack in his work, is the brother of him that wasteth his own works."[5]

We have said that fear is not suitable to command: the lazy person is always fearful, everything seems impossible to him. "The slothful man saith: There is a lion without, I shall be slain in the midst of the streets."[6] And again, "The slothful man saith: There is a lion in the way, and a lioness in the roads. As the door turneth upon its hinges, so doth the slothful upon his bed." Plenty of movement, little action. And finally: "The slothful hideth his hand under his armpit, and it grieveth him to turn it to his mouth."[7]

How can one who cannot help himself possibly help others? "Fear

---

[1] Prov. 12:24. [2] Ibid., 12:24. [3] Ibid., 13:4.
[4] Ibid., 21:25–26. [5] Ibid., 18:9. [6] Ibid., 22:13.
[7] Ibid., 26:13–15.

casteth down the slothful: and the souls of the effeminate shall be hungry."[8]

Negligence pulls down roofs; languishing hands let rain into the house from all sides.[9]

Everything is weak under the slothful. "In all thy works be quick, and no infirmity shall come to thee."[10]

Public affairs are indeed difficult, and one surmounts the difficulty only by indefatigable effort. Many enterprises fail every day, for it is only in virtue of acting ceaselessly that one assures the success of his plans. "In the morning sow thy seed, and in the evening let not thy hand cease: for thou knowest not which may rather spring up, this or that: and if both together, it shall be the better."[11]

2nd Proposition
There is a false firmness

The invincible stubbornness of Pharaoh makes this clear. This is hardness, not firmness. That hardness is fatal to him and to his kingdom. Scripture reveals this in the whole Book of Exodus.

The power to command pushed too far: never to bend, never to condescend, never to relax, to persist in wanting to be obeyed at any price whatsoever – this is a terrible scourge of God on kings and on peoples.

He who said: "Winnow not with every wind,"[12] had said a little beforehand, "do not strive against the stream of the river."[13] There is [such a thing as] excessive thoughtlessness, but also excessive inflexibility.

A false firmness, urged on Roboam by inexperienced young men, caused him to lose ten tribes. The people asked for a little relief from the very high taxes demanded by Solomon: either because they were complaining groundlessly of a prince who had made gold and silver common in Jerusalem, or because Solomon had indeed put a strain on them during the time that he gave himself up to his passions. The old men who understood the state of affairs and the temper of the Jewish people, advised him to appease them with gentle words, followed by some action. "If thou wilt yield to this people today, and

---

[8] Ibid., 18:8. [9] Eccles. 10:18. [10] Ecclus. 31:27.
[11] Eccles. 11:6. [12] Ecclus. 5:11. [13] Ibid., 4:32.

Characteristics of royalty (continuation)

condescend to them, and grant their petition, and wilt speak gentle words to them, they will be thy servants always."[14]

But the reckless young men whom he consulted afterwards mocked the foresight of the old men, and urged on him, not a simple refusal [of the people's request], but a refusal accompanied by hard words and intolerable threats. "My little finger, he said to them, is thicker than the back of my father. And now my father put a heavy yoke on you, but I will add to your yoke: my father beat you with whips, but I will beat you with chains of iron . . . And the king condescended not to the people: for the Lord was turned away from him, and wanted to accomplish what he had declared against Solomon: that, in punishment of his crimes, he would divide his kingdom after his death." [15]

Thus the hardness of Roboam was a scourge sent by God, and a just punishment of Solomon as much as of him.

The young people whom he consulted were not lacking in pretexts: [but] one must sustain authority, and he who lets himself go at the beginning will finally wind up with a foot on his throat. But beyond all that it was necessary [for Roboam] to know the present disposition [of the people], and to yield to a force which could not be vanquished. Even good maxims, pushed too far, bring about the loss of everything. He who wants never to bend, breaks all at once.

3rd Proposition
The prince must, by himself, begin by commanding with firmness, and make himself master of his passions

"Go not after thy lusts, but turn away from thy own will. If thou give thy soul to her desires, she will make thee a joy to thy enemies."[16] Thus one must resist his own wants, and first of all be firm against himself.

The first of all empires is the one that one has over his desires. "Thy lust shall be under thee, and thou shalt have dominion over it."[17]

This is the source and the foundation of all authority. He who exercises it over himself, deserves to exercise it over others. He who is

---

[14] 3 Kings 12:7. [15] Ibid., 10, 11, 15; 11:31.
[16] Ecclus. 18:30–31. [17] Gen. 4:7.

Softness, irresolution, false firmness

not the master of his passions has no strength: for he is weak in principle.

Sedecias, who said to the great, "the king can refuse you nothing,"[18] was weak before them only because he was weak in himself, and did not know how to master his fear.

Evilmerodac, felled by the same passion, let himself be mistreated and pulled about by the great, who said to him: "Deliver Daniel to us, or we will kill you."[19]

If Darius had had enough control over himself to sustain justice, he would have had authority over the great who demanded the same prophet of him, and would not have had the weakness to sacrifice an innocent person to their jealousy.[20]

Pilate had succumbed internally to the temptation of popularity when he let himself be forced to crucify Jesus Christ. In vain did he have in hand the whole of Roman power in Judaea; he was not powerful, because he could not resist known iniquity.

David, however great a king he may have been, was no longer powerful when his power only served him to undertake actions which he bewailed for the rest of his life, and which he would have wanted never to have done.

Solomon was no longer powerful, when his power made him the weakest of all men.

Herod was not powerful at all when, desiring to save St. John the Baptist (whose head was demanded by an unfortunate creature), he dared not do it because "he would not displease her."[21] His crime was influenced by his regard for those present, before whom he feared seeming weak if he failed to fulfil the oath he had sworn. "And the king was struck sad: yet because of his oath, and for them that sat with him at table, he commanded it to be given."[22]

It is the greatest of all weaknesses, to fear appearing weak.

All of this makes it clear that there is no power at all, if one is not first of all powerful over himself; nor true firmness, if one is not first of all firm against his own passions.

"One must want to have a good will," says St. Augustine, "before wanting to have a great power."[23]

---

[18] Jer. 38:5. [19] Dan. 14:28. [20] Ibid., 6:12ff.
[21] Mark 6:26. [22] Matt. 14:9. [23] St. Augustine, *De Trinitate* XIII. 13.

4th Proposition
The fear of God is the true counter-weight to power: the prince fears him the more when he fears only him

In order to establish public peace solidly, and to strengthen a state, we have seen that the prince has had to receive a power independent of any other power there may be on earth. But, for all that, he must not forget himself, nor fly into rages: the less he has to account to men, the more he has to account to God.

The wicked who have nothing to fear from men are all the more unfortunate, since like Cain they are saved for divine vengeance.

"The Lord set a mark on Cain, that whosoever found him should not kill him."[24] It was not that he pardoned this parricide; but it required a divine hand to punish him as he merited.

He treated kings with the same strictness. Their impunity with respect to men submits them to more terrible punishments before God. We have seen that the primacy of their condition draws on them a primacy of punishment. "For to him that is little, mercy is granted: but the mighty shall be mightily tormented . . . But a greater punishment is ready for the more mighty."[25]

Consider how God strikes them in this life. See how he treats an Achab; how he treats an Antiochus; how he treats a Nabuchodonosor, whom he relegates among the animals: a Balshazar, to whom he announces his death and the ruin of his kingdom in the midst of a great feast given for the whole court: finally how he treats so many evil kings: he does not spare greatness, but rather makes it serve as an example.

What will he not do against impenitent kings, if he treats so roughly a David humbled before him and asking pardon? "Why therefore hast thou despised the word of the Lord, to do evil in my sight? Thou hast killed Uriah the Hethite with the sword, and hast taken his wife to be thy wife, and hast slain him with the sword of the children of Ammon. Therefore the sword shall never depart from thy house, because thou hast despised me . . . Thus saith the Lord: Behold, I will raise up evil against thee out of thy own house, and I will take thy wives before thy eyes, and give them to thy neighbor, and he shall lie with thy wives in the sight of the sun. For thou didst it secretly: but I will do this thing

---

[24] Gen. 4:15.   [25] Wisd. 6:6,7,9.

in the sight of all Israel, and in the sight of the sun, for thou hast made the enemies of the Lord blaspheme."[26]

God acted as he had spoken, and it is not necessary to relate here the revolt of Absalom and all its consequences.

These chastisements make one tremble. But everything strict and vengeful which God does on earth is only a shadow in comparison with the rigors of future time. "It is a terrible thing to fall into the hands of the living God."[27]

He lives eternally; his anger is implacable and always living; his power is invincible; he never forgets; he never yields; nothing can escape him.

[26] 2 Kings 12:9–14.   [27] Heb. 10:31.

FIFTH BOOK

Fourth and final characteristic of royal authority

First Article

Royal authority is subject to reason

1st Proposition
Government is a work of reason and intelligence. – "Now, listen, O kings, and be instructed, judges of the earth"[1]

All men are created capable of understanding. But principally you upon whom reposes an entire nation, you who should be the soul and intelligence of a state, in whom must be found the first reason for all its movements: the less it is necessary for you to justify yourself to others, the more you must have justification and intelligence within yourself.

The contrary of acting from reason is to act out of passion or anger. To act out of anger, as Saul acted against David, driven by his jealousy or possessed by his black melancholy, entails all kinds of irregularities, inconsistencies, inequalities, anomalies, injustice, and confusion in one's conduct.

Though one has only a horse to lead and a flock to guide, one cannot do it without reason. How much more is needed for the leadership of men and a rational flock!

"The Lord took David from the care of his sheep to have him conduct Jacob, his servant, and Israel, his inheritance. And he led them in the innocence of his heart with an able and intelligent hand."[2]

Everything among men is accomplished through intelligence and

---

[1] Ps. 2:10.   [2] Ps. 77:70–72; Ps. 78:70–72.

Characteristics of royalty (continuation)

through counsel. "Houses are built out of wisdom and become solid through prudence. Ability fills the granaries and amasses riches. The wise man is courageous. The able man is robust and strong because war is waged by strategy and by industry, and salvation is found where there is much counsel."[3]

Wisdom herself says: "It is through me that kings rule and through me that legislators prescribe what is just."[4]

She is so born to command that she gives the empire even to those born in servitude. "The wise servant will command the children of the house who lack wisdom, and he will apportion their lots."[5] And furthermore: "Free people will subject themselves to a judicious servant."[6]

God, upon installing Joshua, orders him to study the law of Moses, which was the law of the kingdom, "in order," he says, "that you should understand all that you do."[7] And furthermore: "and then you will carry out your designs and you will understand what to do." David said as much to Solomon in the last instructions he gave to him upon dying. "Take care to observe the laws of God so that you may understand all that you do and to which side you are to turn.[8]

"So that you may not be turned, turn yourself knowingly. Let reason direct all your movements. Know what you do and why you are doing it."

Solomon had learned from God himself how much wisdom is necessary to govern a great people. "God appeared to him in a dream during the night, and said to him: Ask what thou wilt that I should give thee. And Solomon said: Thou hast shown great mercy to thy servant David my father, even as he walked before thee in truth, and justice, and an upright heart with thee: and thou hast kept thy great mercy for him, and hast given him a son to sit on his throne, as it is this day. And now, O Lord God, thou hast made thy servant king instead of David my father: and I am but a child, and know not how to go out and come in (that is to say, I do not know how to conduct myself: where to begin or to end matters). And thy servant is in the midst of the people which thou hast chosen, an immense people, which cannot be numbered nor counted for multitude. Give therefore to thy servant an understanding heart, to judge thy people, and discern between good and evil. For who shall be able to judge this

---

[3] Prov. 24:3–6.   [4] Prov. 8:15.   [5] Prov. 7:2.
[6] Ecclus. 10:28.   [7] Josh. 1:7–8.   [8] 3 Kings 2:3.

people, thy people which is so numerous? And the word was pleasing to the Lord that Solomon had asked such a thing. And the Lord said to Solomon: Because thou hast asked this thing, and hast not asked for thyself long life, or riches, nor the lives of thy enemies, but hast asked for thyself wisdom to discern judgment, Behold I have done for thee according to thy words, and have given thee a wise and understanding heart, insomuch that there hath been no one like thee before thee, nor shall arise after thee. Yea and the things also which thou didst not ask, I have given thee: to wit riches and glory, so that no one hath been like thee among the kings in all days heretofore."[9]

This dream of Solomon's was an ecstasy in which the mind of this great king, separated from the senses and united to God, enjoyed true knowledge. He saw, while in this state, that wisdom is the sole grace that a prince should ask of God.

He saw the weightiness of the affairs and the immense multitude of the people whom he had to lead. So many temperaments, so many interests, so many artifices, so many passions, so many surprises to fear, so many things to consider, so many people from every side to hear and know: what mind could be equal to it?

I am young, he said, and I still do not know how to conduct myself. He was not lacking in spirit, any more than in resolution. For he had already spoken in a masterly tone to his brother Adonias: and from the beginning of his reign he had done his part at a decisive juncture, with as much prudence as could be desired: and all the same he trembled still, when he saw this immense chain of cares and of matters that accompany royalty: and he saw well that he could only find his way out through consummate wisdom.

He asked it of God, and God gave it to him: but at the same time he gave him all the rest which he had not asked, that is to say riches and glory.

He teaches kings that they will lack nothing when they have wisdom, and that she alone draws all other goods to them.

We find a fine commentary on Solomon's prayer in the book of Wisdom, which makes this wise king speak as follows: "Wherefore I wished, and understanding was given me: and I called upon God, and the spirit of wisdom came upon me. And I preferred her before kingdoms and thrones, and esteemed riches nothing in comparison of

---

[9] 3 Kings 3:5–13; 2 Par. 1:7–12.

her. Neither did I compare unto her any precious stone: for all gold in comparison of her, is as a little sand, and silver in respect to her shall be counted as clay. I loved her above health and beauty, and chose to have her instead of light: for her light cannot be put out. Now all good things came to me together with her, and innumerable riches through her hands."[10]

2nd Proposition
True firmness is the fruit of intelligence

"Consider what is right [*droit*], and let thy eyes go before thy steps. Make straight the path for thy feet, and all thy ways shall be established."[11] Whoever looks before him walks safely.

Just as much as firmness is necessary in government, so too it requires wisdom.

The nature of wisdom shows itself in consistent conduct. "A holy man continueth in wisdom as the sun: but a fool is changed at the moon."[12]

The wisest of all kings says these words in Wisdom: "Counsel and equity is mine, prudence is mine, strength is mine."[13]

These things are inseparable, if understood correctly. "A wise man is strong: and a knowing man, stout and valiant."[14]

Those who are brutal have only a false boldness. "Nabal was imperious, and no one in his house dared to speak to him."[15] So much so that he thought he had nothing to fear from David, and said insolently: "Who is David? And what is the son of Isai?"[16] As soon as he learned that David had vowed his ruin (though they told him that his wife had appeased David), "his heart died within him, and he became as a stone. And after ten days had passed, he died."[17]

Roboam was viewed with contempt because of his lack of sense. "Solomon left behind him of his seed, the folly of the nation. Even Roboam that had little wisdom, who turned away the people through his counsel."[18]

Since he had no wisdom, he had no firmness; and his own son was constrained to say: "Roboam was unexperienced, and of a fearful heart, and could not resist the rebels."[19] Instead of unexperienced

---

[10] Wisd. 7:7–11. [11] Prov. 4:25–26. [12] Ecclus. 27:12. [13] Prov. 8:14.
[14] Prov. 24:5. [15] 1 Kings 25:17. [16] 1 Kings 25:10. [17] 1 Kings 25:37–38.
[18] Ecclus. 47:27–28. [19] 2 Par. 13:7.

and fearful, the Hebrew [text] says: "He was a child with a tender heart." It was not that he failed to make war on them: "Roboam and Jeroboam had war between them all their days."[20]

He was not accused at all of lacking military courage; rather he did not have that strength which knows how to take good advice, and follow it resolutely. If one noticed the tone in which he spoke to the people, one would have thought him firm and resolute. But he was firm only in words, and at the first sign of sedition one sees him shamefully taking flight. "And king Roboam sent Aduram, who was over the tributes, and the children of Israel stoned him, and he died; and king Roboam made haste to get up into his chariot, and fled into Jerusalem. And Israel revolted from the house of David unto this day."[21]

See the man who prided himself on being more powerful than Solomon: he spoke proudly, when he thought that he could frighten an imploring people. At the first riot he himself trembled, and he strengthened the rebels through his hasty flight.

It was not in this way that his grandfather David acted. When he learned of the revolt of Absalom, he saw what he had to fear and promptly withdrew, but in good order and without too much haste: "walking on foot with his guards, and the best troops he had; and he stationed himself in a deserted place which was difficult of access, while waiting for news from those whom he had left behind to observe the movements of the people."[22]

It is true that he went showing signs of misery, "walking barefoot and with his head covered, he and all the people weeping."[23] This came from a good king and a good father, who saw his well-loved son at the head of rebels and [knew] how much blood would have to be spilled, and that it was his sin which drew all these miseries on his house and his people.

He abased himself at the hand of God, awaiting the outcome with steadfast courage: "If I find grace in the sight of God, he will reestablish me in Jerusalem. But if he shall say to me: Thou pleasest me not: I am ready, let him do that which is good before him."[24]

Being thus resolved, he provided for everything with an admirable presence of mind; and he found without hesitating that fine means by which the counsels of Absalom and Achitopel disappeared.[25]

[20] 2 Par. 12:15. [21] 2 Par. 10:18–19. [22] 2 Kings 15:14.
[23] 2 Kings 15:14,15,17,18,28. [24] 2 Kings 15:25–26. [25] 2 Kings 15:33–34.

And when after the victory he saw Seba son of Bochri, who was gathering the rest of the seditious, he did not rest on the advantage which he had just gained. "And he said to Abisai: Now will Seba the son of Bochri do us more harm than did Absalom: take thou therefore the servants of thy lord, and pursue after him, lest he find fenced cities, and escape me."[26] By this order he assured public tranquillity, and stifled sedition at its birth.

Here is a truly strong man, who knew how to fear when he must, and who knew how to take good advice appropriately.

3rd Proposition
The prince's wisdom makes the people happy

"An unwise king shall be the ruin of his people: and cities shall be inhabited through the prudence of the rulers."[27]

See the happy results of the wise government of Solomon. "Judah and Israel were innumerable . . . eating and drinking and rejoicing. And they dwelt without any fear, every one under his vine, and under his fig-tree."[28]

"Gold and silver were as plentiful in Jerusalem as stones; and cedars were as common as sycamores which grew in the plains."[29]

Under a wise prince everything abounds – men, the goods of the earth, gold and silver. Good order brings about all good things.

The same thing happened under Simon the Maccabee. His characteristic trait was wisdom. Among the Maccabees, the children of Mathathias, Judas was the strong one,[30] Simon the wise. Mathathias had known it well, when he spoke thus to his children: "Simon is a man of counsel: give ear to him always, and he shall be a father to you."[31]

We have already seen how happy the people were under his guidance; but we must look at particular details.

He had found matters in a bad condition: "under him the Jews were freed from the yoke of the Gentiles."[32]

"And all the land of Juda was at rest all the days of Simon, and he sought the good of his nation: and his power and his glory pleased them well all his days . . . He took Joppe for a harbor, and made an

---

[26] 2 Kings 20:6. [27] Ecclus. 10:3. [28] 3 Kings 4:25,26.
[29] 3 Kings 10:27. [30] 1 Macc. 2:66. [31] Ibid., 2:65.
[32] 1 Macc. 13:41.

entrance to the isles of the sea. And he enlarged the bounds of his nation, and made himself master of the country. No one could resist him. And every man tilled his land with peace: and the land of Judah yielded her increase, and the trees of the field their fruit. The ancient men sat all in the streets, and treated together of the good things of the land, and the young men put on them glory, and the robes of war. And he provided victuals for the cities, and he appointed that they should be furnished with ammunition, so that the fame of his glory was renowned even to the end of the earth. He made peace in the land, and Israel rejoiced with great joy. And every man sat under his vine, and his fig-tree, and there was none to make them afraid. There was none left in the land to fight against them; enemy kings were discomfited in those days. And he strengthened all those of his people that were brought low, and he sought the law and took away every unjust and wicked man. He glorified the sanctuary, and multiplied the vessels of the holy places . . .[33] In fine he did justice, he protected the faith, and thought only of the happiness and greatness of his people."[34]

What can a wise prince not do? Under him wars succeed; peace is established; justice reigns; the laws govern; religion flourishes; commerce and navigation enrich the country; the earth itself seems to produce its fruits more willingly. Such are the effects of wisdom. Has not the wise man good reason to say: "all good things came to me together with her"?[35]

If one owes all these benefits to the care and prudence of a single man, can one love him enough? We see too that the greatness of Simon was the joy of his people. There was nothing they did not grant him.[36]

When God wants to make a people happy, he sends it a wise prince. Hiram, admiring Solomon who knew how to do everything appropriately, wrote to him: "Because the Lord hath loved his people, therefore he hath made thee king over them. And he added, saying: Blessed be the Lord the God of Israel, who made heaven and earth, and who hath given to king David a wise and knowing son, endued with understanding and prudence."[37]

"Blessed are thy men, and blessed are thy servants, who stand before thee always, and hear thy wisdom, cried the Queen of Sheba.

[33] 1 Macc. 14:4–15.   [34] Ibid., 4–15.   [35] Wisd. 7:11.
[36] 1 Macc. 14:14,35,46.   [37] 2 Par. 2:11,12.

Characteristics of royalty (continuation)

Blessed be the Lord thy God, whom thou hast pleased, and who hath set thee upon the throne of Israel, because the Lord hath loved Israel for ever, and hath appointed thee king, to do judgment and justice."[38]

4th Proposition
Wisdom saves states sooner than force

"A little city, and few men in it: there came against it a great king, and invested it, and built bulwarks round about it, and the siege was perfect. Now there was found in it a man poor and wise, and he delivered the city by his wisdom . . . And I said that wisdom is better than strength."[39]

It is thus that Solomon explains to us the effects of wisdom. He repeats it once again: "Better is wisdom, than weapons of war: and he that shall offend in one, shall lose many good things."[40]

Battles are hazardous, and war is unfortunate for both parties: wisdom, which takes care of everything and neglects nothing, takes paths which are not only gentler and more reasonable, but also more certain.

In the revolt of Seba against David, the rebel withdrew into Abela, an important city, which Joab did not delay in besieging by order of David.[41] While the walls were being ruined, a woman of the city asked to speak to Joab, and held this conversation with him in the name of the city (which she represented as speaking to him). "A saying was used in the old proverb: They that inquire, let them inquire in Abela."[42] (This city had the reputation of having many wise citizens, whom men came to consult from all sides.) "Am not I she that answer truth in Israel, and thou seekest to destroy the city, and to overthrow a mother in Israel (that is, a capital city)? Why wilt thou throw down the inheritance of the Lord? And Joab answering said: God forbid that I should, I do not throw down, nor destroy . . . But Seba hath lifted up his hand against king David: deliver him only, and we will depart from the city. And the woman said to Joab: Behold his head shall be thrown to thee from the wall. She spoke to the assembled people, and spoke wisely; such that they resolved to do what she had said, and Joab dismissed the army."[43]

There is a case of a city saved by wisdom. Wisdom terminated in

---

[38] 3 Kings 10:8–9. [39] Eccles. 9:14–16. [40] Ibid., 18.
[41] 2 Kings 20:14. [42] Ibid., 18. [43] Ibid., 19–22.

one stroke, without risking anything, and sacrificing only the guilty one, a war which had given David so much apprehension.

Bethulia, besieged by Holofernes, was saved by the counsels of Judith, who first stopped people from following the pernicious decision to surrender already taken in the Council, and then caused their enemies to perish through conduct as wise as it was bold.[44]

Thus one sees that wisdom is the surest defense of states. War puts everything at risk. "The empire of the wise shall be steady."[45]

"Wisdom hath strengthened the wise more than ten princes of the city."[46]

5th Proposition
The wise are feared and respected

David was valiant, and knew perfectly the art of war. This was not, however, the thing that most frightened Saul. "And Saul saw that he was exceeding prudent, and began to beware of him."[47]

David himself most feared Achitopel, of all the people who were with Absalom, because at this time "everyone consulted Achitopel, as if a man should consult God."[48]

It was as much the wisdom as the power of Solomon which kept his neighbours in [a state of] fear, and preserved his kingdom in profound peace.

Because Josaphat was wise, instructed in the law and taking care to instruct the people, all his neighbors feared him. "And the fear of the Lord came upon all the neighboring kingdoms . . . and they dared not make war against Josaphat. The Philistines brought presents to him, and the Arabs paid tribute to him."[49]

Josaphat was bellicose: but Scripture attributes all these fine effects to the piety and the wisdom of this king, who had not made war during the time that he was so redoubtable to his neighbors.

If wisdom makes the prince respected outside [his kingdom], one should not be astonished that it makes him respected within. When Solomon had rendered that memorable judgment by which he showed so much discernment, "all Israel heard the sentence which the king had pronounced, and they feared the king, seeing that the wisdom of God was in him to do judgment."[50]

[44] Jth. 8:9,10,28; 9:10. [45] Ecclus. 10:1. [46] Eccles. 7:20. [47] 1 Kings 18:15.
[48] 2 Kings 16:23. [49] 2 Par. 17:10–11. [50] 3 Kings 3:28.

Characteristics of royalty (continuation)

There is something divine in never being mistaken; and nothing inspires so much respect and so much fear.

And see how Scripture marks exactly the natural effect of each thing. The fine grace of Solomon had already attracted popular love to him. "He sat on the throne of his father, and he pleased all."[51]

Here is something greater still. It shows an exquisite discernment; and everyone feared him with that respectful fear which holds everyone in his duty.

It was thus with good reason that Solomon was made to say that "wisdom is better than strength, and a wise man is better than a strong man."[52]

6th Proposition
It is God who gives wisdom

"All wisdom is from the Lord God, and hath been always with him, and is before all time. Who hath numbered the sand of the sea, and the drops of rain, and the days of the world? Who hath measured the height of heaven, and the breadth of the earth, and the depth of the abyss? Who hath searched out the wisdom of God that goeth before all things? Wisdom hath been created before all things, and the understanding of prudence from everlasting. The word of God on high is the fountain of wisdom, and her ways are everlasting commandments. To whom hath the root of wisdom been revealed, and who hath known her wise counsels? To whom hath the discipline of wisdom been revealed and made manifest, and who hath understood the multiplicity of her steps? There is one most high Creator Almighty, and a powerful king, and greatly to be feared, who sitteth upon his throne, and is the God of dominion. He created her in the Holy Ghost, and saw her, and numbered her, and measured her. And he poured her out upon all his works, and upon all flesh according to his gift, and hath given her to them that love him." In this way Ecclesiasticus begins.[53]

God alone is wise; in him is the fountain of wisdom, and it is he alone who gives it.

It is from him that the wise man requests wisdom. "God of my fathers, and Lord of mercy, who hast made all things with thy word . . .

---

[51] 1 Par. 24:23.   [52] Wisd. 6:1.   [53] Eccles. 1:1–10.

give me wisdom, that sitteth by thy throne . . . Thou hast chosen me to be king . . . and hast commanded me to build a temple . . . And thy wisdom with thee, which knoweth thy works, which then also was present when thou madest the world, and knew what was agreeable to thy eyes, and what was right in thy commandments. Send her out of thy holy heaven, and from the throne of thy majesty, that she may be with me, and may labor with me, that I may know what is acceptable with thee: For she knoweth and understandeth all things, and shall lead me soberly in my works, and shall preserve me by her power. So shall my works be acceptable, and I shall govern thy people justly, and shall be worthy of the throne of my father."[54]

Whoever so desires wisdom, and asks it of God with this ardor, never fails to obtain it. "I have given thee a wise and understanding heart."[55] And again: "God gave to Solomon wisdom and understanding exceeding much, and largeness of heart (that is to say intelligence) as the sand that is on the sea shore."[56]

God gave him wisdom, for understanding the law and wise maxims; prudence, to make him apply them; broadened knowledge (that is to say a great capacity) to understand the difficulties and the *minutiae* of public affairs. God alone gives all this.

7th Proposition
Wisdom must be studied

It is true that God gives it; but he gives it to those who look for it.

"I love them that love me, says Wisdom herself, and they that in the morning early watch for me, shall find me."[57]

"The beginning of wisdom is a true desire to know."[58]

"Love ye therefore my words, she says, and desire to understand them, and you shall have instruction."[59]

"Wisdom . . . is easily seen by them that love her, and is found by them that seek her. She preventeth them that covet her, so that she first showeth herself unto them. He that awaketh early to seek her, shall not labor: for he shall find her sitting at his door. To think therefore upon her, is perfect understanding: and he that watcheth for her, shall quickly be secure. For she goeth about seeking such as are

---

[54] Wisd. 9:1–12.   [55] 3 Kings 3:12.   [56] 3 Kings 4:29.
[57] Prov. 8:17.   [58] Wisd. 6:18.   [59] Ibid., 12.

worthy of her, and she showeth herself to them cheerfully in the ways, and meeteth them with all providence."[60]

She is good, she is accessible: but one must love her, and work to possess her.

One must not complain of the pains one takes in this search, for one is soon recompensed. "My son, from thy youth up receive instruction, and even to thy grey hairs thou shalt find wisdom. Come to her as one that ploweth, and soweth, and wait for her good fruits. For in working about her thou shalt labor a little, and shalt quickly eat of her fruits.[61] Put thy feet into her fetters, and thy neck into her chains, thy shoulder under her yoke . . . For in the latter end thou shalt find rest in her, and she shall be turned to thy joy."[62]

8th Proposition
The prince must study, and cause to be studied, useful things; what his studies must be

One must not imagine the prince book in hand, with a worried countenance and eyes profoundly attached to reading. His main book is the world: his study is to be attentive to what goes on in front of him, in order to profit from it.

It is not that reading is useless to him, and the wisest of kings did not neglect it.

"And whereas Ecclesiastes was very wise (it is Solomon who speaks), he taught the people, and declared the things that he had done: and seeking out, he set forth many parables. He sought profitable words, and wrote words most right, and full of truth. The words of the wise are as goads, and as nails deeply fastened in, which by the counsel of masters are given from one shepherd."[63] It was the king who both took pains himself, and caused others to take pains, in looking for words which are helpful in life.

"More than these, my son, require not." That is, confine yourself to profitable things, put aside merely curious books; "of making many books there is no end: and much study is an affliction of the flesh."[64]

The true studies are those which teach things which are useful to human life. These are the ones that are worthy of the application of an able prince. As for the others, it is enough for him to excite the

[60] Ibid., 13–17. [61] Ecclus. 6:18–20. [62] Ibid., 25,26,19.
[63] Eccles. 12:9–11. [64] Ibid., 12.

industry of the learned by rewards – of which the greatest, in well-made minds, is always the approval and the esteem of an acknowledged master.

It is not fitting for a prince to tire himself by long and curious readings. Let him read few books; let him, like Solomon, read sensible and useful words. Above all let him read the Gospel, and let him meditate on it. There is his law, the will of the Lord.

9th Proposition
The prince must know the law

He is made to judge, and that is the first function of royalty. "Make us a king, to judge us." And again: "we also will be like all nations, and our king shall judge us."[65]

We have seen, too, that God commands kings to write out the law of Moses, to have an authentic copy always by them, and to read it every day of their life.[66]

It is for this reason that during their rites the law was placed in their hands. "They brought the king's son out of the temple, and put the crown upon him, and the testimony, and gave him the law to hold in his hand, and they made him king: and Joiada the high priest and his sons anointed him . . . and all the people cried: God save the king."[67]

The prince must also believe that in the New Testament he receives the Gospel from the hand of God, to rule himself by this writing.

The people must know the law, no doubt, at least in its main points, and be instructed in the rest in other cases: for the people must practise it. But the prince, who must additionally practise it as an example to others, and who must judge according to its decrees, must know it much better.

One does not know what he is doing, when he proceeds without any rule, and when he has no law for his guide: surprise, prejudice, interest and passion obscure everything. "An ignorant prince oppresses many without thinking, and makes calumny triumph."[68]

"Because the commandment is a lamp, and the law a light."[69] The prince who follows it sees clearly, and the whole state is enlightened.

"If the eye of the state (that is to say the prince) is darkened, the

---

[65] 1 Kings 8:5,20. [66] Deut. 17:18–19. [67] 2 Par. 23:11.
[68] Prov. 28:16. [69] Prov. 6:23.

darkness itself how great it shall be: thy whole body shall be darksome."⁷⁰

Let him then know the depths of the law, by which he must govern. And if he cannot descend into all the individual ordinances which public affairs generate every day, let him at least know the great principles of justice, in order never to be taken by surprise. It was Deuteronomy (the foundation of the law) which God obliged him to study and know.

How serious is the life of the prince! He must ceaselessly meditate on the law. Thus there is nothing among men which is more serious and more grave, than the office of royalty.

10th Proposition
The prince must know public affairs

Thus one saw Jephtha, the chosen prince of the people of God, prove by his discussion of the rights of this people, that the King of the Ammonites was unjustly making war on them.[71]

One saw the matter discussed with all possible exactitude. In this discussion, principles of law [*droit*] were linked by Jephtha with research into facts and the knowledge of ancient things. This one calls knowing matters [thoroughly].

The prince, who knew these things, placed reason visibly by his side: his peoples were encouraged to sustain the war through certainty of their righteous cause; his enemies were slowed down; his neighbors had nothing to say.

A comparable discussion did much honor to Simon the Maccabee. "The king of Asia sent Athenobius to demand the citadel of Jerusalem, together with Joppe and Gazara, important places, which he maintained belonged to his kingdom."[72]

Simon, on receiving this demand, first drew the necessary distinctions. He distinguished between the old lands which had always belonged to the Jews, and those which they had recently conquered.

"We have neither taken other men's land, neither do we hold that which is other men's: but the inheritance of our fathers, which was for some time unjustly possessed by our enemies. But we having opportunity claim the inheritance of our fathers."[73]

[70] Matt. 6:2,3.   [71] Judg. 11:15.   [72] 1 Macc. 15:28.   [73] Ibid., 33–34.

We have seen the offers for Joppe and for Gazara, though they had been taken in a good and just war: and he was so reasonable that "Athenobius answered him not a word."[74]

It is fine and useful that matters of a certain importance be discussed, as far as may be, by the prince himself, with so much reasoning-power. If he trusts too much to others, he opens himself to being deceived, or to seeing his rights neglected. No one sees matters more clearly than he who has the main interest in them.

11th Proposition
The prince must know how to recognize [suitable] occasions and times

This is one of the main elements in the science of [public] affairs, which all depend on this.

"All things have their season, and in their times all things pass under heaven. A time to be born and a time to die. A time to plant, and a time to pluck up that which is planted. A time to kill, and a time to heal. A time to destroy, and a time to build. A time to weep, and a time to laugh. A time to mourn, and a time to dance. A time to scatter stones, and a time to gather. A time to embrace, and a time to be far from embraces (that is to say a time to join with, and a time to break with) . . . A time to keep silence, and a time to speak . . . A time of war, and a time of peace . . . God himself does all in certain times."[75]

If all things depend on time, the science of time is thus the true science of [public] affairs, and the true work of the wise man. Thus, it is written that "the heart of a wise man understandeth time and answer."[76]

This is why matters require a great deal of application and work. "There is time and opportunity for every business, and great affliction for man. Because he is ignorant of things past, and things to come he cannot know by any messenger. It is not in man's power to stop the winds, neither hath he power in the day of death, neither is he suffered to rest when war is at hand."[77] No one does as he wants: *force majeure* dominates everywhere: the moments pass rapidly and with great haste: whoever misses them, misses everything.

This science of time was the most praiseworthy thing in the wisdom

---

[74] Ibid., 35. [75] Eccles. 3:1–11. [76] Eccles. 8:5. [77] Ibid., 6–8.

of Solomon. "Blessed be the Lord the God of Israel . . . who hath given to king David a wise and knowing son, endued with understanding and prudence, to build a house to the Lord, and a palace for himself."[78] In a state of profound peace, and of great abundance, after the preparations made by his father – this was the time to undertake such great works.

Because the Maccabees took their time well, they engaged the Romans to protect them; and they freed themselves from the kings of Syria, who oppressed them. "And Jonathan saw that the time served him, and he chose certain men and sent them to Rome, to confirm and to renew the amity with them."[79]

One would have to transcribe the whole of sacred and profane history, to show what timely and untimely things can achieve in [public] affairs [*ce que peuvent dans les affaires les temps et les contres-temps*].

Moreover there are certain times to be observed in protecting decorum, and in maintaining order. "My son, observe the time, and fly from evil."[80]

Time regulates all actions, down to the least. "Woe to thee O land, when thy king is a child, and when the princes eat in the morning. Blessed is the land, whose king is noble, and whose princes eat in due time for refreshment, and not for riotousness."[81]

12th Proposition
The prince must know men

It is, without doubt, his most important business to know what to make of men, and what they are fit for.

Above all other things it is necessary that he know the disposition of his people; and this is what the wise man recommends to him in the image of the shepherd: "Be diligent to know the countenance of thy cattle, and consider thy own flocks."[82]

Without regard for earthly stations, he must judge each person by what he is at bottom. "Despise not a just man that is poor, and do not magnify a sinful man that is rich."[83] And again: "Praise not a man for his beauty, neither despise a man for his looks. The bee is small among flying things, but her fruit hath the chiefest sweetness."[84]

[78] 2 Par. 2:12. [79] 1 Macc. 12:11. [80] Ecclus. 4:23. [81] Eccles. 10:16–17.
[82] Prov. 27:23. [83] Ecclus. 1:26. [84] Ecclus. 11:2–3.

Royalty is subject to reason

It is necessary above all that he know his courtiers. "According to thy power beware of thy neighbor, and treat with the wise and prudent."[85]

Otherwise everything in the state will happen by chance, and that which the wise man deplores will come about. "I saw that under the sun the race is not to the swift, nor the battle to the strong, nor bread to the wise, nor riches to the learned, nor favor to the skillful: but time and chance in all."[86]

This is what happens under an inconsiderate prince, who does not know how to choose men, but who takes those who turn up by chance or circumstance or his own humor.

In such a reign, surprise and error confound everything.

"There is an evil that I have seen under the sun, as it were by an error proceeding from the face of the prince: A fool sat in high dignity, and the rich sitting beneath."[87]

The prince who chooses badly is punished by his own choice: "He that sendeth words by a foolish messenger, is lame of feet and drinketh iniquity."[88]

David, from having known men, saved everything during the revolt of Absalom. He saw that all the power of the rebel faction was in the counsels of Achitopel, and turned his whole mind to his destruction. He knew the ability and the fidelity of Chusai. He was a wise old man who, seeing David constrained to take flight, "came to meet him with his garment rent and his head covered with earth. And David said to him: If thou come with me thou wilt be a burden to me: but if thou makest a show of following Absalom's party, thou shalt defeat the counsel of Achitopel."[89]

He was not deceived in this thought. Chusai kept Absalom from following the advice of Achitopel, which was ruining David without recourse.[90] Achitopel also felt that matters were lost, and he killed himself by hanging.[91]

David, not content with sending Chusai, surrounded him with reliable persons. It was essential not to make a mistake, for with the smallest *faux pas* the precipice was inevitable. See then what David said to Chusai: "What thing soever thou shalt hear out of Absalom's house, thou shalt tell it to Zadoc and Abiathar the priests: they have two sons by whom thou shalt send me all the news."[92]

---

[85] Ecclus. 9:21.   [86] Eccles. 11:11.   [87] Eccles. 10:5–6.   [88] Prov. 26:1,6.
[89] 2 Kings 15:32–34.   [90] 2 Kings 17:7.   [91] Ibid., 23.   [92] 2 Kings 15:35–36.

Chusai did not fail. After having shattered the plans of Achitopel, he sent to David (*via* these two men) news of everything that had happened,[93] and gave him advice which saved the state.

Thus David, from having known the men of whom he made use, regained the upper hand, and restored a situation which had become almost desperate.

By contrast Roboam, from having inadequately known the disposition of his people, as well as the mind of Jeroboam (who stirred them up), lost ten tribes – that is to say more than half his kingdom.

The prince who accustoms himself to knowing men well, seems to be inspired from on high in everything – so much does he look to the end. Joab had sent a clever woman to insinuate something to David. This prince already knew whence this advice came. "Hide not from me, he said to this woman, the thing that I ask thee . . . Is not the hand of Joab with thee in all this? The woman answered, and said: By the health of my soul, my Lord, O king, it is neither on the left hand nor on the right, in all these things which my lord the king hath spoken: for thy servant Joab, he commanded me, and put all these words into the mouth of thy handmaid . . . But thou, my lord, O king, art wise, according to the wisdom of an angel of God, to understand all things upon earth."[94]

This is what Solomon meant in that fine saying: "Divination is in the lips of the king, his mouth shall not err in judgment."[95]

This wise king had tested it, in the memorable judgment between two mothers that he rendered. Since he knew the nature and the effects of the passions, malice and dissimulation could not hide themselves from his eyes. "And all the people knew that the wisdom of God was in him."[96]

Besides the fact that great experience and a knowledge of men gives an assiduous prince thoughtful discernment, God indeed helps him in his industriousness: for "the heart of the king is in his hands."[97]

It was God who placed in David's heart those salutary counsels which returned the crown to his head. This was not the prudence of David: "by the will of the Lord the profitable counsel of Achitopel was defeated."[98]

---

[93] 2 Kings 17:15. [94] 2 Kings 14:18–20. [95] Prov. 16:10.
[96] 3 Kings 3:28. [97] Prov. 21:1. [98] 2 Kings 17:14.

David, moreover, had first turned towards God. "Infatuate, O Lord, I beseech thee, the counsel of Achitopel."[99]

Here then are two things which the prince must do: first, to apply himself with all his power to know men well; second, in this effort, to await illumination from on high, and to ask for this with ardor. For the business is delicate and shrouded.

There is nothing to be added to what Ecclesiasticus has to say on this subject. "Every counsellor giveth out counsel, but there is one that is a counsellor for himself. Beware of a counsellor, and know before what need he hath: for he will devise to his own mind: Lest he thrust a stake into the ground, and say to thee: Thy way is good; and then stand on the other side to see what shall befall thee. Do not consult, then, with a suspect man; look to the views of each and every one. Nor with a woman touching her of whom she is jealous, nor with a coward concerning war, nor with a merchant about traffic, nor with a buyer of selling (each will assert himself, and look to his profit). Nor with an envious man of giving thanks, nor with the ungodly of piety, nor with the dishonest of honesty, nor with the field-laborer of every work. Nor with him that worketh by the year of the finishing of the year, nor with an idle servant of much business; give no heed to these in any matter of counsel. But be continually with a holy man, whomsoever thou shalt know to observe the fear of God, whose soul is according to thy own soul: and who, when thou shalt stumble in the dark, will be sorry for thee. And establish within thyself a heart of good counsel: for there is no other thing of more worth to thee than it. The soul of a holy man discovereth sometimes true things, more than the seven watchmen who sit in a high place to watch. But above all things pray to the most High, that he may direct thy way in the truth."[100]

13th Proposition
The prince must know himself

But of all the men the prince must know, the one it is most important for him to know well is himself. "My son, prove thy soul in thy life: and if it be wicked, give it no power"[101] – that is to say, do not let yourself be driven by its desires. The Greek [text] says: "My son,

---

[99] 2 Kings 15:31. [100] Ecclus. 38:8–19. [101] Ibid., 30.

Characteristics of royalty (continuation)

prove thy soul; know what is bad for it, and guard against giving that to it."

Everything is not suitable for everyone: one has to know what he is fit for. Some man who would be great if employed in certain things, makes himself contemptible when he gives himself over to things which are improper for him.

To know one's own defects is a great art: for one corrects them, or one makes up for them by other means. "Who can understand his sins?"[102] says the Psalmist. No one knows them by himself; one must have some faithful friend who will show them to him. The wise man counsels us: "He that loveth correction, loveth knowledge; but he that hateth reproof is foolish."[103]

Indeed it is a trait of madness to adore all one's thoughts, to believe oneself to be without defect, and not to be able to suffer being informed of it. "The fool when he walketh in the way . . . esteemeth all men fools."[104] And again: "Advise not with fools, for they cannot love but such things as please them."[105]

By contrast the wise man says: "Who will set scourges over my thoughts, and the discipline of wisdom over my heart, that they spare me not in their ignorances, and that their sins may not appear: lest my ignorances increase, and my offenses be multiplied, and my sins abound, and I fall before my adversaries, and my enemy rejoices over me?"[106]

This is what happens to the madman, who does not want to know his faults. Princes, who are accustomed to flattery, are subject to this defect more than all other men. Among an infinity of examples, I shall report only one.

Achab did not want to hear at all the only prophet who told him the truth, because he said it without flattery. "Josaphat, king of Judah, said to Achab, king of Israel: Is there not here some prophet of the Lord, that we may inquire by him? And the king of Israel said to Josaphat: There is one man left, by whom we may inquire of the Lord: Micheas the son of Jemla; but I hate him, for he doth not prophesy good to me, but evil."[107]

Micheas had tried to make him take back his crimes, and warned him of the just judgments of God so that he could escape them. Achab could not endure his words. He preferred to be surrounded by

---

[102] Ps. 18:13.   [103] Prov. 12:1.   [104] Eccles. 10:3.   [105] Ecclus. 8:20.
[106] Ecclus. 23:2–3.   [107] 3 Kings 22:7–8; 2 Par. 18:6–7.

a company of flattering prophets, who only sang his praises and his imaginary triumphs. He wanted to be deceived, and he was. God delivered him over to this spirit of error, which filled the heart of his prophets with flatteries and illusions in which he unfortunately believed: and he perished in the war in which his prophets had predicted so much happy success.

The pious King Josaphat, on the contrary, reprimanded the King of Israel, who did not want anyone to hear this prophet of doom. "Speak not so, O king of Israel."[108] One must listen to those who show us, on behalf of God, both our faults and his judgments.

The same King Josaphat, on returning from the war where he had been with Achab, listened submissively to the prophet Jehu, who said to him: "Thou helpest the ungodly, and thou art joined in friendship with them that hate the Lord . . . thou didst deserve indeed his wrath; but good works are found in thee."[109]

He walked in the ways of his father David who, receiving with respect the just criticisms of the prophets Nathan and Gad,[110] recognized his faults, and obtained forgiveness of them.

It is not only the prophets who must be heard: the wise man views all those who prudently reveal his faults as men sent by God to enlighten him. One should pay no attention to social status: the truth always preserves its natural authority in any mouth whatsoever. "They that are free shall serve a servant that is wise: and a man that is prudent and well-instructed will not murmur when he is reproved."[111]

The man who can endure correction is truly master of himself. "He that rejecteth instruction, despiseth his own soul: but he that yieldeth to reproof possesseth understanding."[112]

14th Proposition
The prince must know what happens within and without his kingdom

Under an able and well-informed prince, no one dares to do evil. One believes him always present, and even the diviner of thoughts. "Detract not the king, no not in thy thought; do not speak against him

---

[108] 3 Kings 22:8; 2 Par. 18:7.   [109] 2 Par. 19:2–3.
[110] 2 Kings 12; 24.   [111] Ecclus. 28.
[112] Prov. 15:32.

in thy private chamber; because even the birds of the air . . . will tell what thou hast said."[113]

News flies to him from every quarter: he knows how to discriminate between these items, and nothing escapes his knowledge.

The soldier who was commanded by Joab, his general, to do something against the orders of the king, said to him: "Whatever sum you might give me, I would not do as you say. For the king has forbidden it: and if I did not fear my own conscience, this could not have been hid from the king; and would you have stood by me?"[114]

"And Nathan said to Bethsabee the mother of Solomon: Hast thou not heard that Adonias the son of Haggith reigneth, and our lord David knoweth it not? Save thy life and that of Solomon; go quickly, and speak to the king."[115] An evil which is known is half cured; hidden wounds become incurable.

So much for domestic matters. As for external affairs: Amasias King of Judah, swollen by the recently achieved victory over the Edomites, wanted to test his forces against those of the more powerful King of Israel. "Joas king of Israel said to him: A thistle of Lebanon sent to a cedar tree . . . saying: Give thy daughter to my son to wife. And the beasts of the forest that are in Lebanon, passed and trod down the thistle. Thou hast beaten and prevailed over Edom, and thy heart hath lifted thee up: be content with the glory, and sit at home. Why provokest thou evil, that thou shouldst fall, and Judah with thee? Amasias did not take this advice; he marched against Joas; he was beaten and taken prisoner. Joas broke down four hundred cubits of the walls of Jerusalem, and took away the treasures of the house of the Lord and of the house of the king."[116] If Amasias had known the strength of his neighbors, he would not have believed that he could conquer a king more powerful than himself, simply because he had vanquished a more feeble one: and this ignorance caused his ruin.

By contrast Judas the Maccabee – from having known perfectly the conduct and the counsels of the Romans, their power, and their way of making war, indeed their secret jealousy of the kings of Syria[117] – made them into guaranteed protectors who gave the Jews the means to throw off the Gentile yoke.

Let the prince, then, be well informed, and let him spare nothing to achieve that. It is to him principally that this word of the wise is

[113] Eccles. 10:20.   [114] 2 Kings 17:12–13.   [115] 3 Kings 1:11–13.
[116] 4 Kings 14:9–14.   [117] 1 Macc. 8:1–3.

addressed: "Buy truth."[118] But let him take care not to pay deceivers, and not to purchase lies.

15th Proposition
The prince must know how to speak

"Works shall be praised for the hand of the artificers, and the prince of the people for the wisdom of his speech."[119]

One expects only great things of him. Job felt his obligation in this matter, and the expectation of the people, when he said: "They that heard me, waited for my sentence, and being attentive held their peace at my counsel. To my words they durst add nothing."[120]

It is not enough to offer up wise speeches, nor to say fine things: one must speak appropriately. "A parable coming out of a fool's mouth shall be rejected: for he doth not speak it in due season."[121]

This is why the wise man thinks of what he says, in order to speak only when it is necessary. "The heart of the wise shall instruct his mouth: and shall add grace to his lips. Well ordered words are as a honey-comb: sweet to the soul, and health to the bones."[122]

"The words of the mouth of a wise man are grace: but the lips of a fool shall throw him down headlong. The beginning of his words is folly, and the end of his talk is a mischievous error."[123]

If nothing is more agreeable than a speech made appropriately, nothing is more shocking than an ill-considered one. "A man without grace is as a vain fable, it shall be continually in the mouth of the unwise."[124]

To speak inappropriately is a thing not merely disagreeable but harmful. "He who holds forth wounds himself with a sword; but the tongue of the wise is health."[125] And again: "He that keepeth his mouth, keepeth his soul: but he that hath no guard on his speech shall meet with evils."[126]

The vain discourser bears the stamp of madness. "The madman speaks without cease."[127] And again: "Hast thou seen a man hasty to speak? Folly is rather to be looked for, than his amendment."[128]

A tongue guided by wisdom is an instrument good for everything.

---

[118] Prov. 23:23. [119] Ecclus. 9:24. [120] Job 29:21–22.
[121] Ecclus. 20:22. [122] Prov. 16:23–24. [123] Eccles. 10:12–13.
[124] Ecclus. 20:21. [125] Prov. 12:18. [126] Prov. 13:3.
[127] Eccles. 10:14. [128] Prov. 29:20.

Characteristics of royalty (continuation)

Do you want to soothe an irritated man? "A mild answer breaketh wrath, but a harsh word stirreth up fury."[129] And again: "A peaceable tongue is a tree of life, but that which is immoderate shall crush the spirit."[130]

Should you want to win over someone who is discontented, a word will do you more good than a gift. "Shall not the dew assuage the heat, so also the good word is better than the gift."[131]

Thus one must be the master of his tongue. "The heart of the wise man instructs his mouth," as we have just seen. And again, "the heart of fools is in their mouth: and the mouth of wise men is in their heart."[132] The itching to speak carries away the one; circumspection limits all the words of the other: the one becomes heated in speaking, he embarks; the other weighs everything in an accurate scale, and says only what he wants.

16th Proposition
The prince must know how to keep quiet: secrecy is the soul of deliberation [l'âme des conseils]

"It is good to hide the secret of a king."[133]

Secrecy in deliberation is an imitation of the deep and impenetrable wisdom of God. "The heaven above, and the earth beneath, and the heart of kings is unsearchable."[134]

There is no power where there is no secrecy. "As a city that lieth open and is not compassed with walls, so is a man that cannot refrain his own spirit in speaking."[135] He is attacked, and he is pushed back from every side.

If speaking too much bears the stamp of madness, knowing how to keep quiet is a mark of wisdom. "Even a fool, if he will hold his peace, shall be counted wise."[136]

The wise man questions more than he speaks: "In many things be as if thou wert ignorant, and hear in silence and withal seeking."[137]

Thus without uncovering yourself, you will uncover others. The desire to show that one knows keeps one from entering into and understanding many things.

Thus one must speak with measure. "A fool uttereth all his mind: a wise man deferreth, and keepeth it till afterwards."[138]

---

[129] Prov. 15:1. [130] Ibid., 4. [131] Ecclus. 18:16. [132] Ecclus. 21:29.
[133] Tob. 12:7. [134] Prov. 25:3. [135] Ibid., 28. [136] Prov. 17:28.
[137] Ecclus. 32:12. [138] Prov. 29:11.

Royalty is subject to reason

He does not always keep quiet, but "a wise man will hold his peace till he see opportunity: but a babbler, and a fool, will regard no time."[139]

"There is one that holdeth his peace, because he knoweth not what to say: and there is another that holdeth his peace, knowing the proper time."[140]

So many great kings, who have let escape rash words that have caused so much disquiet, justify this saying of the wise man: "He that keepeth his mouth and his tongue, keepeth his soul from distress."[141]

"Who will set a guard before my mouth, and a sure seal upon my lips, that I fall not by them, and that my tongue destroy me not?"?[142]

17th Proposition
The prince must foresee

It is not enough for the prince to see: he must foresee. "The prudent man saw the evil, and hid himself; the simple passed on, and suffered loss."[143]

"In the good day enjoy good things, and beware beforehand of the evil day: for God hath made both the one and the other."[144]

One need not have a foresight that is full of care and disquiet, which troubles in time of good fortune; but one must have a foresight full of precaution, which keeps bad fortune from taking us unprepared.

"Remember poverty in the time of abundance, and the necessities of poverty in the day of riches. From the morning until the evening the time shall be changed."[145]

We have seen David, from having foreseen the future, ruin the party of Absalom, and stifle the rebellion of Seba at its birth.[146]

Roboam, Amasias, and the others whose aberrations we have seen, foresaw nothing, and fell. Examples of both kinds of happening are innumerable.

There is hardly a man touched by a great present evil who makes no effort to pull himself out of it: thus the whole of wisdom lies in foreseeing.

The man gifted with foresight takes care of small things, because

---

[139] Ecclus. 20:7. [140] Ibid., 6. [141] Prov. 21:23.
[142] Ecclus. 22:33. [143] Prov. 22:3. [144] Ecclus. 12:15.
[145] Ecclus. 18:25–26. [146] 2 Kings 15; 20.

he sees that great ones depend on them. "He that contemneth small things, shall fall little by little."[147]

In most matters it is not so much a thing itself as its consequences which one must fear; whoever does not understand this understands nothing.

Health depends more on precautions than on remedies. "Learn before thou speak; before sickness take a medicine."[148]

If individuals are short-sighted, that may be bearable. The prince must always be far-seeing, and not close himself up within his own world. "The life of a man is in the number of his days: but the days of Israel are innumerable."[149]

O prince! look then to posterity. You will die: but your state must be immortal.

18th Proposition
The prince must be capable of instructing his ministers

That is to say, he must be possessed of reason. The able prince makes able ministers, and shapes them through his maxims.

This is the meaning of Ecclesiasticus: "A wise judge shall teach his people, and the government of a prudent man shall be steady."[150] And again: "A wise man instructeth his own people, and the fruits of his understanding are faithful."[151]

The example of Josaphat – equally wise, valiant and pious – teaches us what is to be done.

In the third year of his reign, he sent five lords of the court "to instruct the people in the cities of Judah, and with them eight Levites and two priests . . . And they taught the people in Judah, having with them the book of the law of the Lord; and they went about all the cities of Judah, and instructed the people."[152]

Notice always that the law of the Lord was the law of the kingdom, in which the people were instructed; and the king took care that they be instructed in it. Since this law contained religious and political things together, he sent priests with court-lords to instruct the people. But let us see what followed.

"And he set judges of the land in all the fenced cities of Judah, in every place. And charging the judges, he said: Take heed what you

---

[147] Ecclus. 19:1. [148] Ecclus. 18:19–20. [149] Ecclus. 37:28.
[150] Ecclus. 10:1. [151] Ecclus. 37:26. [152] 2 Par. 17:7–9.

do: for you exercise not the judgment of man, but of the Lord: and whatsoever you judge, it shall redound to you. Let the fear of the Lord be with you, and do all things with diligence: for there is no iniquity with the Lord our God, nor respect of persons, nor desire of gifts."[153]

Besides these tribunals erected in the cities of Judah, he erected a more noble tribunal in the capital of the kingdom. "In Jerusalem also Josaphat appointed Levites, and priests and chiefs of the families of Israel, to judge the judgment and the cause of the Lord for the inhabitants thereof. And he charged them, saying: Thus shall you do in the fear of the Lord faithfully, and with a perfect heart. Every cause that shall come to you of your brethren . . . wheresoever there is question concerning the law, the commandment, the ceremonies, the justifications: show it them, that they may not sin against the Lord, and that wrath may not come upon you and your brethren: and so doing you shall not sin."[154]

Thus an able prince gives order that the people be instructed in the laws: and he himself instructs his ministers, so that they act according to the rule.

Article II

Means by which the prince can acquire necessary knowledge

1st Proposition
First means: to love the truth, and declare that one wants to know it

We have shown the prince by the word of God how much he needs to be instructed, and in how many things: let us give him the means to acquire the necessary kinds of knowledge, always following the divine word as our guide.

[153] 2 Par. 19:5–7.   [154] Ibid., 8–10.

The first means of knowing the truth which the prince has, is to love it ardently and to show that he loves it: then it will come to him from all sides, because everyone will know that it gives him pleasure to be told it.

"Birds resort unto their like: so truth will return to those that practice her."[1] The true look for the true: the truth comes easily to a mind disposed to receive it through the love one has for it.

By contrast their whole heart will be filled with error and flattery, if they are of the humor of those "who say to the seers: See not; and to them that behold: Behold not for us those things that are right: speak unto us pleasant things, see errors for us."[2]

Few say this with their mouths; many say it in their hearts. The world is full of these madmen of whom the wise man speaks: "A fool receiveth not the words of prudence: unless thou say those things which are in his heart."[3]

It is not sufficient for the prince to say, in general, that he wants to know the truth – and to ask, as did Pilate of Our Lord, "What is truth?"[4] and then to go suddenly without waiting for the answer. One must say it and mean it in good faith.

Some inform themselves of the truth in the manner of something fully received and *en passant*, as it seems that Pilate did in this instance. Others, without taking pains to know it, inform themselves by ostentation, to be honored for this search. Such was Achab, King of Israel, in whom we see all the marks of this last kind of man.

"At bottom he loved only flattery, and feared the truth. This is why he hated Micheas – for the sole reason that he prophesied only evil to him."[5]

Pulled back from this unjust aversion by Josaphat, King of Judah, he dared not refuse to listen to this true prophet: but in letting him be interrogated by a flattering courtier, Achab caused him to be told secretly what we have already seen: "The words of the prophets with one mouth declare good things to the king: let thy word therefore be like to theirs."[6]

However, when Achab appeared before Josaphat and the world, he made a show of wanting to know the truth. "Micheas, said Achab, shall we go to war? I ask you once again, in the name of God, to tell me only the truth."[7]

---

[1] Ecclus. 27:10. [2] Isa. 30:10. [3] Prov. 18:2. [4] John 18:38. [5] 3 Kings 22:8; 2 Par. 18:7.
[6] 3 Kings 22:13; 2 Par. 18:12.   [7] 3 Kings 22:15–16; 2 Par. 18:14–15.

But as soon as the holy prophet began to explain the truth to him, he became angry; and, at the end of his speech, he had him put in prison. "Did I not tell thee, that he prophesieth no good to me, but always evil?"[8]

It was thus that he spoke to Josaphat, almost as soon as Micheas had opened his mouth; and when he had said all, "the king of Israel said: take Micheas, and let him abide with the governor of the city, and with Joas the son of Amalech. And tell them: thus saith the king: Put this man in prison, and feed him with bread of affliction, and water of distress, till I return in peace."[9]

This was how that fine semblance of Achab's of wanting to know the truth ended up. Thus Micheas, judging him unworthy of knowing it, finally said to him in an ironic tone: "Go, everything will succeed for you."[10]

Finally, urged in the name of God to tell the truth, the prophet revealed to all the world this terrible vision: "I saw the Lord sitting on his throne, and all the army of heaven standing by him on the right hand and on the left: And the Lord said: Who shall deceive Achab king of Israel, that he may go up, and fall at Ramoth Galaad? And one spoke words of this manner, and another otherwise. And there came forth a spirit, and stood before the Lord, and said: I will deceive him. And the Lord said to him: By what means? And he said: I will go forth, and be a lying spirit in the mouth of all his prophets. And the Lord said: Thou shalt deceive him, and shalt prevail: go forth, and do so. Now therefore, continued Micheas, behold the Lord hath given a lying spirit in the mouth of all thy prophets that are here, and the Lord hath spoken evil against thee."[11]

Who would not tremble in seeing such terrible judgments? But who would not admire their justice? God punishes by flattery the kings who love flattery, and gives over to the spirit of lying the kings who look for lying and false indulgence.

Achab was killed; and God thereby showed that he who looks to be deceived, finds deceit to his cost.

"Thou art just, O Lord, and thy judgment is right."[12]

---

[8] 3 Kings 22:18; 2 Par. 18:17.
[9] 3 Kings 22:26–27; 2 Par. 18:25–26.
[10] 3 Kings 22:15; 2 Par. 18:14.
[11] 3 Kings 22:19; 2 Par. 18:18.
[12] Ps. 118:137.

2nd Proposition
Second means: to be attentive and studious

It is in vain that one has the truth before his eyes: if he does not open them, he does not see it. To open one's eyes to the soul – that is to be attentive. "The eyes of a wise man are in his head: the fool walketh in darkness."[13] One demands of the imprudent and the reckless: Fool, what are you thinking of? Where are your eyes? You do not have them in your head, nor in front of you: you do not see before your feet: that is, you think of nothing; you do not have the slightest attention.

It is as if one had no eyes at all, and no ears. "This people sees not with its eyes, and hears not with its ears."[14] Or, as St. Paul translates it, "With the ear you shall hear, and shall not understand; and seeing you shall see, and shall not perceive."[15]

This is why the wise man tells us "the hearing ear, and the seeing eye, the Lord hath made them both."[16]

This gift of God is not made for those that sleep, and who think of nothing. One must stimulate oneself and be studious. "Let thy eyes look straight on, and let thy eyelids go before thy steps. Make straight the path for thy feet, and all thy ways shall be established."[17] Look before walking: pay attention to what you do.

One should never precipitate himself. "Where there is no knowledge of the soul, there is no good: and he that is hasty with his feet shall stumble. The folly of a man supplanteth his steps: and he fretteth in his mind against God."[18]

Be attentive, then, and studious, in all things. "Before judgment prepare thee justice, and learn before thou speak. Before sickness take a medicine, and before judgment examine thyself, and thou shalt find mercy in the sight of God."[19]

Thoughtfulness in everything: that is what saves us. "Counsel shall keep thee, and prudence shall preserve thee. That thou mayst be delivered from the evil way, and from the man that speaketh perverse things: who leave the right way, and walk by dark ways."[20]

In the midst of the disguises and artifices that reign among men, it is only attention and vigilance that can save us from surprises.

Whoever considers men attentively is rarely mistaken. Jacob recognized, from the face of Laban, that the dispositions of his heart

---

[13] Eccles. 2:14. [14] Isa. 6:10. [15] Acts 28:26. [16] Prov. 20:12.
[17] Prov. 4:25–26. [18] Prov. 19:2–3. [19] Ecclus. 18:19–20. [20] Prov. 2:11–13.

had changed. He saw that the face of Laban was not its usual self. And on that basis he made the decision to withdraw.[21]

For, as Ecclesiasticus says (according to the Vulgate): "One recognizes plans of vengeance in the changes of the face."[22] And again: "The heart of a man changeth his countenance, either for good, or for evil."[23]

But this is not easy to discover; it requires great application. "The token of a good heart, and a good countenance thou shalt hardly find, and with labor."[24]

Let the prince, then, consider all things attentively: but let him above all consider men attentively. Nature has imprinted on the outside an image of the inside. "A man is known by his look, and a wise man, when thou meetest him, is known by his countenance. The attire of the body, and the laughter of the teeth, and the gait of the man, show what he is."[25]

One need not, all the same, believe in first impressions. There are deceiving appearances; there are deep dissimulations. The surest course is to observe everything, but to believe only in actions [*œuvres*]. "By their fruits ye shall know them,"[26] that is to say by their actions – so says truth itself. And elsewhere: "The tree is known by its fruit."[27]

Then too one must take note of what Ecclesiasticus says: "There is one, that slippeth with the tongue, but not from his heart. For who is there that hath not offended with his tongue?"[28] As if it said: Do not pay attention to every word, or to every mistake that lets slip. It is in seeing the effects of words and actions that you will come to a rightful judgment.

Nothing is less attentive and less studious than children. The wise man wants to draw us out of this state, and make us more serious, when he tells us: "Forsake childishness, and live, and walk by the ways of prudence."[29]

The man who is not attentive, falls into one of these two faults: either he is led astray, or he is virtually benumbed by a profound lethargy. The first of these faults makes one scatter-brained, the second stupid – conditions which, pushed to a certain point, are two species of madness.

Here, in two words, are two tableaux painted by the hand of the

[21] Gen. 31:2,5. [22] Ecclus. 18:24. [23] Ecclus. 13:31.
[24] Ibid., 32.   [25] Ecclus. 19:26–27. [26] Matt. 7:16,20.
[27] Matt. 12:33. [28] Ecclus. 19:16–17. [29] Prov. 9:6.

wise man: "Wisdom shineth in the face of the wise: the eyes of fools are in the ends of the earth."[30]

See how serious the former is; the other, while one is talking to him, throws his ill-considered glances here and there: his mind is far from you; he does not listen to himself; and his distracted looks show how vague his thoughts are.

But here is another kind of character, who is neither less bad nor less vividly represented. "He speaketh with one that is asleep, who uttereth wisdom to a fool: and in the end of the discourse he saith: Who is this?"[31]

How frequent is this sleep among men! How few there are who are attentive, and also how few who are wise! This is why Jesus Christ, finding the whole human race dozing, woke it up with the words that he repeated so often: "Watch, be attentive, think what you do."[32]

"Take ye heed, watch and pray . . . And what I say to you, I say to all: Watch. You do not know at what hour the thief will come."[33]

He who does not watch is always surprised. What an error if the prince, who wants watchful sentinels around him, should permit to fall asleep within himself that attention without which there is no sure safeguard!

The prince is himself a sentinel established to guard the state: he must watch more than all the others. Unhappy people! Your sentinels (your princes, your magistrates, your priests, in a word all your pastors who must watch to lead you) – "your watchmen, I say, are all blind, they are all ignorant: dumb dogs not able to bark, seeing vain things, sleeping and loving dreams. And most impudent dogs, they never had enough: the shepherds themselves knew no understanding; all have turned aside into their own way, everyone after his own gain, from the first even to the last. Come, they say, let us take wine, and be filled with drunkenness: and it shall be as today, so also tomorrow, and much more."[34]

See the language of those who believe that matters take care of themselves, and that he who has lasted will last by himself, without thought. Then, however, the fatal moment suddenly arrives. "MANE, THECEL, PHARES: God hath numbered the days of thy reign, and hath finished it. Thou art weighed in the balance, and art found wanting.

---

[30] Prov. 17:24.
[31] Ecclus. 22:9.
[32] Matt. 24:42,43; 25:13; 26:38,41; Luke 17:3; 21:34.
[33] Mark 13:33,35,37.
[34] Isa. 56:10–12.

Thy kingdom is divided, and is given to the Medes and the Persians . . . And the same night Balthazar the Chaldean king was slain, and Darius the Mede succeeded to the kingdom."[35]

3rd Proposition
Third means: to take counsel, and to give full freedom to one's counselors

"Be not wise in thy own conceit." Do not believe that your eyes are sufficient to see everything.[36]

"The way of a fool is right in his own eyes." He thinks he is always right. "He that is wise hearkeneth unto counsels."[37]

A presumptuous prince, who does not listen to counsel, and believes only his own thoughts, becomes intractable, cruel and furious. "It is better to meet a bear robbed of her whelps, than a fool trusting in his own folly."[38]

The fool who trusts in his folly, and the presumptuous man who finds good only what he thinks, is already described by these words of the wise: "A fool receiveth not the words of prudence: unless thou say those things which are in his heart."[39]

How fine it is to hear Solomon, the wisest king who ever was, speaking in this way! How truly wise he shows himself to be, in recognizing that his own wisdom is not enough for him!

We see, too, that in asking God for wisdom, Solomon asked for an understanding heart. "Give therefore to thy servant an understanding heart" – a heart capable of taking counsel, not proud, not prejudiced, not obsessed – "to judge thy people."[40] Who ever is incapable of [receiving] counsel, is incapable of government.

To have an understanding heart is not at all to cling stubbornly to one's thoughts: it is to be able to enter into those of others, according to these words from Ecclesiasticus: "Stand in the multitude of ancients that are wise, and join thyself from thy heart to their wisdom."[41]

Thus did David. We have seen how prudent he was; we see him, too, always listening, and entering into the thought of others, not at all obsessed with his own. He listens with patience to that wise woman from the city of Thecua, who dared to come and talk to him about the

---

[35] Dan. 5:25–31. [36] Prov. 3:7. [37] Prov. 12:15. [38] Prov. 17:12.
[39] Prov. 18:2. [40] 3 Kings 3:9. [41] Ecclus. 6:35.

Characteristics of royalty (continuation)

greatest affairs of state and his own family. "Let thy handmaid speak one word to my lord the king. And he said: Speak." She continued: "Why hast thou offended the people of God? And why hath the king committed this sin, of not calling back Absalom, whom he exiled?"[42] David listened quietly, and found that she was right.

When Absalom, abusing David's goodness, had perished in his rebellion, this good father gave himself over to grief. Joab came to him, to urge how important it was not to show so much affliction over the death of this rebel. "Thou hast shamed this day the faces of all thy servants, that have saved my life, and the lives of thy family . . . Thou lovest them that hate thee, and thou hatest them that love thee: and thou hast shown this day that thou carest not for thy nobles, nor for thy servants: and I now plainly perceive that if Absalom had lived, and we all had been slain, then it would have pleased thee. Now therefore arise, and go out, and speak to the satisfaction of thy servants: for I swear to thee by the Lord, that if thou wilt not go forth, there will not tarry with thee so much as one this night: and that will be worse to thee, than all the evils that have befallen thee from thy youth until now."[43]

David, consumed by grief as he was, entered into the thoughts of a man who had, in appearance, treated him badly, but who in fact counselled him well; and by believing him David saved the state.

Thus it is that in taking counsel and in giving all freedom to one's advisors, one discovers the truth, and one acquires true wisdom. "I, wisdom, dwell in counsel, and am present in learned thoughts."[44] And again: "War is managed by due ordering: and there shall be safety where there are many counsels."[45]

It is there that an abundance of expedients is to be found. "The knowledge of a wise man shall abound like a flood, and his counsel continueth like a fountain of life."[46]

"In all thy works let the true word go before thee, and steady counsel before every action."[47]

"Designs are brought to nothing where there is no counsel: but where there are many counsellors, they are established."[48]

"My son, do thou nothing without counsel, and thou shalt not repent when thou hast done."[49]

---

[42] 2 Kings 14:12–13.   [43] 2 Kings 19:5–7.   [44] Prov. 8:12.
[45] Prov. 24:6.   [46] Ecclus. 32:24.   [47] Ecclus. 37:20.
[48] Prov. 15:22.   [49] Ecclus. 32:24.

Besides the fact that things ordinarily succeed through good counsel, there is this consolation: that one need blame himself for nothing when he has accepted it.

It is a wonderful thing to see what small things can become when they are guided by good counsels. Mathathias could oppose to the redoubtable power of Antiochus King of Syria, who was oppressing Judaea, nothing but his family and a small number of friends. But since he had already arranged matters and [provided for] counsel, he laid the foundations of the people's deliverance. "Your brother Simon is a man of counsel: give ear to him always, and he shall be a father to you. Judas, the man of war, will command the troops, and will make war for the people. And you shall take to you all that observe the law of God. Revenge ye the wrong of your people."[50] A good plan, good counsel, a good captain to carry it out – this is an assured means of attracting people to your cause. There is a regulated government, and the small beginning of a great thing.

4th Proposition
Fourth means: to choose one's counsel

"Open not thy heart to every man."[51] And again: "Be in peace with many, but let one of a thousand be thy counsellor."[52]

This is why councils must be reduced to a few persons. The kings of Persia had only seven counsellors, or seven principal ministers. We have seen that they "were always near his person, and all he did was by their counsel."[53]

David had fewer still. "Jonathan, David's uncle, a wise and learned man, was his counsellor. He and Jahiel, the son of Hachamoni, were with the king's sons. And Achitopel, was the king's counsellor, and Chusai the Arachite, the king's friend. And after Achitopel was Joiada the son of Banaias, and Abiathar. And the general of the king's army was Joab."[54] And it was with him that David managed the business of war.

Thus one must have several counsellors, for they enlighten each other, and one alone cannot see everything: but they must be reduced to a small number.

Firstly, because secrecy is the soul of a council. "Nabuchodonosor

---

[50] 1 Macc. 2:65–67. [51] Ecclus. 8:22. [52] Ecclus. 6:6.
[53] Esther 1:13. [54] 2 Par. 27:32,34.

assembled the senators and captains, and communicated to them the secret of his counsel."[55]

It was an angel who said to Tobias: "It is good to hide the secret of a king, but honorable to reveal and confess the works of God."[56]

The counsel of kings is a mystery: their secrecy, which looks to the salvation of the whole state, partakes of something religious and sacred, as does their person and their ministry. This is why the Latin interpreter [of Scripture] has translated *secret* by the words *mystery* and *sacrament*, to show us how much the secrecy of the prince's counsels must be religiously looked after.

For the rest, when the angel says that it is good to hide the secret of the king, but that it is good to reveal the works of God, what is meant is that the counsels of kings can be turned aside, if once discovered; but the power of God encounters no obstacle to his plans; and God does not hide them through fear or precaution, but because men are not worthy of knowing them, nor capable of bearing them.

Let the prince's counsel then be secret: and to that end let him be surrounded by few persons. For words escape easily, and pass too rapidly from one mouth to another. "Advise not with fools, who will not be able to keep your secret."[57]

Another reason obliges the prince to reduce his counsel to a few persons: which is that the number of those who are capable of such a charge is rare.

For it a profound wisdom is first of all necessary – a rare thing among men: a wisdom which penetrates the most secret plans, and which as it were deters what is still more hidden. "Counsel in the heart of a man is like deep water, but a wise man will draw it out."[58]

Such a wise man is not easily found. But I know not whether it is not still more rare and difficult to find faithful men. "Blessed is he that findeth a true friend."[59] And again: "A faithful friend is a strong defense: and he that hath found him, hath found a treasure. Nothing can be compared to a faithful friend, and no weight of gold and silver is able to countervail the goodness of his fidelity."[60]

The difficulty lies in recognizing these true and wise friends. "There is a man that is subtle and a teacher of many, and yet is

[55] Jth. 2:2.   [56] Tob. 12:7.   [57] Ecclus. 8:2.
[58] Prov. 20:5.   [59] Ecclus. 25:12.   [60] Ecclus. 6:14–15.

unprofitable to his own soul;[61] he that speaketh sophistically is hateful: he shall be destitute of every thing..."[62] There is a wise man that is wise to his own soul... and the fruits of his understanding are faithful"[63] – that is to say, their counsels are salutary.

As for false friends, they are innumerable. "Every friend will say: I also am his friend: but there is a friend, that is only a friend in name. Is not this a grief even to death? But a companion and a friend shall be turned to an enemy. O wicked presumption, whence camest thou to cover the earth with thy malice, and deceitfulness? There is a companion who rejoiceth with his friend in his joys, but in the time of trouble, he will be against him. There is a companion who condoleth with his friend for his belly's sake, and he will take up a shield against the enemy."[64] And again: "There is a friend for his own occasion, and he will not abide in the day of thy trouble. And there is a friend that turneth to enmity; and there is a friend that will disclose hatred and strife and reproaches. And there is a friend a companion at the table, and he will not abide in the day of thy distress. A friend if he continue steadfast shall be to thee as thyself, and shall act with confidence among them of thy household. If he humble himself before thee, and hide himself from thy face, thou shalt have unanimous friendship for good."[65]

Among so many false sages and false friends, one must make a prudent choice, and entrust oneself only to a few persons.

There is no surer tie of friendship than the fear of God. "He that feareth God, shall likewise have good friendship: because according to him shall his friendship be."[66] Hence this wise counsel: "Be continually with a holy man, whomsoever thou shalt know to observe the fear of God. Whose soul is according to thy own soul; and who, when thou shalt stumble in the dark, will be sorry for thee."[67]

Notice in all these precepts that the wise man gives you a delightful choice: and that it is necessary to withdraw into the smaller number.

But above all one must consult God. Whoever has God for his friend will be given friends by God. "A faithful friend is the medicine of life and immortality: and they that fear the Lord, shall find him."[68]

---

[61] Ecclus. 37:21. [62] Ibid., 23. [63] Ibid., 25–26.
[64] Ibid., 1–5. [65] Ecclus. 6:8–12. [66] Ibid., 17.
[67] Ecclus. 37:15–16. [68] Ecclus. 6:16.

5th Proposition
Fifth means: to listen and be informed

There are some persons whom one must consult in the ordinary course of affairs, and others whom one must listen to.

The prince must hold counsel with very few persons. But he should not confine to so small a number all those whom he hears: otherwise, should it happen that there be just complaints against his counsellors, or things which they do not know or resolve to keep from him, he would never know anything about it.

We have seen David listen (in important matters) even to a woman, and follow her advice: so much did he love reason and truth, from whatever quarter they came.

The prince must listen, and inform himself from every side, if he wants to know. There are two things: he must listen and notice what comes to him, and he must carefully inform himself of everything which does not reach him clearly enough. "If thou wilt incline thy ear, thou shalt receive instruction: and if thou love to hear, thou shalt be wise."[69]

Following so much instruction drawn from sacred writers, let us not refuse to hear a prince who was an unbeliever, but a great and able statesman [*politique*]. It was Diocletian who said: "Nothing is more difficult than governing well: four or five men can unite and collaborate to deceive the emperor. He, who is closed up in his cabinet, does not know the truth. He can only know what he is told by these four or five men who are close to him. He puts incapable men in important posts, and keeps men of merit out of them. It is thus, this prince said, that a good emperor, a vigilant emperor, who takes care of everything, is sold out. *Bonus, cautus, optimus, venditur imperator.*"

Doubtless this is true, if he listens to only a few people, and does not deign to inform himself of what is happening.

6th Proposition
Sixth means: to be careful of whom one believes, and to punish false reports

Owing to the ease of receiving opinions from several quarters, one must be fearful: firstly, that the prince not denigrate himself by listen-

---
[69] Ibid., 34.

The prince and necessary knowledge

ing to unworthy persons. That woman whom David heard so peacefully[70] was a wise woman and known as such. Ecclesiasticus, which so recommends that we listen, insists that those to whom we give ear be honorable elders and sensible men. "Stand in the multitude of ancients that are wise, and join thyself from thy heart to their wisdom . . . and if thou see a man of understanding, go to him early in the morning, and let thy foot wear the steps of his doors."[71]

Secondly, one must fear that the prince who listens too much may be burdened with false opinions, or let himself be surprised by bad reports.

"He that is hasty to give credit, is light of heart, and shall be lessened."[72]

Believe not every word, then.[73] "Weigh everything in an accurate scale." "Count and weigh,"[74] says Ecclesiasticus.

One must understand, and not believe: that is to say weigh the reasons – and not believe the first to come along, on his word. "The innocent believeth every word: the discreet man considereth his steps."[75]

Solomon, who speaks thus, had profited from this sage opinion of the King his father: "Take care that thou mayest understand all thou dost, and whithersoever thou shalt turn thyself."[76] It is as if he said: Turn yourself to more than one side; for the truth must be sought in several places: human affairs need to be attempted by diverse means; but to whatever side you turn, turn with knowledge and do not believe without reason.

Above all, beware of false reports. "A prince that gladly heareth lying words, hath all his servants wicked."[77]

You will be judged by the persons in whom you believe. "The evil man obeyeth an unjust tongue: and the deceitful hearkeneth to lying lips."[78]

"A thief is better, says the sage, than a man that is always lying."[79] The liar, by his artifices, steals from you the greatest of all treasures – which is the knowledge of that truth without which you cannot do justice, nor make any good choice, nor (in a word) the slightest good.

Take care that the liar, who has sharpened his tongue and prepared his words to cut somebody's throat, not be able to cover his evil

---

[70] 2 Kings 14:2.   [71] Ecclus. 6:35–36.   [72] Ecclus. 19:4.   [73] Ibid., 16.
[74] Ecclus. 42:7.   [75] Prov. 14:15.   [76] 3 Kings 2:3.   [77] Prov. 29:12.
[78] Prov. 17:4.   [79] Ecclus. 20:27.

Characteristics of royalty (continuation)

designs by an appearance of zeal. Miphiboseth, son of Jonathan (devoted to David), was betrayed by his servant Siba who, wanting to ruin him to gain his property, appeared before David with refreshments while David was flying before Absalom. "And the king said: Where is thy master's son? And Siba answered the king: He remained in Jerusalem, saying: Today will the house of Israel restore me the kingdom of my father."[80]

See how one paves the way for the blackest calumnies, by a show of zeal.

Malice sometimes puts on other coverings. It poses as simple and sincere. "The words of the double-tongued are as if they were harmless; but they pierce the heart."[81]

It also poses as amusing, and insinuates itself by mockery. But from that dangerous quarrels can arise: "Cast out the scoffer, and contention shall go out with him, and quarrels and reproaches shall cease."[82]

In whatever form scandal-mongering may appear, fear it like a serpent. "If a serpent bite in silence, he is nothing better that backbiteth secretly."[83]

The sovereign remedy against false reports is to punish them. If you want to know the truth, O prince, let no one lie to you with impunity. No one so lacks respect for you, as he who dares to bear scandals and calumnies to your sacred ears.

One cannot easily lie to someone who knows how to inform himself, and to punish those who deceive him.

The punishment for false reports which I recommend to you, is to deny all credibility to those who make them, and to drive them away from you. "Remove from thee a forward mouth, and let detracting lips be far from thee."[84]

To listen to scandal-mongers, or even to tolerate them, is to participate in their crime. "Strive not with a man that is full of tongue, and heap not wood upon his fire."[85] Do not keep scandal-mongering alive by listening to it and tolerating it. And again: "Do not light the fire of the sinner, for fear that his flame will consume you."[86]

It is not only pieces of malicious gossip that are to be feared; false praises are no less dangerous, and those traitors who sell their princes maintain sycophants to praise them before those princes. All malicious actions, among the great, are carried out under the pretext of zeal. Tobias the Ammonite, who wanted to ruin Nehemias, caused

---

[80] 2 Kings 16:3.   [81] Prov. 18:8.   [82] Prov. 22:10.   [83] Eccles. 10:11.
[84] Prov. 4:24.   [85] Ecclus. 8:4.   [86] Ibid., 13.

him to be given apparently important advice. "There are designs against your life; they want to kill you this very night; consult with me; let us hold counsel in the most secluded part of the temple. And I understood, Nehemias says, that Samaia had been hired by Tobias and Sanaballat. Tobias undertook secret dealings in Judaea; he had a number of principal men on his side, who praised him before me, and reported all my words to him."[87]

O God! How can one save himself among so many traps, if he does not know how to guard himself against speeches full of artifice, and speak cautiously? "Hedge in thy ears with thorns"; do not give admission to every kind of speech: "Hear not a wicked tongue: make doors and bars to thy mouth . . . and make a balance for thy words."[88]

O prince! Without these precautions your affairs may suffer: but if your great power should save you from these evils, it is the greatest of all evils for you to make innocents suffer, if wicked tongues have turned you against them.

How fine it is to hear David singing on his lyre: "I walked in the innocence of my heart, in the midst of my house. I did not set before my eyes any unjust thing: I hated the workers of iniquities. The perverse heart did not cleave to me: and the malignant, that turned aside from me, I would not know. The man that in private detracted his neighbor, him did I persecute. With him that had a proud eye, and an insatiable heart, I would not eat. My eyes were upon the faithful of the earth, to sit with me: the man that walked in the perfect way, he served me. He that worketh pride shall not dwell in the midst of my house: he that speaketh unjust things did not prosper before me. In the morning I put to death all the wicked of the land: that I might cut off all the workers of iniquity from the city of our Lord."[89]

What a splendid court, where one sees so much simplicity and innocence, together with so much courage, so much ability and wisdom!

7th Proposition
Seventh means: to consider time past, and one's own experiences

In all things, time is an excellent counsellor. Time uncovers all secrets; time brings about suitable occasions; time confirms good counsels.

[87] Neh. 6:10–19. [88] Ecclus. 28:28–29. [89] Ps. 100:2–8.

Characteristics of royalty (continuation)

Above all, he who would judge the future well, must consult time past.

If you want to know what will bring about good and evil in future ages, consider what has brought them about in past times. There is nothing better than time-tested things. "Pass not beyond the ancient bounds which thy fathers have set."[90] Preserve the ancient principles on which your monarchy was founded, and which have sustained it.

Imitate the kings of Persia, who had always close to them "those wise counsellors, who knew the laws, and the judgments of their forefathers."[91]

Hence the chronicles of these kings, and the annals of past ages which Assuerus had brought to him in the night, when he could not sleep.[92]

All the ancient monarchies – that of the Egyptians, that of the Hebrews – kept similar chronicles. The Romans imitated them. All the nations, indeed, which have wanted to have regular counsels, have carefully noted past events, to consult them in times of need.

"What is it that hath been? The same thing that shall be. What is it that hath been done? The same that shall be done. Nothing under the sun is new, neither is any man able to say: Behold this is new: for it hath already gone before in the ages that were before us."[93]

This is why, as it is written in Wisdom: "She knoweth things past, and judgeth of things to come."[94]

"A fool multiplieth words. A man cannot tell what hath been before him: and what shall be after him, who can tell?"[95]

Pay no attention to those vain and limitless arguments which are not grounded in experience. It is only the past that can teach you, and guarantee the future.

Thus it is that Scripture is always summoning experienced elders to counsel. The passages are innumerable. Here is one worthy of notice: "Let not the discourse of the ancients escape thee, for they have learned of their fathers. For of them thou shalt learn wisdom, and instruction of understanding, and to give an answer in time of need."[96]

Job, deploring human ignorance, shows us that if there is some spark of wisdom among us, it is in old men that it will be found. "Whence then cometh wisdom, he said, and where is the place of

---

[90] Prov. 22:28. [91] Esther 1:13. [92] Esther 6:1. [93] Eccles. 1:9–10.
[94] Wisd. 8:8. [95] Eccles. 10:14. [96] Ecclus. 8:11–12.

understanding? It is hid from the eyes of all living, and the birds of the air know it not (that is, the highest minds). Destruction and death have said: With our ears we have heard the fame thereof."[97] Experienced elders, on the edge of the tomb, have heard something about it.

Job had said the same thing in other words: "In the ancient is wisdom, and in length of days prudence."[98]

It is through experience, then, that minds are refined. "If the iron be blunt . . . with much labor it shall be sharpened: and after industry shall follow wisdom."[99]

"Give an occasion to a wise man, and wisdom shall be added to him."[100] Employment and experience will fortify him.

Through experience one will even profit from his faults. "What doth he know, that hath not been tried? A man that hath much experience shall think of many things . . . He that hath no experience knoweth little: and he that hath been experienced in many things, multiplieth prudence. I have learned a great deal through my mistakes and in my travels; the knowledge which I have acquired has surpassed all my reasonings: I have found myself in great dangers, and my experience has saved me."[101] It is thus that wisdom takes shape: our very mistakes enlighten us, and whoever knows how to profit from them is wise enough.

Labor, then, O prince, to fill yourself with wisdom! Experience all by itself will give it to you, provided you pay attention to what goes on before your eyes. But apply yourself early: otherwise you will find yourself as little advanced in old age, as you were in childhood.

"The things thou hast not gathered in thy youth, how shalt thou find them in thy old age?"[102]

"Forsake childishness, and live, and walk by the ways of prudence."[103]

8th Proposition
Eighth means: to get used to deciding for oneself

Here there are two things: the first, that one must know how to decide: the second, that one must know how to decide by himself. It is to these two things that one must get accustomed early.

[97] Job 28:20–22. [98] Job 12:12. [99] Eccles. 10:10.
[100] Prov. 9:9. [101] Eccles. 34:9–12. [102] Eccles. 25:5.

Characteristics of royalty (continuation)

One must, then, first of all, know how to decide. To listen, to inform oneself, to take counsel, to choose one's counsel, and all the other things which we have seen, look only to this end: that is to say, deciding.

One must not however be among those who, by dint of listening, seeking and deliberating, get lost in their thoughts and do not know what to decide – men of great deliberation and great theories, but no performance. In the end they lose everything.

"In much work there shall be abundance: but where there are many words, many propositions, unlimited reasonings, there is oftentimes want."[104] One must conclude and act.

"Be not hasty in thy tongue: and slack and remiss in thy works."[105] Be not one of those speechifiers who have fine principles in their mouths, which they do not know how to apply: and fine political reasonings, of which they make no use. Take your part, and turn to action.

"Be not over just: and be not more wise than is necessary, lest thou become stupid"[106] – immobile in action, unable to realize a plan.

This too-just and too-wise man is one who, through weakness and incapacity to decide, is over-scrupulous about everything, and finds infinite difficulties in everything.

There is a certain good sense which brings one to do his part without equivocation. "God made man right, and he hath entangled himself with an infinity of questions."[107] Even after the Fall, our nature retains something of this rightness [*droiture*]: it is by it that one must decide, and not always abandon himself to new doubts.

"He that observeth the wind, shall not sow: and he that considereth the clouds, shall never reap."[108] Whoever wants too much assurance and too much foresight will do nothing.

It is not given to men to find perfect certainty in their counsels and in their affairs. After having reasonably considered things, one must take the better part, and leave the rest to Providence.

For the rest, once one has seen clearly, and has determined himself through solid reasons, one should not change lightly. This we have already seen. "Winnow not with every wind, and go not into every way: for so is every sinner (he who has acted badly) proved by a double tongue."[109] He speaks, and retracts; he decides in one way,

[103] Prov. 9:6. [104] Prov. 14:23. [105] Eccles. 4:34. [106] Eccles. 7:17.
[107] Ibid., 30. [108] Eccles. 9: 4. [109] Eccles. 5: 11.

and acts in another. "Be steadfast . . . in the truth of thy judgment, and let thy speech be one."[110]

When I say that one must know how to form a resolution, I mean that one must form it by himself: otherwise we do not form it, but it is given us; it is not we who turn, rather we are turned.

Let us always come back to David's words to Solomon: "Take care, my son, that thou mayest understand all thou dost; and whithersoever thou shalt turn thyself."[111]

"The wise man understands his ways."[112] He has his end, he has his plans, he considers whether the means proposed to him lead to his end. "The imprudence of fools erreth."[113] For want of having a fixed goal, they know not where to go; they go where they are pushed.

Whoever lets himself be led in this way sees nothing; he is a blind man following his guide.

"Let thy eyes go before thy steps,"[114] the wise man has told us. Your eyes, and not those of others. See that everything is explained to you, see that everything is told you: open your eyes and walk; go forward only with good reason.

Listen, then, to your friends and your counsellors: but do not abandon yourself to them. The counsel of Ecclesiasticus is admirable: "Separate thyself from thy enemies, and take heed of thy friends."[115] Take care that they do not deceive themselves; take care that they do not deceive you.

If you blindly follow someone who has the skill to get at your weak point, and to take hold of your mind, it will not be you who reigns – it will be your servant and your minister. And what the wise man says will happen to you: "By three things the earth is disturbed . . . the first by a slave when he reigneth."[116]

What a reputation that King of Judaea gave himself, of whom it is written in the *Acts [of the Apostles]*: "Herod was angry with the Tyrians and the Sidonians. But they with one accord came to him, and having gained Blastus, who was the king's chamberlain, they obtained what they wanted."[117]

Ceremonially one comes to the prince: in fact one negotiates with the minister. The prince is bowed to; the minister has the effective authority.

One still blushes for Assuerus, King of Persia, when one reads in

[110] Ibid., 12. [111] 3 Kings 2:3. [112] Prov. 14:8. [113] Ibid., 8.
[114] Prov. 4:25. [115] Eccles. 6:13. [116] Prov. 30:21–22. [117] Acts 12:30.

the story about the ease with which he let himself be led by his favorite Aman.[118]

"Establish within thyself a heart of good counsel: for there is no other thing of more worth to thee than it. The soul of a holy man discovereth sometimes true things, more than seven watchmen that sit in a high place to watch."[119] One cannot repeat too often this counsel of the wise.

It is difficult, in your youth, for you to disbelieve anyone: for experience is lacking at this age: the passions are then too impetuous; deliberations are too prompt. But if you wish to become soon capable of acting by yourself, believe in such a way that the reasons for everything are explained to you: and accustom yourself to relishing good ones. "From thy youth up receive instruction, and even to thy grey hairs thou shalt find wisdom."[120]

And notice here that true wisdom must always grow: but it must begin with docility. This is why we have heard Solomon, at the beginning of his reign, and in his earliest youth, asking for a docile heart. And the book of Wisdom makes him say: "I was a witty child and had received a good soul"[121] – that is to say, inclined toward the good and capable of receiving counsel.

By this means he arrived, in a short time, at the highest degree of wisdom. Just as much will come to you. If you listen at the beginning, you will soon deserve to be listened to. If you are docile for a while, you will soon become master and doctor.

9th Proposition
Ninth means: to avoid unfortunate subtleties

We have already seen a fine idea of this in these words from Ecclesiasticus: "There is a man that is subtle and a teacher of many, and yet is unprofitable to his own soul . . . he that speaketh sophistically, is hateful: he shall be destitute of every thing."[122] By dint of over-refining they abandon good sense, and everything escapes them.

That which I here call unfortunate subtleties does not involve merely the coarser subtleties, or the over-subtle refinements, but in general all those subtleties which use bad means.

They never fail to embarrass him who uses them. "He that walketh

---

[118] Esther 3:8.   [119] Ecclus. 38:17–18.   [120] Ecclus. 6:18.
[121] Wisd. 8:19.   [122] Ecclus. 37:21–23.

uprightly shall be saved: he that is perverse in his ways shall fall at once,"[123] says the wisest of kings.

Nothing exposes itself more quickly than unfortunate subtleties. "He that walketh sincerely, walketh confidently; but he that perverteth his ways, shall be manifest."[124]

The deceiver never fails to be the first deceived. "The way of the wicked shall deceive them; the deceitful man shall not find gain."[125] And again: "He that diggeth a pit, shall fall into it; and he that breaketh a hedge, a serpent shall bite him."[126]

Consider the vivid portrait of the deceiver and the impostor that the wise man paints for us. "A man that is an apostate, an unprofitable man, walketh with a perverse mouth. He winketh with the eyes, presseth with the foot, speaketh with the finger (he has secret dealings with everybody). With a wicked heart he deviseth evil, and at all times he soweth discord. To such a one his destruction shall presently come, and he shall suddenly be destroyed, and shall no longer have any remedy."[127]

If such conduct is odious in individuals, how much more unworthy is it in the prince, who is the protector of good faith!

Remember the truly noble and truly royal words of King John, who, urged to violate a treaty, answered: "If good faith had perished all over the earth, it should be found again in the hearts and mouths of kings."

"They that act wickedly are abominable to the king: for the throne is established by justice. Just lips are the delight of kings: he that speaketh right things shall be loved."[128]

This is how a king acts, when he thinks of what he is and wants to act in a kingly way.

10th Proposition
Model of true subtlety and wisdom in the conduct of Saul and of David, to serve as a proof and example of the preceding proposition

We can know the difference between truly wise men and deceivers, by the example of Saul and David.

Saul's beginnings were magnificent: he feared the burden of

[123] Prov. 28:18. [124] Prov. 10:9. [125] Prov. 12:26–27.
[126] Eccles. 10:8. [127] Prov. 6:12–15. [128] Prov. 16:12–13.

Characteristics of royalty (continuation)

royalty; he had hidden himself in his house, and could scarcely be found when he was elected.[129] After his election, he continued to live there in the same simplicity, and dedicated to the same works, as before. The state's needs obliged him to use authority; he made himself obeyed by his people; he defeated his enemies, and his heart became swollen; he forgot God.[130]

Jealousy took hold of his mind. He had loved David.[131] He could no longer endure him, after his services had brought much glory on him. He dared not drive away so great a man from the court, for fear of an outcry against himself, but he distanced him on the pretext of giving him an important command.[132] Thereby he gave David the means to augment his reputation, and gave him new helps.

Finally this jealous prince resolved to ruin David; and he did not see that he himself was losing the best servant he had in his whole kingdom. His jealousy provided him with black arts to succeed in his plan. "Saul promised his daughter to David: but, in order that she might be the occasion of his ruin, Saul had David told by his courtiers: Behold thou pleasest the king, and all his servants love thee."[133] But all this was done to ruin him. On the pretext of doing him honor, he exposed him to dangerous situations; he engaged him in almost inevitable perils. "You will be my son in law, he said, if you kill a hundred Philistines. David did it, and Saul gave him his daughter. But he saw that the Lord was with David: he feared him, and hated him all his life."[134]

His son Jonathan, who loved David, did what he could to appease his jealous father. Saul dissimulated, and deceived his own son, the better to deceive David. He made him return to the court. David distinguished himself through new victories; and Saul was again carried away by jealousy. While David was playing his lyre before him, he wanted to run him through with his spear. David fled, and was obliged to slip away from the court.[135]

Saul recalled him by new signs of affection, and always set new traps for him. David fled once again.[136]

The unhappy King, who saw David's glory always growing, and saw that his own servants – including his relatives and even his own son –

[129] 1 Kings 10:21; 11:5.
[130] 1 Kings 11: 15.
[131] 1 Kings 16:21.
[132] 1 Kings 18.
[133] Ibid., 21–22.
[134] Ibid., 25–29.
[135] 1 Kings 19.
[136] 1 Kings 20.

The prince and necessary knowledge

indeed loved so accomplished a man, spoke to him in this way: "Hear me now, ye sons of Jemini (he was himself of this race): will the son of Isai give every one of you fields, and vineyards, and make you all tribunes, and centurions? That all of you have conspired against me, and there is no one to inform me, especially when even my son hath entered into league with the son of Isai? There is not one of you that pitieth my case, nor that giveth me any information; you prefer to serve my rebellious subject, who undertakes constant attempts against my life."[137]

He could not speak more artfully, to interest his servants in the ruin of David. He found flatterers who entered into his unjust plans. David, quite faithful to the king, was treated as a public enemy. "The Ziphites went to warn Saul that David was hidden among them in a forest. And Saul said to them: Blessed be ye of the Lord, for you have pitied my case. Go, therefore, I pray you, and use all diligence, and curiously inquire, and consider the place where his foot is, and who hath seen him there. For he is a cunning man, who knows well that I hate him. Consider and see all his lurking holes, wherein he is hid, and return to me with the certainty of the thing, that I may go with you. And if he should even go down into the earth to hide himself, I will search him out in all the thousands of Judah."[138]

How much artifice, how much precaution, how much dissimulation, how many unjust accusations! But how many orders precisely given, and with how much attention and vigilance! All this to oppress a faithful subject.

This is what one calls pernicious subtlety. But we are going to see, in David, a true wisdom.

The more Saul strove, by flattering him, to make him forget himself, and flew into rages over proud words, the more David's natural modesty inspired respectful words in him. "Who am I, or what is my life, or my father's family in Israel, that I should be the son in law of the king?"[139]

And again: "Doth it seem a small matter to you to be the king's son in law? But I am a poor man, and of small ability."[140]

He never defended himself against the malicious acts of Saul by any violent means. He made himself redoubtable only by that prudence which made him foresee everything. "And David behaved

[137] 1 Kings 22:7–8.   [138] 1 Kings 23:19–23.
[139] 1 Kings 18:18.   [140] Ibid., 23.

Characteristics of royalty (continuation)

wisely in all his ways, and the Lord was with him. And Saul saw that he was exceeding prudent, and began to beware of him."[141]

He made use of innocent skills to escape the hands of so artful and powerful an enemy. He escaped secretly by a window; and Saul's minions found in his bed, which they searched, only a well-covered statue, which had served to conceal his flight from his domestics.[142]

If he used his prudence to protect himself against the King's jealousy, he used it much more against the enemies of the state. "When the Philistines marched in campaign, David observed them better than all the other captains of Saul; and his name became very famous."[143]

Since he was a good and grateful friend, he made himself faithful friends who would never deceive him. Samuel gave him sanctuary in the house of the prophets.[144] Achimelech, the great priest, had been killed for having served David innocently; his son Abiathar was saved. "Abide thou with me, he said to him, fear not: for he that seeketh my life, seeketh thy life also, and with me thou shalt be saved."[145]

His ability and his virtue so drew to him Jonathan, son of Saul, that far from wanting to enter into the bloody plans of the King his father, he never omitted anything to save David. In this he rendered a service to Saul himself, whom he kept from soaking his hands in innocent blood.

Though David knew that Jonathan was not deceiving him, still, since he knew Saul better than did Jonathan, he did not rest entirely on the assurances given him by his friend. "Jonathan said to him: God forbid, thou shalt not die: for my father will do nothing great or little, without first telling me: hath then my father hid this word only from me? no, this shall not be . . . But David said to him: Thy father certainly knoweth that I have found grace in thy sight, and he will say: Let not Jonathan know this, lest he be grieved. But truly as the Lord liveth, and thy soul liveth, there is but one step (as I may say) between me and death."[146]

In order, then, not to be deceived by Saul's schemes, he gave Jonathan the means to uncover them; and they agreed between themselves on a signal which Jonathan would give to David in time of peril.[147]

[141] Ibid., 14–15.
[142] 1 Kings 19:11–12.
[143] 1 Kings 18:30.
[144] 1 Kings 19:18–20.
[145] 1 Kings 22:23.
[146] 1 Kings 20:2–3.
[147] Ibid., 5,6; 20–22.

Since he saw that he had nothing to hope for from Saul, he provided for the safety of his father and mother, by placing them in the hands of the King of Moab, "till I know what God will do for me."[148] There was a man who thought of everything, and who chose his protectors well. For the King of Moab deceived him not at all. By this means he had only himself to think of. Nothing could be more industrious nor more innocent than the whole course of his conduct.

Constrained to take refuge in the territories of Achis, King of the Philistines, the satraps came and said to the King: "Here is David, this great man, who has defeated so many Philistines." David thought about this speech, and knew so well how to feign madness that Achis, instead of fearing and stopping him, had him driven from his presence and gave him means to save himself.[149]

Surrounded three or four times by the whole army of Saul, he found means of extricating himself, and of twice having Saul in his hands.[150]

Thus was confirmed that which David himself so often sang in his Psalms: "The evil one has fallen into the pit which he dug; his foot hath been taken in the very snare which he hid."[151]

When this faithful subject found himself master of the life of his king, he drew no other advantage from it than that of letting him know how deeply he respected him, and of confounding the calumnies of his enemies. "He cried to him from afar: My lord and my king, why dost thou hear the words of men that say: David seeketh thy hurt? Behold this day thy eyes have seen, that the Lord hath delivered thee into my hand? . . . But I said: I will not put out my hand against my lord, because he is the Lord's anointed . . . Reflect, and see, that there is no evil in my hand, nor iniquity, neither have I sinned against thee. But thou liest in wait for my life, to take it away. The Lord judge between me and thee, and the Lord revenge me of thee: but my hand shall not be upon thee . . . After whom dost thou come out, O king of Israel? After whom dost thou pursue? After a dead dog, after a flea. Be the Lord judge, and judge between me and thee, and see, and judge my cause, and deliver me out of thy hand."[152]

By this wise and irreproachable conduct, he obliged his enemy to recognize his mistake. "Thou art more just than I, Saul said to him."[153]

[148] 1 Kings 22:3. [149] 1 Kings 21:11–15. [150] 1 Kings 24; 26.
[151] Ps. 7:16; 9:16. [152] 1 Kings 24:18. [153] Ibid., 18.

The anger of this unjust king was not appeased, for all that. "And David said in his heart: I shall one day or other fall into the hands of Saul: is it not better for me to flee, and to be saved in the land of the Philistines, that Saul may despair of me, and cease to seek me in all the coasts of Israel?"[154]

Finally he made his treaty with Achis, King of Geth, and treated him so tactfully that, without ever doing anything against his king and against his nation, he kept himself always in Achis' good graces.[155]

You see Saul and David, both of them sensible and able, but in different ways. On one side, a perverse intention; on the other, an upright [*droite*] intention. On one side, Saul, a great king who, allowing no limits to his malice, used every means, without reserve, to ruin a good servant of whom he was jealous. On the other side David, a private individual abandoned and betrayed, found it necessary to defend himself only by permitted means, without detracting from what he owed to his prince and to his country. And nonetheless true wisdom, closed up within such narrow limits, was superior to that false wisdom which omitted nothing to satisfy itself.

Article III

On dangerous curiosities and kinds of knowledge: and on the confidence one must place in God

1st Proposition
The prince must avoid strange and superstitious consultations

Such are consultations with soothsayers and astrologists – something which the ambition and the weakness of the great makes them seek out so often. "Neither let there be found among you any one . . . that consulteth soothsayers, or observeth dreams and omens, neither let

---

[154] 1 Kings 27:1.   [155] 1 Kings 27; 28.

there be any wizard. Nor charmer, nor any one that consulteth pythonic spirits . . . or that seeketh the truth from the dead. For the Lord abhorreth all these things, and for these abominations he will destroy them at thy coming. Thou shalt be perfect, and without spot before the Lord thy God. These nations, whose land thou shalt possess, hearken to soothsayers and diviners: but thou art otherwise instructed by the Lord thy God."[1] He wants you to know the truth through him alone: and if he does not want to reveal it to you, you can only abandon yourself to his providence.

The astrologers are included in these curses of God. See how he speaks to the Chaldeans, the inventors of astrology, in which they gloried. "A sword is upon the Chaldeans, saith the Lord, and upon the inhabitants of Babylon, and upon her princes, and upon her wise men. A sword upon her diviners, and they shall be foolish: a sword upon her valiant ones, and they shall be dismayed. A sword upon their horses, and upon their chariots, and upon all the people that are in the midst of her: and they shall become as women: a sword upon her treasures, and they shall be made a spoil."[2]

None is more feeble and more timid than those who put their trust in forecasters: deceived by their vain omens, they lose heart, and remain without defense.

Thus perished Babylon, mother of astrologers, in the midst of the rejoicings and the triumphs of which their divines sang. Isaiah, foreseeing her fall, spoke to her in these terms: "Stand now with thy enchanters, and with the multitude of thy sorceries, in which thou hast labored from thy youth, if so be it may profit thee any thing, or if thou mayest become stronger. Thou hast failed in the multitude of thy counsels: let now the astrologers stand and save thee, they that gazed at the stars, and counted the months, that from them they might tell thee the things that shall come to thee. Behold they are as stubble, fire hath burnt them, they shall not deliver themselves from the power of the flames."[3]

Those who pride themselves on predicting uncertain events, make themselves like to God. For listen how he speaks: "Who hath wrought and done these things, calling the generations from the beginning? I am the Lord, I am the first and the last."[4]

"Bring me your gods, O Gentiles, says the Lord, that I may try

[1] Deut. 18:10–14.   [2] Jer. 50:35–37.
[3] Isa. 47:12–14.   [4] Isa. 41:4.

them. Speak, if you have something to say, saith the king of Jacob: let them come, and tell us all things that are to come. Show us the things that are to come hereafter, and we shall know that ye are gods."[5]

And again: "Hear ye, O house of Israel. Thus saith the Lord: Learn not according to the ways of the Gentiles: and be not afraid of the signs of heaven, which the heathens fear. For the laws of these people are vain."[6]

The ignorant Gentiles adored the planets and the other stars; attributed to them empires, virtues, and divine influences, through which they dominated the world and ruled events; they assigned to them times and places, where they exercised their dominion. Judicial astrology is a remnant of this doctrine, as impious as it is fabulous. Fear, then, neither eclipses, nor comets, nor the planets, nor the constellations which men have composed through their fantasies, nor those conjunctions esteemed fatal, nor the lines formed on the hands or on the face, nor the images called talismans, impregnated with celestial virtues. Fear neither pictures, nor horoscopes, nor the omens that are drawn from them. All these things – which rest on nothing better than pompous words – are at bottom reveries which frauds sell at a high price to the ignorant.

These curious sciences, which serve to cover spells and evil spells, are condemned in all states – and nonetheless often sought after by the very princes who forbid them. Misery to them, once again misery! They want to know the future – that is, penetrate the secret of God. They will fall into the curse of Saul. This king had forbidden soothsayers, yet he consulted them. A divining woman said to him, without knowing who he was, "Thou knowest that Saul hath rooted out the soothsayers from this land: why then dost thou lay a snare for my life? ... As the Lord liveth, answered Saul, there shall be no evil happen to thee for this thing. And the woman said to him: Whom shall I bring up to thee? And he said, Bring me up Samuel. And when the woman saw Samuel, she cried out with a loud voice, and said to Saul: Why hast thou deceived me? For thou art Saul. And the king said to her: fear not; what hast thou seen? And the woman said to Saul: I saw gods ascending out of the earth. And he said to her: What form is he of? And she said: An old man cometh up, and he is covered with a mantle. And Saul understood that it was Samuel, and he bowed

---

[5] Ibid., 21–23. [6] Jer. 10:1–3.

himself with his face to the ground, and adored. And Samuel said to Saul: Why hast thou disturbed my rest, that I should be brought up? . . . Why askest thou me, seeing the Lord hath departed from thee, and is gone over to thy rival? For the Lord will do to thee as he spoke by me, and he will rend thy kingdom out of thy hand, and will give it to thy neighbor David. Because thou didst not obey the voice of the Lord, neither didst thou execute the wrath of his indignation upon Amalec. Therefore hath the Lord done to thee what thou sufferest this day. And the Lord also will deliver Israel with thee into the hands of the Philistines: and tomorrow thou and thy sons shall be with me."[7] That is to say, among the dead.

At this terrible sentence, Saul collapsed in fear, and was beside himself.[8] And the next day the prediction was fulfilled.[9]

It was not in the power of a witch to summon up a holy soul: nor in the power of the demon who appeared, according to some, in the form of Samuel, to tell the future so precisely. God conducted this event, and wanted to teach us that, when it pleases him, he permits us to find the truth by illicit means, for the just punishment of those who use them.

Do not be astonished, then, to see what the astrologers predict sometimes come to pass. For without falling back on chance – and that which is chance with respect to men is design with respect to God – consider that, by a terrible judgment, God himself hands over to seduction those who look for it. He abandons the world – that is, those who love the world – to those seducing spirits whose toys the ambitious and vainly curious are. These deceiving and malignant spirits dupe and deceive curious (and thereby credulous) souls through a thousand illusions. One of their secrets is astrology, and the other kinds of divination, which sometimes succeed, depending on whether God finds it just to hand over a mad curiosity either to error or to just torture.

It was thus that Saul found, through his curiosity, his own death-sentence. It was thus that God doubled his torment, punishing him not only through the evil which befell him, but still more through foreseeing it. If it is a kind of punishment to hand over curious men to raging terrors, it is another to deliver them up to caressing hopes. In the end their credulity, which makes them trust in others rather than

---

[7] 1 Kings 28:9–19.   [8] Ibid., 20–21.   [9] 1 Kings 31.

Characteristics of royalty (continuation)

in God, merits being punished in several ways: that is to say not only by lies, but also by the truth, so that their rash curiosity will turn them toward every sort of evil.

This is what St. Augustine teaches, basing it on Scripture, in the second book of *On Christian Doctrine*, chapters xx and the following.

Protect yourselves well, O kings, O great of the earth, from being approached by these deceivers and ignorant ones, who are called seers: "who think that which they know not,"[10] as the wisest of kings says.

Do not look among them for interpreters of your dreams, as if they were mysterious. "The hopes of a man that is void of understanding are vain and deceitful: and dreams lift up fools. The man that giveth heed to lying visions, is like to him that catcheth at a shadow, and followeth after the wind. The vision of dreams is the resemblance of one thing to another: as when a man's likeness is before the face of a man." (These are only impure vapors which arise in the brain through ill-chosen nourishment.) "What can be made clean by the unclean, and what truth can come from that which is false? Deceitful divinations and lying omens are the dreams of evil-doers, and vanity. And the heart fancieth as that of a woman in travail: except it be a vision sent forth from the most High, set not thy heart upon them. For dreams have deceived many, and they have failed that put their trust in them."[11]

2nd Proposition
One must not over-rate human counsels, or their wisdom

"A man cannot tell what hath been before him: and what shall be after him, who can tell him?"[12]

Thus "he that trusteth in his own heart, is a fool."[13] And again: "Extol not thyself in the thoughts of thy soul like a mad bull, lest thy strength be quashed by folly. And it eat up thy leaves, and destroy thy fruit, and thou be left as a dry tree";[14] your glory and your power will disappear.

The Egyptians prided themselves on an extraordinary wisdom in their counsels. See how God speaks to them: "The princes of Tanis are become fools, the wise counsellors of Pharaoh have given foolish

---

[10] Prov. 23:7.   [11] Ecclus. 34:1–7.   [12] Ecclus. 10:14.
[13] Prov. 28:26.   [14] Ecclus. 6:2–3.

On dangerous curiosities

counsel: how will you say to Pharaoh: I am the son of the wise, the son of ancient kings? Where are now thy wise men? Let them tell thee, and show what the Lord of hosts hath purposed upon Egypt. The princes of Tanis are become fools, the princes of Memphis are gone astray, they have destroyed Egypt, the stay of the people thereof. The Lord hath mingled in the midst thereof the spirit of giddiness: and they have caused Egypt to err in all its works, as a drunken man staggereth and vomiteth. And there shall be no work for Egypt: she will do neither great nor small things. In that day Egypt shall be like unto women, and they shall be amazed, and afraid, because of the moving of the hand of the Lord of hosts, which he shall move over it." [15]

When one sees his enemies take feeble advice, one must not for all that take pride in it, but reflect that it is the Lord who sends them this spirit of distraction to punish them, and fear a similar judgment.

If God withdraws, says the holy prophet, "wisdom shall perish from their wise men, and the understanding of their prudent men shall be hid."[16]

"It is he that bringeth the searchers of secrets to nothing, that hath made the judges of the earth as vanity."[17]

Tremble then before him, and beware of presuming human wisdom.

3rd Proposition
One must consult God by prayer, and place one's confidence in him, by doing what one can on his own side

We have seen that it is God who gives wisdom. We have just seen that it is God who takes it away from the proud. One must, then, ask him for it humbly.

This is what Ecclesiasticus teaches us when – after having prescribed to us what prudence can achieve, in the oft-cited Chapter XXXVII – it concludes in this way: "But above all these things pray to the most High, that he may direct thy way in truth."[18] He alone knows it thoroughly; it is from him that we must ask knowledge of it.

But whoever asks God for wisdom, must on his side do all that he can. It is on this condition that God permits us to draw confidence

---

[15] Isa. 19:11–17.   [16] Isa. 29:14.
[17] Isa. 40:23.   [18] Ecclus. 37:19.

from his power and his goodness. Otherwise it is tempting God, and imagining vainly that he will send his angels to sustain us, when we shall have thrown ourselves down – as Satan dared to advise Jesus Christ.[19]

Article IV

Consequences of the preceding doctrine: concerning majesty and its adjuncts

1st Proposition
What majesty is

I do not call majesty that pomp which surrounds kings, or that external show which dazzles the vulgar. That is the reflection of majesty, but not its true self.

Majesty is the image of the greatness of God in a prince.

God is infinite, God is all. The prince, in his quality of prince, is not considered as an individual; he is a public personage, all the state is comprised in him; the will of all the people is included in his own. Just as all virtue and excellence are united in God, so the strength of every individual is comprehended in the person of the prince. What greatness this is, for one man to contain so much!

The power of God can be felt in a moment from one end of the world to the other: the royal power acts simultaneously throughout the kingdom. It holds the whole kingdom in position just as God holds the whole world.

If God were to withdraw his hand, the entire world would return to nothing: if authority ceases in the kingdom, all lapses into confusion.

Consider the prince in his cabinet. From thence flow the commands which coordinate the efforts of magistrates and captains, of citizens and soldiers, of provinces and armies, by land and by sea. It is the image of God, who directs all nature from his throne in the highest heaven.

[19] Matt. 4:6–7.

Majesty and its adjuncts

"What is done solely at the emperor's bidding?" asks St. Augustine. "He has only to move his lips, the least of all movements, and the whole empire stirs. It is he who does all things by his command, in the image of God. He spoke, and it was done; he commanded, and all was created."[1]

We admire his works: nature is a subject for the curious to debate. "God hath set the world in their heart, so that no man can find out the work that God maketh from the beginning to the end."[2] We see some portion of it, but the depths are impenetrable. And so too is the secret of the prince.

The intentions of a prince are only known by their execution. The counsels of God are revealed in the same way: until then none penetrates them except those to whom God imparts knowledge.

If the power of God extends everywhere, magnificence accompanies it. Nowhere in the universe is there a lack of striking marks of his goodness. You see order, justice, and peace throughout the realm. These are the natural effects of the authority of the prince.

Nothing is more majestic than all-embracing goodness: and there is no greater debasement of majesty than the misery of the people caused by some prince.

The wicked seek to hide themselves in vain; the light of God pursues them everywhere, his arm will strike them down, whether in the highest heaven or in the lowest depths. "Where shall I go before your spirit and where shall I flee before your face? If I climb to heaven you are there. If I throw myself into the depths of hell, I find you there. If I rise in the morning and retreat to the most distant seas it is your hand that leads me there and your right hand holds me there. And I have said that perhaps the shadows will cover me, but night has been as day around me. Before you, darkness is not dark. The night is lighted as the day. Darkness and light are one and the same."[3] The evil find God everywhere, high and low, night and day. Whatever morning they get up, he warns them. However far they should travel, his hand is on them.

Thus God enables the prince to discover the most deep-laid plots. His eyes and hands are everywhere. We have seen how the birds of the air bring him news of what happens.[4] He even receives from God, in the course of handling affairs, a degree of penetration akin to the

---

[1] St. Augustine, *In Psalmos* CXLVIII.
[2] Eccles. 3:11.   [3] Ps. 138:7–12.   [4] Eccles. 10:20.

power of divination. Once he has penetrated intrigue, his long arms seek out his enemies at the ends of the earth and uncover them in the deepest abysses. Against such power there is no sure refuge.

Finally, gather together all that we have said, so great and so august, about royal authority. You have seen a great nation united under one man: you have seen his sacred power, paternal and absolute: you have seen that secret reason which directs the body politic, enclosed in one head: you have seen the image of God in kings, and you will have the idea of majesty of kingship.

God is holiness itself, goodness itself, power itself, reason itself. In these things consists the divine majesty. In their reflection consists the majesty of the prince.

So great is this majesty that its source cannot be found to reside in the prince: it is borrowed from God, who entrusts it to the prince for the good of his people, to which end it is well that it be restrained by a higher power.

An undefinable element of divinity is possessed by the prince, and inspires fear in his subjects. The king himself would do well to remember this. "I have said, Ye are gods; and all of you are children of the most High. But ye shall die like men, and fall like one of the princes." I have said: you are gods; this signifies that you possess in your authority, you bear on your forehead, the stamp of the divine. You are children of the most High:[5] it is he who has established your power for the good of the human race. But, O gods of flesh and blood, of mud and dust, you will die like other men, you will fall like the greatest. Greatness divides men for a little while; a common fall levels them all in the end.

O kings, be bold therefore in the exercise of your power: for it is divine and beneficial to the human race; but wield it with humility. It is conferred on you from without. In the end it leaves you weak, it leaves you mortal, it leaves you still sinners: and it lays upon you a heavier charge to render to God.

2nd Proposition
That magnanimity, magnificence and all the great virtues are part of majesty

Greatness demands the greatest things: with the highest greatness are associated the highest virtues.

[5] Ps. 81:6–7.

Majesty and its adjuncts

The prince should think of great things: "Let the prince think princely thoughts."[6]

Base thoughts are unbecoming to majesty. Saul was chosen king; at the same time God "gave him another heart, and he was turned into another man."[7]

Be silent, base thoughts: yield to royal thoughts.

Thoughts worthy of royalty are those which concern the general good; great men are not born for themselves alone: great powers, which are in the sight of all the world, are created for the good of all.

The prince is by his office the man furthest removed from small interests, the most interested in the public good; his true interest is that of the state. He can therefore never take too noble a view; he can never be too far above petty thoughts and narrow views [*des pensées particulières*].

Thus Saul, changed into another man during the time that he was faithful to the grace of his ministry, was above everything.

Above royalty, whose burden he understood and whose splendor he spurned. This we have already seen.[8]

Above sentiments of vengeance – for on a day of victory, when all the people wanted him to immolate his enemies, he offered a sacrifice to God in the form of clemency.[9]

Above himself, and above all the feelings that blood inspires: ready to devote to the people his own person and that of his well-loved son Jonathan.[10]

What shall we say of David, who was given this fine and just praise? "For even as an angel of God, so is my lord the king, that he is neither moved with blessing nor cursing."[11] He always aimed at the public good, whether ungrateful men blamed his conduct, or whether it received the praises of which it was worthy.

That is true magnanimity, which was not swollen by praise, which was not cut down by blame, which was moved only by truth.

One joyfully abandons his whole fortune to the guidance of such a prince. "Thou my lord the king art as an angel of God, do what pleaseth thee."[12] So spoke Miphiboseth, grandson of Saul who was betrayed by his servant Siba.

Indeed David was filled only with great things – with God and the public good.

We have seen that, despite the rebellions and the ingratitude of his

---

[6] Isa. 32:8.   [7] 1 Kings 10:6, 9.   [8] 1 Kings 10; 11.   [9] 1 Kings 11:12–13.
[10] 1 Kings 14:41.   [11] 2 Kings 14:17.   [12] 2 Kings 19:27.

Characteristics of royalty (continuation)

people, he drew divine vengeance from them to him as the only guilty one. "Strike, Lord, strike the guilty one, and spare the innocent people."[13]

How sincerely did he admit his fault – so rare a thing in a king! With what zeal did he atone for it! "I have sinned, he said, in numbering the people. O Lord! Pardon me, for I have acted too foolishly."[14]

We have seen him scorn his life in a hundred battles: and afterwards we have seen him place himself above the glory of fighting, by preserving himself for his state.

But how far above resentment and doing harm was he! We have admired his joy, when Abigail stopped him from avenging himself with his own hand. We have seen him spare Saul, his persecutor – though he knew that in avenging himself he would assure himself of the crown, whose succession belonged to him. What loftiness of courage, to place himself so easily above the sweetness of reigning, and of that of vengeance!

When Saul and Jonathan were killed, David bewailed both of them: David sang their praises. It was not only Jonathan, his intimate friend, whose loss he deplored: he cried for his persecutor. "Saul and Jonathan, lovely, and comely in their life, even in death they were not divided. Ye daughters of Israel, weep over Saul, who clothed you with scarlet in delights, who gave you ornaments of gold for your attire," and so on.[15]

He did not conceal the virtues of an unjust predecessor, who did everything he could to ruin him: he celebrated them, and immortalized them through incomparable poetry.

He did not merely bewail Saul: he avenged him, and punished with death the one who had prided himself on having killed him. "I ran him through with my sword, said this traitor, after having removed the diadem that was on his head, and the bracelet that was on his arm, and have brought them hither to thee, my Lord."[16]

These rich presents did not save this parricide. "Why didst thou not fear to put out thy hand to kill the Lord's anointed?"[17]

Let it be, if you like, royalty's self-interest which made David avenge his predecessor: this was still a feeling which was above vulgar thoughts, which David banished – so far [was he] from showing joy at a death which delivered him from so powerful an enemy and placed

[13] 2 Kings 24:17. [14] Ibid., 17. [15] 2 Kings 1:17,23,24.
[16] 2 Kings 1:10. [17] 2 Kings 1:14.

the diadem on his head, which at once vindicated him and assured the public peace together with the life of kings.

He still had a redoubtable enemy: this was a son of Saul who divided the kingdom; it seemed that policy might bring him to treat still more considerately the old who had challenged Saul – for this great, brave man did not want to be delivered from his enemies through assassination-attempts and crimes.

A little later, in fact, some evil men brought him the head of this second enemy. "Behold the head of Isobeth the son of Saul thy enemy who sought thy life: but the Lord hath revenged my lord the king . . . But David answered: . . . as the Lord liveth, who hath delivered my soul out of all distress, the man that told me, and said: Saul is dead, who thought he brought me good tidings, I apprehended, and slew him, who should have been rewarded for his news. How much more now when wicked men have slain an innocent man in his own house, upon his bed, shall I not require his blood at your hand, and take you away from the earth?"[18]

He caused them to be killed immediately, and hung up in a public place their bloody hands, and their feet which had run to murder, so that all Israel should know that he did not want such services.

That which shows that he acted in all things from the noblest motives, was the care he took with the survivors of the house of Saul. "Is there any one, think you, left of the house of Saul, that I may show kindness to him for Jonathan's sake?"[19] He found Miphiboseth, son of Jonathan, to whom he gave [a place at] his table, after having given him all the lands of Saul's house.

While kings from a new royal family dream only of weakening and destroying the survivors of the houses that held the throne before them, David sustained and helped up the house of Saul and Jonathan.

In a word, all the actions and all the words of David breathed forth something so great, and in consequence so royal, that one need only read his life and hear his speeches to have an idea of magnanimity.

To magnanimity corresponds magnificence, which joins great expenditures to great plans.

David again offers us a fine model of this. His victories were marked by the magnificent gifts which he gave to the sanctuary, which he enriched with the spoils of subjugated kingdoms.[20]

[18] 2 Kings 4:8–11. [19] 2 Kings 9:1.
[20] 2 Kings 8:11; 1 Par. 18:11.

Characteristics of royalty (continuation)

What a fine thing it is to see this great man – after having gloriously completed so many wars – passing his old age in making preparations and plans for that magnificent temple, which his son built after his death!

"He assembled at great expense all the most excellent workers; he amassed immense weights of iron and brass; the cedars which he brought in were beyond price: he consecrated to this great work a hundred thousand talents of gold and six million talents of silver; the rest was beyond counting. Solomon my son is young, he said, and the house which I would have to be built to the Lord, must be such as to be renowned in all the world: therefore I will prepare him necessaries."[21]

After such magnificent preparations, he thought he had done nothing. "I have, he said, offered all these things to God from my poverty."[22] He found everything he had prepared to be poor, because this royal expenditure equalled neither his desires nor his ideas – such great ones did he have.

We shall speak more conveniently in another place of the magnificence of Solomon and the other great kings of Judah. And to define in what magnificence consists, we shall see that it appears in great works consecrated to the use of the public, in those works that attract glory to the nation, which impress respect on subjects and on foreigners, and render immortal the names of princes.

[21] 1 Par. 22:1–5,14.   [22] Ibid., 14.

SIXTH BOOK

The duties of subjects toward the prince, based on the preceding doctrine

First Article

On the service one owes to the king

1st Proposition
One owes the prince the same service one owes to his country

No one can have any doubts about this, since we have seen that the whole state is in the person of the prince. In him [is found] the will of the whole people. It is for him alone to make everything converge in the public good. One must render concurrent the service which one owes to the prince and that which one owes to the state, viewed as inseparable things.

2nd Proposition
One must serve the state, as the prince understands it

For we have seen that in him resides the reason which guides the state.

Those who think to serve the state otherwise than by serving the prince (by obeying him), attribute to themselves a part of the royal authority: they trouble the public peace, and the concord of all the members with the head.[1]

---

[1] 2 Kings 19:22.

Such were the children of Sarvia, who through false zeal wanted to ruin those whom David had pardoned. "What have I to do with you, ye sons of Sarvia? Why are you a Satan this day to me?"

The prince sees [both] farther and higher; one must believe that he sees better, and one must obey without a murmur, since murmuring shows a disposition to sedition.

The prince knows the whole secret and the whole outcome of [public] affairs. To fail to observe his orders for a moment is to expose everything to chance. "David said to Amasa: Assemble to me all the men of Judah against the third day, and be thou here present. So Amasa went to assemble the men of Judah, but he tarried beyond the set time which the king had appointed him. And David said to Abisai: Now will Seba the son of Bachri do us more harm than did Absalom: take thou therefore the servants of thy Lord, and pursue after him."[2]

Amasa had not understood that obedience consists in punctuality.

3rd Proposition
It is only public enemies who separate the interest of the prince from the interest of the state

In the ordinary style of sacred Scripture, the enemies of the state are also called the enemies of the king. We have already observed that Saul called his enemies, the Philistines, enemies of the people of God.[3] David, having defeated the Philistines, [spoke in this way]: "God, he said, has defeated my enemies."[4] There is no need to relate further examples of a thing which is too clear to need proof.

Thus one should never think that he can attack a people without attacking its king, nor that one can attack a king without attacking a people.

The speech made by Rabsaces, general of the army of Sennacherib King of Assyria, was too crude to delude anyone. His master had sent him to exterminate Jerusalem, and to transport the Jews far from their country. He made a show of taking pity on a nation reduced to desperate straits by war, and tried to stir them up against their king, Ezechias. This is how he spoke before the whole people to the envoys of this prince: "Hath my master sent me to thy master [Ezechias] and to thee, to speak these words, and not rather to the men that sit upon

---

[2] 2 Kings 20:4–6.   [3] 1 Kings 14:23.   [4] 2 Kings 5:20.

the wall, that they may eat their own dung, and drink their urine with you? Then Rabsaces stood, and cried out with a loud voice in the Jews' language, and said: Hear the words of the great king, the king of the Assyrians. Thus saith the king: Let not Ezechias deceive you, for he shall not be able to deliver you out of my hand . . . Do not harken to Ezechias. For thus saith the king of the Assyrians: Do with me that which is for your advantage, and come out to me: and every man of you shall eat of his own vineyard, and of his own fig-trees: and you shall drink water of your own cisterns. Till I come, and take you away to a land, like to your own land, a fruitful land, and plentiful in wine, a land of bread and vineyards, a land of olives, of oil and honey, and you shall live, and not die. Hearken not to Ezechias, who deceiveth you."[5]

To flatter a people in order to separate it from the interests of its king, is to make the cruellest of all wars upon it, and to add sedition to its other misfortunes.

Let the nations then detest the Rabsaces and all those who pretend to love them, while they attack their king. One never attacks the body so much as when one attacks the head, though one can seem for a while to flatter the other members.

4th Proposition
The prince must be loved as a public good, and his life is the object of the people's good wishes

From this comes the cry, Long live the king!, which has been passed on from the people of God to all the peoples of the world. At the election of Saul, at the coronation of Solomon, at the rite of Joas, one heard this cry from the whole people: Long live the king, long live the king, long live King David, long live King Solomon![6]

When one approached kings, one began with these vows: "O King, live for ever! May God preserve your life, O King my Lord!"[7]

The prophet Baruch, during the [Babylonian] captivity, commanded the whole [Jewish] people "to pray for the life of Nabuchodonosor . . . and for the life of Balthasar his son."[8]

The whole people "offered sacrifices to God in heaven, and prayed for the life of the king and his children."[9]

---
[5] 4 Kings 18:27–32.
[6] 1 Kings 10:24; 3 Kings 31, 34, 39; 4 Kings 11:12; Rom. 13:15.
[7] Neh. 2:3.   [8] Bar. 1:11.   [9] Ezra. 6:10.

The duties of subjects

St. Paul has ordered us to pray for the powers that be,[10] and has based the preservation of public tranquillity on their being preserved.

Men used to swear by the life of the king as by a sacred thing: and the Christians, too religious to swear by mere creatures, have revered this oath, adoring the orders of God in the health and life of princes. We have seen the passages.

The prince is a public good whom each must preserve jealously. "Why have our brothers from Judah hidden the king from us, as if it were for them alone to guard him?",[11] and the rest which we have seen.

From this follow these words, already noticed: "The people said to David: You will not fight with us: it is better that you stay in the city to save us all."[12]

The life of the prince is viewed as the salvation of the whole people: this is why each is careful of the life of the prince as if it were his own, or rather more than his own.

"The anointed of the Lord, whom we regard as the breath of our mouth":[13] that is to say, who is as dear to us as the air we breathe. It was thus that Jeremiah spoke of the king.

"Then David's men swore unto him, saying: Thou shalt go no more out with us to battle, lest thou put out the lamp of Israel."[14]

See how the prince is loved: he is the light of the whole kingdom. What is loved as much as light? It is the joy and the greatest good of the universe.

Thus a good subject loves his prince as he loves the public good, as he loves the safety of the whole state, as he loves the air he breathes, the light of his eyes, his life and more than his life.

5th Proposition
The death of the prince is a public calamity: and men of good will view it as divine punishment of a people

When the light is extinguished, everything is in darkness, everyone is in mourning.

It is always a public misfortune when a state changes hands, because of the firmness of established authority and the weakness of a new reign.

It is a divine punishment for a state, when it changes masters often.

---

[10] 1 Tim. 2:2. [11] 2 Kings 19:42. [12] Ibid., 42.
[13] Thren. 4:20. [14] 2 Kings 21:17.

On the service one owes to the king

"For the sins of the land many are the princes thereof: and for the wisdom of a man, and the knowledge of those things that are said, the life of the prince shall be prolonged."[15] It is a state misfortune to be deprived of the counsels and the wisdom of an experienced prince, and to be submitted to new masters who often learn to be wise only at the people's expense.

And so when Josiah had been killed at the battle of Mageddo, "all Judah and Jerusalem mourned for him: particularly Jeremiah, whose lamentations for Josiah all the singing men and singing women repeat unto this day."[16]

And it is not only good princes such as Josiah, whose death is accounted a public misfortune: the same Jeremiah deplores the death of Sedecias as well – the same Sedecias of whom it is written that "he did evil in the eyes of the Lord his God, and did not reverence the face of Jeremiah the prophet speaking to him from the mouth of the Lord."[17] Far from respecting this holy prophet, he had persecuted him. And nonetheless, after the ruin of Jerusalem, when the imprisoned Sedecias had been blinded, Jeremiah, who deplored the misfortunes of his people, deplored as one of its greatest misfortunes the misfortune of Sedecias. "The anointed of the Lord, who was as the breath of our mouth, is taken in our sins: to whom we had said: Under thy shadow we shall live among the Gentiles."[18] A captive king, a king despoiled of his state and even deprived of sight, is regarded as the mainstay and the consolation of his people, captive with him. This fragment of majesty still seemed to spread its splendor over a desolated nation: and the people, touched by the misfortunes of its prince, deplores them more than its own. "The Lord, they said, hath cast down his house; he hath caused feasts and sabbaths to be forgotten in Zion, and hath delivered up king and priest to reproach, and to the indignation of his wrath . . . The gates of Jerusalem are sunk into the ground . . . her king and her princes are among the Gentiles."[19]

The prophet regards the misfortune of the prince as a public misfortune and as a chastisement by God of the whole people – even the misfortune of a wicked prince; for he does not lose through his crimes the character of the Lord's anointed, and the sacred unction which consecrated him keeps him always venerable.

That is why David bemoans, with the whole people, the death of

[15] Prov. 28:2. [16] 2 Par. 35:24–25. [17] 2 Par. 36:12.
[18] Thren. 4:20. [19] Thren. 2:6,9.

The duties of subjects

Saul (evil as he was). "The illustrious of Israel are slain upon thy mountains: how are the valiant fallen? Tell it not in Geth, publish it not in the streets of Ascolon: lest the daughters of the Philistines rejoice, lest the daughters of the uncircumcised triumph. Ye mountains of Gelboa, let neither dew, nor rain, come upon you, nor offerings; for there was cast away the shield of the valiant, the shield of Saul as though he had not been anointed with oil."[20] And the rest which we have related.

Thus it is that the death of the prince, however wicked, however reprobate, brings joy to the enemies of the state and misery to its subjects. All bemoan him; all are in mourning for his death: even the most insensible things, such as mountains, indeed all nature, feel the effects of it.

6th Proposition
A man of good will prefers the life of the prince to his own, and exposes himself to save it

We have already seen it: a people is about to fight, but is heedless of its peril, provided the prince is safe.[21]

The way in which the prince is protected, in the city and in the country, makes this clear. When David entered the tent of Saul at night, it was necessary to pass through Abner and the whole people, who were sleeping around him.[22] And David, having taken the king's cup and spear[23] to show that he had been master of his life, "cried out from afar to Abner and the whole people: Art not thou a man? . . . Why then hast thou not kept thy lord the king? For there came one of the people in to kill the king thy Lord. Long live the Lord, you all deserve death, who have not kept your master, the Lord's anointed. And now where is the king's spear, and the cup of water, which was at his head?"[24]

The people must guard the prince; they must encamp around him; someone must have made the camp collapse, to be able to reach the prince; one must stay up so that the prince can sleep in safety; whoever fails to protect him is worthy of death.

When the king was in the city, the people and even the great themselves slept by his door. "Uriah (though he was a commander)

---

[20] 2 Kings 1:19–21. [21] 2 Kings 17; 21. [22] 1 Kings 26:7.
[23] Ibid., 12. [24] Ibid., 12.

slept before the gate of the king's house, with the other servants of his lord."[25]

During the rebellion of Absalom, Ethai the Gethite marched before him at the head of six hundred men of Geth, all brave soldiers. They were foreign troops, whose fidelity David wanted to test; and he said to Ethai: "Why comest thou with us? Return and dwell with the king, for thou art a stranger, and art come out of thy own place. Yesterday thou camest, and today shalt thou be forced to go forth with us? But I shall go whither I am going: return thou, and take back thy brethren with thee, and the Lord will show thee mercy, and truth, because thou hast shown grace and fidelity. And Ethai answered the king, saying: As the Lord liveth, and as my lord the king liveth; in what place soever thou shalt be, my lord, O king, either in death or in life, there will thy servant be. And David said to Ethai: Come, and pass over."[26] Through this response, David recognized him as a man who knew what it means to serve kings.

Article II
On the obedience due to the prince

1st Proposition
That subjects owe their prince complete obedience

If the prince is not scrupulously obeyed, public order is overthrown, and there is no further unity, and in consequence no further cooperation or peace in a state.

This is why we have seen that whosoever disobeys public authority is judged worthy of death. "And the man that will do presumptuously, and will not hearken unto the priest or unto the judge, even that man shall die: and thou shalt put away the evil from Israel."[1]

God has established these powers in order to prevent disorder, and we hear St. Paul say in his name: "Let every soul be subject unto the higher powers. For there is no power but of God: the powers that be are ordained of God."[2]

---

[25] 3 Kings 11:9.   [26] Ibid., 10.   [1] Deut. 17:12.   [2] Rom. 13:1–2.

"Put them in mind to be subject to principalities and powers, to obey them scrupulously, to be ready for every good work."[3]

God has made kings and princes his lieutenants on earth, in order to make their authority sacred and inviolable. This leads St. Paul to observe once again that they are "the ministers of God," in accordance with what is written in the Wisdom of Solomon,[4] "that the princes are the ministers of his kingdom."[5]

From this St. Paul concludes: "that ye must needs be subject, not only for wrath, but also for conscience' sake."[6]

St. Peter also says: "Submit yourselves to every ordinance of man for the Lord's sake: whether it be to the king, as supreme; or unto governors, as unto them that are sent by him . . . For this is the will of God."[7]

As we have already seen, the words of the two apostles refer to this when they say: "Servants, be obedient to your masters with all fear, not only to the good and gentle, but also to the froward.[8] Not with eye-service, as men-pleasers; but as the servants of Christ, doing the will of God from the heart."[9] Everything that we have seen of the sacred character of royal power confirms the truth of what we say here: and nothing is better founded on the word of God than the obedience which is due by reason of religion and conscience to legitimate authority.

For the rest, when Jesus said to the Jews: "Render unto Caesar that which is Caesar's,"[10] he did not examine how the power of the Caesars had been established: it was sufficient that he found them established and reigning, and he intended that the divine order and the foundation of public peace should be respected in the form of their authority.

2nd Proposition
That there is only one exception to the obedience due to the prince, which is when his commands run contrary to God's

Subordination requires this. "Submit yourselves . . . to the king, as supreme; or unto governors, as unto them that are sent by him."[11]

---

[3] Titus 3:1. [4] Rom. 13:4. [5] Wisdom 6:5.
[6] Rom. 13:5. [7] 1 Pet. 2:13–15. [8] Ibid., 18.
[9] Eph. 6:5; Col. 3:22. [10] Matt. 22:21. [11] 1 Pet. 2:13–14.

And again: "There are divers degrees, the one above the other: the powerful man is subject to one more powerful, and the king gives commandments to all his subjects."[12]

Obedience is due to each according to his rank, and the governor must never be obeyed if his orders are prejudicial to the prince's.

Above all empires is the empire of God. It is the only empire which can truly be called absolutely sovereign, and from which all others derive: from his all power comes.

Since then one must obey the governor, if there is nothing in his commands which seems contrary to the king's, so the king's orders must be obeyed, if there is nothing in them which seems to conflict with the commandments of God.

For the same reason, just as one must not obey the governor against the orders of the king, even less must one obey the king against the commandments of God.

It was for this reason that the apostles replied to the magistrates: "We ought to obey God rather than men."[13]

3rd Proposition
One owes tribute to the prince

If, as we have seen, one must expose his life for his country and for his prince, still more must one give a part of his goods to maintain public expenses. And this is what one calls tribute.

This is taught by St. John the Baptist. "The publicans (it was they who received taxes and public revenues) came also to be baptized, and said to him: Master, what shall we do to be saved?"[14] He did not say to them: Quit your jobs, for they are wrong and contrary to conscience; "but he said to them: Do nothing more than that which is appointed you."[15]

Our Lord decides this matter. The Pharisees believed that the head-tax which was paid to Caesar in Judaea was not due him. They justified themselves on religious grounds, saying that the people of God should never pay tribute to an infidel prince. They wanted to see what Our Lord would say on this subject: for if he spoke on behalf of Caesar, that would be a way for them to disparage him among the people; and if he spoke against Caesar, they would hand him over to

---

[12] Eccles. 5:7–8.   [13] Acts 5:29.   [14] Luke 3:12.   [15] Ibid., 13.

The duties of subjects

the Romans. Thus they sent to him their disciples, who asked him: "Is it lawful to give tribute to Caesar, or not? But Jesus knowing their wickedness, said: Why do you tempt me, ye hypocrites? Show me the coin of the tribute. And they offered him a penny. And Jesus saith to them: Whose image and inscription is this? They say to him: Caesar's. Then he saith to them: Render therefore to Caesar the things that are Caesar's; and to God the things that are God's."[16]

It is as if he had said: Do not go on using religious pretexts to avoid paying tribute. God has his rights, distinct from those of the prince. You shall obey Caesar: the coinage which you use in your commerce was struck by Caesar's order: if he is your sovereign, recognize his sovereignty by paying to him the tribute he imposes.

Thus the tributes which one pays to the prince are a recognition of supreme authority; and one cannot refuse them without rebellion.

St. Paul teaches this expressly: "The prince is God's minister to thee, for good, the avenger of evil acts. Wherefore be subject of necessity, not only for wrath, but also for conscience' sake. For therefore also you pay tribute. For they are the ministers of God, serving unto this purpose. Render therefore to all men their dues. Tribute, to whom tribute is due: custom, to whom custom; fear, to whom fear; honor, to whom honor."

One sees by these words of the apostle that one must pay tribute to the prince religiously and in good conscience, just as one must render him the honour and the subjection which is due his minister.[17]

And reason [also] makes it clear that all [the members of] the state must contribute to the public necessities which the prince provides.

Without this he can neither support nor defend individuals, nor the state itself. The kingdom will suffer, and individuals will perish in the ruins of the state. Such that, in truth, tribute is nothing else than a small part of one's goods, which one pays to the prince in order to give him the means of saving everything.

4th Proposition
The respect, fidelity and obedience which one owes to kings, cannot be changed on any pretext

That is to say that one must always respect and always serve them, whoever they be, good or bad. "Servants, be subject to your masters,

[16] Matt. 22:17–21.   [17] Rom. 13:4–7.

not only to the good and gentle, but also to the hard and regrettable."[18]

The state is in peril and the public peace is no longer secure, if anyone is permitted to rise up against princes for any reason whatsoever.

The sacred unction is upon them; and the high ministry which they exercise in the name of God protects them from every insult.

We have seen David not only refuse to plot against the life of Saul, but tremble at having dared to cut the hem of his garment, though this was part of a good plan. "God forbid that I should raise my hand against the Lord's anointed. After which David's heart struck him, because he had cut off the hem of Saul's robe."[19]

The words of St. Augustine on this passage are remarkable. "You will object against me," he said to the Donatist Bishop Petilian, "that he who is not innocent cannot be possessed of holiness. I ask of you, if Saul was not possessed of sanctity in virtue of his consecration and the royal unction, what was it in him that caused David to venerate him? For it is because of this holy and sacred unction, that he honored him during his lifetime and avenged his death. And he trembled, heart-struck, when he cut the hem of the robe of this unjust king. You see, then, that Saul, who was not innocent, nonetheless had sanctity: not a holy life, but the sanctity of the divine sacrament, which is holy even in evil men."[20]

He calls sacramental the royal unction: either because he (with all the Fathers) gives this name to all sacred ceremonies, or more particularly because the royal unction of kings, among the ancient [Jewish] people, was a sacred sign instituted by God, to make them capable of their charge, and to pre-figure the unction of Jesus Christ himself.

But what is still more important is that St. Augustine here recognizes, following Scripture, a sanctity which is inherent in the royal character, which cannot be effaced by any crime whatsoever.

It is, he says, this sanctity which David – unjustly pursued to the death by Saul, though himself sanctified to succeed him – respected in a prince reproved by God. For David knew that it is for God alone to do justice to princes; and that it is for men to respect the prince as long as it pleases God to preserve him.

We see too that Samuel, after having declared to Saul that God had

---

[18] 1 Pet. 2:18.   [19] 1 Kings 24:6–7.
[20] St. Augustine, Lib. I cont. Petil., c. XLVIII, 112.

rejected him, did not fail to honor him. "And Saul said to Samuel: I have sinned because I have transgressed the commandment of the Lord . . . But now bear, I beseech thee, my sin, and return with me, that I may adore the Lord. And Samuel said to Saul: I will not return with thee, because thou hast rejected the word of the Lord, and the Lord hath rejected thee from being king over Israel. And Samuel turned about to go away; but Saul laid hold upon the skirt of his mantle, and it rent. And Samuel said to him: The Lord hath rent the kingdom of Israel from thee this day, and hath given it to thy neighbor who is better than thee. But the triumpher in Israel will not spare, and will not be moved to repentance: for he is not a man that he should repent. I have sinned, answered Saul, yet honor me now before the ancients of my people, and before Israel, and return with me, that I may adore the Lord thy God. So Samuel turned again after Saul, and Saul adored the Lord."[21]

One cannot tell a prince more clearly of his reprobation; but in the end Samuel let himself be swayed, and consented to honor Saul before the great and the people: showing us by this example that the public good does not permit one to expose the prince to contempt.

Roboam treated the people harshly; but the revolt of Jeroboam and of the ten tribes who followed him – though permitted by God in punishment of the sins of Solomon – did not fail to be treated with detestation in the whole of Scripture, which declared that in revolting against the house of David, they were revolting against God, who ruled through that house.[22]

All the prophets who lived under evil kings – Eliah and Eliseus under Achab and under Jezebel in Israel, Isaiah under Achaz and under Manasses, Jeremiah under Joachim, under Jechonias, under Sedecias – in a word, all the prophets under so many impious and wicked kings, neither failed in obedience nor inspired rebellion, but rather always submission and respect.

We have just heard Jeremiah, after the ruin of Jerusalem and the complete overturning of the throne of the kings of Judah, speaking still with deep respect of his king Sedecias: "The breath of our life, the anointed of the Lord, is taken in our sins: to whom we said: Under thy shadow we shall live among the Gentiles."[23]

Good subjects did not take themselves to be relieved of the respect

[21] 1 Kings 15:24–31.   [22] 2 Par. 13:5–8.   [23] Thren. 4:20.

which they owed their king, even after his kingdom was overturned, and he was taken captive with his whole people. They respected, even in chains (and after the ruin of the kingdom), the sacred character of royal authority.

5th Proposition
Open impiety, and even persecution, do not free subjects from the obedience which they owe princes

The royal dignity is holy and sacred even in pagan princes: we have seen that Cyrus is called by Isaiah "the anointed of the Lord."[24]

Such were the pride and impiety of Nabuchodonosor that he strove to be the equal of God, and sought to put to death those who refused him sacrilegious rites; yet Daniel said to him: "Thou, O king, art a king of kings; for the God of heaven hath given thee a kingdom, power, and strength, and glory."[25]

This is why God's people prayed for the lives of Nabuchodonosor and of Belshazzar,[26] and of Ahasuerus.[27]

Ahab and Jezebel executed all the prophets of the Lord: Elijah lamented this before the Lord,[28] but always remained obedient.

At this time the prophets wrought amazing miracles to preserve the king and the kingdom.[29]

Elisha did the same under Jehoram, the son of Ahab, who was as impious as his father.[30]

Nothing has ever equaled the impiety of Manasseh, who sinned and caused Judah to sin before the Lord, whose worship he sought to abolish, persecuting the faithful servants of God and making Jerusalem run with their blood.[31] And yet Isaiah and the holy prophets who reproached him for his crimes never aroused the least rebellion against him.

This doctrine has been maintained in the Christian religion.

It was under Tiberius, not only a pagan but also an evil man, that our Lord said to the Jews: "Render unto Caesar that which is Caesar's."[32]

St. Paul appealed to Caesar,[33] and recognized his power.

He ordered prayers to be said for the Emperors,[34] although the

[24] Isa. 45:1. [25] Dan. 2:37. [26] Bar. 1:11. [27] 1 Esdr. 6:10.
[28] 3 Kings 19:10–14. [29] 3 Kings 20. [30] 4 Kings 3; 6; 7.
[31] 4 Kings 21:2,3,16. [32] Matt. 22:21. [33] Acts 25:10–12. [34] 1 Tim. 2:1–2.

The duties of subjects

emperor reigning at that time was Nero, the most impious and wicked of all men.

His reason for ordering the prayer was the need for public tranquillity, which requires that all live together in peace, even under wicked and persecuting princes.

He and St. Peter commanded the faithful to obey the powers that be.[35] We have seen their words; and have also seen which were the powers under whose forms the apostles bade the faithful respect the authority of God.

Because of this apostolic doctrine the first Christians, though persecuted for three hundred years, never raised the least opposition within the Empire. We learn their sentiments from Tertullian and see them continued throughout the history of the Church.

They continued to pray for the emperors even in the midst of the torments to which they were unjustly condemned. "Be of good courage, O worthy judges," said Tertullian, "and tear from the Christians a soul which bursts forth with praise of the Emperor."[36]

Constantius, the son of Constantine the Great, although protector of the Arians and persecutor of the orthodox, found the Church unshakably loyal.

His successor, Julian the Apostate, who restored the pagan cults proscribed by his predecessors, found the Christians no less faithful and no less zealous in his service in spite of this, so well were they able to separate the prince's impiety from the sacred dignity of his sovereign majesty.

Many heretical emperors followed: Valens, Justin, Zeno, Basiliscus, Anastasius, Heraclius, Constantius. Though they deposed orthodox bishops and even Popes, and deluged the Church with bloodshed and massacre, they never saw their authority questioned or undermined by the Catholics.

In fine, for seven hundred years there was not a single example of disobedience to the emperor on religious pretexts. In the eighth century the whole empire remained faithful to Leo the Isaurian, the leader of the Iconoclasts and persecutor of the faithful. Under his son, Constantine Copronymus, who inherited his heresy and violence as well as his crown, the faithful in the East offered only their patience in opposition to his persecution. But during the decline of the Empire, when the Caesars were barely able to defend the Orient into

---

[35] Rom. 13:5; 1 Pet. 2:13,14,17,18. [36] *Apol.* 30.

which they had retreated, Rome was forced to separate itself from the emperors, after having been abandoned for two hundred years to the fury of the Lombards, and having been forced to seek the protection of the Franks [*des Français*].

Rome endured her sufferings for long before taking this extreme course, and only embraced it after the emperors had come to regard the capital of their empire as a land left to abandonment and exposed to invasion.

6th Proposition
Subjects have nothing to oppose to the violence of princes but respectful remonstrances, without mutiny and without murmurings, together with prayers for their conversion

When God wanted to deliver the Israelites from the tyranny of Pharaoh, he did not permit them to proceed by mere *de facto* means against a king whose inhumanity to them was unheard of. They asked with respect, its just complaints by permitted means. Pharaoh, desert.

We have seen that princes must listen to individuals: how much more then must they listen to a whole people, which brings to them, with respect, its just complaints by permitted means. Pharoah, hardened and tyrannical as he was, at least took care to listen to the Israelites. He listened to Moses and Aaron.[37] He received in audience "the officers of the children of Israel, who came to complain to him with loud cries, saying: Why dealest thou so with thy servants?"[38]

Let it then be permitted to an oppressed people to have recourse to the prince through his magistrates and by legitimate paths: but let it always be with respect.

Remonstrances which are full of bitterness and murmuring are the beginning of a sedition which must not be suffered. Thus the Israelites murmured against Moses, and never offered him a quiet remonstrance.[39]

Moses never ceased to listen to them, to soften them, to pray for them, and gave a memorable example of the goodness that princes must exercise toward their peoples; but God, to establish order, visited great punishments on these seditious people.

When I say that these remonstrances must be respectful, I mean

---

[37] Exod. 5:45.   [38] Ibid., 15.   [39] Num. 11; 13; 14; 20; 21.

that they must truly be so, and not only in appearance, like those of Jeroboam and the ten tribes, who said to Roboam: "Thy father laid a grievous yoke upon us: take off a little . . . of his most heavy yoke, and we will serve thee."[40]

There was in these remonstrances some outward appearance of respect, in that they asked only a small diminution and promised to be faithful. But to make their fidelity depend on the favor they were asking was the beginning of mutiny.

One sees nothing like this in the remonstrances which the persecuted Christians made to the [Roman] emperors. Everything was submissive, everything was modest: God's truth was stated with freedom, but these speeches were so far from using seditious terms that even today one cannot read them without being brought to obedience.

The Empress Justine, mother and tutor of Valentinian II, wanted to oblige St. Ambrose to give a church to the Arians whom she protected, in the city of Milan, residence of the Emperor. The whole people united with its bishop, and assembling at the church awaited the outcome of this affair. St. Ambrose never deviated from the modesty of a subject and a bishop. He made his remonstrances to the Emperor: "Do not believe," he told him, "that you have the power to take from God what is his. I cannot give you the church which you demand: but if you take it, I must not resist."[41] And again: "If the Emperor wants to have the goods of the Church, he can take them; none of us will oppose this: let him take them from us, if he wills; I do not give them, but I do not refuse them."[42]

"The Emperor," he added, "is in the Church; but not above the Church. A good emperor, far from rejecting the help of the Church, seeks it out. We say these things with respect; but we feel obliged to set them out with freedom."[43]

He kept the assembled people in such a respectful condition, that not one insolent word escaped them. They prayed, they sang the praises of God, they awaited his help.

There is a resistance worthy of a Christian and of a bishop. However, since the people were assembled with their pastor, it was said at the palace that this holy pastor aspired to tyranny. He

---

[40] 3 Kings 12:4; 2 Par. 10:4.
[41] St. Ambrose, *Sermo contra Aurentium de Bascilicis tradendis*, Epist. XXI.16.22.
[42] Ibid., 33.   [43] Ibid., 36.

answered: "I have a defense: but in the prayers of the poor. These blind and lame men, these cripples and ancients, are stronger than the most courageous soldiers."[44] See the forces of a bishop, see his army!

He had other arms still: his patience, and the prayers which he made to God. "Since they call my action a tyranny," he said, "I do have arms: I have the power to offer my body in sacrifice. We have our tyranny and our power. The power of a bishop is his weakness. I am strong when I am weak, as St. Paul said."[45]

While awaiting the violence with which the Church was threatened, the holy bishop was at the altar, asking of God with tears that no blood be spilled, or at least that God should be content with his. "I began," he says, "to weep bitterly in offering the sacrifice: praying God to help us in such a way that no blood would be shed in the cause of the Church: or at least that no more than mine should be spilled, either among the people or even among the impious."[46]

God listened to such ardent prayers: the Church was victorious, and it cost the blood of no one.

Only a little later, Justine and her son, abandoned by nearly everyone, had recourse to St. Ambrose, and found faithfulness and zeal for their service only in this bishop, who had opposed their plans in the cause of God and of the Church.

This is what respectful remonstrances can achieve: this is what prayers can achieve. Thus did Queen Esther: having conceived a plan to sway her husband Assuerius (who had resolved to sacrifice all the Jews to the vengeance of Aman), she said to Mordechai: "Go, and gather together all the Jews whom thou shalt find in Susan, and pray ye for me. Neither eat nor drink for three days and three nights: and I with my handmaids will fast in like manner, and then I will go in to the king, against the law, not being called, and expose myself to death and to danger."[47]

When she appeared before the king, "the burning eyes of this prince had shown the wrath of his heart . . . but God changed the king's spirit into mildness, remembering the prayers of Esther and of the Jews."[48] And the Jews were delivered through the queen.

Thus when the prince of the apostles was made a prisoner by Herod, "the whole Church prayed for him without respite."[49] And

---

[44] Ibid., Epistl. XXI, 33. [45] Ibid., Epistl. XXIII.
[46] Ibid., Epistl. v. [47] Esther 4:16.
[48] Esther 15:10–11. [49] Acts 12:5.

God sent his angel to deliver him. These are the arms of the Church: vows and persevering prayers.

St. Paul, a prisoner for Jesus Christ, had only this help and these arms. "But withal prepare me also a lodging: For I hope that through your prayers I shall be given unto you."[50]

Indeed he left prison, "and was delivered out of the mouth of the lion."[51] Thus he called Nero, the enemy not just of Christians, but of the whole human race.

If God does not listen to the prayers of his faithful, if in order to test and to punish his children he permits persecution to warm against them, they must then remember that Jesus Christ has sent them "as sheep in the midst of wolves."[52]

There is a doctrine which is truly holy, truly worthy of Jesus Christ and of his disciples.

Article III

Two difficulties drawn from Scripture: David and the Maccabees

1st Proposition
The conduct of David does not favor rebellion

David, persecuted by Saul, did not content himself with taking flight: rather "he assembled his brothers and his relatives, and all that were in distress and oppressed with debt, and under affliction of mind; and he became their prince, and there were with him about four hundred men."[1]

He remained in this condition in Judah, armed against Saul who had declared him his enemy, and who pursued him as such with all the forces of Israel.[2]

Finally he retired into the kingdom of Achis, King of the Philistines, with whom he treated, and obtained the city of Siceleg.[3]

Achis so regarded David as the sworn enemy of the Israelites, that

---

[50] Philem. 22.   [51] 2 Tim. 4:17.   [52] Matt. 10:16.
[1] 1 Kings 22:1–2.   [2] Ibid., 6–7; 24:2–3; 26:1–4.   [3] Ibid., 27:6.

he led him with himself in going to combat them, and said to David: "I will appoint thee to guard my life for ever."[4]

Indeed David and his people marched in the train with Achis, and he did not withdraw from the army of the Philistines until the satraps, who distrusted him, obliged the king to dismiss him.[5]

It seems that he withdrew regretfully. "But what have I done, he said to Achis, and what hast thou found in me thy servant, from the day that I have been in thy sight until this day, that I may not go and fight against the enemies of my lord the king?"[6]

To be armed against his king, to treat with his enemies, to go to war with them against his people – there is everything that can make a subject a rebel.

But to justify David, one need only consider all the circumstances of the story.

He was not a subject like the others; he was chosen by God to succeed Saul, and Samuel had already consecrated him.[7]

Thus the public good, as much as his individual interest, obliged him to preserve his life, which Saul wanted unjustly to deprive him of.

His intention, however, was not to remain in Israel, with the four hundred men who followed his orders. "And David departed into Maspha of Moab with his father and his mother . . . until it should please God to declare his will to him."[8]

This was an order of God brought by the prophet Gad,[9] who obliged him to remain in the land of Judah, where he was better loved (since this was his tribe).

Furthermore he never engaged in any combat against Saul, nor against his people. He fled from desert to desert, solely to keep from being taken captive.

Being in Carmel, in the richest country of the Holy Land and in the midst of the estates of Nabal, the most powerful man in the country, he never took so much as a lamb from an immense flock; and far from vexing Naval, he defended him against a race of enemies.[10]

However cruel may have been the persecution raised against him, he never lost the love which he had for his prince, whose person he always regarded as sacred.

"He knew that the Philistines were attacking the city of Ceila, and were pillaging the environs. He went there with his men; he cut the

---

[4] 1 Kings 28:1–2.   [5] 1 Kings 29.   [6] Ibid., 8.   [7] 1 Kings 16:12–13.
[8] 1 Kings 22:34.   [9] Ibid., 5.   [10] 1 Kings 25:15–16.

Philistines to pieces; he took their baggage-trains and their loot; he saved the people of Ceila."[11]

"And the men that were with David, who opposed his plans, said to him: Behold we are in fear here in Judaea; how much more if we go to Ceila against the bands of the Philistines?"[12] But David's zeal prevailed over their fear.

It is thus that, though hounded to excess, he never lost the desire to serve his prince and his country.

It is true that in the end he went over to Achis, and treated with him. But though he had the dexterity to persuade this prince that he would go against the Jews,[13] in fact he took nothing except from the Amalecites and from other enemies of the people of God.

As for the city which King Achis gave him, he incorporated it into the kingdom of Judah;[14] and the treaty which he made with the enemy profited his country.

If, in order not to defy Achis, he followed him when he marched against Saul; if for the same reason he claimed to withdraw only regretfully, this was simply the same dexterity which had [earlier] saved his life.

One must hold it as certain that, in this last encounter, he would no more have been able to fight against his own people, than he had done hitherto. He was at the back of the camp with the King of the Philistines,[15] to whom it seemed that the custom of these peoples forbad them to risk themselves.

To know what he would have done in the melee, if combat had actually reached King Achis – this is what one cannot guess. These great men, abandoned to divine Providence, learn at the last moment what they are to do; and after pushing human prudence as far as it can go, they find, when they have reached its limit, a divine aid which, against all hope, extricates them from difficulties in which it seems they must be inevitably shrouded.

2nd Proposition
The wars of the Maccabees do not authorize rebellion

After being conquered by the Assyrians, the Jews were subject in turn to the power of the Persians, of Alexander the Great and finally of the kings of Syria.

---

[11] 1 Kings 23:1–5.   [12] Ibid., 3,4,5.   [13] 1 Kings 27.
[14] Ibid., 6.   [15] 1 Kings 29:2.

David and the Maccabees

They remained in this condition for about three hundred and fifty years, and for one hundred and fifty of these they accepted the kings of Syria, until the persecution of Antiochus IV Epiphanes caused them to take up arms against him under the leadership of the Maccabees. For a long time they made war, during the course of which they treated with the Romans and Greeks against the kings of Syria, their legitimate lords, whose yoke they finally overthrew and established princes of their own nation.

Here is a manifest rebellion: if it is not, this instance would seem to show that a tyrannical government, and above all a violent persecution for the sake of true religion, exempts a people from the obedience they owe to their princes.

It is not to be doubted that the war of the Maccabees was just, for God himself approved it: but if we examine the actual circumstances of the event, we see that this example does not sanction later revolts for religious motives.

The true religion until the coming of the Messiah was to be preserved in the race of Abraham and by succession through the blood line.

It was to be preserved in Judaea, in Jerusalem, in the Temple, the place chosen by God for the offering of sacrifices and for rites not permitted anywhere else.

The very essence of this religion thus required that the children of Abraham should continue for ever, and in the land given to their fathers, to live there according to the law of Moses, the observances of which had been freely allowed by the kings of Persia and the other rulers down to the time of Antiochus.

This family of Abraham living in the Holy Land were to be removed from there only once, at the express command of God, but not into eternal banishment.

On the contrary, the prophet Jeremiah who had brought the people the commandment to go to Babylon,[16] where it was God's will that they should suffer the pain due their crimes, at the same time promised that after three score years and ten of captivity they would be reestablished in their own land, there to observe the law of Moses as before, and to practice their religion as usual in the rebuilt Temple in Jerusalem.[17]

The people thus reestablished were to live there until the coming of

---

[16] Jer. 21:7–9.
[17] Jer. 25:12; 27:11–12; 29:10–14; 30:3.

Christ; at which time God would cause a new people to arise, no longer of the race of Abraham, but of all the nations of the world, and would scatter the Jews unfaithful to their Messiah in captivity throughout the world.

But before this the Messiah was to be born of this people, and was to begin among the Jews in Jerusalem that Church which was to fill the whole universe. This great mystery of religion is attested by all the prophets, and it is not the place here to rehearse all the passages [where they do so].

On this basis, it may be seen that by the extinction of the race of Abraham, or by their expulsion from their country at the time of the kings of Syria, religion would be betrayed and the worship of God destroyed.

It only remains now to examine Antiochus' intentions.

He commanded that the Jews should forsake their law to live after the manner of the Gentiles, sacrificing to the same idols and giving up their temple, which he desecrated by erecting the statue of Olympian Zeus on the altar of God.[18]

He decreed the punishment of death for those who disobeyed.[19]

This he carried out: all Judaea ran with the blood of its sons.[20]

He assembled all his forces "to destroy the Israelites and the remains of Jerusalem, and to wipe out from Judaea the memory of the people of God, there to establish strangers, and to parcel out the land by lot."[21]

He had resolved to sell to the Gentiles all who escaped death; and the merchants of the neighboring peoples flocked with money to buy them.[22]

It was in this desperate extremity that Judas Maccabaeus took up arms with his brothers and what remained of the Jewish people. When they saw the pitiless king directing all his power to "the total ruin of the nation, they said to one another: 'let us not suffer our people to be destroyed, but let us fight for our country and our religion, lest it perish with us.' "[23]

If subjects owe nothing further to a king who abdicates his kingship and completely gives up the government, what are we to think of a ruler who would plan to spill the blood of all his subjects and then,

---

[18] 1 Macc. 1:43–57.
[19] Ibid., 52.
[20] Ibid., 60–64; 2 Macc. 6:8–10.
[21] 1 Macc. 3:35–36.
[22] Ibid., 41; 2 Macc. 8:11,14,34,36.
[23] 2 Macc. 8:42–43.

once tired of massacres, would sell the rest to strangers? Can he renounce more clearly his intention to have them for his subjects, or proclaim himself more flagrantly to be no more the king and father, but the enemy of all his people?

This is what Antiochus did towards the Jews, who saw themselves not only abandoned, but exterminated in a body by their king, although they were innocent of any fault, as Antiochus himself was forced to admit in the end. "I remember the wrongs I did in Jerusalem, and the unjust commandments that I made to annihilate all the inhabitants of Judaea."[24]

But the Jews were even better justified, because in accordance with the dispensation of the time and of their people, their religion would perish with them; and for them to give up their land was to give up their religion as well. They could not therefore allow themselves to be sold or carried off or massacred: in this case the law of God manifestly enjoined them to resist.

God also did not fail to reveal his will to them, by miraculous victories and by the strict command which Judas received when he saw the spirit of the prophet Jeremiah "who placed a golden sword in his hands, saying: 'receive this sacred sword sent of God, in the knowledge that with its aid you shall overthrow the enemies of Israel.' "[25]

It is for God to choose the means by which his people shall be preserved. When Assuerus, misled by the wiles of Haman, wished to destroy the whole Jewish people, God prevented this impious design by changing the king's heart by means of his queen Esther, for the king had been drawn into this crime through unfortunate weakness rather than stubborn wickedness. But for the proud Antiochus who openly made war against heaven God prepared a more terrible downfall, and filled his people with a courage against which no wealth, strength, or numbers could be more than a forlorn hope.

God gave them so many victories that finally the kings of Syria made peace with them, recognizing the princes they had chosen from among themselves, and treating them as friends and brothers, so that all the sanctions of legitimate authority combined to establish them.[26]

---

[24] 1 Macc. 15:12.   [25] Ibid., 15–16.
[26] 1 Macc. 11: 24–31; 14:38–42; 15:1–2.

SEVENTH BOOK

On the particular duties of royalty

First Article

General division of the prince's duties

The subjects have learned their obligations. We have given the princes the first idea of theirs. We must go into detail; and in order that nothing be omitted, let us make an exact allotment of these duties.

Government's end is the good and the preservation of the state.

To preserve it, it is first necessary to maintain a good constitution internally.

Secondly, to profit from the help which the state is given.

Thirdly, the state must be spared the difficulties by which it is threatened.

It is thus that the human body preserves itself: by maintaining a healthy constitution; by making use of the aid which human weakness must rely on; by obtaining suitable remedies for the problems and the illnesses which may attack it.

The healthy constitution of the state's body consists in two things: religion and justice. These are the internal, constitutive principles of states. By the one, God is given his due; by the other, men are given what suits them.

Essential to royalty and necessary for government are arms, counsel, and riches or finance, under which trade and taxes will be spoken of. We shall finally conclude with precautions against the drawbacks which accompany royalty and the remedies which can be brought to bear upon them.

The prince knows all his individual duties when he knows how to do all these things. This is what we shall teach him in the books that follow. Let us begin to explain to him what he owes to religion.

Article II

On religion, inasmuch as it is the good of nations and of civil society

1st Proposition
In the ignorance and corruption of mankind, a few principles of religion have always been preserved

It is true that St. Paul, speaking to the peoples of Lycaonia, said "that God had let all the nations proceed in their own paths,"[1] as if he had abandoned them entirely to themselves and to their own thoughts regarding the worship of God, leaving them no guiding principle. He adds, however, in the same place, "that he did not allow himself to go without witness, lavishing gifts from heaven, giving rain and weather proper for bearing fruit, filling our hearts with fitting nourishment and joy."[2] This he would not have told these ignorant people, if despite their barbarism, they had retained no idea of divine power and goodness.

These barbarians also demonstrate a knowledge of the deity, to whom they wished to make sacrifice.[3] And this kind of tradition of divinity and sacrifice, and the worship established to recognize it, is found from the earliest times so universally among nations possessing some form of organization, that it can only have come from Noah and his descendants.

Thus, although the same St. Paul, speaking to the Gentiles converted to the faith, told them "that they were previously without God in this world,"[4] he does not mean that they were absolutely without a deity, since elsewhere he reproaches the Gentiles for "allowing themselves to be drawn to the worship of deaf and dumb idols."[5]

If, then, he also reproaches the Athenians[6] for their times of ignorance, when they lived without knowledge of God, it is simply to tell them that they had only a confused knowledge of God, riddled with error, although they were not entirely destitute of the knowledge

---

[1] Acts 14:15.   [2] Ibid., 16.   [3] Ibid., 10–12.
[4] Eph. 2:12.   [5] 1 Cor. 12:2.   [6] Acts 17:30.

of God, since they adored him unknowingly,[7] and in their ignorance paid him some sort of worship.

Similar ideas of the deity are found throughout the world, from ancient times;[8] this is why there is no race without religion, at least among those which are not absolutely barbaric, without civility and without polity.

2nd Proposition
There was something solid and inviolable about the religious ideas these people had

"For cross to the island of Cethim, said Jeremiah, or send to Cedar (the most distant countries of the East and the West): carefully consider what is happening there, and see if a single of these nations has changed its gods, even though they are not gods."[9] These principles of religion were therefore reputed to be inviolable; and it is also for this reason that it has been so difficult to convert these nations.

3rd Proposition
These principles of religion, although turned to idolatry and error, sufficed to establish a stable state and government

Otherwise, it would follow that there would be no genuine and legitimate authority outside the true religion and the true Church. This is contrary to all the passages where it has been seen that the government of empires, although idolatrous and infidel, was holy, sacred, ordained by God and binding in conscience.

The sanctity of the oath, recognized by all nations, proves the truthfulness of our proposal.

St. Paul observes two things in the sanctity of the oath.[10] One, that something greater than oneself is sworn by. The other is that something immutable is sworn by. From this the same apostle concluded "that the oath creates the final strengthening among men, the last and final decision of affairs."[11]

A third condition must still be added: that one swears by a power

---

[7] Ibid., 23. [8] Cicero, *De natura deorum* II.IV.12.
[9] Jer. 2:10–11. [10] Heb. 6:13,16–18.
[11] Ibid., 16.

which penetrates the most secret of consciences; it cannot be deceived, nor can the punishment for perjury be avoided.

This being admitted, and the oath being established among all nations, this religion simultaneously establishes the greatest possible security among men, who assure one another by what they judge most sovereign, most stable, and which alone makes itself felt by conscience.

This is why it has been established that in two cases where human justice is impotent – one being when it is necessary to negotiate between two equal powers which have nothing above them, and the other being when it is necessary to judge hidden things and the only witness or arbitrator is conscience – the only way to make matters certain is by the sanctity of the oath.

For this it is not absolutely necessary to swear by the true God: it is enough that each swear by the God he recognizes. Thus, as St. Augustine remarks,[12] treaties with barbarians were strengthened by oaths to their gods: *Juratione barbarica*. The Father proves this by the oath that strengthened the peace treaty between Jacob and Laban, each swearing by his God: Jacob by the true God, "who had been feared and revered by his father Isaac."[13] The idolatrous Laban swore by his own gods, as it will seem to those who well understand it.

It is thus that religion, true or false, establishes good faith between men; for although it is an impiety for an idolater to swear by false gods, there is nothing blasphemous about the good faith of an oath that strengthens a treaty: on the contrary, it is in itself sacred and holy, as the same doctor teaches in the same place. That is why God has not failed to be the avenger of false oaths among infidels, because even though oaths to false gods are an abomination before him, he is no less the protector of good faith, which it is hoped will be established by this means.

We have seen that nations which do not know the true God have not failed to strengthen their laws through the oracles of their gods, seeking to establish justice and authority, that is to say tranquillity and peace, by the most sacred means to be found among men.

By this they maintained that their laws and their magistrates became sacred and holy. And even God did not disdain punishing the blasphemy of peoples which profaned the temples they believed to be

---

[12] St. Augustine, *Epist. XLVII ad Public.*, 2.
[13] Gen. 31:53.

holy and the religions they believed to be genuine, because he judges each by his conscience.

If it were asked what must be said of a state where public authority was established without religion, it would be clear from the beginning that chimerical questions need not be answered. Such states never existed. Peoples without religion are, at the same time, without organization, without genuine subordination, and are entirely primitive. Men who are not bound in conscience cannot protect one another. In empires where the histories report that scholars and magistrates despise religion, and have no god in their hearts, the people are driven by other principles, and they have public worship.

If, nevertheless, some [states] were to be found where the government was established without any religion – though these do not exist and it seems cannot exist – the good of society would have to be preserved as much as possible. This state would be better than absolute anarchy, which is a state of war of all against all.

4th Proposition
Because the true religion is founded upon sure principles, it makes state constitutions more stable and solid

Although it is true that false religions, since they possess elements which are good and true (through their recognition of a deity to whom human affairs are subject), could be absolutely sufficient for the constitution of states, they nevertheless always leave doubt and uncertainty in the heart of conscience, which does not allow the establishment of a perfect stability.

One is ashamed in one's heart of the fables of which false religions are composed, and of what one sees in the writings of the pagan sages. If the only evil were worshiping dumb and unfeeling objects, such as stars, the earth and the elements, or believing the deity representable, attaching virtue to wood, stone, and metal, and worshiping idols, that is to say the work of one's hands, it is so senseless and so low that one cannot help but blush inside. This is why the pagan sages believed none of it, although externally they conformed to popular customs, for which St. Paul reproached them.[14]

Herein lies irreligion; and atheism takes root easily in such reli-

---

[14] Rom. 1:20.

gions, as is shown by the example of the Epicureans, with whom St. Paul argued.[15]

This sect acknowledged gods only in speech and out of prudence, to spare themselves from hatred and public punishment. But everyone knew, moreover, that the gods which the Epicureans acknowledged, uncaring in human matters, powerless and without providence, did no good and in no way supported public faith. Nevertheless they were tolerated, even though at base their deism was a true atheism, and though their doctrine which flattered the senses, won a public advantage among those who pride themselves on cleverness.

The Stoics, who opposed them, and with whom St. Paul also argued,[16] did not have an opinion which was more favorable to the deity, since they made a god of their sage, and even preferred him to Jupiter.

Thus, false religions had nothing that could endure. Also, they are made up only of blind zeal, seditious, turbulent, selfish, full of ignorance, confused and without order or reason, as seen in the confused and tumultuous congregation of the Ephesians, and in the senseless outcries in favor of their great Diana.[17] This is far removed from the proper order and reasonable stability which constitutes states; it is, however, the inevitable result of error. The solid foundation of states must be sought, then, in truth, which is the mother of peace; and truth is only to be found in the true religion.

Article III

That the true religion is known through perceptible marks

1st Proposition
The manifest mark is its antiquity

"Remember the old days: think of all the particular generations. Ask your father, and he shall tell you."[1] It is the witness Moses bore to all

[15] Acts 17:18.   [16] Ibid., 18.   [17] Acts 19:24,28,34.   [1] Deut. 32:7.

The true religion

the people in this last canticle which he left to them as the summary and eternal memorial of his instruction. From this he concluded: "Is it not God who is your father, who has possessed you, who has made you, who has created you?"[2] It is upon this that he founds religion.[3]

Solomon says the same thing: "Do not go beyond the limits your fathers have established."[4] Change nothing, invent nothing.

Jeremiah still acknowledged this great character in religion, to destroy the novelties the people were introducing. "Hold to the great paths," he said, "and inform yourselves of ancient ways, and which is the good way. March to it, and you shall find the solace and revival of your souls."[5]

All of this means that, from whatever perspective religion is examined, at any time, one will always see one's ancestors, and even one's father, before himself. One will always find established boundaries, which it is not permitted to go beyond. One will always see the beaten path before himself, in which one never goes astray.

The apostles gave the Christian Church the same character. "O Timothy (O man of God, O pastor, O preacher, whoever you may be, and from whatever time), protect the trust which has been imparted to you (something which has been left to you, which you will always find completely established in the Church), avoiding profane novelties in speech." The apostle repeats this twice.[6]

The means for this, which the apostles left to the Church, is this, which St. Paul points out to the same Timothy: "My son, strengthen yourself through the grace that is in Jesus Christ. And what you have heard from me in the presence of several witnesses, leave it behind and entrust it to the faithful men capable of telling it to others."[7]

Jesus Christ had proposed the same means, and had rendered it eternal by telling his apostles, and through them their successors, according to the ministry he entrusted to them: "Go, teach, baptize; I am with you, every day (unceasingly), to the end of time,"[8] because he promises that there will never be a break in the succession of the outside ministry. This is further confirmed by this statement: "You are Peter, and on this rock I shall build my Church, and the gates of Hell shall not prevail against it."[9] From this it follows that, whatever the time or the state, a solid Church will always be found. Jesus Christ

---

[2] Ibid., 7.   [3] Ibid., 6.   [4] Prov. 22:28.   [5] Jer. 6:16.
[6] 1 Tim. 6:20; 2 Tim. 6:16.   [7] 2 Tim. 2:1–2.
[8] Matt. 28:19–20.   [9] Matt. 16:18.

shall always be with his pastors, and consequently the right doctrine will always be established and passed from hand to hand. Because of this, one will say at all times: I believe in the Catholic Church. And always with St. Paul: "If someone tells you, and gives you as the gospel something other than what you have received, let him be anathematized."[10]

On this basis, in whatever state and at whatever time after Jesus Christ one finds oneself, one will always possess the truth, going forward in the path beaten by our fathers, revering the boundaries they have established, and questioning them about what they believed. By this means, step by step, one will find the same Jesus Christ. Having found him, one will still ask his father, and one will discover that he believed in the same God, and awaited the coming of the same Christ, without the occurrence of other changes between yesterday and today, if not that of waiting yesterday, that which today one believes has come. This makes the apostle say: "God whom I serve, according to the faith left to me by my ancestors."[11] And speaking to Timothy: "Remember the faith which is in you, without lies and which first resided (as in a permanent place and in an ordinary residence) in your grandfather and in your mother Eunice."[12] And yet more generally: "Jesus Christ was yesterday, and today he is for all time." From this the same apostle concluded: "Do not let yourself be carried away by changeable and foreign doctrines."[13]

By this means, after the succession of the Church which has its beginning in the apostles and in Jesus Christ, you come to that of the law and its pontiffs, which have their beginning in Moses and Aaron. It is there that Moses teaches us to further question our fathers; and one finds that they worshiped the God of Abraham, Isaac, and Jacob, who worshiped that of Melchisedech, who worshiped that of Sem and Noah, who worshiped that of Adam – when the memory of him was recent, the tradition entirely new, worship very well established and well known. In this way, at whatever given time, going back step by step, one comes to Adam and the beginning of the universe by a manifest series.

[10] Gal. 1:9. [11] 2 Tim. 1:3.
[12] Ibid., 5. [13] Heb. 13:8–9.

2nd Proposition
The manifest mark of all false religions is their innovation

To confound the idolatry of the kings of Judah, even in the darkest times – that of Achaz, Manasses, Amon, Joachaz, and his children, up to the last king, who was Sedecias – one need only say to them, with Moses: "Question your father, ask your ancestors."[14] And without having recourse to them and going back to the origin of forgotten stories, they only needed to be told: Ask Josiah, who is of recent memory: ask Ezechias, ask Manasses himself, whose deviations were the most extreme, and remember the penitence by which God made him return to the worship of his father, Ezechias. Before Ezechias and the time of Achaz, ask Ozias his father, his grandfather Joatham, and his great-grandfather Amasias. Ask Josaphat, ask Asa: see which religion they practiced. To confound Abiam and his father Roboam, son of Solomon, who went astray at the end, make them ask Solomon: if they object to his final actions, remind them of his earlier ones, when the wisdom of God was in him so visibly. Show them David, and Samuel, who anointed him, and Eli, under whom Samuel developed; and step by step all the judges up to Joshua, and immediately before Joshua, Moses himself. But Moses sends you back to your ancestors, and shows you only patriarchs, the memory of whom was new until Abraham, and the others we have mentioned.

It is true that in this succession there have often been poor examples: and this is why it is said of certain kings that they committed evil before the Lord, like Joachim and his successors: "This one committed evil before the Lord, as his fathers did."[15] And generally of the entire people: "They committed evil like their fathers, who did not want to obey the Lord."[16] However, through the succession of bad examples that one often received from one's recent fathers, it was always easy to disentangle those who kept the faith of the old fathers and those who abandoned it. Because of this, it was still said: "Ask your ancestors and the God of your fathers."

---

[14] Deut. 32:7.   [15] 4 Kings 23:32,37.   [16] 4 Kings 17:14.

3rd Proposition
The sequence of the priesthood makes this mark perceptible

The succession of the priesthood also marked the sequence of religion. The blood of Levi, once consecrated to this office, never stopped providing the temple and the altar with ministers. Aaron and his sons, descended from Levi, have always produced pontiffs and priests, and never was the succession of the priesthood interrupted in the smallest measure. And among the priests there were always some who preserved true worship, true sacrifices and the whole religion established by God through Moses. Witness "the priests, children of Zadok, who always preserved the ceremonies of my sanctuary, said the Lord, while the children of Israel and even those of Levi went astray."[17]

Everything that was sung in the Temple, the Psalms of David, and the others that the entire people knew by heart, the very Temple, the very altar, Passover, circumcision, and all the other legal observances, were witnessed by travelers. Everything called to mind David, Moses, Abraham, God, creator of all things, and always, step by step, such that one only needed to open one's eyes to recognize the succession of religion, completely manifest in constant deeds, and without any obstruction, provided only that one wanted to see.

The schism of Jeroboam had similar marks of innovation, for the memory of the Temple built by Solomon was still recent. It is no less obvious that Solomon had only followed the designs of his father. David had done nothing else but show, according to precepts so many times repeated by Moses, the place where the Lord wished to be served.

Thus Jeroboam and the schismatics who followed him had only to ask their fathers, and even to remember, because they had seen with their own eyes, under Solomon, and under David, at a time when the whole people was united in a single worship and when all Israel agreed that it was in its pureness the worship established by Moses, whose oracles were received by everyone.

Jeroboam himself knew perfectly well that Ahias, the Lord's prophet who had predicted that he would be king, served the God of his fathers and detested his golden calves. In his schism he continued to

---

[17] Ezek. 48:11.

consult him, and received harsh answers followed by a prompt effect.[18] It was well known to everyone that Jeroboam's golden calves were erected only by pure policy [*par une pure politique*], against the genuine maxims of religion, as it has been explained elsewhere. And finally, there was nothing more obvious than what Abia, son of Roboam, told the schismatics, to recall them to the unity of their brothers: "God (who has always been our king) still possesses the realm through the children of David. It is true that you have a great people among you, and the golden calves your new gods which Jeroboam has made."[19] "But you have rejected the Lord's priests, the children of Aaron and the Levites" (whom you yourselves recognize with us, and to whom you well know God has given the priesthood through Moses), "and you have made yourselves priests, like the other peoples of the earth" (without succession, without God's order). "The first to arrive is made a priest. For us, our Lord is God himself, whom we have not abandoned; and we continue to recognize the priests he has given us, who are the children of Aaron and the Levites, each in his station. Thus God is in our army with the priests he has established. Children of Israel, do not fight against the Lord, your God; that would be of no use to you."[20] To innovate in religion in such a manifest way was to fight openly against God, and to scorn all his monuments which still remained.

4th Proposition
This mark of innovation is indelible

Length of time did not erase this blemish. David and Solomon were still remembered, under whom all the tribes were united. Jeroboam, who had separated them, was no less distinctly remembered. Two or three hundred years after the schism, Ezechias still told them: "Children of Israel, return to the Lord, God of Abraham, Isaac and Jacob."[21] They were told to return to him, as were those who had been separated from him. "Do not be, he continued, like your fathers and brothers who have withdrawn from the God of their fathers."[22] They were taught to distinguish their recent fathers from the first fathers, from whom they had become separated. "Do not imitate your fathers, who have withdrawn from theirs. Follow the God of your

---

[18] 3 Kings 14:1ff.   [19] 2 Par. 13:8.   [20] Ibid., 9, 10, 12.
[21] 2 Par. 30:6.   [22] Ibid., 7.

fathers and return to the origin. Come to his sanctuary, which he has sanctified for all time."[23] It was not for a while that David and Solomon had built the Temple in execution of Moses' law. "Serve, then, the God of your fathers," the God of Solomon and David, who was uncontestably the God of Moses and Abraham.

The character of the schism lay in breaking this chain. This mark of innovation follows the schismatics from generation to generation, and a sin of this nature can never be erased.

5th Proposition
The same mark is given in order to recognize the schismatics separated from the Christian Church

This is what has happened to those who have created new sects in religion, as much among Christians as among Jews. The apostle St. Jude characterized them as "separating themselves":[24] and he expressly indicated that that was the common instruction which all the apostles had left to the Churches. "For you," he says, "my well-beloved, remember the words of the apostles' prediction: that deceivers would come lately, who would walk in their blasphemies according to their desires."[25] In order to know them without difficulty, here is their mark: "It is they, he adds, who divide themselves." It is an indelible blemish [*tache*]; and the apostles, who feared the seduction of the faithful by these deceivers, agreed to give them this perceptible character. They shall break with everyone; they shall renounce the religion they find established, they will separate themselves from it. They always have this sign of innovation on their brow, according to the apostles' prediction.

No heresy has escaped it, no matter what it may have done. Arians, Macedonians, Nestorians, Pelagians, Eutychians, all the others, in whatever century they may have appeared, near or far from us, carry in their name, which comes from that of their maker, the mark of their novelty. Jeroboam shall eternally be named, who broke off and made Israel sin. Schism is always known by its author. Time does not close the wound: and even if one looks only a little closely, the opening still seems fresh and bloody.

---

[23] Ibid., 8.   [24] Jude 19.   [25] Ibid., 17–19.

6th Proposition
It is not enough to preserve sound doctrine on the basis of faith: one must be united with the true Church everywhere and in all things

The Samaritans worshiped the true God, who was the God of Jacob; and they awaited the Messiah. The Samaritan declares both of these, when she says to the Savior: "Our fathers worshipped on this mountain."[26] And slightly later: "Christ shall come, and shall teach all things."[27] This doctrine, moreover, is known to have been common to the Samaritans and the people of God. Nevertheless, because they were separated from Jerusalem and from the Temple, without communicating with the true Church and the line of the people of God, this woman received this judgment from the mouth of the Son of God: "You worship what you do not know: as for us (as for us other Jews), we worship what we know, and salvation comes from the Jews."[28] Christ shall come from us; it is among us that he must be sought, and there is salvation only among the Jews.[29]

So it is with all schisms; and it is in vain that one thereby glories in having preserved the foundations of salvation.

7th Proposition
One must always return to the origin

No matter how long a schism may have existed, it shall never prescribe against truth. The schism of Samaria had its first origins in that of Jeroboam, and it had subsisted for almost a thousand years, when the Son of God damned it with the judgment we just heard.

The Chuteans, drawn from the Samaritans, had come into the world from the ten separate tribes that the Assyrians had chased from it.[30] Their natural religion was the worship of idols; but instructed by a preacher of the Israelites, they added to this something of the worship of God, depending upon whether the schismatics practiced it. Thus they took their place and succeeded them; but although they later corrected both their false worship of the Israelites and their personal idolatries, no longer worshiping any but the true God, all of this and the long time of their separation was useless; and Jesus

---

[26] John 4:20.   [27] Ibid., 25.   [28] Ibid., 22.
[29] Ibid., 22.   [30] 4 Kings 17:24ff.

Christ decided that there was no salvation for them unless they returned to the true line.

8th Proposition
The schism's origin is easily found

The knowledge of the origin of that of the Samaritans depended upon certain well-known facts, such as the story of Jeroboam and the first separation of the ten tribes after the reign of David and Solomon, where the entire people was united. This beginning shall never be forgotten: one would sooner forget one's mother and father than David and Solomon and Jeroboam; the latter had separated what the two others had preserved in the union which had always been kept before them.

This evil cannot be redressed. After a hundred generations, one still finds the beginning, that is to say, the falseness of this religion. What makes this beginning and the date of the schism manifest in all the separated sects that are, or ever were, is that there is always a point where one is at a loss, where one can go back no further. It was not this way with the true people, to whom the succession of the preachers and Levites bore witness: everything spoke for them, the Temple itself and the holy city, which they possessed for all times. But, on the contrary, the schismatics of Samaria could never establish their succession, nor return to the source, nor consequently erase the mark of breaking apart. This is why the Son of God pronounces against them the condemnation we have heard.

All schisms have the same mark. Although the priesthood or the Christian ministry does not follow the bloodline [*la trace du sang*], like that of the ancient people, the succession is no less assured. The pontiffs, or the bishops of Christianity, follow one another without interruption in the sees, or in doctrine; but the innovator, who changes the doctrine of his predecessor, will be noticed because of his innovation. Catechisms, rituals, prayer-books, the very temples and the altars, where his predecessor and he himself served God before innovating, shall bear witness against him. This is what made Christ say: "You worship what you do not know."[31] You do not know the origin, neither of religion nor of the alliance. "As for us (for the Jews

---

[31] John 4:22.

among whom I count myself), we worship what we know." We know its origin, back to Moses and Abraham: and salvation is only for us.

9th Proposition
A prince should use his authority to destroy false religions in his state

Thus Asa, thus Ezechias, thus Josiah reduced the idols their people worshiped to rubble.[32] It was of no importance to them that they were established by kings. They knocked down their temples and altars; they broke their vessels which served idolatry; they burned their sacred woods; they exterminated their priests and soothsayers; and they purged the earth of all these impurities.[33] Their zeal did not spare the most majestic people, or those who were closest to them, nor the most venerable things, which the people misused through false worship. From his mother Maacha, daughter of Absalom, Asa took away the dignity she aspired to give herself by presiding at the worship of an infamous god; and, to punish her for her blasphemy, he was compelled to strip her of the mark of royalty.[34] The bronze serpent, which Moses had erected in the desert by God's order, was religiously kept. This serpent, which was a prefiguring of Jesus Christ[35] and a monument of the miracles that God had brought about by this statue,[36] was precious to the entire people. But Ezechias did not fail to take it to pieces,[37] and he gave it a scornful name, because the people had made an idol of it and burned incense to it. Jehu is praised by God for putting the false prophets of Baal to death, who seduced the people, without allowing a single one to escape:[38] and in this he was only imitating the zeal of Elia.[39] Nabuchodonosor published an edict throughout his empire in which he recognized the glory of the God of Israel, and mercilessly condemned to death those who blasphemed his name.[40]

---

[32] 3 Kings 15:11–13; 4 Kings 18:4; 23:5ff.
[33] 2 Par. 14:2–5; 15:8; 34:1ff.
[34] 3 Kings 15:2,13; 2 Par. 15:16.
[35] John 3:14.   [36] Num. 31:9.
[37] 4 Kings 18:4.   [38] Ibid., 10:25,26,30.
[39] 3 Kings 18:40. [40] Dan. 3:96,98; 4:4ff.,34.

10th Proposition
One may employ strictness against those who observe false religions: but gentleness is preferable

"A prince is God's minister. It is not in vain that he carries the sword: whoever does evil should fear him as the avenger of his crime."[41] He is the protector of public tranquillity, which rests on religion. He must support his throne, whose foundation is religion, as we have seen.[42] Those who do not wish to put up with the prince's use of strictness in religious matters, on the grounds that religion should be free, are in blasphemous error. Otherwise it would be necessary to allow, in all subjects and in the entire state, idolatry, Mahommedanism, Judaism, any false religion, blasphemy, even atheism: and the gravest crimes would be the least punished.

However, it is only necessary in extreme cases to use severity – especially the most drastic forms. Abia was armed against the rebels and schismatics of Israel: but before fighting, he first made the charitable invitation which we have seen.[43]

These schismatics were beaten down, and their realm destroyed under Ezechias and Josiah; and these princes were very powerful. But without using force, Ezechias sent ambassadors throughout the entire realm, "from Bersabee to Dan, to invite them, in his name and in the name of the entire people, to Passover,"[44] which he prepared with royal magnificence. Nothing but compassion and gentleness are shown in the letters he addresses to them. "And although those from Manasses, Ephraim, and Zebulon insultingly mocked this charitable invitation," he did not make this an occasion to mistreat them, and he pitied them like the sick.

"Do not harden yourselves, he said, against the God of your fathers: surrender yourselves to the Lord, and come to his sanctuary, which he has sanctified for all time. Serve the God of your fathers, and his anger shall be diverted from you. If you return to the Lord, your brothers and your children, whom the Assyrians hold captive, shall find mercy before their masters; and they shall return to this land: for the Lord is good, pitying, and clement; and he shall not turn away from you, if you return to him."[45]

Josiah settled for "knocking down the altar of Bethel, which

---

[41] Rom. 13:4. [42] Ibid., 4. [43] 2 Par. 13:9ff.
[44] 2 Par. 30:5. [45] Ibid., 8–9.

Jeroboam had erected against God's altar, and all the altars erected in the city of Samaria, and in the tribes of Manasses, Ephraim, and Simeon, up to Nephtali."[46] But he had only pity for the children of Israel, and practiced no violence against them, thinking only to bring them gently to the God of their fathers, and making humble prayers be said for the remains of Israel and Judah.[47]

The Christian princes imitated these examples, blending severity and condescension, according to the circumstances. There are false religions which they believed they must banish from their states under penalty of death; but I want to show here only the behavior they practiced against schisms and heresies. They normally banished their instigators. As for the sectarians, by pitying them as if they were ill they employed, above all things, gentle invitations to bring them back. The Emperor Constantius, son of Constantine, had abundant alms brought to the Donatists, adding to them nothing but an exhortation to return to unity, from which they had separated themselves by a clash and an outrageous insolence. When the emperors saw that these stubborn people took advantage of their kindness, and became hardened in their error, they made penal laws, which consisted mainly of considerable fines. They went so far as to strip them of the disposition of their goods, and to make them intestate. The Church thanked them for these laws; but it still requested that capital punishment be avoided, a punishment which princes also ordered only in cases where sedition and sacrilege accompanied heresy. Such was the conduct of the fourth century. In other times, more severe punishments were employed: and that was primarily against sects which a venomous hatred of the Church, a blasphemous clashing, a spirit of sedition and rebellion, carried to fury, violence, and sacrilege.

11th Proposition
To attract people to religion, a prince can do nothing more effective than set a good example

"Just as the judge of people is, so are his ministers: just as the sovereign of a state is, so are its citizens."[48]

"From the age of eight, King Josiah followed in the footsteps of his father, David, turning neither to the left nor the right. At sixteen, and

---
[46] 4 Kings 23:15,19; 2 Par. 34:6.
[47] 2 Par. 34:21.   [48] Ecclus. 10:2.

in the eighth year of his reign, while he was still a child, he began to seek (with a particular care) the God of his father, David."[49] At twenty, and in the twelfth year of his reign, he knocked down the idols, not only in his entire realm, but in the entire realm of Israel, which was part of the former domain of the house of David, although then subjugated by the Assyrians.

"In the eighteenth year of his reign, he renewed the alliance between the entire people and God, standing on the step of the Temple, in view of the entire people, who solemnly swore to follow in all the Lord's ways: and everyone acquiesced to this pact. He stripped all abominations from the face of the earth, and from all areas, then, not only from Judah, but also from Israel. And he saw to it that what remained of Israel (and the ten tribes as much as the others) served the Lord, their God. During all Josiah's days, they did not stray from God, the Lord of their fathers."[50] What force the example of virtue begun in childhood has in a king, when continued throughout the course of his life!

12th Proposition
A prince should study God's law

"When the king is seated on the throne of his empire, he shall have the law of Deuteronomy (which is a summary of the whole of Moses' law) described in a volume, of which he shall receive a copy from the priests of Levi's race: and he shall keep it with him, and he shall read it every day of his life, so that he might learn to fear the Lord, his God, and to keep his word."[51] He should make God's law the fundamental law of his realm.

Here one sees two great precepts for kings. One, to receive God's law from the hands of the Levites, in order that their copy be reliable, unaltered, and consistent with that which is read in the Temple. The other, to take the time to read what he can with attention. God does not order him to read much at once, but to make a habit of meditating upon it, and to count this holy reading among his fundamental concerns. Happy the prince who would thus read the Gospel; at the end he would find himself well recompensed for his effort.

---

[49] 4 Kings 22:1–2; 2 Par. 34:1–3.   [50] 4 Kings 22:3; 23:2ff.
[51] Deut. 17: 18–19.

13th Proposition
The prince is executor of God's law

This is why one of the main ceremonies of the anointing of the kings of Judah was to place God's law in his hands. "They took the king's son, and placed the diadem upon his forehead and God's law in his hands; and the pontiff anointed him with his children and they cried: Long live the king!"[52] Long may he live, using his power to serve God, who provides him with it, and may he put his hand to executing his law!

This is what David ordains to him with these words: "Now, O kings, listen: teach yourselves, arbitrators of the earth: serve the Lord in fear."[53] Serve him like all the others: for you are his subjects with all the others; but serve him as kings, says St. Augustine, by making your royal power serve his worship, and may your laws support his.

Because of this, the laws of the Christian emperors, and in particular those of our former kings, Clovis, Charlemagne, as well as of the others, are full of severe regulations against those who violate God's law: and they were placed foremost, to serve as a foundation for political laws. We shall perhaps see this in greater detail.

14th Proposition
A prince should see to it that the people be instructed in God's law

"In the third year of his reign, Josaphat dispatched the great men of the realm, and with them several Levites and two preachers: and they taught the people, carrying with them the book of the Lord's law; and they went through all the cities of the realm of Judah, and they instructed the people."[54]

A prince should reign only for the good of the people, of whom he is the father and the judge. And, if God so expressly ordered the kings to write the law-book themselves, always to have an authentic copy with them, to read it each day of their life, as we have already noticed, then there is no doubt that this is primarily to make them capable of instructing their people, and to provide them with information about it, as did the valiant and pious King Josaphat.

[52] 2 Par. 23:11.   [53] Ps. 2:10.   [54] 2 Par. 17:7-9.

On the particular duties of royalty

What care, what eagerness to hear this law do we not see in Josiah – to read it to the people himself, as soon as the High Priest Helcias had placed the authentic copy of Deuteronomy in his hands, which had been mislaid since the first years of the reign of the blasphemous Manasses, his grandfather, and which the pontiffs had just rediscovered in the Lord's temple! "When the king had called together all the elders of Judah and Jerusalem, he climbed to the Lord's temple, accompanied by all the men of Judah and the citizens of Jerusalem, by preachers, Levites, prophets, and the entire people, from the smallest to the greatest. They all began to listen in the Lord's house: and the king read them all the words of this book of the covenant, which had been found in the Lord's house."[55]

Scripture makes us understand well enough that the principal cause of the disorders and blasphemies to which the kings of Judah, the predecessors of Josiah, abandoned themselves, as well as the just vengeance the Lord was going to wreak upon them, must be ascribed to their negligence of this law into which they had let the people fall. "Because, said the prince, the Lord's anger has been kindled against us, and is ready to fall on our heads, because our fathers have not listened to the Lord's words, and have not accomplished what has been written in this book."[56]

In fact, their negligence had been carried to such excess that these kings had allowed the authentic copy of the Deuteronomy to be lost, the copy Moses had stored next to the ark of the covenant, which was rediscovered in Josiah's time.

It was also undoubtedly to recompense the zeal with which this holy king was filled on this memorable occasion that God expressly exempted him from the terrible sentence he pronounced against the kings of Judah. "As for the king of Judah, who sent us here to pray and to consult the Lord, answered the prophetess Olda, who was inspired by God, to Josiah's messengers, here is what the Lord, God of Israel, says: Because you have heard the book's words, because you have penetrated its meaning, because you have taught your people of it, because your heart has been softened by it, because you have humbled yourself in hearing the evils with which I threatened Jerusalem and its inhabitants, I have also answered your prayer, says the Lord. I shall make you rest with your fathers: you shall be put in

---

[55] 4 Kings 23:1–2; 2 Par. 34:29–30.
[56] 4 Kings 22:13; 2 Par. 34:21.

your tomb in peace, and your eyes shall not see all the misfortune I must bring on this city and its inhabitants."[57] Just recompense for this pious prince's holy ardor, to hear God's law, to be attentive to it, and to make it known to his people!

Article IV

Errors of men of the world and statesmen concerning the affairs and practices of religion

1st Proposition
False politics views religious affairs with disdain; and no one worries about the subjects which are treated there, or about the persecution which those who follow it must suffer. This is the first error of the powers and statesmen of the world

There is nothing more bizarre than the judgments of statesmen and politicians concerning religious affairs.

Most treat them as trifles and vain subtleties. The Jews brought St. Paul with an obstinate hatred "to the tribunal of Gallio, proconsul of Achaea, and told him that this man wanted God to be worshiped against what the law ordained."[1] They thought they had attracted his attention with such a serious accusation. "But Paul had no sooner opened his mouth (to defend himself) than the proconsul interrupted him, and said from his tribunal on high: If it were a question of some injustice or wrongful action, I would give you all the time you wish. But as for questions of words and names, and disputes over your law, do what you please about it: I do not want to be the judge of these things."[2] He did not say: They are too elevated, and surpass my intelligence; he said that all this is only a dispute over words and vain

---

[57] 4 Kings 22:18–20; 2 Par. 34:26–28.
[1] Acts 18:12–13.   [2] Ibid., 14–15.

subtleties, unworthy of being brought to a serious judgment and of occupying the time of a magistrate.

The Jews, seeing how little the judge troubled himself with their indictments, and seemed to abandon Paul and his companion to their furor, "threw themselves on Sosthenes and beat him"[3] (with no respect for the tribunal of so great a magistrate); "and Gallio cared for none of these things." All seemed to him to be trifles in these religious disputes, and an imprudent ardor of people intoxicated by vain things.

2nd Proposition
Another error of the great men of the world about religion: they fear to go deeply into it

Others seemed to take the matter more seriously. Felix, governor of Judaea, was very well informed about this faith, that is to say about Christianity.[4] This is why, when listening to Paul speak of justice (which magistrates were supposed to render so religiously), of the chastity that should have been guarded with such care and precaution (such harsh words to the worldly, who love only their pleasures), and of the judgment to come, where God would demand an account of all these things with an implacable severity – in order not to go too deeply into such disagreeable subjects, although he could not prevent himself from being frightened about it, Felix told him: "That is enough about it for the moment; I shall call you at a more suitable time."[5] The objects which occupied him further dissipated these fears; avarice dominated him; and he only summoned Paul any longer "in the hope that he would give him money, leaving him captive for two years, nevertheless allowing all his friends to see him."[6]

3rd Proposition
Another procedure of men of the world, who take religion to be madness, without caring about justice, or preventing the persecution of innocence

Festus, the new governor sent to replace Felix, was more or less of Gallio's sentiment, if he did not push things yet further. King Agrippa

---

[3] Ibid., 17.   [4] Acts 24:22.   [5] Ibid., 25.   [6] Ibid., 26.

Errors concerning religion

and Queen Berenice, who later became so famous from the passion that Titus had for her, greatly desired to hear St. Paul, and Festus wanted to give them this pleasure in an official assembly which was held expressly for this and with great pomp.[7] "Besides, he told the king, I have found no evil in this man; but there were disputes between him and the Jews who brought him to me: about their superstitions, and about a certain Jesus who was dead, and of whom Paul assured that he was alive."[8] These people, occupied with society and with their greatness, treat religious affairs and eternal salvation in this way, without even deigning to learn facts as important and extraordinary as those which concerned the Son of God, for all that did nothing for their interests and their pleasures, or for social affairs. St. Paul had begun to speak, and when he began to get to the root of the question, Festus interrupted him;[9] and without respect for the presence of the king and queen, and without waiting for their judgment and for that of the assembly, "he cried out loud: Paul, you are mad; too much study has twisted your mind."[10]

From this one can see that however equitable Festus may have appeared toward St. Paul, when he agreed "that he did not find him criminal, and he could have been sent back if he had not appealed to the emperor,"[11] there entered into this sentiment a secret scorn for the heart of the matter which Festus did not judge important enough to make it the subject of a judgment, or to merit the emperor's knowledge of it. The only question he found here was to know what he would report to the emperor: "I do not know, he said, what to write to the master about it."[12] And he was afraid that it might be believed that he sent him back news of entirely frivolous affairs. For to inform him of miracles or of Jesus Christ's doctrine, or Paul's, and to examine prophecies, which were the apostle's strong point, or to speak seriously of the matter of eternal salvation, was out of the question.

However, this equitable man, who did not want to condemn St. Paul, was not afraid of giving him up to his enemies. For instead of judging him at Caesarea, where everything was arranged for this, and sending him back right away, he proposed to transport him to Jerusalem, to please the Jews, who had plotted to kill him, either on the road or else in Jerusalem, where all the people were theirs. This

---

[7] Acts 25:18. [8] Ibid., 19. [9] Acts 26:1ff.
[10] Ibid., 24. [11] Acts 25:18,25; 26:32. [12] Acts 25:26.

obligated St. Paul to tell Festus: "I have done no wrong to the Jews, as you know perfectly well: no one can give me up to them. I appeal to Caesar, and it is in his tribunal that I should be judged."[13]

Here, then, is everything that Festus found to be real and serious in this affair: to please the Jews, to satisfy the curiosity of Agrippa, and to resolve what had to be written to the emperor. When one wanted to go deeper, and examine the foundation, one was mad.

4th Proposition
Another error: human considerations dictate that those who are well-versed in certain religious points do not dare speak about them

Agrippa, who was a Jew, attached to his religion and well instructed in the prophecies, acted more seriously. St. Paul, who knew him, took him to witness about the facts he put forward concerning Jesus Christ. "And when Festus screamed at him that he was mad: No, no, he said, most excellent Festus, I am not mad: the king knows the truth of what I say, and I speak boldly before him. For all this has not happened in a corner, but before the eyes of the entire public."[14] Then addressing himself to the king himself: "O king Agrippa, he said, do you not believe the prophets? I know you believe them."[15] St. Paul wanted to bind him to say in good faith what he knew of this subject before Festus and the Romans; and he owed this witness to pagans. But he was merely evasive: and without saying anything about all the marvels that occurred in Judaea, and without even daring to testify what he believed about the prophecies which spoke so much of Christ, he simply responded to St. Paul in a jesting manner: "You very nearly persuade me to be a Christian."[16]

This is what the great men of the world, kings, and all the men of the world, thought about the great matter of their time, which was that of Jesus Christ. No one wanted to know it, nor to go more deeply into it, nor to say what they knew about it. After that, who can be surprised that one finds so little about it in profane histories?

---

[13] Ibid., 9–11.   [14] Acts 26:24–26.   [15] Ibid., 27.   [16] Ibid., 28.

5th Proposition
The indifference of the world's sages towards religion

But there was nothing more marvelous then than the Athenians. For all time, Athens had been the seat of politeness, knowledge and wit: philosophers triumphed there; and since, being subjugated by the Romans, it had no longer to deal with war and peace, or affairs of state, it was entirely given over to curiosity: "Such that one thought of nothing else but saying or hearing some novelty,"[17] especially on the subject of doctrine. St. Paul, having arrived there, found himself in the Lyceum with the Stoic and Epicurean philosophers. "He discoursed with them. Some of them said: What does this speechifier mean? And the others: This is assuredly a man who has filled his head with new deities (or as they said), with new demons."[18] They remembered that a similar accusation had been made among them against Socrates: and they still adhered to their old ideas. Whereupon they brought him to the Areopagus,[19] the most famous company of all Greece, and with no other intent than to satisfy the curiosity of the Athenians, and a meeting of the senate was held expressly for this. Paul was listened to, as long as he recited the great principles of philosophy: and Greece was pleased to hear him cite its poets so appropriately. But when he got to the main point, which was to announce to them that Jesus Christ was resurrected, and the miracles that God had performed to show that this Jesus Christ was he whom God had chosen to declare his volition to men, "some mocked Paul";[20] the others, more courteous towards truth, but at base neither better disposed, nor less indifferent, told him honestly: "We shall hear you another time on this subject. And Paul departed thus from among them."[21] Taken further, the matter would have become serious: it would have been truly necessary to convert, and everyone wanted to think only of curiosity and of his pleasure.

Jesus Christ was dealt with similarly, from the beginning. Herod, to whom Pilate had sent him, wanted to see only miracles; he hoped that God would have used his omnipotence to amuse him. Because he did not want to make a game for him of the works of his powerful hand, he scorned him, and sent him back with the white clothing he dressed him in.[22]

[17] Acts 27:21. [18] Ibid., 18. [19] Ibid., 19ff.
[20] Ibid., 32. [21] Ibid., 32–33. [22] Luke 23:8,11.

Pilate did no better. As Jesus had told him: "I was born, and came into this world to bear witness of truth":[23] profound words, by which he wanted to teach him to seek the truth of God. He rejoined: "And what is the truth?"[24] After which he got up and left without informing himself any further, as if he had said: The truth, you say? who knows? and why should we care to know it, this truth? Worldly people, and especially the great, scarcely worry about it: they take only business and pleasure to heart.

We are not better than those of whom we have just spoken: and if we do not so openly scorn Jesus Christ and his doctrine, when it is necessary to come to the most serious part of religion, that is to say practicing and sacrificing one's ambition or one's pleasure to God and to one's salvation, we laugh secretly, to ourselves, at those who recommend it to us: and religion is no less a game to us than to the infidels.

6th Proposition
How politics finally came to persecute religion, with a manifest iniquity

If religion had only been discoursed upon, like a curious subject, perhaps society would not have persecuted it; but since one saw that those who did not follow it were condemned, interests were mixed in with it. The Pharisees could not suffer their avarice being decried, nor the ruination of the domination over consciences which they usurped. Those who made idols, and the others who profited among the pagans from superstitious worship, animated the people. It was remembered "that Diana was the great goddess of the Ephesians, when it was seen that by decrying her, and the majesty of her temple, which everyone revered,"[25] the great consideration and profit that it brought to private individuals and to the public, were beginning to dry up.[26]

Rome itself was angered when people wanted to decry its gods, to whom it imagined that it owed its victories. The emperors were irritated because people no longer wanted to worship them. Roman policy decided that the ancient religion had to be adhered to, and that to suffer change was to expose it to ruin. They wanted to imagine

---

[23] John 18:37.   [24] Ibid., 38.   [25] Acts 19:27–28.   [26] Ibid., 25–26.

Errors concerning religion

seditions, revolts, and civil wars in the establishment of Christianity – although experience showed that in fact [this] religion was established without persecutions having excited even a murmur from the Christians, [not to mention] activity or disobedience, however violent the persecutions may have been. But the proud and corrupted society did not want to let itself be convicted of ignorance and blindness, or to suffer a religion that changed the face of the earth.

7th Proposition
Feeble minds mock the piety of kings

Michol, wife of David, steeped in ostentation and pitiless toward her father, Saul, when she saw her husband the king entirely beside himself in front of the ark he had had brought to Zion with royal pomp, "scorned him in her heart. How wonderful it was, she said, to see the king of Israel with the servants, walking naked like a juggler!"[27] Did he not make a fine character there? But David, although he loved her tenderly, answered her: "Long live the Lord, who has raised me rather than your father and his house: I shall humble myself even further than I have in front of him, and I shall be contemptible in my own eyes;[28] and I glory in humbling myself, as you said, with the servants."[29]

This jesting spirit must not be allowed to dominate in courts, especially in women, even if they were to be queens, since it is this, on the contrary, which must be suppressed the most. God rewarded David's piety, and punished Michol with eternal sterility.[30]

8th Proposition
The seriousness of religion known by great kings. The example of David

The ark was the symbol of God's presence to the ancient people, though far inferior to that which we have in the Eucharist: however, David's devotion to the ark was immense. When he had it transported to Zion, he made great liberalities to the people in honor of such a solemn day. "Victims were sacrificed (the entire length of the path by which the ark passed). They marched to the sound of trumpets,

---

[27] 2 Kings 6:20.   [28] Ibid., 21.   [29] Ibid., 22.   [30] 2 Kings 6:23.

drums, oboes, and every kind of musical instrument." The king, stripped of the royal garb which he did not dare wear before God, "and dressed simply in a linen tunic, followed with the entire people and his captains, in great joy, playing his lyre, and dancing with all his might, beside himself as he was."[31] They were ceremonies which the time justified.

On a more doleful occasion, when in punishment of his sin he fled from Absalom, we have seen that the ark was brought to him as the only thing that could give him consolation. But he did not deem himself worthy of seeing it in the state he was in, where God treated him as a sinner. "Ah, he cried, if I find favor from the Lord (after these days of punishment), he shall show it to me one day in his tabernacle."[32] That was the dearest object of his wishes. And during the time of Saul, banished from his country and from the holy assembly of God's people, he sighed only for the ark. A great example to make known what one should feel in the presence of the Eucharist, of which the ark was only an imperfect pre-figuring.

9th Proposition
A prince should fear three types of false piety: firstly, external piety and piety out of prudence

Two reasons should make a prince fearful of giving too much to external appearances in practices of piety. The first, because he is a public figure [*personnage*]: since he is artificially made and non-natural, he should be careful, by the great consideration he must have for the public, which has its eyes fixed on him. Secondly, because piety is in fact useful in establishing domination, so that unbeknownst to him, a prince could get used to seeing it in this way. Thus Saul said to Samuel, who abandoned him and no longer wanted to attend God's sanctuary with him before all the people: "I have done badly; but honor me before Israel and before my people's senators, and return with me to worship the Lord, your God."[33] He no longer wanted to call him his own; and caring little about religion, he thought no longer of anything but keeping up appearances out of policy.

Thus the kings of Israel sometimes showed themselves to be pious against Baal and his idols. But they were very careful not to destroy

---

[31] Ibid., 13ff.   [32] 2 Kings 15:25.   [33] 1 Kings 15:30.

the golden calves erected by Jeroboam in order to hold the people. For "he had said to himself: the realm will come back to the house of David, if the people will still come up to Jerusalem, to the Lord's house to offer sacrifices there. The people's heart shall turn to Roboam, king of Judah, and they will put me to death, and they will come back to him. Thus, by a considered resolution he made two golden calves, and he told them: Come up to Jerusalem no longer; O Israel, here are your gods, who have drawn you from the land of Egypt."[34]

Thus Jehu massacred all of Baal's priests, and he broke his statue, and set fire to his temple. And as if he had wanted to carry out all the duties of the religion, he took the holy man Jonodab, son of Rechab, in his wagon, to be a witness of his conduct. "Come, he told him, and see my zeal for the Lord. But he did not withdraw from Jeroboam's sins, nor from the golden calves he had erected at Bethel and Dan."[35] For *raison d'état* did not permit it.

Such is the religion of a prudent king. He shows zeal in things that do not harm his ambition, and he even seems to want to satisfy the most upright people: but false prudence prevents him from going the whole way with piety. Joachaz, one of Jehu's successors in the realm of Israel, seemed to want to go further. "God had left Israel to Hazael, king of Syria, and to his son, Benadad: and Joachaz prayed to the Lord, who heard his voice, for he pitied Israel, which these kings had brought to distress."[36] But Joachaz, who seemed with all his heart to want to return to God in his penitence, did not have the force to destroy the golden calves, which were the scandal of Israel: "and he did not withdraw from Jeroboam's sins: God, too, abandoned him. And the king of Syria did to him and his people what is done to the dust that is shaken in a sandbank."[37]

And this whole façade of piety is nothing but hypocrisy: and it is familiar to cunning princes, who think of nothing but amusing the people with appearances. Thus Herod, that old, dissembling politician, feigning zeal for the law of the Jews, to the point of rebuilding the Temple with a magnificence matching Solomon's, at the same time raised temples to Augustus.

And it is known what he wanted to do against Jesus Christ.[38] Looking only at externals, he desired nothing so much as worshiping

---

[34] 3 Kings 12:26–28.   [35] 4 Kings 10:15,28,29.
[36] 4 Kings 13:3–5.   [37] Ibid., 6–7.   [38] Matt. 2:3ff.

this newborn King of the Jews with the Magi. He called together the ecclesiastical council, like a man who wanted nothing else but to be enlightened about the prophecies; but all this hid the dark design of assassinating the Savior, whose title of King of the Jews was odious to his ambition, although the way in which he wanted to appear to men showed well enough that his realm was not of this world.

10th Proposition
The second kind of false piety: forced or selfish piety

Such was Holofernes', when he told Judith: "Your God shall be my God, if he does what you promise for me,"[39] that is to say, [gives] so many victories. The ambitious will worship whomever you please, as long as their ambition is satisfied.

"Herod feared St. John, who took him over (with an invincible strength): for he knew that he was a holy and just man; and he did several things on his advice, which he gladly heard."[40] For we have seen that these politicians sometimes want to satisfy upright people. But all this was nothing but artifice or superstitious terror, since he feared St. John so much, that after cutting off his head he was still afraid that he would be raised from the dead to torment him.[41]

Listen to an Antiochus, that proud King of Syria. "It is just, he said, to be subject to God, and that a mortal should not endeavor to be his equal." And he spoke only of the Athenians being equalled by the Jews (whom he did not judge worthy of being only a burial-ground) and of freeing Jerusalem, which he had so cruelly oppressed, of showering with gifts the Temple he had stripped: and finally of making himself a Jew.[42] But it was because he felt the hand of God, which he imagined he could avoid by all these vain promises. God scorned his forced penitence: "and this wicked one asked for the mercy he did not deserve."[43]

Galerius Maximianus and Maximinus, the two cruellest persecutors of the Christian Church, died with an equally forced and vain admission of their error:[44] and before surrendering them to capital punishment, God had them make honorable amends to his people, whom they had tyrannized for so long.

[39] Jth. 11:21.   [40] Mark 6:20.   [41] Ibid., 16.   [42] 2 Macc. 9:12–17.   [43] Ibid., 13.
[44] Eusebius, *Hist. eccl.* VIII, 16–17; IX, 10: Lactantius, *De mort. persecut.* XXXIII, XLIX.

11th Proposition
The third kind of false piety: piety which is misguided

"Go, and put the wicked people of Amalec to the sword, and spare none of this blasphemous nation, which I have given over to vengeance, said the Lord to Saul. And this prince saved from the booty the ewes and the oxen, to sacrifice them to the Lord. But Samuel told him: Is it victims or sacrifices that the Lord asks, or obedience to his voice? Obedience is better than sacrifice, and it is better to obey than to offer the fat of rams; for to disobey is like someone consulting soothsayers; and not to submit is the crime of idolatry."[45]

The sentence came from above: "God has rejected you, said Samuel, and you shall no longer be king."[46]

Herod, who put St. John the Baptist to death, was not without some religious feeling, [even] in the midst of his greatest crimes. He imprisoned the holy precursor who boldly recaptured him from his incest. Yet at the same time we have seen "that he feared him, knowing that he was a just and holy man; that he had him come often, and even followed his advice."[47] Nevertheless, he surrendered him in the end and, unjustly scrupulous, the sanctity of the oath carried him to his crime. "He was sorry he committed himself; but because of the oath he had sworn and the company, he went on."[48] He was afraid of him, even after he had put him to death. "And hearing the miracles of Jesus, John, whom I have decapitated, lives again in him, and it is his virtue working."[49] He scorned religion; superstition tyrannized him. He listened to and considered the one he held in irons, a prisoner who had influence in the court, and intrepid critic of the prince and the sworn enemy of his mistress, who nevertheless was listened to: a man who was put to death, and who afterwards was still feared. So many fears that struggled against one another: that of losing a holy man, that of hearing overly free reproaches from his mouth, that of disturbing his pleasures, that of appearing weak in company, that of divine justice that never stopped coming back, although so often pushed away: all this made a strange mixture here. One does not know what to believe about such a prince: one thinks now that he is

---

[45] 1 Kings 15:18–23. [46] 1 Kings 15:23.
[47] Mark 6:20. [48] Matt. 14:9. [49] Ibid., 1–2.

somewhat religious, now not at all. It is an inexplicable enigma, and superstition is not coherent.

"They multiply their prayers, they roll from their tongues, but they do not have their hearts in them. But this is imitating the Gentiles, who imagine, said the Son of God, that their prayers are answered because they multiply their words."[50] And from the Lord's mouth is heard: "This people honors me with its tongue, but its heart is far from me."[51]

They spoil very good works: they fast, and carefully observe the Church's abstinences: this is right. But, as the Son of God says, "more important parts of the law are left aside, justice, mercy, fidelity. Some had to be done, without leaving out the others.[52] Do you know which fast I like, said the Lord? Free those who are detained in prisons; relieve a people overwhelmed with a burden it cannot carry; feed the poor; clothe the naked: then your justice will be genuine and resplendent like the sun."[53]

You build magnificent temples; you multiply your sacrifices, and you have masses said at every altar. But Jesus Christ answers: "Go learn what this word means: I like mercy better than sacrifice.[54] The sacrifice which pleases God is a heart that is contrite and lowered before Him.[55] The true and pure religion is comforting widows, and the oppressed, and keeping one's heart free from the contagion of this age."[56]

Therefore, put every work in its place. If in doing the small ones, you do away with the one obligation of doing the great ones, you are among those of whom it is written: "They hatch cockatrice eggs. They have woven spider webs. Their webs are incapable of clothing them and they shall not be covered with their works; for their words are useless words, and their thoughts are vain thoughts."[57]

---

[50] Matt. 6:7. [51] Matt. 15:8; Isa. 29:13. [52] Matt. 23:23.
[53] Isa. 58:6–8. [54] Matt. 9:13. [55] Ps. 50:19.
[56] James 1:27. [57] Isa. 59:4–7.

Article v

What care great kings have taken for the worship of God

1st Proposition
The efforts of Joshua, David, and Solomon to construct the ark of the covenant and to build the Temple of God

Joshua had no sooner conquered and divided the promised land, than, to place it forever under the protection of God, who had given it to his people, "he established the seat of religion at Silo, where he placed the tabernacle."[1] It was necessary to begin in this way, and to place God in possession of this land and of the entire people, whose true king he was.

David subsequently found a more worthy place for the ark and the tabernacle, and he set them up in Zion, where he had them transported in great triumph,[2] and God chose Zion and Jerusalem as the place where he established his name and worship.

He also made, as has been seen, preparations for the Temple, where God wanted to be served with great magnificence, consecrating the spoils of defeated nations there.[3]

He indicated its place, which God himself had chosen, and charged Solomon with building it.

Solomon did this great work with the magnificence we have seen elsewhere. For he wanted to make it proportional, as much as he could, to the greatness of him who wished to be served there. "The house, he said, that I wish to build is large, because our God is above all gods. Who, then, would be powerful enough to build a house worthy of him?"[4]

---

[1] Josh. 18:1. [2] 2 Kings 6:12ff.
[3] 2 Kings 7:1. [4] 2 Par. 2:5.

2nd Proposition
Even the most magnificent things one does for God are always beneath his greatness

This was the feeling of Solomon, after he had built a temple so rich that nothing had ever equaled it. "Is it credible then that God should dwell with men on the earth, he whom heaven and the heaven of heavens cannot contain?"[5] And David, who had made the preparations for it, found all of it poor in comparison with his desire – though he had spared nothing and had consecrated to this work "a hundred thousand talents of gold, a million talents of silver, brass and iron without limit, and all the stones and woods needed for so great an edifice,"[6] without sparing cedar, which was the most precious. "I have, he said, offered all this from my poverty."[7]

3rd Proposition
Princes must sanctify feast-days

Moses put in prison[8] and finally punished with death (by order of God) whoever had violated the Sabbath.[9] The Christian law is gentler, and the Christians, who are more docile, have no need of such strictness: but one must guard against impunity.

Public ordinances are full of penalties against those who violate feast-days, and above all holy Sunday. And kings must oblige magistrates to keep their hands carefully to the complete execution of these laws – against which much is done unless one applies all the necessary remedies.

It is mainly on the sanctification of feast-days that the worship of God depends – a feeling that would dissipate in the continual occupations of life, if God had not consecrated certain days to think more seriously about it, and to renew in oneself the spirit of religion.

The holy kings Ezechias and Josiah are celebrated in the histories of the people of God for having caused the pasch to be solemnized by religion and by extraordinary magnificence. The whole people was filled with joy: "no one had seen anything like it since the time of Solomon." This is what is said about Ezechias' pasch.[10] And about

---

[5] 2 Par. 6:18.   [6] 1 Par. 22:14.   [7] 1 Par. 22:14.
[8] Num. 15:32ff.   [9] Num. 15:32ff.   [10] 2 Par. 30:26.

that of Josiah,[11] this was said: "There was not such a pasch kept under all the preceding kings, nor since the time of Samuel."[12]

The feast-days of the Christians are much more simple, and less restricting – and at the same time much holier and much more consoling than those of the Jews, in which there was only a shadow of the truths which have been revealed to us. And nonetheless we are much more lax in celebrating them.

4th Proposition
Princes must be careful not only of the persons consecrated to God, but also of the goods destined for their subsistence

"Honor God with all thy soul, and give honor to the priests."[13]

"He that heareth you, heareth me; and he that despiseth you, despiseth me," said Jesus Christ himself to his disciples.[14]

"Take heed thou forsake not the Levite all the time that thou livest in the land."[15] The land tells you while nourishing you, that you must provide for the subsistence of the ministers of God, who makes it fruitful.

The whole [Jewish] law is full of similar precepts. Abraham left an example of it for all posterity, in giving a portion of the spoils taken from his enemies to Melchisedech, the High Priest of the most high God, who blessed him and offered a sacrifice for him and for the whole people.[16]

In this Abraham followed an already-established custom. One sees it in all nations, from remotest antiquity. And we have a fine memorial of it in Egypt, under Pharaoh and Joseph. All the people sold their land to the king in order to have bread, "except the land of the priests, which had been given them by the king: to whom also a certain allowance of food was given out of the public stores, and therefore they were not forced to sell their possessions."[17]

The people of Israel did not complain about being charged with the feeding of the Levites and their families, who made up more than a twelfth part of the nation, being one of its most abundant tribes. On the contrary, they nourished them with joy. In the time of David, there were thirty-eight thousand Levites, to count them over thirty

---
[11] 4 Kings 23:22–23. [12] 2 Par. 35:18. [13] Ecclus. 7:33. [14] Luke 10:16.
[15] Deut. 12:19. [16] Gen. 14:18–20. [17] Gen. 47:22.

years' time – without including therein the priests who were descended from Aaron, divided into two main families by the sons of Aaron, and sub-divided in David's time into twenty-four very numerous families issued from these first two.[18] The whole nation maintained them quite abundantly with all things, together with their families. For the Levites had no other possessions or shares among their brethren, save the tithes, the offerings, the oblations, and the rest, that the people gave them. And everyone saw in this maintenance [of the priests] one of the main exercises of religion, and the salvation of the whole people.

5th Proposition
The admirable cares of David

The great kings of the house of David made their reign celebrated through the great care which they took to maintain the order of the ministry, and all the functions of the sacrifice-givers and the Levites according to the law of Moses.

David had given them the example; and he established this fine regulation which was followed and executed by his successors. This king, who was wise and pious as he was warlike and victorious, used up the final years of his life in this great business, while the whole kingdom was at peace: [he was] assisted by the principal men of the kingdom and above all by the sovereign pontiff, together with the heads of the Levitical and sacerdotal families, and by the prophets Nathan and Gad[19] – being himself a prophet and counted in Scripture among the number of men inspired by God.

With this counsel and by a particular inspiration [*une inspiration particulière*], he regulated the hours of the divine service. "And the Levites are to stand in the morning to give thanks, and to sing praises to the Lord: and in like manner in the evening."[20]

He established the necessary subordination in this great body of ministers consecrated to God, by ordering the Levites to serve "each according to his rank, by keeping the sacred rites and all the observances of the sons of Aaron, who presided over these functions by the command of God,"[21] and according to the law of Moses.

Among these Levites, there were three main ones "who served next

---

[18] 1 Par. 23:3ff. [19] Ibid., 2ff; 24:6; 2 Par. 29:25.
[20] 2 Par. 29:30. [21] 1 Par. 23:32; 24:19.

to the king": Asaph, Idithun, and Heman. This last was called the Seer or the prophet of the king:[22] and Asaph prophesied near the king as well; he too was called the Seer,[23] and made himself so famous with his canticles that he was ranked with David. Such were the ecclesiastics (to speak in our fashion) who were nearest to the person of the king: men inspired by God, and the most celebrated of their order. David also kept near him a sacrifice-giver named Ira, who was honored with the title of David's priest or sacrifice-giver.[24]

6th Proposition
The care of sacred places and vessels

King Joas, instructed by the sovereign pontiff Joiada, summoned the Levites, together with the other sacrifice-givers, to make them work on the repairs of the Temple, which they had neglected for several years. He prescribed the order of the work, he regulated the funds: and an officer commissioned by the king supervised them – with the pontiff, or someone appointed by him – in order to put them in the hands of the workers, "who re-established the Temple in its original splendor and solidity. The rest of the money was brought to the king and to the pontiff: and from it they made sacred vessels of silver and of gold, to use in the sacrifice."[25]

Ezechias made himself no less celebrated, when he assembled the Levites and the sacrifice-givers,[26] to oblige them carefully to purify the Temple and the sacred vessels, which had been profaned by impious kings. And he caused David's regulations to be carefully executed.[27]

One cannot sufficiently praise the holy King Josiah, and the care which he took to purify and rebuild the Temple.[28] God inspired a sacred author to give him this praise, to incite kings to similar practices.

7th Proposition
Praises of Josiah and of David

Ecclesiasticus speaks in this way of Josiah: "The memory of Josiah is like the composition of a sweet smell made by the art of a perfumer:

---

[22] 1 Par. 25:2,5,6.   [23] 2 Par. 29:30.   [24] 2 Kings 20:26.   [25] 4 Kings 12:4,7ff.
[26] 2 Par. 29:5,16ff.   [27] Ibid., 25.   [28] 4 Kings 22; 23; 2 Par. 34.

His remembrance shall be sweet as honey in every mouth, and as music at a banquet of exquisite wine. He was directed by God unto the repentance of the nation, and he took away the abomination of wickedness (from the Temple and from the earth). God directed his heart and strengthened his piety in a time of iniquity and of disorder,"[29] in which everything was corrupted by the bad examples of the kings who had preceded him.

The same sacred author also celebrates the praises of David in these words: "In all his works he gave thanks to the holy one . . . he praised him with all his heart (in his divine Psalms which the whole people sang). With his whole heart he loved the Lord, and the God that made him: and he gave him power against his enemies. And he set singers before the altar, and by their voices he made sweet melody. And to the festivals he added beauty, and set in order the solemn times even to the end of his life, that they should praise the holy name of the Lord, and magnify the holiness of God in the morning."[30]

This is how the Holy Spirit praises pious kings, who have taken care to regulate sacred ministers, to decorate the Temple, and to cause the divine service to be accomplished with suitable splendor.

8th Proposition
The care of Nehemias, and how he protected the Levites against the magistrates

One must not forget Nehemias, governor of the people of God under the kings of Persia, and restorer of the Temple and the holy city. He did justice to the Levites who had been deprived of their rights.[31] The sacred singers and all the other ministers who had been forced to retire to their homes and to abandon the service, from not having received the just salary which had been ordained for them, were recalled. He took from Tobias the office which Eliasib the sacrifice-giver, his relative, had given him to enrich him, and disposed according to the old rules the funds destined for the Temple, and the divine service.[32] "He upheld the cause of the Levites against the magistrates (who had failed in their duty to them), and he placed their grain and their revenues in faithful hands: placing in charge of this ministry the priest Selemias and some Levites.[33] Moreover, in taking care of them,

[29] Ecclus. 49:1–4.   [30] Ecclus. 47:9–12.   [31] Neh. 13:10.
[32] Ibid., 5–9.   [33] Ibid., 11–13.

he made them keep carefully the ordinances of David.[34] Subordination was observed: the people did honor to the Levites (by giving them what they owed them): and the Levites rendered to the children of Aaron, who were their superiors. They carefully kept all the observances of their God."[35]

Nehemias kept a steady hand: he commanded the sacrifice-givers and the Levites to be attentive to that which was prescribed to them. "He spoke to the Levites that they should be purified . . . and would not tolerate those who profaned the priesthood, and showed contempt for sacerdotai and Levitical law"[36] – that is to say, the rules which prescribed their functions to them. This made him say, with confidence: "Remember me, O God, for this thing . . . and do not forget the care which I took for the house of my God and for his ceremonies, and for the sacerdotal and Levitical order."[37]

O princes, follow these examples: Take into your care everything that is consecrated to God – and not only the persons but also the places and the goods that ought to be used in his service. Protect the goods of the churches, which are also the goods of the poor. Remember Heliodorus and the hand of God which was upon him, for having wanted to invade the property placed on deposit in the Temple.[38] How much more is it necessary to preserve the goods which were not only deposited in the Temple, but given in funds to the churches!

9th Proposition
A reflection which kings ought to make, following the example of David, concerning their liberalities towards the churches – and how dangerous it is to lay a hand on them

These great goods come from kings, I grant; they have enriched the churches through their liberalities; and the people have done nothing in this line without the concurrence of their authority. But everything which they have given, they had first received from God. "Who am I, said David, and what is my people, that we should be able to promise thee all these gifts for your Temple? All things are thine: and we have given thee what we received of thy hand."[39]

He continues: "We are sojourners before thee, and strangers, as were all our fathers."[40] We have nothing which belongs to us; our very

---

[34] Neh. 12:24,44,45.   [35] Ibid., 46.   [36] Neh. 13:22,29.   [37] Ibid., 14,30,31.
[38] 2 Macc. 3:23ff.   [39] 1 Par. 29:14.   [40] Ibid., 15.

life is not our own. "Our days upon earth are as a shadow, and we have only a moment to live."[41] Everything escapes us, nothing belongs to us. "O Lord our God, all this store that we have prepared to build thee a house for thy holy name, is from thy hand, and all things are thine."[42]

What an attempt, to rob God of what comes from him, what belongs to him, what one gives to him – and to raise one's hand to repossess it from the tops of the altars!

But it is a much greater danger to put one's hand on the ministers of God. "Touch ye not my anointed," says David;[43] God was speaking of Abraham and Isaac, who were ranked among his sacrifice-givers and ministers. "God suffered no man to hurt them; and he reproved kings for their sakes."[44]

"Herod beheaded James, the brother of John: and seeing that it pleased the Jews, he proceeded to take up Peter also. He had him guarded by sixteen soldiers, with a view to bringing him forth to the people, after the pasch."[45] But God, who had destined Peter to suffer in another time and in a more celebrated place, knew not only how to draw him out of prison, but also knew how to make the tyrant feel his powerful hand. For a little while afterwards, given over to an insane pride, in which he let himself be admired and praised as a god, "the angel of the Lord struck him, and he died eaten by worms."[46]

Saul, who caused Abimelech and the other sacrifice-givers to be massacred for having favored David, was in a state of abomination before God and before men. "His officers, whom he commanded to kill them, were horrified to extend their hands against the priests of the Lord." It was only Doeg the Edomite, a stranger of an impious race, who dared to soil his hands with their blood, without respect to the holy garment which they wore.[47] David, from having been the innocent occasion of this sacrilegious murder, shuddered at it: "I am guilty, he said, of his unjustly spilled blood. He took under his protection Abiathar, son of Abimelech. Stay with me, he said, and fear nothing: for he that seeketh my life, seeketh thy life also, and with me thou shalt be saved."[48]

---

[41] Ibid.   [42] Ibid., 16.   [43] Ps. 104:15.
[44] Ibid., 14.   [45] Acts 12:1–4.   [46] Ibid., 22–23.
[47] 1 Kings 22:16–18.   [48] Ibid., 22–23.

10th Proposition
Kings should undertake nothing against the rights and the authority of the priesthood: and they must find it good that the priestly order maintain them against all sorts of enterprises

When Ozias wanted to plot against these sacred rights, and put his hand on the altar of incense, the priests were obliged by the law of God to oppose this – as much for the good of this prince as for the preservation of their right, which was, as has been said, that of God.[49] They did this with vigor: and placing themselves before the king with their pontiff at their head, they said to him: "It doth not belong to thee, Ozias, to burn incense to the Lord, but to the priests, that is, to the sons of Aaron, whom God hath appointed to this ministry. Go out of the sanctuary, do not despise: for this thing shall not be counted to thy glory by the Lord our God."[50]

Instead of yielding to this speech, and to the authority of the pontiff and his priests, "Ozias was angry, and holding in his hand the censer to burn incense, threatened the priests. The earth quaked.[51] And presently there rose a leprosy in his forehead before the priests, who (warned by this miracle) . . . were constrained to thrust him out of the sanctuary. Yea himself also being frightened, hasted to go out, because he had quickly felt the stroke of the Lord. The leprosy did not leave him: it was necessary that he dwell apart according to the law. And his son Jonathan took on the administration of the kingdom, and governed it under the authority of the king his father."[52]

By contrast the pious King Josaphat, far from attempting anything against the sacred rights of the priesthood, distinguished precisely the two functions – the priestly and the kingly – in giving this instruction "to the Levites, to the priests and chiefs of the families of Israel whom he sent out to all the cities for the regulation of their affairs: Amarias the priest your high priest shall be chief in the things which regard God: and Zabadias the son of Ismahel, who is ruler in the house of Judah, shall be over those matters which belong to the king's office: and you have before you the Levites for masters and doctors."[53]

One sees with what exactitude he distinguished matters, and ordained to each the objects of his concern: not permitting his minis-

---

[49] 2 Par. 26:16.   [50] Ibid., 17–18.   [51] Amos 1:1; Zach. 14:5.
[52] 2 Par. 26:19–21.   [53] 2 Par. 19:8,11.

ters to attempt anything against the ministers of sacred things, nor (reciprocally) letting the latter undertake anything against royal rights.

In truth we have seen that kings concerned themselves with sacred things: we have seen at the same time that this was in execution of ancient regulations, and orders already given on God's part; and also [they concerned themselves] with the pontiffs, the sacrifice-givers, and the prophets.

The holy things which are reserved for the priestly order, are even more clearly distinguished in the New Testament from the civil and temporal things reserved for princes. This is why Christian kings, in matters of religion, have been the first to submit themselves to ecclesiastical decisions. A hundred examples could make this clear, if the thing were doubtful: but here is one from among many, which concerns the kings of France.

11th Proposition
The example of the kings of France, and of the Council of Chalcedon

The sectarian followers of Elipandus, Archbishop of Toledo, and of Felix, Bishop of Urgel, who renewed the heresy of Nestorius in Spain, begged Charlemagne to take notice of this disagreement, and to promise to render a decision. This prince took them at their word, and accepted the offer with a view to bringing them back to the unity of the faith, by means of the agreement into which they had entered. But he knew how a prince can serve as arbiter in these matters.[54] He consulted the Holy See, and at the same time the other bishops, whom he found in agreement with their leader: and without discussing further the matter [of Nestorian heresy] in his letter which he wrote to the new doctors, he sent them "the letters, the decisions, and the decrees formulated by the ecclesiastical authority: exhorting them to submit to it, like himself, and not to believe themselves more knowledgeable than the universal Church: telling them at the same time that, in view of the agreement of the authority of the apostolic See and of synodal unanimity, innovators could no longer escape being taken for heretics, and he himself and the other faithful dared have no further communication with them."[55] This is how that prince decided: and his decision was nothing else than an absolute submission to the decisions of the Church.

[54] *Epist. Car. Mag. ad Elipand.*, in *Concil. Gall.*, Vol. II.   [55] Ibid., Vol. II.

Great kings and the worship of God

So much for what regards faith. As for ecclesiastical discipline, it is enough for me to report here the ordinance of an emperor [who was] King of France: "I will, he said to the bishops, that – supported by our help and seconded by our power, as good order requires – you may execute that which your authority demands."[56] Everywhere else the royal power gives the law, and walks first in sovereignty. In ecclesiastical matters it only supports and serves: *famulante, ut decet, potestate nostra*: these are the very words of the prince. In matters not only of faith, but even of ecclesiastical discipline, the decision is for the Church: to the prince belongs the protection, the defense, the execution of the ecclesiastical canons and regulations.

It is the spirit of Christianity that the Church be governed by canon laws. At the Council of Chalcedon the emperor Marcian, hoping that certain rules of discipline would be established in the Church, himself proposed them in person to the Council, that they might be established by the authority of this holy assembly.[57] And in the same Council, being moved by a question in which the laws of the emperor seemed not to be in accord with the canon laws, the judges nominated by the emperor to maintain good order in so numerous a council – at which there were six hundred and thirty bishops – pointed out this contradiction [between Imperial and canon law] to the Fathers, and asked them what they thought about this matter. At once "the holy Council cried in a common voice: Let the canon laws carry the day, let the canons be obeyed"[58] – showing by this response that even if (through condescension and the good of peace) the Church yields in certain matters which concern its governance to the secular authority, its spirit, when it acts freely (which pious princes will always freely grant it) is to act by its own rules, so that its decrees prevail everywhere.

12th Proposition
The priesthood and the empire are two powers [which are] independent, but united

The priesthood in the spiritual [realm] and the empire in the temporal depend only on God.[59] But the ecclesiastical order recognizes the empire in the temporal [sphere]: as kings, in the spiritual [realm],

---
[56] *Lud. Pii Capit.* XI, title IV, in *Concil. Gall.*, Vol. II.
[57] *Conc. Chalced.* act. VI, Vol. VI *Concil.*, col. 575ff.
[58] Ibid., act. XIII, col. 716.   [59] Dante, *De monarchia* III.

recognize themselves as humble children of the Church. Every state in the world turns on these two powers. This is why they owe each other a mutual help. "Zorobabel (who represented the temporal power) shall bear the glory, and rule upon his throne: and the pontiff and the sacrifice-giver shall rule upon his, and the counsel of peace (that is to say a perfect mutual aid) shall be between them both."[60]

13th Proposition
The danger facing kings who choose bad pastors

This is said for the benefit of kings who have received from the Church the right (under whatever form it may be) to name or to introduce bishops and other prelates – but principally for the benefit of the kings of France, who have this right through a perpetual concordat. I do not fear to say that this is the most important part of their cares, and also the most dangerous, for which they will have to render a great account to God.

The whole instruction of the people depends on this.[61] "For the lips of the priest shall keep knowledge, and the people shall seek the law at his mouth.[62] The king himself receives it from his hand.[63] He is the angel (the envoy, the ambassador) of the Lord of hosts.[64] For Christ therefore we are ambassadors, says St. Paul, God as it were exhorting by us."[65]

Experience makes it only too clear that the ignorance or the disorders of pastors have caused almost all the evils of the Church – scandals which have made people down to the very elect (if this were possible) fall into error.

If then pastors are not, as St. Paul says, "workmen that need not be ashamed, rightly handling the words of truth,"[66] this is the greatest temptation of a faithful people.

Jesus Christ established his apostles "to be the light of the world, and placed them on the candlestick to illuminate the house of God"[67] (still more by their good life than by their doctrine). "If then the light that is in thee, be darkness: the darkness itself how great it shall be!"[68]

You, then, who give more weight to ambition or to favoritism than to merit, by putting [in office] persons who are unworthy either

[60] Zach. 6:13.   [61] Mal. 2:7.   [62] Ibid., 7.
[63] Deut. 17:18.   [64] Mal. 2:7.   [65] 2 Cor. 5:20.
[66] 2 Tim. 2:15.   [67] Matt. 5:14-15.   [68] Matt. 6:23.

through ignorance or through the way they live – have you undertaken to render the priesthood and even the Church itself contemptible? Listen to what a prophet says to such pastors: "You have departed out of the way, and you have scandalized the people of God, by not observing the law (which you preach): I have delivered you up to the contempt of the nations (you will fall into disparagement): you will be vile in their eyes."[69]

For what can one do with "an insipid and tasteless salt? It is good for nothing any more, says the son of God, but to be cast out and trodden on by men."[70]

It is written of "Simon the high priest, the son of Onias, that in mounting the holy altar, he honored and ornamented the sacred vesture which he wore."[71] By contrast the pontiffs who are not holy, by going up to the holy altar, dishonor the holy garment which makes them be viewed with so much respect, and tarnish the brightness of the Church and of religion.

What will you do, then, O prince, to avoid the misfortune of giving bad pastors to the Church? Do as St. Paul says: "Let these also first be proved, and then let them minister."[72] If he speaks thus of deacons, what would he say of bishops? The clergy is a militia: do not put at its head him who has never had the command. Consult the views of the public [*la voix publique*]. "It is necessary, says St. Paul, that he whom one wants to make bishops have a good testimony, even from those who are without (even, if possible, from heretics and infidels, but still more from the faithful) – lest he fall into reproach."[73]

Every time it is necessary to appoint a bishop, the prince should believe that Jesus Christ himself speaks to him in this way: O prince who names ministers for me, I want you to give me those who are worthy of me. I made you king: make me reign, and give me ministers who will cause me to be obeyed. Whoever obeys me, obeys you: your people is the people I have placed in your care. My Church is in your hands. This choice was not natural to your office: you have wished to take charge of it; take care, at your peril and in my service.

Kings must not believe, on the pretext that they have the choice of pastors, that they are at liberty to choose according to their liking: they are obligated to choose them in the way that the Church wants them

[69] Mal. 2:8–9.
[70] Matt. 5:13.
[71] Ecclus. 50:1,12.
[72] 1 Tim. 3:10.
[73] Ibid. 7.

chosen. For the Church, leaving them the nomination or the choice, has not claimed to exempt its ministers from its discipline.

The summary of all the laws of the Church, from the Council of Trent, is this:[74] in choosing bishops, one is obligated "to choose those whom one judges in conscience to be most worthy, and most useful to the Church, on pain of mortal sin." A decree that one cannot read too much, or too often inculcate in princes. "What manner of man the ruler of a city is, such also are they that dwell therein,"[75] says the Holy Spirit. Thus "the whole state, and the whole order of the family of Jesus Christ is in peril, if what one hopes to find in the body is not first found in the head," says the Council of Trent.[76] It is the same, in proportion, with all the ministers and the prelates of the Church.

The prince, by a bad choice of prelates, charges himself before God and his Church with the most terrible of accountings: not only with all the evil which is done by unworthy prelates, but still more the omission of all the good which would be done if they were better.

14th Proposition
The prince must protect piety, and cherish men of good will

They are the underpinning of the state. "If there are fifty just in this abominable (let it not be named), if there are forty-five, if there are forty, or thirty, or twenty – if there are so many as ten, I will not destroy it for the sake of these ten just,"[77] the Lord said to Abraham.[78]

15th Proposition
The prince does not suffer impious people, blasphemers, those who swear, perjurors, nor sorcerers

"A wise king scattereth the wicked, and curveth vaults over them."[79] He closes them up in dungeons, from which no one can draw them. Or, as others translate the original text: "He turns the wheels over them."[80] He breaks them, he reduces them to powder, by causing

---

[74] *Sess. XXIV, decr. reform.*, Ch. 1.   [75] Ecclus. 10:2.
[76] *Sess. XXIV, decr. reform.*, Ch. 1.   [77] Gen. 18:26ff.
[78] Ibid., 26ff.   [79] Prov. 20:26.   [80] Ibid., 26.

chariots armed with iron to roll over them: as Gideon did to the followers of Soccoth,[81] and David to the children of Ammon.[82]

The Lord says of Moses: "Bring forth the blasphemer without the camp" (one must not breathe the same air as he, and his last breath exhaled within would infect it): "and let them that heard him, put their hands upon his head (in witness), and let all the people stone him. And thou shalt speak, God added, to the children of Israel: the man that curseth his God, shall bear his sin. And he that blasphemeth the name of the Lord, dying let him die: all the multitude shall stone him, whether he be a native or a stranger."[83] Each must purge himself of the part he could have had in so abominable a crime.

Nabuchodonosor, an infidel prince, astonished by the miracles of God – who had delivered from the flames those three young men who are so famous in sacred history – made this ordinance: "By me therefore this decree is made, that every people, tribe, and tongue, which shall speak blasphemy against the God of Sidrach, Misach, and Abednago, shall be destroyed, and their houses laid waste: for there is no other God that can save in this manner."[84]

The perjurer is an impious man and a blasphemer "who takes the name of God in vain,"[85] and who, by this, treats God as a vain thing: who does not believe that God is just, or powerful, or veritable: who defies him to do evil to him, and no more fears his justice (which he brings down on himself) than if he named a vain and mute idol in place of God.

Swearing frequently verges on blasphemy, and exposes one to perjury.[86] "The speech that sweareth much shall make the hair of the head stand upright: and its irreverence shall make one stop his ears[87] ... A man that sweareth much, shall be filled with iniquity, and a scourge shall not depart from his house."[88]

It is for the same reason that the prince must exterminate from the face of the earth sorcerers and magicians, who attribute divine power to themselves or to demons. And one knows what happened to Saul, for having himself violated the ordinance which he had made against this impiety.[89]

[81] Judg. 8:16.
[82] 2 Kings 12:31; 1 Par. 20:3.
[83] Lev. 24:14ff.
[84] Dan. 3:96.
[85] Exod. 20:7.
[86] Ecclus. 27:15.
[87] Ibid., 15.
[88] Exod. 23:12.
[89] 1 Kings 28.

16th Proposition
Blasphemies cause kings and armies to perish

Sennacherib, King of Assyria, after having made blasphemy-filled threats against Ezechias and his people, sent them ambassadors with a letter containing these words:[90] "Let not thy God deceive thee, in whom thou trustest . . . Have the gods of the nations delivered any of them? . . . Where are the king of Emath, and the king of Arphad, and the kings of so many vanquished peoples," who have uselessly invoked their gods against me? "This day, saith Ezechias, is a day of tribulation, and of rebuke, and of blasphemy (but, O Lord, we can do nothing about it). This whole people makes useless efforts, like those of a woman whose child is ready to be born, and hath not strength. But it may be that God will hear the blasphemies of his enemies (who compare him to the idols of the Gentiles). And Ezechias took the letters from the hand of the ambassadors, and he went into the Temple, and he showed them quite open, before the Lord."[91] He had no stronger arms. And the blasphemies of this impious prince caused him to perish, he and his army: and in one night a hundred and eighty-five thousand men had their throats cut by the hand of an angel.[92]

Though God does not always carry out such striking executions, he knows how to avenge blasphemies in ways equally efficacious, but more hidden. He who had sent his angel against Sennacherib, inspired in Judas Maccabeus an invincible courage against Nicanor. The impious one perished together with his immense army, which menaced heaven: "the hand which he had raised against the Temple was affixed to it. His head was exposed from the top of a tower. And his tongue, with which he had said, Is there a powerful God in heaven, as I am powerful upon the earth?, was given as prey to the birds of heaven. And all the heavens blessed the Lord in saying: Blessed be God, who has preserved his Temple."[93]

---

[90] 4 Kings 19:10–13. [91] Ibid., 3–4.
[92] Ibid., 14,15,35. [93] 2 Macc. 15:4,5,32–34.

17th Proposition
The prince is the religious observer of his oath

We have seen the qualities of the oath, indicated by St. Paul:[94] and first of all, "that men swear by one greater than themselves."[95]

This bears on kings in a quite special way. One swears by something greater than oneself: that is to say one swears by his sovereign, by his judge. God is the sovereign of kings and of supreme powers. He is their special judge, because he alone can judge them, and because he must judge them even when he would not judge the rest of men.

"Men swear, the Apostle adds, by something immutable." This he explains by saying that "men swear by something which cannot lie, nor deceive anyone."[96] And this is what ought to be ordained principally with respect to kings: for, everyone being so ready to flatter them and to deceive them, one must take for their judge and witness the one [God] who does not flatter them.

The prince swears to God in his [coronation] rites (as we are going to see at greater length) to maintain the privileges of the churches; to preserve the Catholic faith which he has received from his fathers; to stop acts of violence, and to render justice to all his subjects. This oath is the foundation of public tranquillity: and God is the more obligated (by his own truth) to see it upheld, since he is its sole avenger.

There is another kind of oath, which sovereign powers swear to their equals, to keep the faith of treaties. For since in every treaty one submits to some judge as executor, those who have only God for their judge have recourse to him in the case of treaties – as the final appeal of public peace.

From all this it follows that princes who fail in their oaths (God forbid that this should ever happen to them), as far as this lies in them, make vain everything that is most solid among men, and at the same time make impossible both social life and the repose of the human race. In this way they make both God and men their just and irreconcilable enemies – since, to conciliate them, there remains nothing beyond that which they have rendered null.

---

[94] Heb. 6:13.   [95] Ibid., 16.   [96] Ibid., 18.

Whoever does not feel how terrible this is, has nothing more to feel than hell itself, and a divine vengeance manifestly and pitilessly declared.

18th Proposition
In which we treat the oath from the coronation-rites of the kings of France

The consecrating archbishop, or the bishops, speak to the king in these terms from the beginning of the rites, in the name of all the churches which are subject to him: "We implore you to grant to us and to our churches, which you preserve and defend, the canonical privilege, together with the law and the justice which is their due."[97] This includes the ecclesiastical immunities, equally established by canon law and by the [civil] laws. And the king responds: "I promise to preserve, for you and for your churches, the canonical privilege, together with the law, and the justice which is due them. And I promise to grant them the defense of these things, as a king ought lawfully to grant it in his kingdom to a bishop, and to the Church which is committed to his care."[98]

Then one sings the *Te Deum*. And the king, standing, makes the following promises: "I promise in the name of Jesus Christ, these three things to the Christian people subject to me. First, that the whole Christian people of the Church of God preserve for all time a true peace, under our orders. In the second place, that I forbid all rapacity and iniquity. In the third place, that in every judgment I ordain equity and pity."

After the litanies have been recited, the prostrated prince raises himself up, and is interrogated in this way by the metropolitan *seigneur*: "Will you uphold the holy faith, which has been left to you by Catholic men, and observe it through good works? And the king responds: I will. The metropolitan continues: Will you be the tutor and the defender of the churches and of the ministers of the Church? And the king responds: I will. The metropolitan finally asks: Will you govern and defend your kingdom, which has been given you by God, according to the justice of your fathers? And the king responds: I will; and so far as it is possible for me, with the grace of God, [I will be] a

---

[97] *Ceremonial français*, ed. T. and D. Godefroy (Paris, 1649), Vol. I, p. 14.
[98] Ibid., p. 14.

consolation to everyone. Thus I promise to act faithfully, in everything and everywhere."[99]

Finally he is asked "if he will defend the holy churches of God, and their pastors, and all the people subject to him, justly and religiously, by a royal providence, according to the customs of his fathers.[100] And after he has answered that he will do all this with all his power, the bishop asks the people if they will not undertake to submit to such a prince (who promises them justice and every kind of good), and subject themselves to his reign with a firm fidelity, and obey his commands, according to the words of the apostle:[101] Let every soul be subject to the higher powers: be it the king, as above all the others.[102] Then let it be answered in a single voice, by all the clergy, and all the people: Let it be thus; let it be thus. Amen. Amen."[103]

After the customary unction, the bishop offers this prayer: "Grant him, Lord, that he may be the strong defender of his country, the consoler of the churches and the holy monasteries, with great piety and a royal munificence. Let him be the most courageous and the most powerful of all kings: the conqueror of his enemies. Let him cut down those who rise up against him, and the pagan nations. Let him be terrible to his enemies, by the great force of the royal power. Let him appear magnificent, lovable and pious to the great of the kingdom: and let him be feared and loved by everyone."[104]

In giving him the sceptre, the hand of justice and the sword, the archbishop says to him: "Let this sword be blessed, that it may be (according to God's order) the defender of the holy churches.[105] And one warns the prince to remember him of whom it was said by the prophet: Put your sword by your side, O most powerful[106] – in order that equity have all its force; that the ramparts of iniquity be powerfully destroyed; and finally that you merit, through the care you take for justice, to reign eternally with the son of God, whose image you are."[107]

The king also promises "to preserve the sovereignty, the rights and the nobilities of the crown of France: without alienating them or conveying them to anyone; and to exterminate in good faith, according to his power, all heretics identified and condemned by the Church."[108] And he affirms all these things by an oath.

[99] Ibid., p. 16.   [100] Ibid., pp. 16–17.   [101] Rom. 13:1.   [102] 1 Peter 2:13.
[103] *Ceremonial français*, pp. 18–19.   [104] Ibid., p. 19.   [105] Ibid., pp. 20–21.
[106] Ps. 44:4.   [107] *Ceremonial français*, p. 21.   [108] Ibid., p. 33.

In the blessing of the sword, God is asked "that the sword be in the hand of him who desires to arm himself with it, for the defense and the protection of the churches, of widows, of orphans, and of all the servants of God."[109] In this way one shows that force is established only in favor of justice and reason, and to sustain weakness.

Riches, abundance of goods of all sorts, splendor and royal magnificence, are asked of God for the king, through this prayer: "Deign, Lord, that the dew of heaven and the fat of the earth, the wheat, the wine, the oil, and all the richness and abundance of fruits, be given to the king, and continued by divine largesse. Such that, during his reign, health and peace will be in the kingdom: and such that the glory and majesty of the royal dignity will shine in the palace in the eyes of everyone, and cast everywhere beams of the royal power."[110]

This splendor must convey to all minds an impression of the power of kings, and seem to be an image of the celestial court.

What accounting will not princes who neglect to keep promises so solemnly sworn have to make to God!

19th Proposition
In doubtful cases, one must decide in favor of an oath

It is this that Joshua did. The city of Gabaon was one of those that God had destined for the residence of his people, and whose inhabitants he had ordered, without pity, to be put to the sword, because of their crimes, as well as all the others. The Amorrhites, inhabitants of Gabaon, frightened by the victories of Joshua and of the Israelites, made use of subtlety; and, feigning to come from far-away countries, they approached them saying that they "came from far away, wondering at the prodigies which God had wrought on the [Israelites'] behalf, to submit to their empire."[111] They did everything which was necessary to deceive Joshua and the other leaders, who guaranteed them their life with an oath.

Three days later, the truth was known. The question was that of knowing whether one should hold to a sworn alliance. Two strong reasons opposed this: one was the fraud of these peoples, who had been pardoned on the strength of a false statement; the other was the command of God, who ordained that they be entirely exterminated.

[109] Ibid., p. 34.   [110] Ibid., p. 35.   [111] Josh. 9:3–6.

But Joshua and the leaders of the people held to the oath and the alliance.

On the question of surprise, it was said that one must inform himself of the truth before committing himself, and "consult the mouth of the Lord"[112] (which Joshua had failed to do); but that, the commitment having been made, and the name of God having been interposed, one had to hold fast to it.

To the divine command to run all these people through with the sword Joshua and the leaders opposed an older and more important commandment, that of not taking the name of God in vain. "We have sworn to them in the name of the Lord the God of Israel, and therefore we may not touch them."[113] The whole people, murmuring a little earlier, saw the force of this reason, and approved the decision of Joshua and his chiefs.

God himself confirmed it, when he delivered Gabaon from the Amorrhite kings who held the besieged city, through that famous victory in which Joshua stopped the sun.[114]

And long afterwards, during the lifetime of David – since during the reign of Saul this cruel prince had wanted to move this question again, in order to kill the Gabaonites under a pretext of zeal – God sent the plague in punishment of this attempt, and did not let himself yield until the cruelty of Saul had been rigorously punished in his family:[115] whether because it had concurred [in Saul's attempt], or whether in just punishment of another crime. Thus the decision of Joshua was confirmed by a manifest declaration of the will of God: and the whole people adhered to it down to the latest times.

The power of the decision had a perpetual effect: and not only under the kings, but also in the times of Esdras and the return from captivity.[116]

It is thus that the Gabaonites were saved. The faith of the people of God, the holiness of oaths, the majesty and the justice of the God of Israel, shone magnificently on this occasion: and it left to posterity a memorable example of interpreting treaties in favor of [keeping] an oath.

---

[112] Ibid., 14.   [113] Ibid., 19.   [114] Josh. 10.   [115] 2 Kings 21:1ff.
[116] 1 Esdr. 2:70; 7:7,24; 8:17,20; Neh. 7:60; 10:28.

Article VI

Religious motives peculiar to kings

1st Proposition
It is God who makes kings, and who establishes reigning houses

Saul was looking for the she-asses of his father Cis; David was grazing the sheep of his father Isai, when God elevated them from so low a condition to royalty.[1]

Since he gives kingdoms, he cuts them in half when it pleases him. He caused Jeroboam to be told by his prophet: "I will rend the kingdom out of the hand of Solomon, and will give thee ten tribes . . . because he [Jeroboam] hath forsaken me, and hath adored Astarthe the goddess of the Sidonians, and Chamos the god of Moab, and Moloch the god of the children of Ammon . . . But one tribe shall remain to him for the sake of my servant David, and Jerusalem the city, which I have chosen."[2]

The prophet Jehu, son of Hanani, was ordered to say to Baasa, the third king of Israel after Jeroboam, "I have exalted thee out of the dust, and made thee prince over my people Israel: and thou hast walked in the way of Jeroboam, and hast provoked my anger against thee: I will cut down the posterity of Baasa, and the posterity of his house."[3]

By the same authority a prophet went to Jehu, son of Josaphat, son of Namsi: "and finding him amidst the great said loudly: O prince, I must talk with thee. And Jehu said: Unto whom of all of us? And he said: To thee, O prince. And he took him, according to the order he had received from God, into the most secret chamber of the house, and said to him: The Lord hath anointed thee king over the people of Israel: and thou shalt cut off the house of Achab thy master."[4]

God exercises the same power over infidel nations. "Go, he said to the prophet Elias, and return on thy way through the desert to

---

[1] 1 Kings 9; 10; 16. [2] 3 Kings 11:31–33.
[3] 3 Kings 16:1–3.   [4] 4 Kings 9:5–7.

Damascus: and when thou art come thither, thou shalt anoint Hazael to be king over Syria."[5]

By these extraordinary acts, God only shows more clearly that he operates in all the kingdoms of the universe, to which he gives such masters as please him. "I am the Lord, he said; I made the earth, and the men, and the animals . . . and I have given it to whom it seemed good in my eyes."[6]

It is again God who establishes reigning houses.[7] He said to Abraham: "Kings shall come out of thee,"[8] and to David: "The Lord will make thee a house,"[9] and to Jeroboam: "If thou art faithful to me, I will make thee a house, as I did for David."[10]

He determines the time that royal houses will last. "Thy children shall sit upon the throne of Israel to the fourth generation, he said to Jehu."[11]

"I have given all these lands into the hand of Nabuchodonosor king of Babylon . . . And all nations shall serve him, and his son, and his son's son, till the time come."[12]

And all this is the consequence of the eternal counsel, by which God has resolved "to make all men issue from one alone, to dwell upon the whole face of the earth, determining appointed times, and the limits of their habitation."[13]

2nd Proposition
God inspires obedience in nations, and lets spread in them a spirit of uprising

God, who keeps in check the waves of the sea, is also the only one who can keep the indocile humor of the nations under the yoke. And this is why David sang to him: "Blessed be the Lord my God, my protector in whom I hope, who submits my people to my power."[14]

He acted on the hearts of the new subjects whom he had given to Saul: "And a part of the army, whose hearts God had touched, followed Saul."[15]

In inspiring obedience in subjects, he also places a secret confidence in the heart of the prince, which makes him command without

---

[5] 3 Kings 19:15.   [6] Jer. 27:5.
[7] Cf. Bossuet, *Oraison funèbre de Marie-Thérèse d'Autriche.*
[8] Gen. 17:6.   [9] 2 Kings 7:11.   [10] 3 Kings 11:38.   [11] 4 Kings 10:30.
[12] Jer. 27:6–7.   [13] Acts 17:26.   [14] Ps. 143:1–2.   [15] 1 Kings 10:26.

fear: "And God gave unto Saul another heart."[16] He who viewed himself hitherto as the least of the whole people of Israel, took in hand the command of peoples and of armies, and felt in himself all the power needful to act as a master.

After the prophet sent by God had spoken to Jehu in order to make him king, "the servants of his lord [Achab] said to him: Why came this mad man to thee? And he said to them: everything he will have said is false; but rather do thou tell us."[17] This is what they said, being little-disposed, as one can see, to believe the prophet in this matter. But Jehu had no sooner revealed to them that the prophet had consecrated him as king than "they made haste and taking every man his garment laid it under his feet, after the manner of a judgment seat, and they sounded the trumpet, and said: Jehu is king."[18] And they forgot Joram, their legitimate king, for whom they had just risked their lives in a bloody battle against the King of Syria, and in the siege of Ramoth Galaad – so promptly did God change their hearts.

One must always remember that these extraordinary things only serve to manifest that which God does ordinarily in a way which is equally efficacious, though more hidden. At the same time that he inspired the great to follow Jehu by a secret judgment of his providence, he spread among the people a spirit of universal rebellion, and nothing in the kingdom could sustain itself. Jehu marched, with his band of conspirators, to Jezrahel, where the king was. When he was seen arriving, Joram sent to ask him whether he came in a spirit of peace.[19] What hast thou to do with peace? he said to him who brought him the message. Go behind, and follow me. Joram sent out another to make the same demand: he received the same answer, and he imitated the first by joining forces with Jehu. The king, who received no answer, advanced in person with the King of Judah, thinking to astonish Jehu by the presence of two kings united, one of them his sovereign. "And when Joram saw Jehu, he said: Is there peace, Jehu? And he answered: What peace can there be for thee? . . . But Jehu bent his bow with his hand, and shot Joram between the shoulders: and the arrow went out through the heart of Joram, who fell dead at his feet."[20] He stayed in the palace of Queen Jezebel, mother of Joram: "she appeared at the window richly adorned, her eyes colored with an exquisite make-up. Who is this?, said Jehu. And he comman-

[16] Ibid., 9. [17] 4 Kings 9:11–12.
[18] Ibid., 13. [19] Ibid., 18–21. [20] Ibid., 22–24.

ded the eunuchs of this princess to throw her down headlong."[21] After this bloody execution, he sent orders to Samaria to kill all the children of the king:[22] and all the great of the kingdom resolved that they should die, to the number of seventy, whose heads were brought to Jehu: and he invaded the kingdom without resistance. God avenged in this way the impieties of Achab and of Jezebel, on them and on their house.

This is the spirit of revolt which he sends, when he wants to overturn thrones. Without authorizing rebellions, God permits them, and punishes crimes by other crimes, which he also punishes in his good time, always terribly and always justly.

3rd Proposition
God decides the fortune of states

"The Lord God shall strike Israel as a reed is shaken in the water: and he shall root up Israel out of this good land, which he gave to their fathers; and like a breath of wind he will transport them to Babylon."[23] So great is the ease with which he overturns the most flourishing kingdoms.

4th Proposition
The happiness of princes comes from God, and often has great reversals

Swollen by a long series of prosperities, a foolish prince says in his heart: I am happy, everything succeeds for me; fortune, which has always been favorable to me, governs everything among men, and no evil will ever come to me. "I am queen," said Babylon, who gloried in her vast and redoubtable empire: "I am seated" (on my happy and tranquil throne): "I shall be always dominant; I shall not sit as a widow, nor ever be deprived of any good; I will never know what it is to be barren or weak."[24] You do not dream, fool, that it is God who sends you your felicity: perhaps to blind you, and to make your misfortune more intolerable. "I have given all these lands into the hands of Nabuchodonosor king of Babylon: moreover also the beasts of the field I have given him to serve him . . . But the nation and the

---

[21] Ibid., 30–33. [22] Ibid. 10:1ff.
[23] 3 Kings 14:15. [24] Isa. 47:7–8.

kingdom that will not suffer the yoke shall perish: I will visit upon that nation with the sword, and with famine, and with pestilence, until I destroy them entirely,"[25] in order that nothing be lacking in the happiness or the misery of his enemies.

But all this is only for a time, and this excess of happiness has a prompt reversal. "For while he was walking in his Babylon, in the halls and in the courts, and was saying in his heart: Is it not this great Babylon, which I have built with my power and my shining glory?," without casting even the smallest glance on the supreme power, from whom all this happiness came to him: "A voice came down from heaven, and said to him: Nabuchodonosor, it is to thee that I speak. Thy kingdom shall pass from thee at this moment: And they shall cast thee out from among men, and thy dwelling shall be with cattle and wild beasts . . . till thou know that the most High ruleth in the kingdom of men, and giveth it to whomsoever he will."[26]

O prince! Take care, then, not to consider your happiness as something attached to your person; if you do not think at the same time that it comes from God, who can equally give it and take it away, "these two things shall come upon thee suddenly in one day, barrenness and widowhood."[27] All evils will overwhelm you. "For when they shall say, peace and security: then shall sudden destruction come upon them."[28]

Thus King Belshazzar, in the middle of a royal feast which he undertook with great joy[29] with his lords and courtiers, dreamed only of "praising his gods of gold and silver, of brass and of marble," which crowned him with so many pleasures and with so much glory – when those three so-famous fingers appeared in the air, and wrote his [death] sentence on the wall: "Mane, Thecel, Phares. God has numbered thy days, and thy reign is finished. Thou art weighed in the balance, and art found wanting. Thy kingdom is divided, and is given to the Medes and Persians."[30]

[25] Jer. 27:6–8.   [26] Dan. 4:26–29.   [27] Isa. 47:9.
[28] 1 Thess. 5:3.   [29] Dan. 5:1ff.   [30] Ibid., 1ff.

5th Proposition
There is no chance in the governance of human affairs: and fortune is only a word which has no sense

It was in vain that the blind children of Israel "set a table for fortune, and offered libations upon it."[31] They called fortune the queen of heaven, the ruler of the universe, and said to Jeremiah:[32] O prophet, "we no longer wish to listen to your speech: we want to act according to our will. We shall sacrifice to the queen of heaven: and we will pour out drink offerings to her, as we and our fathers have done, our princes and our kings. Everything succeeds for us, and we will be overflowing with good things."

It is thus that, seduced by a long string of happy successes, the men of the world attribute everything to fortune, and know no other divinity. They call the queen of heaven that dominant and favorable star which, in their opinion, makes all their plans prosper. It is my star, they say, it is my ascendancy, it is the powerful and benign heavenly body which declared my nativity, which places all my enemies at my feet.

But the world contains neither fortune nor dominant stars. Nothing dominates save God. "The stars, like his army, march at his order: each shines in the post it has been given.[33] They were called, and they said: Here we are: and with cheerfulness they have shined forth to him that made them."[34]

6th Proposition
Since everything in the world flows from wisdom, nothing happens by chance

"God poured wisdom out upon all his works.[35] God saw all, numbered all, measured all.[36] God has ordered all things in measure, and number, and weight."[37] Nothing is excessive, nothing is lacking. With respect to the whole, nothing is larger or smaller than is necessary: that which seems defective from one side, serves in a superior and hidden order, which God knows. Everything is spread from generous hands: and nonetheless everything is done and given with measure. "The very hairs of our head are all numbered.[38] The days of man are

---

[31] Isa. 45:11.   [32] Jer. 44:16–17.   [33] Bar. 3:34.   [34] Ibid., 35.
[35] Ecclus. 1:10.   [36] Ibid., 9.   [37] Wisd. 11:21.   [38] Matt. 10:30.

short, and the number of his months is with thee: thou hast appointed his bounds which cannot be passed."[39] Even a sparrow does not fall on the ground without your heavenly father."[40] That which would prevail on one side, has its counter-weight on the other: the scale is accurate, and the equilibrium perfect.

Where wisdom is infinite, there is no room left for chance.

7th Proposition
There is a particular providence [une providence particulière] in the governance of human affairs

"It is the part of man to prepare the soul: and of the Lord to govern the tongue."[41]

"The heart of man disposeth his way: but the Lord must direct his steps."[42]

In vain does one rehearse in his mind all his speeches and all his plans: the occasion always brings with it something unexpected, such that one always says and does more or less than one had thought. And this place, unknown to me in their own actions and in their own thought-processes, is the secret place in which God acts, the spring which he moves.

If he governs men as individuals [les hommes en particulier] in this fashion, for a much stronger reason does he so govern them in state-bodies and in kingdoms. It is also in affairs of state "that we are (principally) in his hand, we and our works, and all wisdom, and the knowledge and skill of works."[43]

"God hath made in particular the hearts of men; he understandeth all their works. That is why, the Psalmist adds, the king is not saved by a great army . . . but by the powerful hand of God."[44] He who governs the hearts of all men, and who holds in his hand the spring that makes them move, has revealed to a great king [the fact] that he exercises this sovereign right especially over the hearts of kings: "As the division of waters (is in the hands of him that controls them), so the heart of the king is in the hand of the Lord: whithersoever he will he shall turn it."[45] He governs particularly the prime mover, through whom he sets human affairs in motion.

---

[39] Job 14:5. [40] Matt. 10:29. [41] Prov. 16:1. [42] Ibid., 9.
[43] Wisd. 7:16. [44] Ps. 32:15–16. [45] Prov. 21:1.

8th Proposition
Kings, more than all others, must abandon themselves to the providence of God

All the preceding propositions end up at this one. The greater is the work of kings, the more it surpasses human weakness, the more God has reserved it to himself, the more the prince who manages it must unite himself with God, and abandon himself to his counsels.

In vain does a king imagine that he is the arbiter of his fate, because he is the arbiter of that of others: he is more governed than governing: "There is no wisdom, there is no prudence, there is no counsel against the Lord."[46]

"For the thoughts of mortal men are fearful, and our counsels uncertain."[47]

"There are many thoughts in the heart of a man (they render him timid and irresolute): but the counsels of God are eternal."[48]

The latter alone exist always, they are invincible.

9th Proposition
No power can escape the hands of God

Solomon, well warned by a prophet that Jeroboam would one day divide his kingdom, tried to have him killed: but in vain, since he found a safe retreat with Sesac, King of Egypt.[49]

Achab, King of Israel, was warned by Micheas that he would perish in a battle. "I will change my dress, he said, and so I will go to the battle." But while the enemy looked for him in vain, and turned all its effort against Josaphat King of Judah, who alone appeared in royal garments, "it happened that one of the people shot an arrow at a venture, and struck the King of Israel between the neck and the shoulders. I am wounded, he cried: turn thy hand, he continued to him that drove his chariot, and carry me out of the battle." But the blow which he had received was mortal; and he died the same evening.[50]

Everything seemed to conspire to save him. For though there was an order to attack him alone, he was not recognized: and Josaphat, who was mistaken for him, was delivered – God turning aside the

---

[46] Prov. 2:30. [47] Wisd. 9:14. [48] Prov. 19:21.
[49] 3 Kings 11:40. [50] 2 Par. 18:27–34.

blows which were visited on him. Achab, who was not shot at because he could not be recognized, was hit by an arrow by chance. But that which seems to be shot by chance, is secretly guided by the hand of God.

Only a moment more was needed to save Achab: the sun was going to set; the night was going to separate the combatants: but it was necessary that he perish: "And he was killed with the setting of the sun."[51]

It was in vain that Sedecias believed, during the taking of Jerusalem, that he had avoided by flight the hands of Nabuchodonosor, to whom God wanted to deliver him: "He was captured with his children, who were killed before his eyes: and then they blinded him,"[52] after this sad spectacle.

David was more wise and far-sighted than any man of his age; and he used all his skill to cover up his crime. But God saw it: "Thou didst it secretly: but I will do this thing in the sight of all Israel, and in the sight of the sun"[53] (though you had thought what you did enveloped in impenetrable shadows).

Subtleties are useless: everything that a man does to save himself, only hastens his ruin. "He is fallen into the hole he made; and the snare we set captures us."[54]

There is no recourse, then, save abandoning oneself to God with a full confidence.

10th Proposition
These sentiments produce a true piety in the heart of kings

Such was the piety of David. Fleeing before his son Absalom, abandoned by all his own, he said to Zadok the priest and to the Levites, who brought him the ark of the covenant of the Lord: "Carry back the ark of God into Jerusalem: if I shall find grace in the sight of the Lord, he will bring me again, and he will show me it, and his tabernacle. But if he shall say to me: Thou pleasest me not, I am ready: let him do that which is good before him."[55] I am submitted to his will.

His servants dissolved in tears, seeing him obliged to flee with so much haste and ignominy; but David, with an intrepid heart, revived

---

[51] Ibid., 34. [52] Jer. 39:4–7. [53] 2 Kings 12:12.
[54] Ps. 7:16; 34:8; Ecclus. 27:29. [55] 2 Kings 15:24–26.

their courage. He even wanted, through a generosity which was natural to him, to send back six hundred of his most valiant soldiers, with Ethai the Gethite (who commanded them), in order not to expose them to a ruin which seemed inevitable. "Why comest thou with us? For myself, he added, I shall go where I must go."[56] What courage, what greatness of soul! And at the same time, what resignation to the will of God! He recognized the divine hand which was justly pursuing him, and put all his confidence in that same hand which alone could save him.

11th Proposition
This piety is active

There is an abandoning [of oneself] to God which comes from power and piety; there is a kind which comes from laziness. To abandon onself to God without doing what one can on one's own side, involves laxness and nonchalance.

The piety of David does not have this low character at all. At the same time that he submissively awaited what God would ordain for the kingdom and for his person during the revolt of Absalom, he – without losing a moment's time – gave all the necessary orders to the troops, to his counsellors, and to his principal confidants, to guarantee his retreat and reestablish matters.[57]

God wills it: to act otherwise is to tempt him, despite his prohibition: "Thou shalt not tempt the Lord thy God."[58] It is not in vain that he has given you wisdom, foresight, liberty: he wills that you make use of them. Not to do so, and to say in one's heart: I shall abandon everything to the will of chance, and believe that there is no wisdom among men, on the pretext that it is subordinated to that of God, is to dispute with him, to will to shake off the yoke, and act as a desperate person.

12th Proposition
The prince who has failed must not lose hope, but return to God for penitence

Thus Manasses, King of Judah, after so many impieties and adulteries, after having spilled so much innocent blood, to the point of

---

[56] Ibid., 19–21.   [57] 2 Kings 15; 18.   [58] Deut. 6:16.

engulfing the walls of Jerusalem,[59] struck by the hand of God, "and delivered to his enemies who carried him to Babylon, bound with chains, prayed to the Lord his God in his distress, and did penance exceedingly before the God of his fathers; and he entreated him, and besought him earnestly. And God heard his prayer, and brought him again to Jerusalem into his kingdom; and Manasses knew that the Lord was the true God."[60] But one must remark well that the penitence of this prince was serious, his humility sincere, and his prayers urgent.

God sometimes does not fail to pay attention to the penitence of impious people when they, being converted, are frightened by his threats. Achab, having heard the threats which God was making through the prophet Elias, was frightened by them. "He rent his garments, and put haircloth upon his flesh, and fasted and slept in sackcloth, and walked with his head cast down (this head earlier so proud). God the Lord said to Elias: Hast thou not seen Achab humbled before me? Therefore, because he hath humbled himself for my sake, I will not bring the evil in his days, but in his son's days will I bring the evil upon his house."[61]

God seems to take pleasure in seeing great kings and proud kings humbled before him. It is not that the greatest kings are more [important] than other men in his eyes, before whom everything is equally nothing: but that their humiliation is all the greater an example to the human race.

One would never finish if one wanted to speak here of the penitence of David, so famous throughout the world. It so effaced all his sins, that it even seems as if God had entirely forgotten them. David remained as he was before, a man after God's heart: the model for good kings and the father *par excellence* of the Messiah. God gave to him, and even augmented, not only the spirit of justice, but still more the spirit of prophecy and other extraordinary gifts – such that one can say that he lost nothing.

---

[59] 4 Kings 31:2,16.   [60] 2 Par. 33:11–13.   [61] 3 Kings 31:27–29.

13th Proposition
Religion provides princes with particular motives of penitence

"To thee only have I sinned," said David.[62] To thee only, since thou hast made me independent of every power save thy own.[63] Such is the first motive: "To thee only have I sinned." I must, then, through this special motive of [compensating for] the offense which I have committed against thee, devote myself entirely to penitence.

The second motive is this: if princes are exposed to more dangerous temptations, God has given them greater means to make reparations through their good works.

The third is that the prince – whose sins are more striking – must also expiate them by a more edifying penitence.

14th Proposition
The kings of France have a particular obligation [une obligation particulière] to love the Church, and to be attached to the Holy See

"The holy Roman Church, the mother, the nurse, and the mistress of all the churches, must be consulted concerning all doubts which have to do with faith and morals: principally on the part of those who, like us, have been fathered in Jesus Christ by his ministry, and nourished by her [the Church] with the milk of Catholic doctrine." These are the words of Hincmar, the celebrated Archbishop of Reims.[64]

It is true that a part of this kingdom, for example the Church of Lyon and its neighbors, have received the faith from a mission which came to them from the East, and through the ministry of St. Polycarp, disciple of the apostle John. But, since the Church is one throughout the universe, this Eastern mission is no less favorable to the authority of the Holy See, than one which has come directly from it. This is clear from the doctrine of St. Irenius, Bishop of Lyon, who, from the second century, insisted so strongly on the necessity of uniting with the Roman Church: "as the principal Church of the universe, founded by the two principal Apostles, St. Peter and St. Paul."[65]

---

[62] Ps. 50:6.   [63] Ibid., 6.
[64] Hincmar, *De divortio Lotharii et Tetbergae*, preface.
[65] St. Irenée de Lyon, *Libros quinque adversus haereses* 1.3.

On the particular duties of royalty

The Gallican Church has been founded by the blood of an infinity of martyrs. Here I want to name only St. Pothin, and St. Irenius, the holy martyrs of Lyon and of Vienne, and St. Denis together with his holy companions.

The Gallican Church has furnished the most learned, the most holy, the most celebrated bishops who ever were: I will make mention only of St. Hilary and of St. Martin.

When the time came for the Roman empire to fall in the West, God, who handed over to the barbarians so fine a part of this empire, and that which included Rome (since become the head of the [Catholic] religion), destined for France kings who were to be the defenders of the Church. In order to convert them to the faith together with that whole bellicose nation of the Franks, he created that apostolic man, St. Remy[66] – through whom he renewed all the miracles which had burst on the scene in the founding of the most celebrated churches, as St. Remy himself observes in his testament.[67]

This great saint, this new Samuel, called to consecrate kings, consecrated those of France in the person of Clovis,[68] as he himself says, "to be the perpetual defender of the Church and of the poor,"[69] who are the most worthy object of royalty. He blessed them and their successors, whom he always called his children, and prayed to God day and night that they might persevere in the faith – a prayer answered by God with a quite particular prerogative, since France is the only kingdom in Christendom which has seen on its throne only kings who were children of the Church.[70]

All the saints who then existed were delighted by the baptism of Clovis; and during the decline of the Roman empire, they thought to see in the kings of France "a new light for the whole West and the whole Church."[71]

Pope Anastasius II also believed that he saw in the newly converted kingdom of France "a column of iron, which God has raised for the sustenance of his holy Church, while charity was growing cold everywhere else"[72] and even the emperors had abandoned the faith.

Pelagius II expected from the descendants of Clovis – as charitable

---

[66] *Test. S. Remig.*, in Flodoard, *Historia Ecclesiae Remensis* I.XVIII.
[67] Ibid., I.XVIII.   [68] Ibid., I.XVIII.
[70] Ibid., I.XVIII.   [69] Ibid., I.XVIII.
[71] *Epist. Avit. Vienn. ad Clodov.*, in *Con. Gall.*, Vol. 1, p. 154.
[72] Anastasius II, *Ep. II ad Clod.*, Vol. IV, *Conc.*, col. 1282.

neighbors of Italy and of Rome – the same protection for the Holy See which he had received from the emperors.[73] St. Gregory the Great went beyond his holy predecessors when, touched by the faith and the zeal of these kings, he placed them "as much above other sovereigns, as sovereigns are above individuals."[74]

The children of Clovis, not having walked in the paths which St. Remy had prescribed to them, God created another family to reign in France. The Popes and the whole Church blessed it in the person of Pepin, who was its head.[75] The Empire was established there, in the person of Charlemagne and his successors. No royal family was ever so beneficent towards the Roman Church. The family derived its whole temporal greatness therefrom; and the empire was never better united with the sacerdotal realm, nor more respectful toward the Popes, than when it was in the hands of the kings of France.

After these blessed days, Rome had some unfortunate masters: and the Popes had everything to fear, as much from the emperors as from a seditious people. But they always found in our kings the charitable neighbors that Pope Pelagius II had hoped for. France, more favorable to their sacred power than Italy and even Rome itself, became a kind of second See for them, where they held their councils, and from which they made their oracular utterances heard by the whole Church – as can be seen in the Councils of Troyes, of Clermont, of Toulouse, of Tours, and of Reims.

A third family had ascended the throne. A family, if possible, more pious than the two others, under whom France was declared by the Popes to be "a realm beloved and blessed by God, whose glory is inseparable from that of the Holy See."[76] A family, too, which alone in the entire universe can look back on seven hundred years of wearing the crown and ruling without interruption: and what is still more glorious, always Catholic – God, in his infinite mercy, not having permitted that a prince who had mounted the throne in a state of heresy should persevere in it.

Since it appears, from this survey of our history, that the greatest glory of the kings of France comes to them from their faith, and from the constant protection which they have given to the Church, they will

---

[73] Pelagius II, *Ep. ad Aunach.*, Vol. IV, *Conc. Gall.*, p. 376.
[74] Gregorius Magnus, *Epist.* I, VI; Ep. VI, Vol. II, col. 795.
[75] Paul I, *Ep. X ad Franc.*, *Conc. Gall.*, Vol. II, p. 59.
[76] Alexander III, *Ep. XXX, Conc.*, col. 1212, Vol. X.

not allow their glory to be weakened: and the reigning family will hand it on to its posterity until the end of time.

It produced St. Louis, the holiest king ever seen among the Christians. All the princes of France who remain today are descended from him. And, as Christ said to the Jews: "If ye were Abraham's children, ye would do the works of Abraham,"[77] it remains to me only to say to our princes: "If you are the children of St. Louis, do the works of St. Louis."

[77] John 8:39.

EIGHTH BOOK

The particular duties of royalty, continued: of justice

First Article

That justice is founded on religion

1st Proposition
God is the judge of judges, and presides over judgments

"God hath stood in the congregation of the gods: and being in the midst of them he judgeth gods."[1]

These gods that God judges are the kings and the judges gathered under their authority to do justice. He calls them gods because the word for God in the language of Scripture is a word for "judge": and thus the authority to judge is a participation in the supreme justice of God, with which he has endowed the kings of the earth.

That which principally brings them to merit the name of "gods" is the independence with which they must judge, without respect of persons, and without fearing the great any more than the small – "for the judgment is God's," as Moses said,[2] when one must judge with an independence like that of God, neither fearing nor favoring anyone.

It is said that God judges these earthly gods, because he carries out a perpetual examination of their judgments.

The Psalm continues, and makes God speak in this way: "How long will you judge unjustly, and accept the persons of the wicked?"[3] This touches the root of all injustice, which consists in considering persons rather than the right [*droit*].

---

[1] Ps. 71:1.   [2] Deut. 1:17.   [3] Ps. 81:2.

The duties of royalty: of justice

"Judge for the needy and fatherless: do justice to the humble and the poor. Rescue the poor; and deliver the needy out of the hand of the sinner."[4]

"Judge for the needy." That is to say, if he has right on his side: for God forbids elsewhere that "thou favor a poor man in judgment."[5] For one should no more judge through pity than through indulgence or through anger, but only through reason. What justice requires is equality between citizens, and that he who oppresses always be weakest in the sight of justice. This is what is meant by the word, rescue. This indicates a strong action against the oppressor, in order to oppose force by force: the force of justice against the force of iniquity.

After this severe reprehension and this supreme command, God complains, in the continuation of the Psalm, of those judges who do not hear his voice. "They have not known nor understood: they walk in darkness: all the foundations of the earth shall be moved."[6] Nothing is assured among men if justice is not done.

This is why God regards unjust judges with anger, and makes them remember that they are mortal. "I have said: You are gods"[7] (and I do not retract that): "and all of you the sons of the most High" (through this flowing of God's sovereign justice over your persons): "but you like men shall die, and shall fall (in the grave) like all princes."[8] You will be judged with them.

After this it remains only to turn towards God, and to say to him: There is no justice among men: "Arise, O God, judge thou the earth: for thou shalt inherit among all the nations."[9]

It is thus that the Holy Spirit, in this divine Psalm, shows us justice founded on religion.

2nd Proposition
Justice belongs to God: and it is he who gives it to kings

"Give to the king thy judgment, O God: and to the king's son thy justice: To judge thy people with justice, and thy poor with judgment."[10] This was David's prayer for Solomon.

The people, whom the king must judge, are the people of God

---

[4] Ibid., 3–4.   [5] Exod. 23:3.   [6] Ps. 81:5.   [7] Ibid., 6.
[8] Ibid., 7.   [9] Ibid., 8.   [10] Ibid., 2.

rather than his. The poor belong to God by a more particular title, since he has declared himself their father.

It is thus to him that justice and judgment belong, as property: and it is he who gives it to kings. That is to say, he gives them not only the authority to judge, but also the inclination and the industry to do it as he wants, in accordance with his eternal laws.

3rd Proposition
Justice is the true nature of a king, and it is she who shores up his throne

David knew and predicted the happy reign of Solomon. "In his days shall justice spring up, and abundance of peace, till the moon be taken away."[11] Justice rises like a beautiful sun, during the reign of a good king: peace follows her as an inseparable companion. The same David announces it thus: "Let the mountains receive peace for the people: and the hills justice."[12] She will fall on the mountains and in the valleys, like the rain that waters them and fertilizes them. The throne of the king will be strengthened: "it will be stable, like the sun and like the moon."[13] Or, as another Psalm says, "his throne will remain as the sun before me: and as the moon perfect for ever, and a faithful witness in heaven"[14] (through the regularity of its course) of the immutability of God's designs.

If any empire ought to expand, it is that of a just prince. Everyone wants him for a master. "And he shall rule from sea to sea, and from the river (the heart of his domain) unto the ends of the earth. Before him the Ethiopians shall fall down: and his enemies shall lick the ground. The kings of Tharsis and the islands shall offer presents: the kings of the Arabians and of Saba shall bring gifts. And all kings of the earth shall adore him: all nations shall take pleasure in serving him."[15]

This is the description of the reign of Jesus Christ: and the reign of a just prince is an image of it: "for he shall deliver the poor from the mighty: and the needy that had no helper."[16] The poor would remain without assistance; but they have found a sure help in the prince. He is a second redeemer of the people, after Jesus Christ: and his love for justice has its effect.

---

[11] Ibid., 7.   [12] Ibid., 3.   [13] Ibid., 5.
[14] Ps. 88:38.   [15] Ps. 81:8–11.   [16] Ibid., 12–13.

4th Proposition
Under a just God, there is no purely arbitrary power

Under a just God, there is no power which by its nature is liberated from all law – natural, divine, or human.

At least there is no power on earth which is not subject to divine justice.

All judges, and even the most sovereign, whom God for that reason calls gods, are examined and corrected by a greater judge. "God is seated in the midst of gods, and there he judges the gods,"[17] as has just been said.

Thus all judgments are subject to revision by a more august tribunal. God also says for this reason: "When I shall take a time, I will judge justices."[18] The judgments rendered by human judges will pass in review before my eyes.

Thus the most sovereign and the most absolute judgments are, like others with respect to God, subject to correction: with this difference only, that it is done in a hidden way.

The judges of the earth pay little attention to this review of their judgments, because it produces no visible effects and is reserved for another life: but it is all the more terrible for that, since it is inevitable. When the time for these divine judgments is at hand, "there will be no help, neither from the east, nor from the west, nor from the desert hills" (those remote places from which hidden help often comes) "for God is the judge,"[19] against whom there is no recourse.

"He has in his hand the cup of his vengeance, full of a strong and fiery wine":[20] full of a justice that will not be tempered by any sweetening mixture. On the contrary, "it will be mixed with bitterness": with harmful and poisoning liquors. This is a second reason to fear the terrible examination of human judgments; it will be done in an age in which justice will be perfectly pure, and will be carried out in its full and inexorable rigor. "This cup is in the hand of the Lord and he hath poured it out from this to that," and he presents it to be drunk. He presents it to hardened and incorrigible sinners, and above all to unjust judges: "it will have to be swallowed whole, to the very dregs." For them there will be no more pity: such that this vengeance will be eternal.

[17] Ibid., 1.
[18] Ps. 84:3.
[19] Ibid., 7–8.
[20] Ibid., 9.

Article II

On government which is called arbitrary

1st Proposition
There is among men a kind of government which is called arbitrary, but which is not found among us in well-ordered states

Four attributes accompany these kinds of government.

Firstly: subject peoples are born slaves, that is to say truly serfs; and among them there are no free persons.

Secondly: no one possesses private property: all the sources [of wealth] belong to the prince, and there is no right of inheritance, even from father to son.

Thirdly: the prince has the right to dispose as he wishes, not only of the goods, but also of the lives of his subjects, as one would do with slaves.

And finally, in the fourth place: there is no law but his will.

This is what is called arbitrary power. I do not wish to examine whether it is permissible or illicit. There are nations and great empires which are content with it; and it is not for us to awaken doubts in them about the form of their government. It suffices for us to say that it is barbarous and odious. These four characteristics are quite far from our own customs [*mœurs*]; and so among us there is no arbitrary government.

It is one thing for a government to be absolute, and another for it to be arbitrary. It is absolute with respect to constraint – there being no power capable of forcing the sovereign, who in this sense is independent of all human authority. But it does not follow from this that the government is arbitrary, for besides the fact that everything is subject to the judgment of God (which is also true of those governments we have just called arbitrary), there are also [constitutional] laws in empires, so that whatever is done against them is null in a legal sense [*nul de droit*]: and there is always an opportunity for redress, either on other occasions or in other times. Such that each person remains the legitimate possessor of his goods: no one being able to believe that he can possess anything with security to the prejudice of the laws – whose vigilance and action against injustices and acts of violence is deathlesss, as we have explained more fully elsewhere. This is what is called legitimate government, by its very nature the opposite of arbitrary government.

Here we shall only touch on the first two attributes of this power that is called arbitrary, which we have just treated. As for the last two, they seem to be so contrary to humanity and to society, that they are too visibly opposed to legitimate government.

2nd Proposition
In legitimate government, persons are free

It is only necessary to recall the passages in which we have established that government is paternal, and that kings are fathers: their subjects were thus children, who differ from slaves in that they are born free and innocent.

Government is established to free all men from all oppression and from all violence, as has been often demonstrated. This constitutes the state of perfect liberty: there being fundamentally nothing less free than anarchy, which takes away all legitimate claims among men, and knows no law other than force.

3rd Proposition
The ownership of goods is legitimate and inviolable

We have seen the distribution of lands under Joshua, according to the orders of Moses.[1]

This is the means which insures their cultivation: and experience shows that land which is held not only in common, but also without legitimate and permanent ownership, is neglected and abandoned. This is why it is not permitted to violate this order [of Moses'] – as the following example shows in a terrible way.

---

[1] Josh. 13; 14ff.

4th Proposition
The story of Achab King of Israel, of Queen Jezebel his wife, and of Naboth, is considered

"Naboth the Jezrahelite, who was in Jezrahel the royal city, had at that time a vineyard near the palace of Achab king of Samaria. And Achab spoke to Naboth, saying: Give me thy vineyard, that I may make me a garden of herbs, because it is nigh, and adjoining to my house; and I will give thee for it a better vineyard: or if thou think it more convenient for thee, I will give thee the worth of it in money. And Naboth answered: The Lord be merciful to me, and not let me give thee the inheritance of my fathers (something prohibited by the law of God). And Achab came into his house angry and fretting, because of the word that Naboth had spoken to him . . . and casting himself upon his bed, he turned his face to the wall, and would eat no bread.

And Jezebel his wife went in to him, and said to him: What is the matter that thy soul is so grieved? and why eatest thou no bread? And he told her of his proposition to Naboth, and of his answer. Jezebel rejoined: Thou art of great authority indeed, and governest well the kingdom of Israel. Arise, and eat bread, and be of good cheer; I will give thee the vineyard. So she wrote letters in Achab's name, and sealed them with his ring, and sent them to the ancients, and the chief men that were in his city, and that dwelt with Naboth. And this was the tenor of the letters: Proclaim a fast, and make Naboth sit among the chief of the people. And suborn two men, sons of Belial, against him, and let them bear false witness: that he hath blasphemed God and the king: and then carry him out, and stone him, and so let him die. This order was executed, and the great gave an account of the execution to Jezebel. Having learned this, the queen said to Achab: Arise and take possession of the vineyard of Naboth, who would not agree with thee, and give it thee for money: for he is dead. Achab then went to take possession of this vineyard.

And the word of the Lord came to Elias the Thesbite (his prophet), saying: Arise, and go down to meet Achab king of Israel . . .: behold he is going down to the vineyard of Naboth, to take possession of it. And thou shalt speak to him, saying: Thus saith the Lord: Thou hast slain an innocent, moreover also thou hast taken possession. And after these words thou shalt add: In this place, wherein the dogs have licked the blood of Naboth (unjustly stoned as a criminal and blasphemer), they shall lick thy blood also."[2]

Achab thought to elude the strictness of this just sentence by starting a private quarrel with Elias (who had been ordered to pronounce this sentence), saying to him: "Hast thou found me thy enemy, to treat me in this way? Yes, Elias said to him (in the name of the Lord). I have found thee my enemy, because thou art sold (like a slave to iniquity), to do evil in the sight of the Lord. And for my part, said the Lord, I will visit evil upon thee (the evil of a just torment for the evil thou hast unjustly committed): I will cut down thy posterity, and everything that belongs to thee, sparing nothing; and I will not let survive a dog of the house of Achab, and the last in Israel. And I will make thy house like the house of Jeroboam and that of Baasa, both king of Israel, which I exterminated entirely: since like them thou hast provoked my anger, and made Israel to sin (by thy scandalous example and thy unjust orders). And the Lord pronounced against Jezebel: The dogs shall lick the blood of Jezebel in the field of Jezrahel. If Achab die in the city, the dogs shall eat him: but if he die in the field, the birds of the air shall eat him."[3]

Scripture adds that "there was not such another as Achab, who was sold to do evil in the sight of the Lord. His wife Jezebel (whom he had believed in his first crime) set him on."[4] She acquired all power over his mind, to his cost: and he was the most wretched as well as the most abominable of all kings: "pushing abomination to the point of adoring the idols of the Amorrhites, whom the Lord destroyed by the swords of the children of Israel."[5]

In execution of this sentence, Achab and Jezebel perished, just as God has predicted. Divine vengeance also pursued, with pitiless rigor, the vestiges of their blood: and their posterity of both sexes was exterminated, without even one remaining.[6]

The crime which God punished with so much strictness was Achab's and Jezebel's depraved will to dispose as they liked – independently of the law of God which was also that of the kingdom – of the goods, the honor, and the life of a subject, and also to make themselves the masters of public judgments, backed by royal authority.

They wanted to force this subject to sell his inheritance. This is

[2] 3 Kings 21:1–19. [3] Ibid., 20–24. [4] Ibid., 25.
[5] Ibid., 26. [6] 4 Kings 9–11.

precisely what those good kings, David and Solomon, never did during the time they were building the magnificent palaces of which Scripture speaks. The law decreed that each should keep his inheritance from his fathers, for the preservation of the goods of the tribes. This is why God counted among Achab's crimes, not only the fact that he had killed, but that he had moreover possessed that which could not belong to him. It is, however, expressly indicated that Achab offered the just value of the piece of land he wanted to be ceded to him, and even [that he offered] an advantageous exchange. This shows how holy and inviolable the right of legitimate property was reputed to be, and how much the invasion of it was condemned.

Nonetheless Achab was in a fury over the refusal of Naboth. He could neither drink nor eat, and counted as nothing so great a kingdom and so many possessions, if he could not add a vineyard to it to enlarge his garden. So poor is royalty in itself, and so incapable is it of contenting a disordered mind!

His wife Jezebel came along: and instead of curing this sick mind, she on the contrary persuaded him, by her mocking manner, that he had lost all authority, if he did not give way to his fantasies. Finally, without preserving any form of judgment, she herself ordained the paths which we have seen.

She even sacrificed religion to her unjust designs. She wanted to make use of a public religious fast to sacrifice a good man to the vengeance of the king, and to that idea of authority which consists of doing whatever one wants.

Naboth's standing did not stop her. He was a man of importance, since he was ranked among the first men of the people. Jezebel made a show of preserving his rank and his dignity to ruin him more certainly: adding derision to violence and injustice, she believed herself queen at this price, and thought to bring royalty to the king her husband.

At the same time, divine justice declared itself. Achab was punished in two ways: God gave him over to crime, to deliver him more justly to punishment.

Jezebel had only too much power over this prince: for Elias had no sooner exterminated the false prophets of Baal, than the king gave leave to Jezebel to sacrifice so great a prophet to the revenge of this woman, as imperious as she was impious.[7] But, since she had made

[7] 3 Kings 19:1–2.

him master of what he wanted by such detestable means, she had more power than ever over the mind of this wretched prince, who yielded to all the desires of his wife, as if sold to iniquity.

As he was going from crime to crime in an abandoned fashion, he was also thrown from torment to torment – he and his family, who were all sacrificed to a just, perpetual and inexorable vengeance. And it is thus that all those who wanted to introduce arbitrary power into the kingdom of Israel were punished.

However, in the midst of these chastisements, in which the divine hand was so set against a royal family, God – always just and always the avenger of royal dignity (of which he is the source) – preserved that dignity in its entirety on this occasion, since the injustice of Achab was not that of punishing by death someone who spoke against the king, but that of having imputed such an attempt to a man who was innocent of it. So that it is obvious that this is something worthy of the highest torment, and that this crime – speaking ill of the king – is treated as being almost equivalent to blaspheming against God.

Article III

On legislation and on judgments

1st Proposition
Both terms are defined

The law gives the rule: and judgments are the application of it to human affairs and to particular questions, as has been said.

"If from a sincere heart you speak justice: judge right things, ye sons of men."[1] If you love the justice dictated by the law, put it then into practice: and let it be the only rule of your judgments.

---

[1] Ps. 57:2.

2nd Proposition
The first effect of justice and the laws, is to preserve the rights granted by earlier princes, not only for the whole body of the state, but for each part of which it is composed

Thus was preserved for the tribe of Judah the prerogative which it had always enjoyed – that of marching at the head of the tribes.

Thus did the tribe of Levi eternally enjoy the rights given by the law, according to the favorable interpretations of the ancient kings.

Thus was preserved for the tribes of Gad and of Ruben that which had been granted by Moses,[2] for having been the first to cross the Jordan.

Thus were the Gabaonites always maintained, in fulfilment of the treaty made with them by Joshua: also was their fidelity unwavering.

The good faith of princes binds that of subjects, who remain in [a state of] obedience not only through fear, but also, inviolably, through affection.

3rd Proposition
Praiseworthy customs take the place of laws

Before David mounted the throne, a dispute arose between the soldiers who had been in combat, and those who had remained behind, by his order, to guard the supplies: this wise prince judged in favor of the latter, and pronounced this sentence: "Equal shall be the portion of him that went down to battle, and of him that abode at the baggage; and they shall divide alike. And this hath been done from that day forward, and since was made a statute, and an ordinance, and as a law in Israel."[3]

The preservation of these ancient laws and of these praiseworthy customs, provides great kingdoms with an idea not only of fidelity and of wisdom, but even of immortality – which brings the state to be regarded, like the universe, as governed by counsels of an immortal duration.

---

[2] Num. 32:33; Josh. 13:8.
[3] 1 Kings 30:24–25.

4th Proposition
The prince owes justice, and is himself the chief judge

"Make us a king, to judge us, as all the nations have."[4] This was the idea of the people, when they asked Samuel for kings. And thus the word king is a word for judge.

When Absalom aspired to royalty, "he went to the city-gates and into the public ways, interrogating those who came from every quarter to the king's judgment, and said: . . . Thy words seem to me good and just. But there is no man appointed by the king to hear thee. And he added: O that they would make me judge over the land, that all that have business might come to me, that I might do them justice."[5] He dared not say: who will make me king? Rebellion would have been too openly declared; but it was the name of king that he was demanding under that of judge.

He decried the government of the king his father, saying that there was no justice – which was a calumny, for far from neglecting justice, David rendered it himself with marvelous care. "And David reigned over all Israel: and David did judgment and justice to all his people."[6]

Nathan went to David to bring him the complaint of a poor man, from whom an unjust rich man had taken an ewe-lamb that he loved: and David, annoyed, received the complaint.[7] It was [in the form of] a parable: but since parables are drawn from things in common use, this one shows the custom of bringing the complaints of individuals to kings: and David rendered justice, saying: "He shall restore the ewe fourfold."[8]

"I am a widow woman who had two sons, said the woman of Thecua to this same David, . . . and they quarreled with each other in the field, and there was none to part them: and the one struck the other, and he died of it: and the family is pursuing his brother, to punish him with death. They are depriving me of my sole heir, and they seek to quench my spark which is left, and will leave my husband no name, nor remainder upon the earth. And the king said to her: Go in peace to thy house, and I will give charge in thy favor."[9]

She added: "Upon me, my lord, be the iniquity, and upon the house of my father: but may the king and his throne be guiltless."[10] One would not think the king guiltless, or his throne stainless, if he

---

[4] 1 Kings 8:5.   [5] 2 Kings 15:2–4.   [6] 2 Kings 8:15.   [7] 2 Kings 12:1ff.
[8] Ibid., 6.   [9] 2 Kings 14:5–8.   [10] Ibid., 9.

refused to give justice. And David answered: "If any one shall say ought against thee, bring him to me, and he shall not touch thee any more."[11]

The family's pursuit [of the fratricide] seemed just according to the letter of the law, which condemned a murderer to death: this was a case of having recourse to the grace and the clemency of the prince, in a cause so favorable to an afflicted mother.

The woman pressed David by saying: "Let the king remember the Lord his God, that the next of kin be not multiplied to take revenge, and that they may not kill my son." She did not fear to bring David before the judge of kings. And this just prince approved her plea, and said to her: "As the Lord liveth, there shall not one hair of thy son fall to the earth."[12]

We are familiar with the judgment of Solomon, which drew to him the respectful fear of the whole people, which makes kings obeyed and establishes their empire.

5th Proposition
The ways of justice are easy to know

The path of justice is not one of those tortuous paths which, in the manner of labyrinths, make you constantly fear being lost. "The way of the just is right, the path of the just is right to walk in, and there is no detour."[13]

Even a pagan said that one should not do that which is doubtful and ambiguous. Equity, this author continues, shines brightly by itself; but doubt seems to envelop any secret plan of injustice.[14]

If you would know the way of justice, walk uncovered in the country: go where your sight takes you, and "let your eyes, as the sage says, go before your steps."[15] Justice does not hide herself.

It is true that, on many points, she is dependent on positive laws; but the language of the law is simple, wishing neither to shine nor subtilize, wishing only to be clear and precise.

Nonetheless, since it is impossible that there not be difficulties and complicated questions, the prince – in order not to be deceived, and to provide room for a greater illumination of the truth – furnishes the remedy which is about to be explained.

[11] Ibid., 10.   [12] Ibid., 11.   [13] Isa. 26:7.
[14] Cicero, *De officiis* I. 1.9,30.   [15] Prov. 4:25.

6th Proposition
The prince establishes tribunals, and names their members with great care, and instructs them in their duties

This was the practice of Moses himself,[16] for fear of using himself up in useless work.

This is what he explained to the people in these terms: "I alone am not able to bear your business, and the charge of you and your differences. Let me have from among you wise and understanding men, whose conduct is approved . . . And I took out of your tribes men wise and honorable, and I made them your judges, saying to them: Hear the people, and pronounce that which shall be just between the citizen and the stranger, without distinction of persons, judging the little as well as the great: neither shall you respect any man's person, because it is the judgment of God. And if any thing seem hard to you, refer it to me, and I will hear it."[17]

One sees three things in these words of Moses'. In the first place: the establishment of judges under the prince. In the second place: the choice of them, and the qualities with which they must be adorned. In the third place: the reserving of the most difficult matters to the prince himself.

These judges were established in all the cities and in each tribe; and Moses had ordained it thus.[18]

Following this example, we have seen the tribunals established by Josaphat[19] – a prince zealous for justice, if ever there was one among the kings of Judah and on the throne of David.

These tribunals were of two sorts. There were those of all the particular cities; and there was a supreme one in the capital of the kingdom, under the eyes of the king – following the example of, and perhaps to perpetuate, the great senate of seventy that Moses had established.

We have also noticed the care he took to instruct the judges in person, after the example of Moses.[20] This had two good effects: the first, to make the prince's ability felt; and the second, to carve the rules of justice more deeply in hearts. Thereafter one saw these two kinds of tribunals preserved among the Jews.

In those solemn actions which had to do with some great good to

---

[16] Exod. 18:13ff. [17] Deut. 1:12–17. [18] Deut. 16:18.
[19] 2 Par. 19:5–8. [20] Ibid., 9–10.

the state, the good kings such as Josiah "gathered together all the ancients of Judah and Jerusalem."[21] He learned, from their conversation, what was to be done for the common good – both of the state in general, and of the cities in particular.

Article IV
On the virtues which must accompany justice

1st Proposition
There are three main ones, indicated by the learned and pious Gerson, in a sermon delivered before the king: constancy, prudence, and clemency

Justice must be rule-governed, firm, and constant: otherwise it is uneven in its conduct, and more bizarre than steady; it acts according to the humor that dominates it.

It must know how to recognize the true and the false, in the facts which are presented to it: otherwise it is blind in applying it. This discernment is an advantage that it draws from prudence.

Finally it must occasionally be relaxed: otherwise it is extreme and unbearable in its rigor: and this softening of the rigor of justice is the effect of clemency.

Constancy affirms it in its principles; prudence enlightens it in questions of fact; clemency lets it tolerate and pardon weakness. Constancy supports it; prudence applies it; and clemency tempers it.[1]

2nd Proposition
Constancy and firmness are necessary to justice, against the iniquity which dominates in the world

The human race, from its beginning, had become so criminal in the eyes of God, that he resolved to destroy it through the Flood: "seeing

---
[21] 4 Kings 23:1.
[1] Gerson, *De justitia* (1408), in *Opera* (1706 edn.), Vol. IV.

that the wickedness of men was great on the earth, and that all the thought of their heart was bent upon evil at all times."[2] See this unhappy firmness in evil-doing, from the beginning of the world. This naturally invincible inclination of the human heart towards evil, makes Scripture say too that "sin is at the door"[3] – which is to say that it does not cease in urging us to open to it.

All the waters of the Flood were unable to efface a sin which is so inherent in the human heart. "Go about, said Jeremiah, through the streets of Jerusalem, and see, and consider, and seek in the broad places thereof, if you can find a man that executeth judgment, and seeketh faith."[4] Through a false constancy they are confirmed in vice: "they have made their faces harder than the rock, and they have refused to return from their injustices."[5]

"Woe is me, said Micheas; . . . there is none upright among men; they all lie in wait for blood, every one hunteth his brother to death. A cruel and barbarous hunt has come about, in which each seeks to catch not animals but his friends as prey. Believe not a friend, and trust not in a magistrate: keep the doors of thy mouth from her that sleepeth in thy bosom. For the son dishonoreth the father, and the daughter riseth up against her mother . . . and a man's enemies are they of his own household."[6] All the families are divided, and ties of blood no longer have place.

If, in this disorder of human affairs, you think you can find a refuge in public justice, you deceive yourself. It no longer rules or has firmness. "Whatever a great man dares to demand, the judge believes himself bound to give him, as a debt."[7] The evil of their hands they call good; there is no more law among men.

"Magistrates (who ought to sustain the weak) are as roaring lions who devour them; judges are ravenous wolves, who do not even keep till morning the prey they have taken at night."[8] They satisfy their insatiable appetite in the field [*sur-le-champ*].

It is thus that men are naturally wolves to each other. David was first to complain of it. "There is not any man just on earth, he said, there is none that understandeth, there is none that seeketh after God. All have turned out of the way; they are become unprofitable together. There is none that doth good, there is not so much as one."[9]

[2] Gen. 6:5.   [3] Gen. 4:7.   [4] Jer. 5:1.
[5] Ibid., 3.   [6] Mic. 7:1,2,5,6.   [7] Ibid., 3.
[8] Soph. 3:3.   [9] Ps. 13:2–3; Rom. 3:10ff.

Against this overflowing of iniquity there is only one sure dike, which is the firmness of justice.

3rd Proposition
If justice is not firm, it is swept away by this deluge of injustice

If the duty of the judge is, as Ecclesiasticus says, "to penetrate the cabals of iniquity (like a battalion called together), it is necessary to the realization of this duty that justice be not only strong, but even that it be invincible and intrepid."[10] Otherwise what Isaiah said will come about: "Judgment is turned away backward, and justice hath stood far off (pushed back by so great a confluence of contrary interests); and equity could not come in against such great obstacles."[11]

If the respect which is kept for the name of justice is weakened, one renders it only half-heartedly, and merely to save appearances. Thus, said the prophet, "injustice has prevailed: there is a judgment, but opposition is more powerful. Therefore the law is torn in pieces (one keeps a part and despises the rest); and judgment cometh not to the end."[12] Justice half-rendered is only the color of justice, and is all the more dangerous.

"Justice, the wise man said, is perpetual and immortal."[13] Equality is the soul of this virtue. It is in vain that some magistrate prides himself sometimes on doing justice; if he does not render it entirely and throughout, the unevenness of his conduct means that justice cannot achieve what it might according to the rules – for the rule ceases to be a rule, when it is not perpetual and does not walk with an even step.

In the midst of so many contradictions, it is a kind of combat to render justice, in which "if you have not gone up to face the enemy or you have not set up a wall for the house of Israel (like a strengthened dike), and for the people of God,"[14] you are vanquished.

One must be, by a firm resolution and a strong habit, like "a fortified city (defended on all sides), like a pillar of iron, and a wall of brass":[15] otherwise one is soon overpowered.

The prince must, then, through his constancy and his firmness,

---

[10] Ecclus. 7:6.　[11] Isa. 59:14.　[12] Hab. 1:3–4.
[13] Wisd. 1:15.　[14] Ezek. 13:5.　[15] Jer. 1:18.

render the exercise of justice easy and simple: for these difficult things are not of long duration.

4th Proposition
On prudence, the second virtue which accompanies justice. Prudence can come about from the outside, from factual truth: but it should instruct itself in this matter

"The cry of Sodom and Gomorrha is multiplied, and their sin is become exceedingly grievous. I will go down and see whether they have done according to the cry that is come to me: or whether it be not so, that I may know."[16]

He who knows all and cannot be deceived lowers himself, say the holy Fathers, even to the point of informing himself, in order to be able to instruct princes (who are subject to so much ignorance and so many surprises) in what they have to do.

He gives them three instructions. Firstly, when he says: "I want to know what is going on," he shows them the desire they should have to know the factual truths which they must judge.

Secondly, in making it known that the cry has reached even him, he teaches them that their ears must always be open, always attentive, always ready to hear what is going on.

Finally in adding, "I will go down and see," he shows them that, after having heard, one must come to an exact assessment, and base his judgment only on certain knowledge.

Ordinary reports and noises should excite the prince; but he should yield only to known truth.

Let us add that it is not sufficient to receive [passively] that which presents itself: one must search by himself, and go before the truth, if he would discover it. This we have already seen.

Men, and above all the great, are not too happy when truth reaches them through its own power, nor [when it comes to them] from a single source, nor when it pierces the obstacles with which they surround themselves. Too many people are interested in not knowing truth in its entirety: and too often those who surround them spare each other, so to speak. Often enough one fears to reveal to them those nagging truths which they do not wish to know. Those who are

[16] Gen. 18:20–21.

always with them often think themselves obliged to treat them carefully, either through prudence or through artifice. They must descend from this high peak of greatness, which no one approaches but trembling, and mix in some fashion with the people, in order to see things close up, and collect, here and there, the dispersed traces of the truth.

St. Ambrose has drawn all of this together in a few words: "When God says that he will go down, he has spoken thus for your instructions, that you may learn to look into things with care. I will go down and see, that is to say: Go down from my care to inform you, for fear that, being far away, you do not always see what happens. Come forward, to see things at close range. Those who are placed so high are always ignorant of things."[17]

5th Proposition
On clemency, the third virtue: firstly, that it is the joy of the human race

"In the cheerfulness of the king's countenance is life: and his clemency is like the latter rain."[18] Or, if one likes, more conformably perhaps to the original text: "like the rain of late autumn." Quite literally, one must understand that clemency is just as agreeable to men as a rain which comes in the evening, or in the autumn, to temper the warmth of the day or that of a burning-hot season, and to water the earth which has been dried out by the sun's ardor.

It is permissible to add that, just as the morning designates virtue, which alone can illuminate human life, the evening by contrast represents to us the condition into which we have fallen through our faults – since it is then, indeed, that the day declines, and that reason ceases to enlighten. According to this explanation, the morning dew would be the recompense of virtue, just as the evening rain would be a pardon granted to our faults. And thus Solomon would have us understand that, to delight the earth, and to produce fruits which are suitable for public kindness, the prince must cause to fall on the human race both kinds of dew: in recompensing always those who do good, and pardoning those who fail, provided that the public good and the holy authority of the laws do not come into question.

We have seen David, the model of good kings, promising protec-

---

[17] St. Ambrose, *De Abraham* I. 1. 47.
[18] Prov. 16:15.

tion to a mother, from whom they wanted to take her second son – the last of her hope and of her family – in punishment for the death he had delivered to his brother, through a blow which was more unfortunate than malicious. It is thus that equity often tempers the strictness which justice demands, against him who had deprived his brother of life. David had understood that justice must be exercised with some tempering – that it becomes iniquitous and intolerable when it insists pitilessly on all its rights, and that goodness, which moderates its extreme rigors, is one of its principal parts.

6th Proposition
Clemency is the glory of a reign

Moses, whom Scripture calls a king[19] – and an absolute and strict king, when it was necessary – is renowned as "the gentlest of all men."[20] Naturally, he would have pardoned; when he punished it was not he but the law which exercised rigor for the common good.

"Remember David, and all his meekness."[21] This was what his son Solomon sang at the dedication of the Temple; and it seemed that David's clemency would make all his other virtues forgotten.

Happy the prince who can say, with Job: "From my infancy mercy grew up with me: and it came out with me from my mother's womb."[22]

It was a fine testimonial given to the kings of Israel, even by their enemies: "The kings of the house of Israel are merciful."[23]

7th Proposition
It is a great happiness to save a man

"Deliver them that are led to death: and those that are drawn to death forbear not to deliver."[24]

It is the finest sacrifice one can offer to the Father of all the living to save one of his children – unless he be one of those whose life is the death of others, either through his cruelty or through the examples he sets.

---

[19] Deut. 33:5.   [20] Num. 12:3.   [21] Ps. 131:1.
[22] Job 31:18.   [23] 3 Kings 20:31.   [24] Prov. 24:11.

8th Proposition
To remember that one is mortal gives a motive for clemency

"We all die, said David to that wise woman of Thecua; and like waters that return no more, we fall down into the earth: neither will God have a soul to perish, but recalleth, meaning that he that is cast off should not altogether perish. [And the woman said:] Why then do you not think to recall one who is banished and disgraced?"[25]

Life is so unhappy in itself, and flows by so fast, that one should not, if possible, let such brief days pass by in despondency. Mortality makes us weak: and in this state of fragility one easily makes mistakes; one must then bring oneself to be indulgent, and excuse the weaknesses of the human race.

9th Proposition
The day of a victory, which makes us the masters of our enemies, is a suitable day for clemency

Saul defeated the Ammonites. And his faithful subjects, who saw his throne shored up by this victory, [and who were] indignant against those of the people who a little earlier had been contemptuous of the new king, said to Samuel: "Who is he that said: Shall Saul reign over us? Bring the men and we will kill them. And Saul said: No man shall be killed this day, because the Lord this day hath wrought salvation in Israel."[26] And we should imitate his pity.

It is again a reason for pardoning, when God delivers our enemies into our hands, by a particular grace and providence.

"Strike them with blindness,"[27] said Eliseus of the Syrians who were making war on the Israelites. "And the Lord struck them with blindness." And in this state the prophet led them into Samaria. "And the king of Israel said to Eliseus, when he saw them: My father, shall I not kill them? Thou shalt not kill them, answered Eliseus: for thou didst not take them with thy sword, or thy bow, that thou mayst kill them: but set bread and water before them, that they may eat and drink, and go to their master."[28]

---

[25] 2 Kings 14:13–14.
[26] 1 Kings 11:12–13.
[27] 4 Kings 6:18.
[28] Ibid., 21.

A prince never shows himself so great before his enemies, as when he treats them with generosity and clemency.

10th Proposition
In acts of clemency, it is often suitable to leave some element of punishment, out of reverence for the laws and as an example

"Behold I am appeased by your reasons with respect to Absalom, despite the terrible assassination attempt he made on his brother Amnon, said David to Joab. Let him return into his house; but let him not see the face of the king. Thus he was called back to Jerusalem: and he dwelt two years there, without daring to present himself before the king."[29]

Moses had given a similar example, when his sister Mary, who had become leprous for having disobeyed him, asked pardon of Moses through the intercession of Aaron. "And Moses cried to the Lord, saying: O God, I beseech thee heal her. But the Lord answered: If her father (for some fault), had spitten upon her face, ought she not to have been ashamed for seven days at least? Let her be separated seven days without the camp, and afterwards she shall be called again."[30]

11th Proposition
There is a false indulgence

Such was that of David towards his elder son, whose crime greatly saddened him (but this was not sufficient: he ought to have been punished). Because "he would not afflict the spirit of his son Amnon, whom he greatly loved," he left his assassination-attempt unpunished – which caused the vengeance of Absalom, who killed his brother.[31]

This great king was also too indulgent toward the enterprises of Absalom and of Adonias. The latter "exalted himself excessively in David's old age. Neither did his father rebuke him at any time, saying: Why hast thou done this?"[32] And his excessive easiness had the consequences which one knows well enough.

We know too the indulgence of Heli, a sovereign pontiff and a man otherwise holy, and the strange way in which God punished him.[33]

---

[29] 2 Kings 14:21,24,28. [30] Num. 12:13–14. [31] 2 Kings 13:21,28,29.
[32] 3 Kings 1:5–6. [33] 1 Kings 3:13; 4:14ff.

These are dangerous faults; and one sees that men of good will, who are naturally given to indulgence, must watch themselves more closely than other men.

12th Proposition
When crimes are multiplied, justice must become more severe

So it has appeared since the beginning of the world, in these words of Lamech, of the race of Cain, to his two wives Ada and Sella: "Hear my voice, ye wives of Lamech, hearken to my speech. For I have slain a man to the wounding of myself, and a stripling to my own bruising. Seven-fold vengeance shall be taken for Cain: but for Lamech seventy times seven fold."[34]

Men grow accustomed to crime; and the habit of seeing it makes it less horrible to them. But it is not so with justice. Vengeance grew heavier upon Lamech who, far from profiting from the punishment of Cain (one of his ancestors), and of distancing himself from crime because of this domestic example, seems rather to have taken Cain for a model.

The just severity which God so visibly reveals in the holy books, when crimes have multiplied and have reached a certain excess, should be in some way a model for princes in the governance of human affairs.

Article V

Obstacles to justice

1st Proposition
First obstacle: corruption and presents

"Thou shalt not accept persons nor gifts: for gifts blind the eyes of the wise, and change the words of the just."[1]

Moses does not say: they blind the eyes of the wicked, and change

---

[34] Gen. 4:23–24.   [1] Deut. 16:19.

their words. He says: they blind the eyes of the wise, and change the words of the just. Before the judge spoke well: the present has arrived, and he is no longer the same man: a new jurisprudence (which his interest furnishes to him) makes him change his language. It is not always large presents which produce this effect: small ones given at the right time sometimes show a secret eagerness for friendship which inclines and wins the heart.

Those who, by their dignity, are above this kind of corruption, have other presents to fear – praise and flattery. Let them keep well in mind this word of the wise: "Praise not any man before his death."[2] All praise given to the living is suspect: "Love justice, you that are the judges of the earth."[3] Do not be the victim of a subtle flatterer.

Services rendered to the state constitute another way of seducing kings. "Have no regard for persons," says the Lord. Services demand another kind of justice, which is that of recompense. Prince, you owe it; but do not pay this debt at someone else's expense.

2nd Proposition
Prejudice: the second obstacle

It is a kind of folly which keeps one from reasoning. "A fool receiveth not the words of prudence,"[4] and wants to hear only what he has in his heart.

The prejudiced man does not hear you: he is deaf: the place is filled up, and truth finds no room for itself.

Solomon opposed this humble prayer to prejudice: "Give to thy servant an understanding heart . . . And God gave to Solomon largeness of heart as the sand that is on the sea shore,"[5] capable of everything.

The mind of the prince must be a clear and smooth mirror, in which everything that arrives, from whatever side it may be, is represented as it is, according to the truth. He is in a perfect equilibrium: he turns neither to the right nor to the left.[6] This is why God has placed him at the pinnacle of human affairs in order that, free from the attacks which come to him from what is beneath him, he may receive impressions only from on high, that is to say, from the truth. "Teach me truth and discipline and knowledge, O Lord."[7]

[2] Ecclus. 11:30.   [3] Wisd. 1:1.   [4] Prov. 18:2.
[5] 3 Kings 3:9; 4:29.   [6] Deut. 5:32.   [7] Ps. 118:66.

There are two ways of avoiding prejudices. The first is to remember that our judgments are reviewed by him who says: "I will judge the justices."[8] Enter into the spirit of the higher judge: strip yourself of your prejudices.

The other means: 'Judge of the disposition of thy neighbor by thyself.'[9] Go out of yourself, then: you will judge purely, and you will do as you would have others do to you.

3rd Proposition
Other obstacles: laziness and haste

"The eyes of a wise man are in his head . . . Be attentive: and let your eyelids go before your steps."[10] Give yourself time to reflect: do not hurry your judgment: do not fear the pain of thinking. "The impatient man can do nothing opportunely, and shall work folly."[11]

To laziness and to haste the prince must oppose attention and vigilance. We have already treated this matter, and it is useless to repeat it here.

4th Proposition
Piety and strictness

In judging pity no one, not even the poor. This we have already seen. "Render pitilessly eye for eye, tooth for tooth, wound for wound."[12] Turn your pity in another direction. It is for the oppressed, and for people who suffer from unjust and violent men, that you must have compassion.

Others always lean toward strictness. But you, prince, must turn neither to the right nor to the left. One turns to the left when, leaning toward laxness and softness, one weakens the severity of the law. One does no better by turning to the right, that is to say by pushing the rigor of the laws too far.

The zeal to discover wrong often makes one do wrong to him that has done none. One wishes to deter the authors of crimes; and rather than leave them unpunished, one charges innocents with them. But the wise men has said: "He that justifieth the wicked, and he that condemneth the just, both are abominable before God."[13]

[8] Ps. 74:3. [9] Ecclus. 31:18. [10] Eccles. 2:14; Prov. 4:25.
[11] Prov. 14:17. [12] Exod. 21:24. [13] Prov. 17:15.

5th Proposition
Anger

Anger is a passion most unworthy of a prince. One must strive to vanquish it, when one loves the justice whose enemy it is. "The patient man is better than the valiant: and he that ruleth his spirit, than he that taketh cities."[14]

The Emperor Theodosius the Great had well understood this saying of the wise. This prince, so many times victorious, and illustrious by his conquests, though naturally given to impetuous anger, profited so well from the counsels of St. Ambrose that in the end (as this Father says[15]) he felt himself obligated when he was begged for pardon: and when he was moved by a specially lively feeling of anger, it was then that he came most easily to acts of clemency.

6th Proposition
Cabals and squabbles

"Loose the bands of wickedness (of unjust men), and let not the innocent be overcome: take this heavy weight from his shoulders."[16]

Be on guard against the protection that riches find. Do not abandon the poor man on the pretext that there is no one to take his defense in hand. This is the effect of money and cabals. "The rich man hath done wrong (to an innocent man), and yet he will fume: but the poor is wronged and must hold his peace."[17] Be watchful, then, and get to the bottom of things – you who love justice.

As for squabbles, it is written: "He that loveth discord, seeketh ruin."[18] Justice must reprimand him for his own good, as well as for that of others.

7th Proposition
Wars and negligence

Too occupied with war, whose action is so lively, one thinks not at all of justice. But it is written of David, in the midst of so many wars, and while he was combating the Moabites, the Ammonites, the Syrians,

---

[14] Prov. 16:32. [15] St. Ambrose, *De obitu Theodosii*, orat. 13.
[16] Isa. 58:6. [17] Ecclus. 13:4. [18] Prov. 17:19.

Obstacles to justice

the Philistines, the Idumeans, and so many other enemies: "David did judgment and justice to all his people."[19] This is truly reigning – to make justice rule in the midst of the tumult of war, such that no one whosoever is deprived of it.

One is ordinarily careful to render justice in great places: and one neglects it in villages and deserted places. By contrast Isaiah writes of a great king (it is Ezechias of whom he speaks) that in his time "judgment dwelt in the wilderness, and held her sessions in the great places"[20] – which he calls Carmel, according to the usage of sacred Scripture. Justice illuminated the most out-of-the-way places: the poor felt its help, and abundance did not corrupt those who rendered it.

8th Proposition
One must regulate the procedures of justice

"Thou shalt follow justly after that which is just."[21] It is not enough to have a good legal claim [*bon droit*]: one must also pursue it in good ways, without fraud, without bending [the rules], without violence, without doing justice for oneself, and waiting for the public power.

[19] 2 Kings 8:15.   [20] Isa. 32:16.   [21] Deut. 16:20.

NINTH BOOK

The supports of royalty: arms, riches or finances, and counsels

Article 1

On war and its just motives, general and particular

1st Proposition
God makes warrior-princes

This is what brings David to say: "Blessed be the Lord my God, who teacheth my hands to fight, and my fingers to war."[1]

2nd Proposition
God gave an express command to the Israelites to make war

God orders his people to make war on certain nations.

Such were the nations of which it is written: "Thou shalt destroy many nations before thee: the Hethite, and the Gergezite, the Amorrhite, the Canaanite, the Pherezite, the Hevite, and the Jebusite: seven nations greater and stronger than thou art; and the Lord thy God shall have delivered them to thee, and thou shalt utterly destroy them.[2] Thou shalt make no league with them, nor show mercy to them."[3]

And again: "Thou shalt not make peace with them, neither shalt thou seek their prosperity all the days of thy life for ever."[4] This was a

---

[1] Ps. 143:1.   [2] Deut. 7:1.
[3] Ibid., 2.   [4] Deut. 23:6.

war carried to the utmost extreme, with fire and blood, irreconcilable, commanded of the people of God.

This is why Saul was punished without pity and deprived of royalty – for having spared the Amalecites,[5] one of the Canaanite peoples cursed by God.

3rd Proposition
God has promised this land to Abraham and his posterity

These were the peoples whose country God had promised to give to Abraham, by these words: "Lift up thy eyes, and look from the place wherein thou art, to the north and to the south, to the east and to the west. All the land which thou seest, I will give to thee, and to thy seed for ever."[6]

And again: "That day God made a covenant with Abraham, saying: To thy seed will I give this land, from the river of Egypt even to the great river Euphrates. The Caneans, the Hethites, the Amorrhites," and the others which have just been named.[7]

4th Proposition
God wanted to chastise the nations, and punish their impieties

They were abominable nations, and from the beginning devoted to every sort of idolatry, injustice and impiety: a race cursed since Cham and Canaan, to whom malice had passed naturally through their corrupt habits. As it is written in the Book of Wisdom: "Lord, thou didst abhor them, because they did works hateful to thee by their sorceries and wicked sacrifices. These people immolated their own children to their gods: they spared neither their hosts nor their friends: and thou hast destroyed them by the hands of our parents, because their malice was natural and incorrigible."[8]

Such were, says the Holy Spirit in this divine book, the ancient inhabitants of the holy land. And this is why God chased them from it by a just judgment to give it to the Israelites.

---

[5] 1 Kings 15:7ff.
[6] Gen. 13:14–15.
[7] Gen. 15:18–21.
[8] Wisd. 12:3–7.

5th Proposition
God had endured these people with a long-suffering patience

"The iniquities of the Amorrhites are not at the full until this present time," said the Lord to Abraham.[9]

Whatever will he may have had to give to so faithful and beloved a servant the heritage which he had promised for his faith, he suspended the actual giving of it by a counsel of pity.

But how much longer would this delay last? Four hundred years, he said, during which time he exhorted his people to patience, and awaited the penitence of his enemies. While waiting, he said, "Thy children will be afflicted for four hundred years."[10] So much did it pain him to dispossess wicked and accursed people of their lands.

Arbiter of the universe, who obliged you to show so much consideration, you who fear no one? – as it is noted in the Book of Wisdom. "What could anyone say to thee, when thou hast caused to perish one of the nations which thou hadst made? Surely thou wishest to show that thou dost all with justice, and that, the more powerful thou art, the more thou lovest to pardon."[11]

6th Proposition
God does not will that ancient inhabitants of lands be dispossessed, or that blood-ties be counted as nothing

Though absolute master of the whole earth, [free] to give it to whomsoever he pleased, God does not use this right and this sovereign domain to dispossess of their lands the peoples who enjoyed them peaceably: and he takes them away to give them to his people only in just punishment of crimes.

It is for this reason that he gave this express order to the Israelites: "You shall pass by the borders of your brethren, the children of Esau, who dwell in Seir, and they will be afraid of you. Take ye then good heed that you stir not against them. For I will not give you of their land so much as the step of one foot can tread upon, because I have given Mount Seir to Esau, for a possession. (You will observe towards them all the laws of commerce and society.) You shall buy meats of

---

[9] Gen. 15:16.   [10] Ibid., 13.   [11] Wisd. 12:13–16.

them for money and shall eat: you shall draw water for money, and shall drink (in a land where it is so rare). You will not pass through their lands, but you will take a roundabout path,"[12] for fear of causing a quarrel with them.

"Act in the same way toward the Moabites and the Ammonites" (descendants of Lot, cousin of Abraham, and like him descended from Thare, their common father). "Do not fight against them: for I will not give thee any part of their land, because I have given it to the children of Lot."[13]

The ancient inhabitants of these lands, which God had given to the children of Esau and to those of Lot, are called giants, and other odious names[14] – names which, in the style of Scripture, signify robust men of great size, but also bloody, unjust, and violent, oppressors and ravishers. And Scripture notes this, to show that God had delivered them to a just vengeance, when he chased them from their lands; especially when this was done by so express a command and a providence so particular [*une providence si particulière*], which he revealed to his people in the conquest of the holy land.

In a word, God wills that men view these lands as given by him to those who first occupied them, and who have remained in tranquil and immemorial possession – without troubling their enjoyment of them, or disturbing the repose of the human race.

God also wills that men preserve the memory of their relatives and of their common origins, however distant they may be.

Thus, however distant from Lot and Esau the Israelites may be, and even without considering that Esau had been a bad brother, God always wills that men remember their common fathers, and that Esau, like Jacob, came from Isaac: because he is the father and the protector of human society, and he wants to make all the ties of blood respected among men, in order (so far as possible) to make war odious in all sorts of ways.

---

[12] Deut. 2:4–6; 2 Par. 20:10.
[13] Deut. 2:19.
[14] Ibid., 10–12,19ff.

7th Proposition
These are other just motives for war: acts of unjust hostility, the refusal of passage demanded on equitable conditions, the law of nations violated in the person of ambassadors

Besides the motive of an express command of God (as just judge), which appears only one time in Scripture, here are some others.

Four conspiring kings entered the lands of the King of Sodom, of the King of Gomorrha and of three other neighboring kings.[15] The aggressors were victorious, and withdrew laden with loot, and leading their captives, among whom was Lot, nephew of Abraham, who was staying in Sodom. But God had prepared a liberator for him. His uncle Abraham pursued these abductors, cut them to pieces, and took back Lot and the captive women, together with an innumerable people and all the loot. God accepted his victory, and caused it to be blessed by his great pontiff, the celebrated Melchisedech, the most excellent prefiguration of Christ.

Og, King of Basan, also came fully armed to a meeting with the Israelites in order to attack them: and they cut him to pieces as an unjust aggressor, and took from him sixty cities, despite the height of their walls and of their towers.[16]

Also, one must not spare unjust aggressors. And, for having refused passage, the strict but just treatment meted out to Sehon, King of Hesebon, is a quite remarkable example.

"The Israelites sent their ambassadors to Sehon, King of Hesebon (to make this peaceable legation to him): We will pass through thy land, but we will take no suspect detour: we will not turn aside, neither to the right hand nor to the left: we will go along by the highway. Sell us meat for money, that we may eat; give us water for money, and so we will drink. We only ask that thou wilt let us pass through."[17]

To further reassure him, they reminded him of their conduct in the case of other peoples. "As the children of Esau have done, and those of the Ammonites. We do not want to stop, and we want only to come to the Jordan, and pass to the land which the Lord our God has given us."[18]

---

[15] Gen. 14.   [16] Deut. 3:1–5.
[17] Deut. 2:26–28.   [18] Ibid., 29.

The highway [is protected by] the law of nations, provided that one does not undertake passage by force, and that one asks it on equitable conditions. Thus war was justly declared on Sehon, whose heart God had hardened, in order to be able to refuse him all pardon afterwards; and he was put under the yoke.

Here then are two just motives for making war: the unjust refusal of passage requested on equitable terms, and the manifest hostility which makes you an unjust aggressor.

One must relate to this last motive that which the people of God did to liberate themselves from an unjustly imposed yoke, to avenge oppressed liberty, and to defend their religion by the express order of God.[19] And such was the motive of the wars of the Maccabees, as has been reported elsewhere.[20]

Finally, the motive of [avenging] the violation of the law of nations in the person of ambassadors is one of the most important.

"Daas, King of the Ammonites, having died, and his son having ascended the throne, David said: I will show kindness to Hanon, as his father showed kindness to me."[21] The Ammonites (who little knew the generous and grateful heart of David), persuaded their king that these ambassadors were spies, who came to find out about the weakness of the place, and to excite the people to rebellion. Thus they inflicted an unworthy treatment on them: and sensing how much they had offended David, they leagued against him with neighboring kings. But David sent Joab against them with an army, and he himself marched in person to win this war, which was happy for him.

This is what motives for war – the kind that is called foreign – come down to, and which are noted in Scripture.

---

[19] 2 Kings 10:2.
[20] 2 Macc. 8: 42–43.
[21] 2 Kings 10: 1–2.

Article II

On unjust motives for war

1st Proposition
First motive: ambitious conquests

This motive appeared soon after the Flood in the person of Nimrod, a savage man, who by his violent temperament became the first of the conquerors.[1] But it is expressly noted that he was among the children of Chus, son of Cham, the only one of the children of Noah who had deserved to be cursed by his father.[2]

The title of "conqueror" was born in this family: and Scripture expresses this event by saying "that he was the first mighty one on earth" – that is to say, he was the first whom the love of power brought to invade neighboring land.

2nd Proposition
Those who love war, and make it to satisfy their ambition, are declared to be enemies of God

"For I will require the blood of your lives at the hand of every beast, and at the hand of man, at the hand of every man, and of his brother, will I require the life of man. Whosoever shall shed man's blood, his blood shall be shed: for man was made to the image of God."[3]

God is so horrified by murder and by the cruel shedding of human blood, that he wills (in some fashion) that even beasts who have spilled it be held guilty. Such would seem to be the meaning of the words, in which God would obligate wild animals to respect the ancient nature of the domination which was given to us over them – though it is nearly effaced by sin. The violation of human life on the part of animals is taken to be an attack; and it is a kind of punishment to which God subjects them, by making them so odious that men seek only to seize and kill them.

The reason for this prohibition is admirable: "For man, he says,

---

[1] Gen. 10:8–11.   [2] Ibid., 8–11.   [3] Gen. 9:5–6.

was made to the image of God." This fine resemblance cannot appear too much on earth. Instead of diminishing it by murder, God wills (on the contrary) that men multiply themselves: "Increase, he said to them, and fill the earth."[4]

If depriving a single man of the divine gift of life is an attempt against God, who has placed in man the imprint of his face, how much more detestable in his eyes are those who sacrifice so many millions of men and so many children to their ambition?

3rd Proposition
The character of ambitious conquerors, drawn by the Holy Spirit

After Nabuchodonosor King of Nineveh and of Assyria had defeated and subjugated Arphaxad King of the Medes, "his empire was exalted and his heart was elevated; and he sent to all that dwelt in Cilicia and Damascus, and Libanus, and to the nations that are in Carmel, to the Arabs, to the inhabitants of Galilee in the great plain of Asdrelon, to the Samaritans, and to the environs of the Jordan, and to all the land of Jesse to the borders of Ethiopia. He sent his envoys to all these peoples to oblige them to submit to his power. But these nations (jealous of their liberty) sent back the ambassadors with empty hands, and without honor. Then the King of Assyria was angry, and swore by his throne and kingdom that he would defend himself against all those countries,"[5] or rather that he would revenge himself for their resistance.

There is the first trait of an unjust conqueror. He has no sooner subjugated a powerful enemy, than he believes that everything is his: there is no people that he does not oppress, and if anyone refuses the yoke, his pride is inflamed. He does not speak of attacking: he believes he has a legitimate right over everyone. Because he is the strongest, he does not view himself as an aggressor; and he calls defense, the plan to invade the lands of free peoples. As if it were rebellion to preserve one's liberty against his ambition, he speaks no longer save of vengeance: and the wars which he undertakes seem to him only the just punishment of rebels.

He disregards this: and not content to invade so many countries

---

[4] Ibid., 7.   [5] Jth. 1:5–12.

On unjust motives for war

which do not stand up against him in the slightest way, he believes that he undertakes nothing worthy of his greatness, if he does not make himself master of the universe. This is the consequence of the character of this unjust conqueror. "The word was given out in the house of the King of Assyria, that he would defend and avenge himself. And he called all the ancients, and all the governors, and his officers of war, and communicated to them the secret of his counsel: and he said that his thoughts were to bring all the earth under his empire."[6]

It was not advice which he demanded of this great assembly: he took for counsel only his untamable pride; and without consulting further, he moved straight to execution: "he gave his orders to Holofernes the general of his armies (a great man of war). And said to him: Thy eye shall not spare any kingdom and all the strong cities thou shalt bring under my yoke."[7]

This is the second trait of this proud character. This proud king had no need of counsel: the assembly of his counsellors was only a ceremony, to declare in a more solemn way that which was already resolved, and to set everything in motion.

But here is a final trait. It is to respect and recognize neither God nor man, and to spare no temple whatever, not even that of the true God – which Nabuchodonosor would have willed to reduce to ashes with the others, in the middle of Jerusalem. For "he had commanded Holofernes to destroy all the Gods of the earth, in order that he only might be called God by those nations which could be brought under him by arms."[8]

This is accomplished in two ways: either by openly attributing to oneself divine honors (as was done by almost all the conquerors of the pagan era); or through [historical] outcomes, when, by an outrageous pride, one attributes one's victories to oneself, to one's power and counsel (without dreaming that there is a God). So that one seems to say in his heart: "I am a god," and even made myself, as it is written by the prophet.[9]

Or, to repeat the words of another Nabuchodonosor: "Is this not the great Babylon, which I have built by the strength of my power, and in the glory of my excellence, to be the seat of my empire?"[10] – without reflecting that there is a god, to whom one owes everything.

[6] Jth. 2:1–3.   [7] Ibid., 4–6.   [8] Jth. 3:13.
[9] Ezek. 28:2.   [10] Dan. 4:27.

Such is the character of ambitious conquerors who, intoxicated by the success of their victorious arms, call themselves the masters of the world, and think their arm their God.

4th Proposition
When God seems to grant everything to such conquerors, he is preparing a strict chastisement for them

"I have given all these lands and all these seas to Nabuchodonosor king of Babylon, my servant"[11] (and the minister of my just vengeance). This is not to say that he gave them to him in order that he might be the legitimate possessor of them; it is to say that by a secret judgment, God abandoned them to the king's ambition, to occupy and to invade them. Nothing will escape his hands: "and even the birds of the air (those things which are most free) will fall into them."[12]

Here, in appearance, was a [divine] favor, well declared: but the reversal was terrible. How is the hammer of the whole earth broken, and destroyed![13] The Lord hath broken the staff with which he struck the rest of the world with an incurable wound.[14] "Behold I come against thee, O proud one, saith the Lord of hosts: for thy day is come, the time of my visitation (by divine justice): God will overturn Babylon, as he overthrew Sodom and Gomorrha, and will leave him no recourse.[15] There is no more cure for her ills! because her judgment hath reached even to the heavens, and is lifted up to the clouds."[16]

5th Proposition
Second unjust motive for war: pillage

For this reason the four kings of whom we just spoke armed themselves: and they carried off the rich booty and the captives that Abraham delivered.[17]

If one puts up with such wars, there will be no more kingdom, nor tranquil province. This is why God opposed to these abductors the magnanimity of Abraham, who kept from the loot which he had recovered, only that which belonged to his allies, the companions of

---

[11] Jer. 27:6.   [12] Dan. 2:38.   [13] Jer. 50:23.   [14] Isa. 14:5–6.
[15] Jer. 50:31,40.   [16] Jer. 51:9.   [17] Gen. 14:9,11,12.

his enterprise. And, in addition, he did not want anyone "on earth to be able to boast of having enriched Abraham."[18]

Often, too, God delivers those who pillage into the hands of other looters. Listen to Isaiah: "Woe to thee, that spoilest, shalt not thou thyself also be spoiled? And thou that despisest (all the laws of justice and believe that thou canst steal everything with impunity), shalt not thyself also be despised by some other more powerful than thee? When thou shalt have made an end of spoiling, thou shalt be spoiled; when being wearied thou shalt cease to despise (in the midst of the perils of an unjust war), thou shalt be despised."[19]

6th Proposition
Third unjust motive: jealousy

"Isaac was enriched, and he went on prospering and increasing till he became exceedingly great: . . . wherefore the Philistines, envying him, practiced hostilities and unjust violence against him. And the king of the country said to him: Depart from us, for thou art become much mightier than we."[20]

Though this reason for harming him was base and unjust, he agreed for the sake of peace, retiring from the vicinity: and the matter ended with a solemn treaty of peace, in which his enemies recognized the wrong which they had done, and the rights of Isaac.

7th Proposition
Fourth unjust motive: the glory of arms and the sweetness of victory. First example

There is nothing more flattering than this military glory: it often decides human affairs with a single stroke, and seems to have a kind of total power in forcing events; and this is why it so strongly tempts the kings of the earth. But we are about to see how vain it is.

Amasias King of Judah, "had won signal victories against the Edomites, and had taken from them the most renowned fortresses. Swollen with this success, he sent ambassadors to Joas king of Israel, and said to him: Come let us see one another (fully armed: let us test our powers). Joas (more moderate) answered him: Thou hast beaten

---

[18] Ibid., 23. [19] Isa. 33:1. [20] Gen. 26:12–16.

and prevailed over Edom, and thy heart hath lifted thee up: be content with the glory and sit at home. Why provokest thou evil, that thou shouldst fall, and Judah with thee? But Amasias did not accept this wise counsel. So Joas king of Israel marched: and he and Amasias king of Judah saw one another in Bethsames, a town in Judah. And Judah was put to the worst before Israel, and they fled every man to his dwellings. But Joas king of Israel took Amasias . . . and brought him into Jerusalem: and he broke down the wall of Jerusalem, four hundred cubits of the walls of this royal city; and he took all the gold, and silver, and all the vessels, that were found in the house of the Lord (that of Obededom, where the ark had rested from the time of David), and in the palace; he took hostages, and returned to Samaria."[21] Such was the fruit of the quarrel which Amasias made with Joas, for no reason other than vain-glory, and to show off his power and the courage of his people.

8th Proposition
Second example of the same motive, which shows how dangerous the temptation is

"Nechao, king of Egypt, came up to fight in Charcamis by the Euphrates: and Josiah went out to meet him. But Nechao sent messengers to him, saying: What have I to do with thee, king of Judah? I come not against thee this day, but I fight against another house, to which God hath commanded me to go in haste: forbear to do against God, who is with me, lest he kill thee. Josiah would not return, but prepared to fight against him, and hearkened not to the words of Nechao from the mouth of God, but went to fight in the field of Mageddo. And there he was wounded by the archers, and he said to his servants: Carry me out of the battle, for I am grievously wounded. And they removed him from the chariot into another, that followed him after the manner of kings, and they carried him away to Jerusalem, and he died, and was buried in the monument of his fathers, and all Judah and Jerusalem mourned for him."[22]

If so good a king lets himself be tempted by the desire for victory, or in any case by that of making war without reason, what shall one not fear from the others?

[21] 4 Kings 14:7–14.   [22] 2 Par. 35:20–25.

9th Proposition
One always fights with a kind of disadvantage, when one makes war without a cause [sans sujet]

One can note through these two examples, that it is a disadvantage to make war without reason.

A good cause adds, to the other advantages of war, both courage and confidence. Indignation against injustice augments power, and makes one fight in a more determined and bold way. One even has reason to believe that one has God on his side – because one defends justice, whose natural protector he is. One loses this advantage when one makes war needlessly or light-heartedly, such that – whatever the outcome may be, according to the terrible and profound judgments of God (who gives victory by his orders and by quite hidden springs, when one does not have justice on his side) – one can say that one fights in such a case with unequal forces.

It is even, perhaps, an effect of the vengeance of God, to be given over to the spirit of war. And it is written of Amasias, on the occasion which we have just seen, that this prince did not want to listen to the wise counsels of the King of Israel, who tried to turn him away from a war unjustly undertaken, "because it was the Lord's will that he should be delivered into the hands of enemies, because of the gods of Edom which he had served."[23]

10th Proposition
One has reason to hope that one has placed God on one's side, when justice is there

"Lord, said Josaphat, the children of Moab and the inhabitants of Mount Seir were spared by our ancestors, when they came out of Egypt: and they turned aside from them, in order not to pass through these lands, and not to have an occasion to fight with these peoples. But they, on the contrary, are assembling an immense army to cast us out of the possessions which Thou hast delivered to us. O our God, wilt thou not then judge them? As for us we have not strength enough to be able to resist this multitude, which cometh violently upon us. But as we know not what to do, we can only turn our eyes to thee."[24]

[23] Ibid., 20.   [24] Ibid., 20:10–12.

Thus prayed Josaphat: and he received from that moment assurances of the protection of God.

11th Proposition
The strongest are, often enough, the most circumspect in taking up arms

We have seen the examples of this in the wars of Amasias and of Josiah. But I shall add one more based on a particular fact.

In a rout of the children of Israel by the party of Isboseth, conducted by Abner against David, "Asael one of the brothers of Joab, who was a most swift runner, like one of the roes that abide in the woods, pursued Abner, and turned not to the right hand nor to the left from following him. And Abner looked behind him, and said: Art thou Asael? And he answered: I am. And Abner said to him: Go to the right hand or to the left, and lay hold on one of the young men and take thee his spoils. But Asael would not leave off following him close.

And again Abner said to Asael: Go off, and do not follow me, lest I be obliged to stab thee to the ground, and I shall not be able to hold up my face to Joab thy brother. But he refused to hearken to him, and would not turn aside: wherefore Abner struck him with his spear with a back stroke in the groin, and thrust him through, and he died upon the spot: and all that came to the place where Asael fell down and died stood still."[25]

One could not show more moderation, despite one's superiority, than did Abner, one of the valiant men of his times, or treat Joab and Asael more considerately.

12th Proposition
Bloody derision of conquerors by the prophet Isaiah

"How art thou fallen from heaven, beautiful star who didst rise in the morning? How art thou fallen to the earth, that didst wound the nations? And thou saidst in thy heart: I will ascend into heaven, I will exalt my throne above the stars of God, I will sit in the mountain of the covenant, in the sides of the north. I will ascend above the height of the clouds, I will be like the most High. But yet thou shalt be

---

[25] 2 Kings 2:18–23.

brought down to hell, into the depth of the pit. They that shall see thee, shall turn toward thee, and behold thee. Is this the man that troubled the earth, and shook kingdoms, that made the world a wilderness, and destroyed the cities thereof, that opened not the prison to his prisoners? All the kings of the nations have all of them slept in glory, every one in his own house. But thou art cast out of thy grave, as an unprofitable branch defiled, which leaves no posterity."[26]

And a little before: "When thou fellest to earth, the whole universe was quiet and still, it was glad and hath rejoiced. The fir trees also have rejoiced over thee, and the cedars of Lebanon, saying: Since thou hast slept, there hath none come up to cut us down. Hell below was in an uproar at thy coming, it stirred up the giants for thee. All the princes of the earth are risen up from their thrones, all the princes of nations. All shall answer, and say to thee: Thou art wounded as well as we, thou art become like unto us. Thy pride is brought down to hell, thy carcass is fallen down: under thee shall the moth be strewed, and worms shall be thy covering."[27]

13th Proposition
Two words of the Son of God, which destroy false glory, and extinguish the love of conquests

There is nothing above these expressions, above the simplicity of these two words of the Son of God: "What doth it profit a man, if he gain the whole world, and suffer the loss of his own soul?"[28]

And again, to strike down false glory with a single word: "They have received their reward."[29] They have prayed in corners of the streets; they have fasted; they have given alms. Let us add: They have practiced these great military virtues, so laborious and so striking, to make men talk: "Amen I say to you, they have received their reward." They wanted to be talked about; they are content; the whole universe talks about them. They enjoy this confused noise with which they were intoxicated: and, vain, as they were, they have received a recompense as vain as their undertakings: *Receperunt mercedem suam, van: vanum*, as St. Augustine says.[30]

What sweating, what labor, said Alexander (but how much blood

---

[26] Isa. 14:12–19.   [27] Ibid., 7–11.
[28] Matt. 16:26.   [29] Matt. 6:2,5.
[30] St. Augustine, *Enarrationes in Psalmos CXVIII, serm.* XII, 2.

spilled) – just to make the Athenians talk! He felt the vanity of this frivolous reward: and at the same time he repaid himself with this smoke.

Article III

On wars between citizens, together with their motives, and the rules which must be followed

1st Proposition
First example. The war between the tribes was undertaken through a false suspicion: in clearing it up, peace was made

The children of the tribe of Reuben and of Gad, and half of the tribe of Manasses, were separated from their brothers by the Jordan: and they erected on the banks of this river an altar of immense size. The rest of the children of Israel, having learned that this altar was being erected over against them in the land of Canaan, all assembled in Silo to fight against them: and while waiting sent a deputation from each tribe, together with Phineas, son of Eleazar the sovereign priest. When they had arrived in the land of Galaad, where they found the Reubenites and the others who were raising this altar, they spoke to them in this way: "What meaneth this transgression of the law of God? Why have you forsaken the Lord the God of Israel, building a sacrilegious altar, and revolting from the worship of him? . . . If you think the land of your possession to be unclean, pass over to the land wherein is the tabernacle of the Lord, and dwell among us: only depart not from the Lord, and from our society, by building an altar beside the altar of the Lord our God: and do not draw down on us his just vengeance, as Achan did by his blasphemy."

"And the children of Reuben and the others responded to this speech: The Lord the most mighty God, he knoweth, and Israel also shall understand, that we are raising this altar only to be an eternal memorial to the right which we have, we and our children, over the holocausts, for fear that one day you will say to us: You have no part in the Lord. Phineas, who was the head of the legation, having listened to this answer, made by the Reubenites and the others, together with their execration of the sacrilege which was imputed to them, made a report to the people, who were satisfied with it; and the new altar was called: Our testimony, that the Lord is God."[1]

One sees here that the tribes were going to arm against their brothers, whom they took to be prevaricators; but that, without going against them, everyone arrived at a perfect understanding, as prudence and charity would have it; and the peace was made.

2nd Proposition
Second example. The people arm in just punishment of a crime, for want of being able to punish the authors of it

A Levite, making his way, lodged in passing in the city of Gabaa, which belonged to the children of Benjamin: he was unworthily treated, he and his wife, who died at their shameless hands.[2] The Levite, to excite public vengeance, divided the dead body into twelve pieces, which he dispersed into all the orders of Israel. At this spectacle, everyone cried: "There was never such a thing done in Israel. Gather together, everyone said to the tribes, and decree in common what ought to be done."[3]

The tribes being assembled, it was ordained that, above all things, the guilty would be demanded [of Gabaa].[4] But, instead of delivering them up, the children of Benjamin undertook their defense; and into Gabaa flowed twenty-five thousand soldiers, all men of might and courage, and well instructed in the art of war: and after various battles with so doubtful an outcome, the tribe of Benjamin was exterminated, except for six hundred men, who had escaped from so many bloody battles.

Besides the difficulty of this war, there was also the extinction of a tribe of Israel to be considered. This is why all the tribes were distressed: "O Lord, shall one of the tribes perish, one of the springs of Israel?"[5] But justice carried the day: and the only thing produced

---

[1] Josh. 22:10–34. [2] Judg. 19:1–27. [3] Ibid., 30.
[4] Judg. 20:1ff. [5] Judg. 21:3,6–7.

by the regret for so considerable a loss, was to aid this miserable tribe in reestablishing itself, so far as possible, by marriage.

3rd Proposition
Third example. They proceeded by arms to the punishment of those who failed to come to the army, having been summoned by public order

This is what happened in the same war, when people lodged an accusation and demanded: "Who are they who did not present themselves at the general assembly? It was found that the inhabitants of Jabes Galaad had been missing: and they chose ten thousand of the best soldiers to put them to the sword."[6]

Gideon had punished, in very nearly the same way, the inhabitants of Soccoth, who, in a spirit of revolt, refused provisions to the army which was marching against the enemy. He took the tower of Phanuel, in which they placed their hope: he demolished it, and put the inhabitants to death.[7]

It is thus that one takes from rebels and mutineers the fortresses which they abuse: and one leaves an example to posterity of the punishment one gives them.

One sees clearly, in these examples, that the public power must be armed, so that force remains always with the sovereign.

4th Proposition
Fourth example. The war between David and Isboseth, son of Saul

The whole kingdom of Saul, after the death of this prince, belonged to David. God was not only the absolute master of it, through his sovereign and universal domain, but also its proprietor in virtue of particular titles over the family of Abraham and over the whole people of Israel. God, then, having given this entire kingdom to David, whom he had consecrated by Samuel, and to his family, one cannot doubt David's right: and nonetheless God willed that he conquer this kingdom which belonged to him by a just title.

The right of David's had been recognized by the whole people, and

---

[6] Ibid., 8–10.   [7] Judg. 8:5ff.

even by the family of Saul. Jonathan, son of Saul, said to David: "I know that thou shalt reign over Israel, and I shall be next to thee: yea, and my father knoweth this."[8] Indeed Saul himself, in one of his good moments, had spoken to David in these terms: "As I know that thou shalt surely be king, swear to me that thou wilt preserve the rest of my family."[9] Thus the right of David was well known.

That which retarded the execution of the will of God, was that Abner son of Ner, who commanded the armies of Saul, made this prince's name worthy, and put his son Isboseth on the throne for seven years – while David reigned at Hebron, over the house of Judah.[10]

However certain and recognized David's right may have been, he did not use his advantages during this war, and was careful of the blood of citizens. During this time the Philistines, enemies of the people of God, attempted nothing, and David had nothing to fear from the hand of strangers: thus he did not press Isboseth, and left him in peace for two years without making the slightest movement. War afterwards flared up: "And there was a very fierce battle between the two parties."[11] But Abner, on a height where he had rallied, with what he had left of the troops most devoted to the house of Saul (who were those of the tribe of Benjamin, from which he came), "cried to Joab, who was bitterly pursuing the disarrayed army: Shall thy sword rage unto utter destruction? Knowest thou not that it is dangerous to drive people to despair? How long dost thou defer to bid the people cease from pursuing after their brethren?" Joab asked for no better, and had no sooner heard Abner's reproach than he answered: "As the Lord liveth, if thou hadst spoke sooner, even in the morning the people should have retired from pursuing after their brethren. Then Joab sounded the trumpet, and all the army stood still, and did not pursue any further, nor fight any more."[12]

One sees in this conduct a disposition to spare fraternal blood – that is to say, that of the tribes which had all issued from Jacob. This was the only memorable combat which was undertaken: and however rough it may have been, they found among the dead only nineteen men from David's side, and from that of Abner, though beaten, only three hundred and sixty.

It will even be noticed that David never went in person to this war,

[8] 1 Kings 23:17.   [9] 1 Kings 24:21–22.   [10] 2 Kings 2:8ff.
[11] Ibid., 17.   [12] Ibid., 26–28.

for fear that the presence of one king might bring about a general combat. This prince did not want to soak his hands in the blood of his subjects: and he took care, as far as he could, of the survivors of the house of Saul, because of Jonathan. There were only individual clashes [*rencontres particulières*] in which, since "David was always prospering and growing stronger, while the house of Saul was decaying daily,"[13] he believed that it was better to let it fall by itself, than to pursue it to the extreme.

Everything in the party of Isboseth turned on the credit of Abner alone. David had only to treat him considerately, and to profit (as he did) from the annoyances which Abner received every day from a master equally feeble and haughty.[14]

Abner, in his soul, knew that David was the legitimate king: and one day, mistreated by Isboseth, he threatened him with making David reign over all Israel, as the Lord had ordained and promised.[15]

He treated indeed, with David, for whom he had won all Israel and the whole tribe of Benjamin, saying to them: "Both yesterday and the day before you sought for David, that he might reign over you. Now then do it: because the Lord hath spoken to David, saying: By the hand of my servant David I will save my people Israel from the hands of the Philistines."[16]

It happened in these circumstances that Joab treacherously killed Abner. "And Isboseth the son of Saul heard that Abner was slain in Hebron: and his hands were weakened, and all Israel was troubled."[17] This was what gave to two captains of thieving bands the boldness to kill Isboseth himself, in broad daylight in his bed, where he was sleeping at noon: and they brought his head to David.[18]

Thus ended the civil war, as David had always hoped, almost without spilling blood in fighting. But David, whose hands were clean, for fear of being thought a party to the assassination of Abner and to that of Isboseth, exonerated himself by two striking actions which won him all hearts.

The circumstances of the time, in which the reign which was beginning was still not very secure, did not permit David to punish Joab – whose person was so important and whose services were so necessary. What he could do about the murder of Abner was to say to the whole army and to Joab himself: "Rend your garments, and gird

---

[13] 2 Kings 3:1.   [14] Ibid., 6–8.   [15] Ibid., 9–10.
[16] Ibid., 17–19.   [17] 2 Kings 4:1.   [18] Ibid., 5–8.

yourselves with sackcloths, and mourn before the funeral of Abner. And David himself followed the bier. And when they had buried Abner in Hebron, David lifted up his voice, and wept at the grave of Abner . . . And the king mourning and lamenting over Abner said: Not as cowards are wont to die hath Abner died. Thy hands were not bound, nor thy feet laden with fetters: but as men fall before the children of iniquity, so didst thou fall. And all the people repeating it wept over him. And when all the people came to take meat with David, while it was yet broad day, David swore, saying: So do God to me, and more also, if I taste bread or anything else before sunset. And all the people, and all Israel understood that day that it was not the king's doing that Abner was slain."[19]

He did more, and "also said to his servants: Do you not know that a prince and a great man is slain this day in Israel? But I am yet weak, though anointed king. These men the sons of Sarvia (these were Joab and his brother Abisai) are too hard for me: The Lord reward him that doth evil according to his wickedness."[20] This was all that was permitted in the circumstances of those times.

As for what regards Isboseth, when the two leaders of the brigades, Baana and Rechab, brought David his head, thinking to render him a great service: "As the Lord liveth, he said, who hath delivered my soul out of all distress, the man that told me, and said: Saul is dead, who thought he brought me good tidings, I apprehended and slew . . . How much more now when wicked men have slain an innocent man in his own bed, shall I not require his blood at your hand?"[21] Thus perished these two thieves, as he had perished who gloried in having killed King Saul. The distinction that David knew, was that the latter was punished as a murderer of the Lord's anointed: and the former were killed for being guilty of the blood of an innocent man who had done them no evil – without calling him the Lord's anointed, which indeed he was not.

One saw, through this conduct of David, that in a civil war a good prince must take great care of the blood of citizens. If murders happen, which might be attributed to him because he profits from them, he must justify himself so highly that the whole people is satisfied.

---

[19] 2 Kings 3:31–37.   [20] Ibid., 38–39.   [21] 2 Kings 4:9–11.

5th Proposition
Fifth and sixth examples. The civil war of Absalom and Seba: with the story of Adonias

No prince was ever born with greater natural advantage, nor more capable of causing great movements and of forming a truly great party within the state, than Absalom son of David. Besides the graces which accompanied his whole person,[22] he was the most accommodating and the most thoughtful of men. He made a show of an immense love of justice, and knew how to flatter by this means all those who seemed to have the slightest reason for complaint.[23] We have observed him elsewhere: and I know not whether we have also remarked that David was perhaps a little slow on that point, during the time he was occupied with Bathsheba. However that may have been, Absalom knew how to profit from the circumstances, in which the reputation of the king his father seemed to be damaged by this weakness, and still more by the odious murder of Uriah, a man so brave, so attached to his service and so faithful to his master.

He was the eldest son of the king: the throne was in sight, and he was so close to it that he scarcely needed to take a step to ascend it.

In order to throw himself into a relief commensurate with so high a birth, "Absalom made himself chariots, and horsemen, and fifty men to run before him";[24] and he imposed on the people with this brilliance. This was a mistake against good policy: one should have permitted nothing extraordinary to so enterprising a spirit. The king, little suspicious of his nature and always too indulgent to his children, did not pull him back from this bold course. Absalom knew how to win him over by his flatteries: and being deprived, in a time of disgrace, of the presence of the king, he had said to him: "wherefore am I come from Gessur where I was banished? It had been better for me to be left there to end my days. Let me see the face of the king, or let him kill me."[25]

When he had sufficiently established his sources of intelligence throughout the kingdom, and thought himself in a state to break out, he chose the city of Hebron, the ancient seat of the monarchy, which was already taken for him, to declare himself. The pretext for distancing himself from the court could not have been more specious, nor

[22] 2 Kings 14:25.
[23] 2 Kings 15:2ff.
[24] Ibid., 1.
[25] 2 Kings 14:32.

more flattering to the king: "While I was banished from your court, I made a vow that, if I returned to Jerusalem to enjoy your presence, I would sacrifice to the Lord in Hebron."[26]

Absalom was no sooner in Hebron, than he gave the signal for revolt to all Israel. And on all sides men cried: "Absalom reigneth in Hebron."[27]

This deceitful prince took with him two hundred men out of Jerusalem,[28] who thought least of all of making Absalom king: but they nonetheless found themselves forced to declare for him. At the same time appeared at the head of his council "Achitopel, the principal minister and counsellor of David,[29] who was consulted like a god, first under David, and then under Absalom."[30] And at the same time Amasa, a renowned captain, was put at the head of Absalom's troops,[31] and this prince forgot nothing which might give repute to his party.

To impress on all minds that matters were irreconcilable, Achitopel advised Absalom, as soon as he had arrived in Jerusalem, to enter the apartment of the king's women in broad daylight – so that everyone might see the outrage which he did to the king, whose couch he soiled, and that everyone would at once sense that he was committed beyond recall, and that there would be no further consideration.[32]

Such was the state of affairs on the rebel side. Let us now consider the conduct of David.

He began, first of all, by giving himself time to reconnoitre; and abandoning Jerusalem, where the rebel was soon to become the strongest (in order to overwhelm him without recourse), he retired to a hidden place in the desert with the elite of his troops.[33]

Since he felt the hand of God, who was punishing him according to the prophecy of Nathan, he truly steeped himself in the humility which was fitting in a guilty person (whom his God was striking) – retiring on foot, weeping, with his whole following, with his head covered, and recognizing the finger of the Lord.[34] But at the same time he did not forget his duty. For having seen that the whole kingdom was in danger through this revolt, he gave all the necessary orders to assure himself the retention of his most faithful servants – such as the legions supported by Phelethi and by Cereth: such as the

[26] 2 Kings 15:7–8.
[27] Ibid., 10.
[28] Ibid., 11.
[29] Ibid., 12.
[30] 2 Kings 16:23.
[31] 2 Kings 17:25.
[32] 2 Kings 16:20–21.
[33] 2 Kings 15:14,18,28.
[34] Ibid., 16,24,30.

foreign troops of Ethai the Gethite, such as Zadok and Abiathar, together with their family.[35] He also dreamt of being warned of the undertakings of the rebel party, dividing his counsels, and of destroying that of Achitopel (which was the most formidable[36]).

After having thus dampened the first fire of the rebellion, and having provided for the most pressing needs by orders which met with success, he put himself in a position to fight. He himself divided his army into three parts (which had to be done), because this division was necessary to allow combat without confusion – given the huge bodies of armies as they existed in those days. He named the officers and the commanders, and said to them: "I shall march at your head."[37] He saw well that the whole monarchy was at stake, and believed that he need not restrain himself, as we have seen him do against Isboseth.

The whole people opposed this, saying to him "that thou alone art accounted for ten thousand: it is better therefore that thou shouldst be in the city to succor us."[38]

We have remarked elsewhere that he did not play at bravery in this difficult moment, but yielded to the wise counsels which had the good of the realm as their object.

He did not forget the duty of a father; and earnestly commanded Joab and the other leaders to save Absalom.[39] The royal blood is a good for the whole state, which David had to take care of – not only as a father, but also as a king.

The outcome of the battle is known: how Absalom perished in it, despite the orders of David; and how, to spare the citizens, those who were fleeing were no longer pursued.[40]

David, however, made a considerable mistake, into which his natural goodness led him. He grieved without measure over the loss of his son, crying ceaselessly in a lamenting tone: "My son Absalom, Absalom my son: would to God that I might die for thee, Absalom my son, my son Absalom."[41]

News of this came to the army, and the victory was changed into mourning: the people were discouraged, and like a people defeated and put to rout, they dared not appear before the king.[42] This is what finally obliged Joab to give him the advice which we have noticed

---

[35] Ibid., 17,22,27.   [36] Ibid., 31,32ff.   [37] 2 Kings 18:1–2.   [38] Ibid., 3.
[39] Ibid., 5,12.   [40] Ibid., 6,7ff.   [41] Ibid., 33.   [42] 2 Kings 19:1–3.

On wars between citizens

elsewhere. And this is what should make princes understand that, in civil wars, despite their own sorrow (against which they must make an effort), they must take part in the public joy which victory inspires; otherwise one alienates all minds, and draws new misfortune on the kingdom.

The rebellion, however, was not without consequences. Seba the son of Bochri, of the family of Jemin (which was that of Saul) aroused the still-excited people by his contemptuous words: "We have no part in David, nor inheritance in the son of Isai . . . " The king recognized the danger, and said to Amasa: Hasten to assemble all the men of Judah. He executed this order slowly, and David said to Abisai: Now will Seba the son of Bochri do us more harm than did Absalom; take thou therefore the servants of the Lord, and pursue after him, lest he find fenced cities, and escape us."[43] Abisai took the legions of Cereth: and of Phelethi, together with the many soldiers he had in Jerusalem. Joab on his side pursued Seba, who was going from tribe to tribe arousing the people, and taking away the choice troops he could. But Joab made it clear to the children of Abela, where the rebel was shut up, that it was not only a question of this one man. Following his persuasion, a wise woman of this country, who complained that so fine a city would be ruined, knew how to save it by having the head of Seba thrown over the walls to Joab.

Thus ended the rebellion, which cost only the blood of the leaders of the rebels. David's diligence saved the state. He had reason to think that this second revolt, which arose out of a popular movement and a feeling of contempt, was more to be feared than that which had been excited by the presence of the king's son. He also knew how useful it was to have a seasoned body of troops under his control; and such were the remedies which he used against the rebels.

One can report in this connection what happened to Adonias, son of David.[44] This prince, taking advantage of the old age of the king his father, whose eldest he was, wanted to seize the kingdom despite him, and entered into an accord to that end with Joab and Abiathar, the important priest. But Zadok, the prince of priests after him, and Banaias (with the troops whose command he had), and the power of the army of David, were not at all for Adonias. David, with this aid, prevented the civil war which Adonias, sustained by a great faction,

---

[43] 2 Kings 20:1–6.   [44] 3 Kings 1:1,7–8.

contemplated, and left the peaceable kingdom to Solomon, to whom he gave it by order of God.

Thus everyone continued to recognize the usefulness of standing troops, through which a king always remains armed and the strongest.

6th Proposition
Last example of civil wars. That which began under Roboam through the division of the ten tribes

The cause of this revolt, in which the kingdom of Israel or the ten tribes was erected, can be treated more appropriately in other places. Here we shall merely remark that:

In the first place, the kings of Judah, after so great a rebellion which divided the kingdom, [who were] obliged to defend themselves not only against foreigners,[45] but also against their rebellious brothers, built in the territories of the tribe of Judah a great number of new fortresses and of arsenals, where there were stores of provisions in abundance, and at the same time all kinds of suits of armor.[46]

In the second place, they readied themselves to reconquer by arms the new kingdom which the rebellion had raised against the house of David. But God, who wanted to show how much the blood of Israel should be dear to its brothers, and that even after the division one should not forget common origins, forbad (through his prophet) the men of Judah from making war on their brothers, rebels and schismatics though they were.[47]

It even came about afterwards – and this should be noted in the third place – that the kingdom of Judah linked itself by a strict alliance to the rebel kingdom. For even though there was, over several reigns, a continual war between the two kingdoms[48] – against the will of God, and perhaps more through the fault of the children of Israel than of those of Judah – nonetheless in the fulness of time the alliance between them was so solidly established that the pious King Josaphat, invited by Achab King of Israel to join his forces with those of Israel (to help them recover from the King of Syria a strong place which they claimed), came in person to say to Achab: "As I am, so art thou: my people and thy people are one: and my horsemen, thy horsemen."[49]

[45] 3 Kings 14:26.   [46] 2 Par. 11:5–12.   [47] 3 Kings 12:24.
[48] 3 Kings 14:30; 15:32.   [49] 3 Kings 22:5.

On wars between citizens

The alliance was afterwards confirmed: and the same Josaphat again responded to Joram King of Israel (who begged him to help him against the King of Moab): "I will come up: he that is mine, is thine; my people, thy people; and my horses, thy horses."[50]

Through this one sees that, for the sake of peace and the stability of human affairs, kingdoms founded at first on rebellion are afterwards viewed as having become legitimate, either through long possession, or through treaties and the recognition of earlier kings.

And notice that the law of possession had force in a kingdom which had joined the revolt against the true religion, to the point of defection.

In the fourth place, legitimate kings should always show themselves most moderate, by striving to recover through reason those who had abandoned their duties. Thus acted King Abia son of Roboam, before coming to actual fighting with the rebels: and the armies being present, he climbed onto a high place, where he delivered this fine speech to the Israelites, with as much force as gentleness: "Hear me, O Jeroboam, and all Israel"[51] – representing to them with lively reasons the wrong which they had done against God and their kings. He was incomparably the strongest: but, still more anxious to recover the rebels than to profit from this advantage, he failed to notice that Jeroboam surrounded him from the rear. He found himself almost enveloped by his enemies. God took his part, and spread terror over the rebels, who took flight.

We shall give as a fifth and final observation, that the kingdom of Israel, though made legitimate and very powerful later on, never equaled the solidity of the kingdom of Judah, from which it had been separated.

Since it was established by division, it was often divided against itself. Kings chased each other out. Baasa chased out the family of Jeroboam, who had founded the kingdom, from the second generation. Zambri, the subject of Baasa, rose up against him, and reigned only seven days. Amri took his place, and forced him to set fire personally to the palace, in which he was burned; the kingdom divided in half. Amri, whose party prevailed and who seemed to have resurrected the kingdom of Israel by beating Samaria,[52] reigned briefly: and his family perished under his grandson. The best-

---

[50] 4 Kings 3:7.   [51] 2 Par. 13:4.
[52] 3 Kings 15:27; 16:9,10,16,18,21,24.

established royal families scarcely lasted four or five generations. And that of Jehu, which God himself had consecrated by Eliseus, soon fell through the revolt of Sellum, who killed the king and seized the kingdom.[53]

By contrast in the kingdom of Judah, where the succession was legitimate, the family of David remained tranquilly on the throne, and there was no more civil war: men loved the name of David and of his house. Among so many kings who reigned over Israel, there was not a single one whom God approved: but there issued from David great and holy kings, imitators of his piety. The kingdom of Judah had the happiness to preserve the law of Moses and the religion of its fathers. It is true that, for their sins, the children of Judah were carried off to Babylonia, and the throne of David was overturned: but God did not leave without recourse the people of Judah, to whom he promised a return to the land of their fathers after seventy years of captivity. But as for the kingdom of Israel, besides the fact that it fell sooner, it was broken up without recourse at the hands of Salmanasar, King of Assyria,[54] and lost itself among the Gentiles.

Such was the nature and the catastrophe of these two kingdoms. That which had been raised by revolt against legitimate kings, though later recognized by those same kings, had within itself a perpetual instability and finally perished hopelessly through its faults.

[53] 4 Kings 9; 10:30; 15:10,12.
[54] 4 Kings 17; 18.

Article IV

Though God made war for his people in an extraordinary and miraculous fashion, he wanted to harden them by giving them warlike kings and great captains

1st Proposition
God made war for his people, from the heights of heaven, in an extraordinary and miraculous way

So Moses had said on the banks of the Red Sea: "Fear not this immense nation by which you are pursued. The Lord will fight for you, and you will only have to remain at rest."[1]

"Besides opening the sea for them, he put his angel, while they passed through, between them and the Egyptians, to keep Pharaoh from approaching them."[2]

On the famous day when the sun stopped at the voice of Joshua, and while the enemy was in flight, God caused great stones to fall from heaven like hail,[3] so that no one would escape, and so that those who had escaped the sword would be overcome by blows from above.

The walls fell before the bow: the rivers returned to their source to give him passage, and everything yielded to him.[4]

Sometimes God sent to their enemies, in their dreams, terrible prognostications of their ruin. They saw the sword of Gideon which pursued them so closely that they could not escape; and they fled in disorder with terrible howling, to the sound of his trumpets and the light of his torches, and turned their swords on one another, not knowing whom to blame for their total collapse.[5]

A comparable furor seized the Philistines, when Jonathan attacked them; and they undertook a horrible carnage of their own troops.[6]

---

[1] Exod., 14:13–14. [2] Ibid., 19,20. [3] Josh. 10:10–13.
[4] Ibid., 3, 7. [5] Judg. 6:13ff. [6] 1 Kings 14:19–20.

God made his thunder rumble over the fleeing,[7] who, frozen with fright, led themselves be killed without resistance.

Sometimes one heard a noise of horses and of armed chariots, which tested the enemy, and made them believe that great help was arriving for the Israelites; such that they fled and abandoned the camp with all the equipment.[8]

At other times, instead of noise, Eliseus made chariots of flame appear before his terrified companions,[9] who believed themselves surrounded by an invisible army which was stronger than that of their enemies the Syrians. The same prophet struck the Syrians with blindness, and led them to the midst of Samaria.[10]

Everyone knows about the carnage done by an angel of God in one night (following the prayer of Ezechias) against eighty-five thousand men from the army of Sennacherib, which was besieging Jerusalem.[11]

But we must end these recitals, with a still more surprising spectacle.

Josaphat, who saw no salvation from the terrifying army of the league of the Idumeans, the Moabites and the Ammonites (sustained by the Syrians[12]), after having begged the help of God, and after having obtained certain assurances from the mouth of a holy prophet (as has been noticed elsewhere), marched against the enemy in the desert of Thecua, and gave this new order of war: "Let the singing men of the Lord be put at the head of the army, and they will sing the divine psalm together: Give glory to the Lord, for his mercy endureth forever."[13] Thus the army changed into a musical choir; scarcely had it begun this divine chant than the enemies who lay in ambush turned on each other, and cut themselves to pieces: such that the children of Judah, arriving at a solitary high-point, saw from afar the whole country covered with dead bodies, without a single man remaining alive among their enemies: and three days did not suffice to gather up their rich spoils. This valley was called the "Valley of Benediction," since it was in blessing God that they defeated an army which seemed invincible. Josaphat returned to Jerusalem in a great triumph; and entering the house of the Lord to the sound of their harps, their lutes,

---

[7] 1 Kings 7:10; Ecclus. 46:20–21.
[8] 4 Kings 7:6–7.
[9] 4 Kings 6:16–17.
[10] Ibid., 18–19.
[11] 4 Kings 19:35.
[12] 2 Par. 20:2ff.
[13] Ibid., 21.

and their trumpets, they continued the praise of God, who had shown his goodness in the punishment of these unjust aggressors.

It was thus that was fulfilled that which had been sung by the prophetess Deborah: "The Lord chose new wars ... war from heaven was made against them, the stars remaining in their order and courses fought against the Sisara."[14] The whole of nature was for us: the stars declared themselves: and the angels who presided over it on the order of God, and in the way known by him, have thrown their javelins from on high.

2nd Proposition
This extraordinary way of making war was not perpetual: ordinarily the people fought fully armed, though God gave the victory no less

Most of the battles of David were carried out in the ordinary way. It was the same with the other kings: and the wars of the Maccabees were not managed otherwise. God wanted to make warriors and wanted to make military virtue shine brightly in his people.

Thus the holy land was conquered by the various exploits of the tribes. They pressed the enemy in his camps and in his cities, because they were vigorous attackers. It was always God who gave suitable resolution to the leaders, and intrepidity and obedience to the soldiers, on these occasions; whereas he sent to the enemy camp terror, discord, and confusion. Jabes, the bravest of all his brothers, invoked the God of Israel, and made him a vow which drew his help to him:[15] but this was while fighting valiantly. Thus [did] Caleb; thus Juda; thus the others. Reuben and Gad conquered the Agarites and their allies, "because they called upon God in the battle, and he heard them, because they had put their faith in him while fighting."[16]

3rd Proposition
God wanted to harden his people: how he did it

"I will not destroy entirely the nations which Joshua left, when he died."[17] Thus God left them in order, and did not want to extermi-

---

[14] Judg. 5:8,20. [15] 1 Par. 4:10.
[16] 1 Par. 5:20. [17] Judg. 2:21,23.

nate them entirely, nor deliver them into the hands of Joshua, "in order that Israel might be instructed by their resistance: and all that had not known the wars of the Canaanites, might learn, they and their children, to fight with their enemies, and be trained up to war."[18]

4th Proposition
God gave his people great captains and warlike princes

This was a new way of shaping them for war. One need only name a Joshua, a Jeptha, a Gideon, a Saul and a Jonathan, a David (and under him a Joab, an Abisai, an Abner and an Amasa), a Josaphat, an Ozias, an Ezechias, a Judah the Maccabee, with his brothers Jonathan and Simon, a John Hyrcanus, son of the latter – and so many others whose names are so celebrated in the sacred books and in the archives of the people of God. One need only, I say, name them, to see in this people more great captains and warlike princes (from whom the Israelites learned war) than are known in other nations.

One even sees, to begin with Abraham, that this great man, so famous for his faith, was no less so for his combats.

All the holy books are filled with the most renowned military exploits, undertaken not just by the whole body of the nation, but also by the particular tribes, in the conquest of the holy land – as it appears in the first nine chapters of the first book of *Paralipomenon*. Thus one cannot doubt that military virtue shone brilliantly in the holy people.

5th Proposition
Even women, among the holy people, excelled in courage, and performed astonishing acts

Thus Jahel, wife of Haben, pierced the temples of Sisara through and through with a nail. Thus on the orders of Barak and of Deborah the prophetess took place the bloody battle in which Sisara was cut to pieces.[19]

The prophetess sang of his defeat in an ode,[20] whose sublime tone surpasses that of the lyrics of Pindar and an Alceas, together with that of a Horace, their imitator.[21] At the end one heard the speech of the mother of Sisara, who looks out of the window, and is astonished not

[18] Judg. 3:1–3.
[19] Judg. 4.
[20] Judg. 5:1–31.
[21] Ibid., 1–31.

to hear the sound of his victory-wagon, while the ablest of her women responds by singing of his victories, representing him as a conqueror destined by fate, with his share of a rich booty (the most beautiful of all women[22]), in the manner of barbarous peoples. In fact, however, he had fallen at the hand of a woman. "So let all thy enemies perish, O Lord, concludes Deborah: but let them that love thee shine, as the sun shineth in his rising."[23] Such was the victory which gave forty years of peace to the people of God.[24]

Everyone will anticipate me here by adding a Judith, with the head of Holofernes which she had cut off – and by this means routed the enemy of the Assyrians, commanded by so great a general.

It was in vain that he assembled so redoubtable an army, that he climbed so many mountains, overcame so many places, crossed so many great rivers, put so many provinces to the torch, received the surrender of so many important cities, from which he chose such brave soldiers as there were to flesh out his troops.[25]

His vigilance in leading his troops, in augmenting them on the march, in visiting their quarters, in determining the ways in which a place could be reduced by cutting its water supply – [all] were useless to him. His head was reserved for a woman, whose master this proud general believed himself to be.

This woman, by her vigorous counsels, had first raised the courage of her citizens: and by the death of a single man, she dispersed the proud camp of the Assyrians. "For their mighty one did not fall by young men, neither did the sons of Titan strike him, nor tall giants oppose him, but Judith the daughter of Merari weakened him with the beauty of her eyes . . . The Persians quaked at her constancy, and the Medes at her boldness."[26] Thus she sang, like another Deborah, over the victory of the Lord through a woman – who during the rest of her life was the ornament of all feasts, and remained forever celebrated for having known how to join power together with chastity.[27]

The Romans boasted of their Cloelia, and her companions, whose boldness in crossing the river astonished and intimidated the camp of Porsenna. Here, without exaggeration, was something greater. And I shall not say more about it.

---

[22] Ibid., 28–30.
[23] Ibid., 31.
[24] Ibid., 32.
[25] Judith 1; 2; 3.
[26] Judith 16:8,12.
[27] Ibid., 25–27.

6th Proposition
Under the proper conditions, war is not only legitimate, but also pious and holy

"And they said every man to his neighbor: Let us raise up the low condition of our people, and let us fight for our people, for our holy laws, and for our holy ceremonies."[28]

It is of such wars that it is truly said: "Sanctify war,"[29] in the sense that Moses said to the Levites: "You have consecrated your hands this day to the Lord,"[30] when you have armed them for his fight.

God ordinarily calls himself the God of armies, and sanctifies them by taking this name.

7th Proposition
God, nonetheless, after all, does not love war, and prefers the peaceful to warriors

"David called his son Solomon, and spoke to him in this way: My son, it was my desire to have built a house for the name of the Lord my God. But the word of the Lord came to me, saying: Thou hast shed much blood, and fought many battles, so thou canst not build a house to my name, after shedding so much blood before me . . ."[31] I have not failed to prepare the charges of the house of the Lord, of gold a hundred thousand talents, and of silver ten million talents: but of brass and of iron there is no weight; timber also and stones I have prepared for all the charges, together with excellent workmen to make use of all this . . . Arise then, and be doing, and the Lord will be with thee."[32]

God did not want to receive the Temple from a bloody hand. David was a holy king, and the model of princes: so pleasing to God that he had deigned to call him a man after his own heart. Never had he spilled any but infidel blood in wars which were called the Lord's wars: and if he had spilled that of the Israelites it was that of rebels, whom he had already spared as much as he could. But it was enough that this was human blood, to cause him to be judged unworthy of presenting the Temple to the Lord, the author and protector of human life.

[28] 1 Macc. 3:43. [29] Jer. 6:4. [30] Exod. 32:29.
[31] 1 Par. 22:6–8; 28:3. [32] 1 Par. 22:14–16.

Such was the exclusion which God pronounced on him in the first part of the prophetic speech. But the second [part] is no less remarkable: it was the choice of Solomon to build the Temple. The title which God gave him was that of "Peaceable."[33] Hands so free of blood were the only ones worthy of raising God's sanctuary. God did not rest with this; he gave the glory of securing the throne to this peaceable one, whom he preferred to warriors by this honor. Still more, he made of this peaceable one one of the most excellent prefigurations of his incarnate Son.[34]

David had conceived the plan of building the Temple from an excellent motive; and he spoke in these terms to the prophet Nathan: "Dost thou see that I dwell in a house of cedar, and the ark of God is lodged within tents and skins?"[35] The great prophet had approved this great and pious plan, by saying to him: "Go, do all that is in thy heart: because the Lord is with thee."[36] But the word of God was addressed to Nathan, the following night in these terms: "Thus saith the Lord . . . Thou shalt not build the Temple in my name. When the days shall be fulfilled . . . one of the sons whom I shall cause to be born from thy blood will build the Temple, and I will establish the throne of his kingdom for ever."[37]

God refused his acceptance to David out of hatred for the blood in which he already saw his hands steeped. So much saintliness in this prince was not able to efface the stain. God loves the peaceable: and the glory of peace he prefers over that of arms, however holy and religious.

[33] Ibid., 9–10. [34] Ibid., 9–10. [35] 2 Kings 7:2; 1 Par. 17:1.
[36] 2 Kings 7:3. [37] Ibid., 5,12,13.

Article v

On military virtues, institutions, orders, and exercises

1st Proposition
Glory preferred to life

Bacchides and Alcimus had twenty thousand men, with two thousand horses, before Jerusalem: and Judas had camped nearby with only three thousand men, drawn from his best troops. When they saw the multitude of the enemy host, they were terrified. This fear dissipated the army, of which there remained only eight hundred men.[1] Judas, whose army had flowed away, and pressed to fight in this condition, without having the time to gather his forces, had his courage broken down. This was his first feeling, which was that of nature. But it could be vanquished by the feeling of virtue. "Judas said to them that remained: Let us arise, and go against our enemies, if we may be able to fight against them. But they dissuaded him, saying: We shall not be able, but let us save our lives now, and return to our brethren, and then we will fight against them: for we are but few. But Judas said: God forbid we should do this thing, and flee away from them: but if our time be come, let us die manfully for our brethren, and let us not stain our glory. At these words he left the camp; the army marched out to fight in good order."[2] The right flank of Bacchides was the stronger: Judas attacked it with his best soldiers, and set it to flight. Those of the left flank, seeing the rout, took Judas from behind, while he was pursuing the enemy: the fight heated up, there were already many wounded on both sides: Judas was killed, and the rest took flight.

There are occasions where the glory of dying courageously is worth more than victory. Glory sustains war. Those who know how to rush to certain death for their country, leave behind a reputation for valor which astonishes the enemy: and by this means they are more useful to their country than if they remained alive.

---

[1] 1 Macc. 9:4–7.   [2] Ibid., 8–11.

It is this which makes the love of glory effective. But one must always remember that it is the glory of defending one's country and its liberty. The Maccabees proposed this law to themselves when they said: "Let us all die in our innocency: and heaven and earth shall be witness for us, that you have attacked us unjustly."[3] And afterwards: "We will fight for our lives and our laws, for our wives and our children."[4] And again: "Is it not better for us to die in battle, than to see the evils of our nation, and of the holies? Nevertheless as it shall be the will of God in heaven, so be it done."[5] And to say all in a word, let us die for our brothers, as the courageous Judas said. Let us leave them the example of dying for our holy laws; and let the memory of our valor make tremble those who would attack men so determined on death. Let it be eternally said in Israel: However weak we may be, let no one attack us with impunity.

2nd Proposition
Necessity gives courage

"It is not now as yesterday, and the day before. For behold the battle is before us, said Jonathan to his people; and the waters of the Jordan on this side and on that side, and banks, and marshes and woods: and there is no place for us to turn aside. Now therefore cry ye to heaven."[6] At the same time they marched against the enemy: Bacchides was pressed by Jonathan, who, seeing him shaken, crossed the Jordan by swimming to pursue him, and himself killed two thousand men.

3rd Proposition
One rushes to certain death

Samson had given the example. After having gouged out his eyes, the Philistines gathered praising their god Dagon, who had given them the victory over so redoubtable an enemy. They made him come to their gatherings and to their banquets as a diversion, and placed him in the middle of the hall, between two pillars which held up the building.[7]

---

[3] 1 Macc. 2:37.   [4] 1 Macc. 3:20–21.
[5] Ibid., 59–60.   [6] 1 Macc. 9:44–46.
[7] Judg. 16:21ff.

Samson, who felt the return of his power with the rebirth of his hair, "said to the lad that guided his step: suffer me to touch the pillars."[8] The whole house was full of men and women: and all the princes of the Philistines were there, to the number of about three thousand, who had come to see Samson, whom they made light of. Then he invoked God in this way: "O Lord God, remember me, and restore to me now my former strength, that I may revenge myself on my enemies (who were the enemies of the people of God, whose leader and judge he was): and for the loss of my two eyes I may take one revenge."[9] At the same moment seizing the two columns which sustained the edifice, the one with his right hand and the other with his left: "Let me die, he said, with the Philistines."[10] In weakening the columns he brought the whole house down on the Philistines, and while dying killed more of them at a single stroke than he had done in his lifetime.

The interpreters [of Scripture] prove very well, through Ecclesiasticus[11] and the Epistle to the Hebrews,[12] that Samson was [divinely] inspired on death, to accustom his people to scorn it.

One can believe that a similar inspiration motivated Eleazar, who saw the people astonished by the prodigious army of Antiochus (and still more by the number and size of his elephants), to go straight to the king, who was recognized by his height and his armor. "He exposed himself to deliver his people and to get himself an everlasting name. And he ran up to the elephant boldly in the midst of the legion, killing on the right hand and on the left, and they fell by him on this side and that side. And he went between the feet of the elephant, and put himself under it: and slew it, and it fell to the ground upon him, and he died there."[13]

These actions of astonishing valor make it clear that anything is possible for him who knows how to despise his life: at once they filled citizens with courage, and the enemy with terror.

4th Proposition
Moderation in victory

The examples of this are infinite. That of Gideon is worthy of note.

The people, freed by his signal victories, came to him in a body to

[8] Ibid., 26. [9] Ibid., 28. [10] Ibid., 30.
[11] Ecclus. 46. [12] Heb. 11:32–34. [13] 1 Macc. 6:43–46.

say: "Rule thou over us, and thy son, and thy son's son, because we owe our liberty to thee." But Gideon, without taking pride in himself and without wishing to change the form of government, answered: "I will not rule over you, neither shall my son rule over you, nor our posterity; but the Lord shall remain the sole sovereign."[14]

From the beginning of the nation, Abraham, after having taken back all the goods of his friends the kings that the enemy had taken away, paid a tithe to the high priest of the Lord, preserved for the allies their share of the booty, without keeping for himself "a single thread or a strap, and gave up everything, and wanted to owe nothing to any mortal."[15]

5th Proposition
To make war equitably

To treat one's old allies considerately, and ask passage of them on just conditions: this is what has been stressed from the beginning of this book.

By the effect of this same equity, one sets limits between neighboring peoples. There were immortal testimonials of what belonged to them. *Tumulus testis*.[16]

"Pass not beyond the ancient bounds which thy fathers have set."[17]

To respect these bounds is to respect God, who had been taken as a witness and who alone was present when they were laid down. "None is witness of our speech but God, who is present and belongeth."[18]

He is also taken to be the avenger of violated faith. "The Lord behold and judge between us when we shall be gone one from the other."[19]

It was also in a spirit of justice that Abraham, who negotiated as an equal, sovereign-to-sovereign, with King Abimelech, reproached him for the violence which had been done to his servants, instead of beginning with him. "But Abimelech answered: I knew not who did this thing, and thou didst not tell me, and I heard not of it till today."[20]

In fine this spirit of equity, which must prevail even amidst arms, appears nowhere more clearly than in the manner of war-making which God prescribed to his people while placing arms in their hands.

[14] Judg. 8:22–23. [15] Gen. 14:23. [16] Gen. 31:48. [17] Prov. 22:28.
[18] Gen. 31:50. [19] Ibid., 49. [20] Gen. 21:25–26.

"If at any time thou come to fight against a city, thou shalt first offer it peace. If they receive it, and open the gates to thee, all the people that are therein, shall be saved, and shall serve thee paying tribute. But if they will not make peace, and shall begin war against thee, thou shalt besiege it. And when the Lord thy God shall deliver it into thy hands, thou shalt slay all that are therein of the male sex, with the edge of the sword, excepting women, children and animals . . ."[21] So shalt thou do to all cities that are at a great distance from thee, and are not of those cities which thou shalt receive in possession."[22] For the latter God ordains no pity, for particular reasons which have already been noticed: but it is an exception which (as they say) proves the rule.

Moses continues on God's behalf: "When thou hast besieged a city a long time, and hast compassed it with bulwarks to take it, thou shalt not cut down the trees that may be eaten of, neither shalt thou spoil the country round about with axes: for it is a tree, and not a man, neither can it increase the number of them that fight against thee (this applies to fruit-trees). But if there be any trees that are not fruitful, but wild, and fit for other uses, cut them down, and make engines, until thou take the city, which fighteth against thee."[23]

Prudence, perseverance, and at the same time justice with mildness, gleam in these words.

6th Proposition
Not to make oneself odious in a foreign land

"You have troubled me by the unjust war that you have made against the children of Sichem: And you make me hateful to the people of that country, whom I have always treated considerately"[24] said Jacob to Simeon and to Levi, his children. He withdrew, and sought after peace.

7th Proposition
A military cry before combat, to know the soldier's disposition

"And when the battle is now at hand . . . the captains shall proclaim through every band in the hearing of the army: What man is there, that hath built a new house and hath not dedicated it? Let him go and

---

[21] Deut. 20:10–13. [22] Ibid., 14–15.
[23] Ibid., 19–20. [24] Gen. 34:30.

return to his house, lest he die in the battle, and another man dedicate it. What man is there, that hath planted a vineyard, and hath not as yet made it be common, whereof all men may eat? Let him do the same. What man is there, that hath espoused a wife? Let him take her, and not leave her to another man."[25]

This cry is meant to insure that soldiers have nothing in their hearts save fighting, and that they have nothing in their memory which could dampen their ardor.

Afterwards one undertook this general cry: "What man is there that is fearful, and faint-hearted? Let him go, and return to his house, lest he make the hearts of his brethren to fear, as he himself is possessed with fear."[26]

The custom of this cry still lasted during the wars of the Maccabees.[27] It left to soldiers only the love of the fatherland, together with the cares of combat, without having regret for their lives.

8th Proposition
The choice of soldiers

When Gideon assembled the army to pursue the Madianites, he received this order from God: "Speak to the people, and proclaim in the hearing of all, Whosoever is fearful and timorous, let him return." Twenty-two thousand men returned, and only ten thousand of them remained. God continued: "Bring them to the waters . . . They that shall lap the water with their tongues, as dogs are wont to lap, thou shalt set apart by themselves: but they that shall drink bowing down their knees to drink at their ease, shall be on the other side: and the number of them that had lapped water, casting it with the hand to their mouth, was three hundred men, whom God chose for combat." And he taught this general that those who are found to be most fit to endure hunger and thirst would be the best soldiers.[28]

9th Proposition
The qualities of a commander

"Take courage, and be strong. Be a man; fear not and be not dismayed."[29]

[25] Deut. 20:2,5–7.   [26] Ibid., 8.   [27] 1 Macc. 3:56.
[28] Judg. 7:3–6.   [29] Josh. 1:6,7,9; 1 Par. 22:13.

This is the first thing required of men who are to command, and the foundation of all the rest.

This is also what Nehemias, governor of Judaea, was told, when timid counsels had been inspired in him: "Who is there that, being as I am, would flee from fear?"[30]

10th Proposition
Intrepidity

"Joshua lifted up his eyes, and saw a man standing over against him holding a drawn sword; and he went to him without fear, and said: Art thou one of ours, or of our adversaries"[31] – as someone might say among us, "who lives?" He learned, on approaching, that this was an angel. "I am prince of the host of the Lord" (this invisible army is always ready to fight for his servants). And Joshua turned his attack into adoration – but after having learned by this trial that nothing is to be feared in war, not even an angel of God in human form.

11th Proposition
A general's order

"What you shall see me do, do you the same"[32] – all eyes on the general and all hearts ready to follow him through all dangers.

Thus spoke Gideon at the beginning of a battle. It is the most noble and proud order that a general ever gave to his soldiers.

12th Proposition
The tribes complained when they were not summoned first to fight the enemy

"The men of the tribe of Ephraim said to Gideon: What is this that thou meanest to do, that thou wouldst not call us promptly when thou wentest to fight against Madian? And they chid him sharply and almost offered violence."[33]

They had been summoned merely to pursue the enemy, already put to rout, and they had cut off the retreat of the Madianites: so far that they had captured Oreb and Zeb, two of their leaders, whose heads

---

[30] Neh. 6:11. [31] Josh. 5:13–16.
[32] Judg. 7:17. [33] Judg. 8:1.

they carried on the ends of their pikes.[34] And the desire to fight was so great, that they murmured against Gideon, as we have just learned.

13th Proposition
A general appeases brave men by praising them

"But Gideon answered them: What could I have done like to that which you have done? Is not one bunch of grapes of Ephraim better than the vintages of Abiezer (however abundant this country may have been)? The Lord hath delivered into your hands Oreb and Zeb: what could I have done like to that which you have done?"[35] Their anger was appeased by this praise.

14th Proposition
To die, or to vanquish

This is what determined soldiers do, who never give up: such were those of whom it is spoken in the war between David and Isboseth.

"Abner said to Joab: Let the young men rise, and play before us" – that is to say, let them fight to the end, in single combat, as used to be done in our tournaments. "Then there arose and went over twelve in number of Benjamin, of the part of Isboseth the son of Saul, and twelve of the servants of David. And every one catching his fellow by the head (perhaps in the manner of gladiators, who had a glove in hand for this purpose), thrust his sword into the side of his adversary, and they fell down dead together." At once their valor was compensated, by calling the field: "The Field of the Valiant of Gabaon."[36] And the title remained in memory of so determined an action.

15th Proposition
To accustom soldiers to have contempt for the enemy

"Open the mouth of the cave, and bring forth to me the five kings that lie hid therein."[37] God had condemned them to death. "And when they were brought out to him, he called all the soldiers, and in their presence gave this order to the chiefs: Go, and set your feet on the necks of these kings. And when they had gone, and put their feet

---

[34] Judg. 7:24–25.
[35] Judg. 8:2–3.
[36] 2 Kings 2:14–16.
[37] Josh. 10:22.

upon the necks of them lying under them, he said again to them: Fear not, neither be ye dismayed, take courage, and be strong: for so will the Lord do to all your enemies, against whom you fight. And after having killed them, he hanged them upon five gibbets, to be a spectacle to the people . . . and they cast them into the cave where they had been taken, and put great stones at the mouth thereof, according to custom, as an eternal monument to posterity."[38]

16th Proposition
On diligence and precautions on expeditions, and in all matters of war

"Prepare you victuals, as much as necessary. In three days (a day to be named) you will pass over the Jordan: and you will enter the land of the enemy."[39]

At the same time Joshua sent out spies, and caused Jericho to be observed. He learned that everything was in a state of terror. He marched the whole night,[40] wanting to mark the beginning of his new principality by some striking action. "I shall begin today, said the Lord, to make your name shine like that of Moses."[41]

Gideon awoke at night, assembled the army, beat the enemy, pursued them without relenting, fell by chance on fifteen thousand men, who remained, seized their commanders (who were resting safely and expected nothing less than an attack), cut everyone to pieces, and returned before the setting of the sun.[42]

In order to profit from his advantage, and seeing that his soldiers had regained their courage, Saul (without losing a moment and without even leaving time for refreshment) took ten thousand men that he found at hand: "Cursed be the man that shall eat food till evening, till I be revenged of my enemies."[43] And he carried out a great slaughter from Machmas to Ailon, in a large country. Not content with this victory, though his soldiers were very tired, "march, he said, and let us fall upon them by night, and let us not lower our heads till morning."[44]

Baasa King of Israel fortified Rama, and by this means stopped the kings of Judah from setting foot on his lands, and assuring himself of a position from which he derived great advantages. But Asa King of

[38] Ibid., 23–27.   [39] Josh. 1:11.   [40] Josh. 2:1,2,24; 3:1.   [41] Josh. 1:7.
[42] Judg. 7:1; 8:11–13.   [43] 1 Kings 14:24.   [44] Ibid., 36.

Judah saw the importance of it. Without sparing either gold or silver, he won over the King of Syria against Baasa: the work was interrupted by this unexpected war, and Baasa withdrew.[45] Asa, without losing any time, "sent word into all Judah, in this absolute form: Let no man be excused. And they took away from Rama the materials for the new fortification: and from them Asa built two fortresses."[46] Such was the effect of his diligence. It weakened the enemy and strengthened him.

One could go on to infinity, if one wanted to relate the examples of activity or vigilance, or precaution in wartime expeditions, furnished by the Joshuas, the Gideons, the Davids, the Maccabees, and the other great captains whose memory has been preserved by sacred history.

17th Proposition
Suitable alliances

We have just seen a fine example of this, when Asa linked himself so opportunely with the King of Syria; other examples would be superfluous; and it is sufficient to notice once that there are occasions on which one should spare nothing.

18th Proposition
The reputation of being a man of war keeps the enemy fearful

"Chusai said to Absalom: Thou knowest thy father, and the brave men that are with him, that they are very valiant, and bitter in their mind, as a bear raging in the wood when her whelps are taken away: and thy father is a warrior, and will not lodge with the people. Perhaps he now lieth hid in pits, or in some other place which he list: and when anyone shall fall at the first, every one that heareth it shall say: There is a slaughter among the people that followed Absalom. And the most valiant men whose heart is as the heart of a lion shall melt for fear: for all the people of Israel know thy father to be a valiant man, and that all who are with him are valiant."[47] He advised that one risk nothing and attack only with certainty – which gave David time to regroup, and assured him the victory. And he stopped in this simple

---

[45] 3 Kings 15:17–21. [46] Ibid., 22. [47] 2 Kings 17:8–10.

way the impetuosity of Absalom, who feared in David the resources which this great captain could find in his warlike ability and in his courage.

19th Proposition
Military honors

Saul, after his victories, erected a triumphal arch,[48] to remind posterity and to rouse them by example and by similar marks of honor.

The constitution of the country did not then permit the erection of statues, which the law of God reproved. They erected altars, to serve as a memorial;[49] or they made mounds of stones.[50]

20th Proposition
Military exercises, or distinctions deserved among men of war

David taught the Israelites to draw the bow,[51] and wrote a canticle for this exercise in praise of Saul, who had apparently established it.

The men of the tribe of Issachar had the reputation of knowing the profession of war better than the others. "There were two hundred men of this tribe who were very able, and knew how to instruct Israel in all sorts of timely and suitable movements; and the rest of the tribe followed their counsels."[52]

In the profound peace of the reign of Solomon, military exercises continued to be honored, and two hundred and fifty chiefs instructed the people.[53]

This prince, peaceable as he was, sustained the warrior temper in his people. He employed foreigners on royal works, but not the children of Israel. He occupied them with war.[54] They were the first captains, and commanded the cavalry and the chariots.

Some, principally the men of Judah and of Nephtali, fought with the buckler and pike; the others joined the bow to the buckler;[55] and each was instructed in the way that these arms were used.

Josaphat, though he made war more for his allies than for himself,

---

[48] 1 Kings 15:12.
[50] Josh. 10:27; 2 Kings 18:17–18.
[52] 1 Par. 12:32.
[54] Ibid., 9.
[49] 1 Kings 14:35.
[51] 2 Kings 1:18.
[53] 2 Par. 8:10.
[55] 1 Par. 8:40; 12:24,34,38.

made himself famous through the good order he established in the military.[56]

The reputation of Ozias was carried quite far by a similar vigilance, which made him add to the pains of his predecessors that of constructing magazines of arms, helmets, bucklers, bows, and slings, together with war-machines of all sorts – not so much those that he kept in the towers as those which he kept standing on the walls, to sting the enemy and to throw great stones.[57] Such that nothing was lacking in the exercise of arms.

Honorable distinctions also inspired the courage of brave men.

Under David a distinction was drawn between these three kinds of titles:[58] the three strong ones (of two different orders), together with the thirty who had a chief. Their actions were noted in the public records. There were some who were called the king's captains, the great or first captains,[59] or the captains of captains.[60]

One sees elsewhere, as an estate, two thousand six hundred principal officers.[61] Under each prince, one recognized those who were established for general commands, those who commanded beneath them, and the whole military order.[62]

God wanted to show, in his own people, a perfectly constituted state, not only with respect to religion and justice, but also with respect to war and peace, and to preserve the glory of warrior-princes.

Article VI

On peace and war: various observations on both of them

1st Proposition
The prince must cherish brave men

Saul, in whom one admires such great qualities, made himself noticed by this one: "Whomsoever Saul saw to be a valiant man, he took him to himself."[1]

[56] 2 Par. 17:2,10,13ff.
[58] 2 Kings 23:9ff; 1 Par. 11:10,11,15ff.
[60] 1 Par. 7:40.
[62] 2 Par. 17:14–19.

[57] 2 Par. 26:8,14,15.
[59] 2 Par. 26:11.
[61] 2 Par. 26:12.
[1] 1 Kings 14:52.

This is the means of drawing brave men to oneself. If you take on one, you gain a hundred more. When men see that it is merit and valor that you seek, they begin to recognize the good you have done to others, and each hopes for it in his turn.

2nd Proposition
There is nothing finer in war than cooperation among the leaders, and the working together of the whole state

Joab, seeing himself virtually surrounded by his enemies, divided the army in two parts, to have a head on both sides: one part against the Ammonites, and one part against the Syrians. "If the Syrians are too strong for me, said Joab to Abisai, then thou shalt help me: but if the children of Ammon are too strong for thee, then I will help thee. Be of good courage, and let us fight for our people, and for the city of our God: and the Lord will do what is good in his sight."[2] Do what one must, be in agreement, be attentive to each other, be resolute in all and subject to God: this is all that good generals should be.

Judas spoke in these terms to his brother Simon: "Choose thee men, and go, and deliver thy brethren in Galilee; and I, and my brother Jonathan, will go into the country of Galaad."[3] He left Joseph son of Zacharia, and Azarias, two chiefs of the army, with the rest of the troops to guard Judaea, forbidding them to fight until his return. Simon with three thousand men, fought fortunately in Galilee, pursued the vanquished quite far, to the very gates of Ptolemai, took a great deal of booty, and led into Judaea those men whom the Gentiles held captive with their wives and children. At the same time Judas and Jonathan crossed the Jordan with eight thousand men, and took many strong places in Galaad: and after having won so many signal victories without loss, they returned in triumph to Zion, where they offered their sacrifices as actions of grace. The holy people got the upper hand over their enemies by this agreement of their three chiefs. Joseph, son of Zacharia, and Azarias, one of the chiefs, shattered this fine concord, and caused a great wound in Israel, as will be shown in a moment.

Under Saul, Jabes Galaad, a city beyond the Jordan besieged by Naas King of the Ammonites, offered to negotiate and to submit

---

[2] 2 Kings 10:11–12.   [3] 1 Macc. 5:17.

himself to his power. Naas answered with bloody derision: "On this condition will I make a covenant with thee, that I may pluck out all your right eyes, and make you a reproach in all Israel. And the ancients of Jabes said to him: Allow us seven days, that we may send messengers to all the coasts of Israel: and if there be no one to defend us, we will come out to thee."[4] Their envoys came then to Gabaa, where Saul made his residence, and they revealed to all the people the condition in which the city found itself: the whole people raised their voice and dissolved in tears. Each cried for a city which they were going to lose, as if one were going to tear off one of their members. Saul arrived during the meeting, following some oxen who came in from the country. For we have already seen, though he was, and was recognized as king, he still clung to his old calling – without fuss and without raising himself higher. Such was the simplicity of those times. Having arrived at the meeting, he said: "What aileth the people that they weep?"[5] So they told him about the condition of Jabes. "The spirit of the Lord came upon Saul . . . and taking both the oxen, he cut them to pieces, and sent them into all the coasts of Israel by messenger, saying: Whosoever shall not come forth and follow Saul, so shall it be done to his oxen."[6] Everyone obeyed; they passed in review; he found under his standard three hundred thousand combatants: and the tribe of Judah alone added thirty thousand to them. He sent back the deputies of Jabes with this precise answer: "Tomorrow you shall have relief." Action followed his words. In the morning, Saul divided his army in three, entered the middle of the enemy camp, and did not cease to kill until the heat of the day: all the enemies were dispersed, and two men together did not remain. This is what can be achieved by the public interest, diligence, the cooperation of the king, of the people and all the powers of the state.

The memory of such a benefit was eternally preserved. The inhabitants of Jabes Galaad, touched by this memory, were faithful to Saul even after his death, and were the only ones in all Israel who rose up for him. David found this to his liking, and had them told: "Blessed be you to the Lord, who have shown mercy to your master Saul, and have buried him. And now the Lord surely will render you mercy and truth, and I also will requite you for this good turn, because you have done this thing . . . For although your master Saul be dead, yet

---

[4] 1 Kings 11:1–3.   [5] Ibid., 5.   [6] Ibid., 6–7.

the house of Judah hath anointed me to be their king. And I will succeed to the friendship that he had for you, as well as to his throne."[7]

3rd Proposition
Not to fight against orders

While Judas and Simon accomplished the exploits which we have seen in Galilee and in Galaad,[8] Joseph and Azarias, the two chiefs to whom they had left the defense of Judaea, together with prohibition of fighting until the whole army was reunited, were flattered by the false glory of making a name for themselves (following their example), by fighting the Gentiles by whom they were surrounded. Thus they went out on a campaign: but Gorgias came out to meet them, and pushed them back to the borders of Judaea.[9] Two thousand men of theirs remained in place, and fright took hold of the whole country, because they would not obey the wise orders which they had received from Judas, imagining that they would share with him the glory of saving the people. "But they were not of the seed of those men by whom salvation was brought to Israel."[10]

Their general knew them better than they knew themselves. They were left to guard the country, and they had only to remain on the defensive. For want of having obeyed, they lost for their troops the advantage of fighting with the whole rest of the army, and under wise leaders.

4th Proposition
It is good to accustom the army to the same general

"All Israel and Judah loved David, even during the lifetime of Saul, because they saw him always marching at their head, and leading them into campaigns."[11] Men grew accustomed [to him], they grew attached, they acquired confidence, they regarded as a father a general who thought of them more than they did of themselves.

This was remembered, when it was time to bring the tribes together to recognize David. "Both yesterday and the day before you sought for David that he might reign over you. Now then do it: and

---

[7] 2 Kings 2:4–7.   [8] 1 Macc. 5:55ff.   [9] Ibid., 55ff.
[10] Ibid., 62.   [11] 1 Kings 17:16.

range yourselves under his standard."[12] It is not an unknown person whom I am suggesting to you, said Abner to all Israel.

5th Proposition
Peace confirms conquests

It is good for a state to be at rest. The peace of Solomon's time secured the conquests of David.[13] The Hethites, the Amorrhites and the other peoples whom the Israelites had not yet entirely cut down were subjugated by Solomon, and became his tributaries.[14]

6th Proposition
Peace is made to strengthen the interior

Whatever peace one enjoys, always surrounded by jealous neighbors, one must never forget war entirely, which may come at a stroke. While you are being left in repose: that is the time to strengthen yourself within.

Solomon provides the example of this. He rebuilt the cities which Hiram had ceded to him, and established Israelite colonies there. He fortified Emath-Suba, a distant place in Syria, and an ancient seat of kings. He built Palmyra in the desert, which several centuries later became a royal city, in which Odenat and Zenobia held their court. In Emath he raised several strong cities, and erected upper and lower Bethoron, and other walled places in which to keep his cavalry and his chariots; and he filled Jerusalem, Lebanon and all the lands under him with his buildings.[15]

The other great kings, Asa, Josaphat and Ozias, imitated him.

"Asa built also strong cities in Judah, for he was quiet, and there had no wars risen in his time."[16] War requires other cares, and does not give this leisure. Thus he took this time to say to the children of Judah: "Let us build these cities, and compass them with walls, and fortify them with towers, and gates, and bars, while all is quiet from wars ... So they built, and there was no hindrance in the building."[17] One notices, in passing, the fortifications which were needed in those times; and none of them was neglected.

[12] 2 Kings 3:17–18.   [13] 2 Par. 8:7–8.   [14] Ibid., 7–8.
[15] 2 Par. 8:2–6.   [16] 2 Par. 14:6.   [17] Ibid., 7.

"Josaphat also built houses like towers, and walled cities; and on every side one saw great works."[18]

"Ozias built towers in Jerusalem over the gate of the corner, and over the gate of the valley, and the rest, in the same side of the wall."[19] These were apparently the most difficult spots to defend, and which one had to try to make impregnable.

7th Proposition
In the midst of vigilant cares, one must always have the uncertainty of events in view

Among the many examples furnished by Scripture of unexpected downfalls, that of Abimelech is one of the most remarkable.

Abimelech, son of Gideon, had persuaded the inhabitants of Sichem to yield to him.[20] This post was important, and it was there that Samaria was later built. He levied troops with the money which they gave him, and seized the place where his brothers were, to the number of seventy, all of whom he massacred with a single stone, with the exception of Joatham, the youngest, who was hidden. He was elected king at an oak-tree near Sichem, though Joatham reproached them for their ingratitude towards the house of Gideon, their liberator: but he was constrained from taking flight out of fear of Abimelech, who remained the master for three years, without any trouble.

After the three years, he sowed a spirit of division between himself and the inhabitants of Sichem, who were beginning to hate him, and the great of Sichem, who had aided him in the terrible fratricide which he had committed against his brothers. At a time when Abimelech was absent, then, they made themselves a chief called Gaal, son of Obed, who, having entered into Sichem, gave courage to the rebelling inhabitants, who went pillaging and ravaging through the environs, and were cursing Abimelech in the midst of their feasts and in the temple of their God. There remained to Abimelech one faithful friend, named Zebul, to whom he had left the governance of the city – who also gave him secret intelligence of everything he had seen, exhorting him to do everything he could without losing time.

Abimelech left at night, and marched towards Sichem, where Gaal

---

[18] 2 Par. 17:12–13.   [19] 2 Par. 26:9.   [20] Judg. 9.

was master: and Gaal was constrained to shut himself up in the place, which Abimelech besieged. The men of Gaal were beaten and defeated for the second time. Abimelech pressed the siege without relaxing, and did not leave a single inhabitant, nor stone on top of stone in the city, which he reduced to a field sown with salt. There remained to the Sichemites an old temple, which they had fortified with care: but Abimelech had a whole forest transported there, and having lit a great fire around it, he killed all his enemies with smoke.

Victorious on that front, he besieged Thebes, which he quickly reduced. There was a high tower in which men and women had taken refuge, with the principal men of the city. Abimelech pressed on with vigor, and was ready to set fire to it, for he had the entire advantage; but a woman, finding at hand a piece of millstone, threw it on his head. He fell dying: and he who made war so ardently and so fortunately, whom nothing could resist, perishing by so weak a hand, caused himself in his despair to have his side pierced by one of his soldiers, "for fear it should be said that he was slain by a woman."[21]

Pride yourself neither in your power, nor in your diligence, nor in your happy successes, above all in unjust and tyrannical enterprises. Death, or some frightful disaster, will come to you from the side that you least expect it; and public hatred, which will arm the feeblest hand against you, will crush you.

8th Proposition
Luxury, splendor, and debauchery blind men of war, and cause them to perish

Ela King of Israel, son of Baasa, made war on the Philistines; and his army besieged Gebbethon, one of their strongest places – without worrying about what was happening in the army and at the court, content to dine well with the governor of Thersa, who was apparently as little careful of public affairs as his master. Zambri, however, to whom (without knowing him well) Ela had given the command of half the cavalry, having surprised him in his cups and half-drunk at the governor's, cut his throat (together with his family and friends) and seized the kingdom. The sound of this news having come to the army which was besieging Gebbethon, it created a king on its side, namely

[21] Ibid., 54.

Amri, who was its general: and Zambri found himself forced to burn himself in his palace, after a reign of seven days.[22]

The affair of Benadad King of Syria is scarcely less surprising. He was besieging Samaria, capital of the kingdom of Israel, with an immense army and thirty-two allied kings.[23] He was at table with them, under cover of his tent, full of wine and anger. Several men were seen coming up to him: they came to tell Benadad that someone had come out of Samaria. "Whether they come for peace, take them alive: or whether they come to fight, take them alive."[24] He never dreamed that seven thousand men were following after. All the Syrians who were thoughtlessly advancing were killed. The Syrian army was put to flight; Benadad also took flight with his cavalry, and left all his spoils to the King of Israel.

To revive his courage, his counsellors diverted him with the superstitions of his religion, saying to him: "Their gods are the gods of the hills, therefore they have overcome us; but it is better that we should fight against them in the plains, and we shall overcome them."[25] But they added to this vain proposal some much more solid advice: "Remove all the kings from thy army (who can only embarrass it), and put captains in their stead: re-establish your army on its old footing; fight them in the plains and in the open, and you will win the victory."[26] The advice was admirable: but Benadad was a timid and vain king, who understood only splendor and pride. And God delivered him again into the hands of the King of Israel, all too happy to find humanity in his conquerors.

9th Proposition
One must above all things know and measure his powers

"What king, about to go to make war against another king, doth not first sit down, and think whether he be able, with ten thousand, to meet him that, with twenty thousand, cometh against him? Or else, whilst the other is yet afar off, sending an embassy, he desireth conditions of peace."[27] This is the word of eternal wisdom.

To negotiate peace, then, one sends presents on ahead, as Jacob

---

[22] 3 Kings 16:8–18.
[23] 3 Kings 20:1ff.
[24] Ibid., 18.
[25] Ibid., 23.
[26] 3 Kings 20:24–25.
[27] Luke 14:31–32.

did to Esau: and like him, one accompanies them with gentle words.[28] For it is written, "The good word is better than the gift."[29]

10th Proposition
There are ways of securing vanquished peoples, after a war finished advantageously

David not only believed it necessary to place garrisons in the cities of Syria, in Damascus and in Edom, which he had conquered: but when the people were still rebellious, he disarmed them again, and had their horses' legs broken.[30]

The violators of treaties were harshly punished. Thus the Israelites, not content to destroy all the cities of Moab, covered their best lands with stones; they stopped up the springs; they cut down the trees, and demolished the walls.[31]

In wars undertaken because of more horrible outrages – as when the Ammonites violated with cruel derision, in the persons of David's ambassadors, the laws which are most sacred among men – a more terrible vengeance was used. He wanted to make an example of them, which would leave eternally in all nations a feeling of terror which would deprive them of the courage to fight, by causing chariots armed with knives to pass over their bodies, in all their cities.[32]

One can take away from this rigor that which the spirit of gentleness and of clemency inspires in the new law: for fear that we will be told, as were those disciples who wanted to strike down everything: "You know not of what spirit you are."[33]

A Christian conqueror must spare blood; and the spirit of the gospel on this point is quite different from the spirit of the law.

11th Proposition
One must observe the beginnings and endings of reigns, with respect to revolts

When Edom was subjugated by David, Adad, a young prince of the royal family, found a way of withdrawing into Egypt, where he was very well received by Pharaoh.[34] When he learned of the death of

---

[28] Gen. 32:3–5; 33:9–11.   [29] Ecclus. 18:16.   [30] 2 Kings 8:4,5,13,14.
[31] 4 Kings 3:4,5,25.   [32] 2 Kings 12:31.
[33] Luke 9:55.   [34] 3 Kings 11:17–18.

David, and of that of Joab (which happened at the beginning of Solomon's reign), and believing the kingdom weakened by the loss of so great a king and by that of so renowned a general, he said to Pharaoh: "Let me go back to my land."[35] This was in order to awaken his friends there, and to sow the seeds of a war which would hatch in its time.

The extreme old age of David gave rise to movements which threatened the state with a civil war.

Adonias, eldest son of David after Absalom, thought to bring his brother back to life by his good looks, by the noise and ostentation of his retinue, and by his ambition.[36] Over Absalom he had this unhappy advantage, that he found David failing – he needed to be, not pushed indeed, but awoken by his servants. He had placed in his party Joab, who commanded the armies, and Abiathar, the sovereign pontiff (earlier so faithful to David), and many others of the king's servants from the tribe of Judah. With this aid he aspired to nothing less than the invasion of the kingdom during the king's lifetime – and against the disposition [of the throne] which David had declared by designating Solomon as his successor and in getting him recognized by all the great men, and by the whole army, as he whom God preferred to all his other brothers, in order to fill him with wisdom, and cause him to build his Temple in the midst of profound peace.[37]

Adonias wanted to overturn so well-established an order. To gather together his party, and to give the signal to his friends to recognize him as king, this young prince made a solemn sacrifice, followed by a superb feast. The whole court watched it. It will be noticed that the principal men of Judah had prayed, with Joab and Abiathar, and all the king's sons with the exception of Solomon: but since neither that prince, nor Zadok the priest, nor Nathan, nor Banaias (very confident in David and the commander of his old troops), all of them attached to the king and to Solomon, were seen there, the plan of Adonias was seen through, and the mystery was revealed. At the same time Nathan and Bathsheba, mother of Solomon, acted in concert before David, speaking to him very bluntly. They opened the eyes of this prince, who up till then had remained tranquil not out of softness, but from confidence in a power as well established as his and in a resolution [to give Solomon the throne] as

[35] Ibid., 21–22. [36] 3 Kings 1:1,2,5ff. [37] 1 Par. 28:1ff.

well explained. The king spoke with as much firmness as authority; his orders were so precise and so promptly executed that, before the end of Adonias' feast, the whole city was resounding with joy at the coronation of Solomon. Joab, bold and experienced as he was, was surprised; the thing was done, and everyone went away ashamed and trembling. The new king spoke to Adonias in a masterly tone: nothing was shaken in the kingdom, and the rebellion which had rumbled was stilled.

It did not return until the beginning of the reign of Roboam. And that is a time of weakness that one must always watch with extra care, if one wants to insure public peace.

12th Proposition
Kings are always armed

We have seen under David the legions of Celethi and Phelethi, which Banaias commanded, always on foot.

He had also preserved a corps of six hundred valiant fighters, commanded by Ethai the Gethite, and the others who had come with his during his disgrace.[38]

I shall not speak of other troops who are maintained [and who are] so necessary to a state. They are all immortal bodies which, by renewing themselves through the same spirit by which they were formed, make their fidelity and their valor eternal.

Men decorated these troops, chosen in a particular way, in order to distinguish them. And this was the destined purpose of the two hundred pikes decorated with gold, and the two hundred bucklers, heavy and weighty, covered with strips of gold, together with three hundred others of a different shape, similarly covered with highly refined gold of great weight, which Solomon kept in his arsenals.[39]

Besides the garrisons that one finds everywhere in the books of Kings and Chronicles, and besides the troops which were on foot, there were an infinite number under the king's control, together with designated chiefs ready for the first order.[40]

One hardly knows where to rank those men of war, who arose to the number of twenty-four thousand, on the first day of each month, with twelve commanders.[41]

---

[38] 2 Kings 15:18–19; 3 Kings 1:8,10,38.
[39] 3 Kings 10:16–17; 2 Par. 9:15–16.
[40] 2 Par. 17:14ff.; 26:12–13.
[41] 1 Par. 27:1ff.

It is not necessary to notice that in order not to weigh down the state with expenses, they were assembled [only] according to need – of which there are plenty of examples.

Thus states remain strong without, against the enemy, and within, against the wicked and rebellious; and the public peace is assured.

TENTH AND FINAL BOOK

Continuation of helps to royalty: Riches or finances
Counsel
The inconveniences and temptations which accompany royalty: and the remedies that one can bring to them

Article 1

On riches or on finances. On commerce, and on taxes

1st Proposition
There are expenses of necessity: there are others of splendor and of dignity

"Who ever makes war at his expense? What soldier does not receive his pay?"[1]

One can rank among these expenses of necessity all those which are necessary for war, such as the fortification of places, arsenals, and magazines and munitions, of which we have spoken.

Expenses of magnificence and of dignity are in their way no less necessary for the sustaining of majesty in the eyes of peoples and of foreigners.

---

[1] 1 Cor. 9:7.

Continuation of helps to royalty

It would be an infinite task to recount the magnificences of Solomon.[2]

First of all in the Temple, which was both the ornament and the defense of the city. Nothing equaled it in all the earth, any more than [anything equaled] the God who was worshiped there. This Temple carried to heaven and to posterity the glory of the nation, and the name of Solomon its founder.[3]

Thirteen whole years were used in building the palace of the king in Jerusalem, with woods, stones, marbles, and the most precious materials – together with the richest and most beautiful architecture that had ever been seen. It was called Lebanon, because of the multitude of cedars which were placed there, in tall columns like a forest, in vast and long galleries, and with a marvelous order.[4]

There everyone admired in particular the royal throne, where everything was radiant with gold, with the superb gallery where it was set up. Its seat was ivory, covered with the purest gold: the six steps by which one mounted the throne, and the step-stool on which one's feet rested, were of the same metal: the ornaments which surrounded it were also of massive gold.[5]

Nearby one saw the particular spot on which justice was rendered, all constructed of similar workmanship.

At the same time Solomon built the palace of his wife the queen, daughter of Pharaoh, where everything sparkled with precious stones, and where, together with magnificence, one saw gleaming an exquisite cleanness.[6]

To achieve these fine works this prince summoned, as much from his kingdom as from foreign countries, artisans who were the most renowned for design, for sculpture,[7] for architecture, whose names are consecrated forever in the records of the people of God, that is to say in the holy books.

Let us add the places destined for the work-crews,[8] where horses, chariots, and harnesses were innumerable.

The tables, and the offices of the king's house for the hunt, for [preparing] nourishment, for the whole royal service, both in their number and in their order, answered to this magnificence.[9]

---

[2] 3 Kings 6–9; 2 Par. 1–7.　　[3] 1 Par. 29:23–25.
[4] 3 Kings 7:1ff.　　[5] 3 Kings 10:18–20; 2 Par. 9:17,19.
[6] 3 Kings 3:1; 9:24; 2 Par. 8:11.　　[7] 2 Par. 2:13–14.
[8] 3 Kings 4:26; 10:26; 2 Par. 1:14; 9:25.　　[9] 3 Kings 4:22–23.

The king was served on golden dishes. All the vases in the house of Lebanon were of gold.[10] And the Holy Spirit does not disdain to descend into all this detail, because it served, in this time of peace, to cause the power of so great a king to be admired and feared, both within and without.

A great queen, drawn by the reputation of so many marvels, came to see them in the most superb conveyance and with camels laden with all sorts of riches.[11] But, although accustomed to the grandeur into which she was born, she remained overcome at the sight of so much magnificence at the court of Solomon. What was most remarkable of all about her voyage, was that she admired the wisdom of the king more than all his other marks of greatness, and that something happened which always happens at the advent of great men – that she recognized in Solomon a merit which surpassed his reputation.

The presents she made him in gold, in precious stones, and in the most exquisite perfumes were immense, but were nonetheless far inferior to those that Solomon gave her. By this the Holy Spirit gives us to understand that one must find in great kings a greatness of soul which surpasses all their treasures, and that it is the former which truly makes a soul royal.

The great works of Josaphat, of Ozias, of Ezechias and of the other great kings of Judah – the cities, the aqueducts, the public baths, and the other things which they built, not only for security and for public convenience, but also for the ornamentation of the palace and of the kingdom – are indicated with care in Scripture.[12] It does not forget the precious furniture which appeared in their palace and that which they had kept there: any more than the cabinets of perfumes, the vessels of gold and of silver, all the exquisite works and the curiosities which were gathered there.

God forbad the ostentation which vanity inspires, and the mad swelling of a heart intoxicated by its riches; but he willed nonetheless that the court of kings be striking and magnificent, to impress a certain respect on peoples.

And even today, at the rites of kings, as we have already seen, the Church offers this prayer: "May the glorious dignity and the majesty of the palace make shine in all eyes the great splendor of the royal

---

[10] 3 Kings 10:21; 2 Par. 9:20.
[11] 3 Kings 10; 2 Par. 9.
[12] 4 Kings 20:13,20; 2 Par. 17; 26; 32:27–29.

power, such that light, like that of a flash of lightning, may illuminate it from all sides."[13] All [these are] words chosen to express the magnificence of a royal court, which is asked of God as a necessary support of royalty.

2nd Proposition
A flourishing state is rich in gold and in silver: and this is one of the fruits of a long peace

So abundant was gold during the reign of Solomon that "there was no silver, nor was any account made of it . . . he made it to be as plentiful as stones, and cedars to be as common as the sycamores which grow (by chance) in the plains."[14]

Since this was the fruit of a long peace, the Holy Spirit takes note of it, in order to make princes love peace, which produces such great things.

3rd Proposition
The first source of such riches is commerce and navigation

"For the king's navy, once in three years, went with the navy of Hiram by sea to Tarsus, and brought from thence gold, and silver, and elephants' teeth, together with the rarest animals."[15]

Solomon had a fleet at Asiongaber near Agilath, on the shore of the Red Sea: and Hiram King of Tyre joined his with it, together with the Tyrians, the people most renowned on earth for navigation and for commerce, who brought back from Ophir (which must have been extraordinary) four hundred and twenty talents of gold, soon to be four hundred and fifty, for Solomon's coffers – together with the most precious woods and precious stones.[16]

The wisdom of Solomon appears here in two ways. The first: that after having recognized the necessity of commerce to enrich his kingdom, he chose a time of profound peace to establish it, in which the state was not overwhelmed by the expense of war. And second, that his subjects not being at all used to commerce and the art of naviga-

---

[13] *Ceremonial français*, pp. 19, 35, 61.
[14] 3 Kings 10:21,27; 2 Par. 9:20,27.
[15] 3 Kings 10:22; 2 Par. 9:21.
[16] 3 Kings 10:26–28; 10:11; 2 Par. 8:17–18.

tion, he knew how to link himself with the ablest traders and the most assured leaders in navigation who existed in the world (that is to say the Tyrians), and to make with them treaties which were so advantageous and so certain.

When the Israelites had instructed themselves in the secrets of commerce, they did without these allies; and the enterprise, unfortunate as it was, of King Josaphat (whose fleet perished in the port of Asiongaber), made it clear that the kings carried on with commerce and the voyages to Ophir – without any further mention of help from the Tyrians.[17]

4th Proposition
Second source of riches: the domain of the prince

In the time of David, there were treasures in Jerusalem: and Azmoth son of Adiel was the guardian of them.[18] As for the treasures which were kept in the cities, in the villages, and in castles or towers, Jonathan son of Chelub had care of those who were occupied with plowing and with works in the countryside. There was a separate administrator for those who grew the vines and took care of the cellars: and this was Semeias and [then] Zabdias. Balanan was appointed to the growing of olives and of figs: and Joas kept a watch on the reservoirs of oil. One sees by all this that the prince had funds, and officers nominated to govern them.

One notices, too, the villages which belonged to him, and the care which he took to surround them with walls.[19] Foodstuffs were grown in the pastures of the mountain of Saron, and in the small valleys which led up to it. Scripture describes horned beasts, camels, and herds of sheep. Each work had its prefect: "and all these were the rulers of the goods and riches of King David."[20]

The same thing continued under the other kings. It is written of Ozias: "that he dug many cisterns, for he had much cattle both in the plains and in the waste of the desert: he had also vineyards and dressers of vines in the mountains, and in Carmel: for he was a man that loved husbandry."[21]

These great kings knew the worth of natural riches, which

[17] 3 Kings 22:49; 2 Par. 20:36–37.   [18] 1 Par. 27:25–28.
[19] 3 Kings 9:19.   [20] 1 Par. 27:29–31.   [21] 2 Par. 26:10.

furnished the necessities of life, and enrich the people more than mines of gold and silver.

The Israelites had learned these useful activities from the beginning. It is written of Abraham "that he was very rich in gold and in silver,"[22] things which – since he did not know the places where nature hides these rich metals – could only have come to him in virtue of his cares for agriculture and for the flocks. From this came the fame of the pastoral life, which this patriarch and his descendants had embraced.

5th Proposition
Third source of riches: tributes imposed on vanquished kings and nations, which were called gifts

Thus David imposed tribute on the Moabites and at Damascus, and established garrisons there to make them render these gifts.[23]

Solomon had subjected all the kingdoms from the river in the land of the Philistines to the borders of Egypt. And all the kings of these countries offered him presents, and owed him certain services.[24]

The amount of gold which was paid each year to Solomon amounted to six hundred talents – besides the amount which the ambassadors of different nations, and rich foreign merchants, and all the kings of Arabia, and the princes of other lands, had grown accustomed to paying him – bringing him gold and silver.[25] It was thus that men sang in advance, under King David, that the daughters of Tyre (that is to say, opulent cities), and their richest merchants would bring their presents to the court of Solomon.[26]

All the kings of neighboring lands sent their presents each year to Solomon, which consisted of gold and silver vases, of rich garments, of arms, of perfumes, of horses, and of mules – that is to say, the best things each country had.[27]

The Ammonites brought their presents to Ozias: and his name was celebrated to the very borders of Egypt.[28]

Among these presents was numbered not only gold and silver, but flocks as well: and it was thus that the Arabs paid each year to Josaphat seven thousand seven hundred rams and as many goats or kids.[29]

[22] Gen. 13:2. [23] 1 Par. 18:2–6. [24] 3 Kings 4:21.
[25] 3 Kings 10:14–15; 2 Par. 9:13–14. [26] Ps. 44:13. [27] 2 Par. 9:23–24.
[28] 2 Par. 26:8. [29] 2 Par. 17:11.

6th Proposition
Fourth source of riches: the taxes that the people pay

In all states, the people contribute to public expenses, that is to say to their own preservation: and the part of their goods which they give up, secures the rest to them, together with their liberty and their tranquillity.

Under Kings David and Solomon, finances were ordered in such a way that there was a superintendent in charge of all taxes, who gave the general orders.[30]

For the details there were twelve intendants distributed by provinces: and these were charged, each in a certain month, with the contributions which were necessary for the expenses of the king and his household. Their department was large, since each one had in his charge sixty large cities, surrounded by walls, with locks of brass.[31]

One reads too of Jeroboam that "Solomon seeing him a young man ingenious and industrious (or active, as the original says), made him chief over the tribute of all the house of Joseph"[32] – that is to say over the two tribes of Ephraim and of Manasses. This shows, in passing, the qualities that a wise king insisted on for such functions, even if his prudence was deceived in the choice of persons.

7th Proposition
The prince must moderate taxes, and not overwhelm the people

"He that strongly squeezeth the paps to bring out milk, straineth out butter: and he that violently bloweth his nose, bringeth out blood: and he that provoketh wrath bringeth forth strife." This is the rule that Solomon gives.[33]

The example of Roboam teaches the duty of kings on this point.

Since this story is well known and has already been touched on above, we shall make only a few observations.

In the first place, concerning the complaints which the people made to Roboam against Solomon, who had raised extraordinary levies.[34] Everything was abundant during this reign, as we have seen.

---

[30] 2 Kings 20:24; 3 Kings 4:6; 12:18; 2 Par. 10:18.
[31] 3 Kings 4:7–13.
[32] 3 Kings 11:28.
[33] Prov. 30:33.
[34] 3 Kings 12:1–4; 2 Par. 10:2–4.

However, since sacred history says nothing against this [popular] reproach, and since on the contrary it passes for proven, one must believe that, at the end of his life, abandoned to the love of women, Solomon's weakness brought him to excessive expenditures, in order to satisfy their avarice and their ambition.

It is misfortune, or rather blindness, into which the wisest kings are led by this deplorable excess.

In the second place, the hard and threatening response of Roboam pushed the people to revolt – whose most remarkable effect was to overwhelm Aduram (who was charged with the care of his tributes) with blows from stones, though he had been sent by the king for the execution of his rigorous conditions. This so terrified this prince that he quickly mounted his wagon and fled toward Jerusalem[35] – so much did he feel imperiled.

In the third place, the harshness of Roboam in refusing all relief to his people, and the obstinate threat to worsen the burden (to the point of intolerable excess), placed this prince among the ranks of the insane. "Solomon was succeeded by the folly of the nation, says the Holy Spirit, and Roboam, that had little wisdom, turned away the people through his counsel."[36] [He did this] to the point that his own son and successor, Abia, called him ignorant, and of a fearful heart.[37]

In the fourth place, this proud and inhuman response was attributed to a blindness permitted by God, and was viewed as an effect of that justice which lets the spirit of giddiness creep into the counsels of kings. "And the king condescended not to the people: for the Lord was turned away from him, to make good his word, which he had spoken in the hand of Ahias the Silonite, which had predicted during Solomon's lifetime the revolt of the ten tribes and the division of the kingdom."[38] Thus when God works to punish fathers, he delivers their children over to bad counsels, and chastises both together.

In the fifth place, what happened next was still more terrible. God permitted that the aroused people forget all respect, by massacring (under the king's eyes) one of his principal ministers, and spurning all movement towards obedience.

In the sixth place, it is not true that this massacre and this rebellion were not crimes. One knows well enough that God permits such

---

[35] 3 Kings 12:18; 2 Par. 10:18. [36] Ecclus. 47:27–28.
[37] 2 Par. 13:7. [38] 3 Kings 12:15; 2 Par. 10:15.

things in some, in order to punish others. The people were wrong: and God punished the enormous injustice of a king who took it as an honor to oppress his people, that is to say his children.

In the seventh place, this harshness of Roboam's effaced at a stroke the memory of David and all his goodness, as well as that of his concepts and of his other great actions. "What portion have we in David, said the people of Israel, and what inheritance in the son of Isai? Return to thy dwellings, O Israel, and do thou, O David, feed thy own house. And Israel went away to their dwellings."[39] Jerusalem, the Temple, religion, the law of Moses, were also forgotten: and the people were now sensible only of God's vengeance.

Finally, in the eighth place, while this plot of the people was inexcusable, God seemed afterwards to want to authorize the new kingdom which was established by the uprising: and he forbad Roboam to make war on the revolted tribes, "for by my will this thing hath been done"[40] – by my express permission and by a just counsel. Jeroboam seemed to become a legitimate king, by the gift of the new kingdom which God made to him. His successors were consistently true kings, whom God had anointed by his prophets. It was not that he loved these princes, who caused all sorts of idolatries and evil actions to reign; but he wanted to leave to kings an eternal reminder which might make them feel how much their harshness towards their subjects was odious to God and men.

8th Proposition
The conduct of Joseph in the time of that terrible famine, by which all Egypt and the neighboring areas were afflicted

Joseph, in selling wheat to the Egyptians, placed all the money in Egypt in the coffers of the king. By this means he also acquired all their animals for the king, and finally all their lands, and even their very persons, which were put into servitude.[41]

Far from this conduct having given offense, severe as it seems, the glory of Joseph was immortal. This wise minister furnished the people with what they needed to sow their lands, which Pharaoh gave them; he limited the taxes which they owed to the king to a fifth part of their

---

[39] 3 Kings 12:16; 2 Par. 10:16.   [40] 3 Kings 12:24; 2 Par. 11:4.
[41] Gen. 47:13–20.

income, and did honor to religion by exempting priestly lands from this tribute. It was thus that he fulfilled the whole duty of a zealous minister towards the king and towards the people, and that he merited the title of Savior of the World.[42]

9th Proposition
Remarks on the words of Jesus Christ and of his apostles, touching on tributes

"Render to Caesar that which is Caesar's, and to God that which is God's,"[43] said Jesus Christ. In order to pronounce this sentence, without asking how and in what order taxes were levied, he considered only the name of Caesar stamped on the public coinage.

His apostle enunciated the same thing: "Render tribute to whom tribute is due; and taxes to whom taxes are due (in money or in kind, as custom decrees); honor to whom honor; fear to whom fear."[44]

St. John the Baptist had said to the publicans charged with raising what was owed to the empire: "Do nothing more than that which is appointed to you."[45]

Religion does not enter into the details of establishing the public taxes, which each nation is familiar with. The sole divine and inviolable rule among all the peoples of the world, is that of not weighing down the people, and to proportion taxes to the needs of the state and to public burdens.

10th Proposition
Reflections on the preceding doctrine, and definition of true riches

One must conclude, from the passages which we have reported, that true riches are those which we have called natural, because they furnish nature with its true needs. The fertility of the earth and that of animals is an inextinguishable source of true goods: gold and silver only arrived afterwards to facilitate exchange.

It is necessary, then, following the example of the great kings whom we have named, to take particular care of the cultivation of the earth, and to maintain pastures for animals, together with the truly fruitful

---

[42] Gen. 41:45. [43] Matt. 22:21.
[44] Rom. 13:7. [45] Luke 3:13.

art of raising flocks, conformably to the word: "Hate not laborious works, nor husbandry ordained by the most High."[46] And again: "Be diligent to know the countenance of thy cattle, and consider thy own flocks."[47]

11th Proposition
Men are the true riches of a kingdom

One is delighted when he sees, under good kings, the incredible multitude of people and the astonishing largeness of the armies. By contrast one is ashamed of Achab and of the kingdom of Israel exhausted of people, when one sees his army encamp "like two little flocks of goats"[48] – while the Syrian army which faced it covered the face of the earth.

In the enumeration of the immense riches of Solomon, there is nothing finer than these words: "Judah and Israel were innumerable, as the sand of the sea in multitude."[49]

But here is the pinnacle of felicity and of richness. It is that this whole innumerable people "ate and drank of the fruit of its hands, every one under his vine and under his fig-tree, and rejoicing."[50] For joy makes bodies healthy and vigorous, and makes profitable the innocent repast that one consumes with his family – far from the fear of the enemy, and blessing (as the author of so many goods) the prince who loves peace even should he be in a state of war, and fears it only from goodness and justice. A sad and languishing people loses courage and is good for nothing: the earth itself resents the casualness with which they fall: and families are weak and desolated.

12th Proposition
Certain means of increasing the people

They must be somewhat comfortable, as has already been seen.

Under a wise prince idleness must be odious, and people must not be left to the enjoyment of unjust repose. It is idleness that corrupts morals and brings about robberies. It also produces beggars, another group that must be banished from a well-regulated kingdom, in remembrance of this law: "There shall be no poor nor beggar among

---
[46] Ecclus. 7:16.　　[47] Ibid., 24; Prov. 27:23.　　[48] 3 Kings 20:27.
[49] 3 Kings 4:20.　　[50] Ibid., 20, 25.

you."[51] One should not find them among the citizens, because they are a charge on the state – they and their children. But to do away with beggary, one must find means to prevent indigence.

Above all one must attend to marriages, make the education of children easy and pleasant, and oppose illicit unions. Faithfulness, holiness, and happiness in marriage is a public interest and a source of felicity for all states.

This law is as much political as [it is] moral and religious: "There shall be no whore among the daughters of Israel, nor whoremonger among the sons of Israel."[52] Let those unions which are meant to bear no fruit, and which have avowed sterility, be cursed by God and man. All the women of the house of Abimelech became sterile by an express judgment of God, because of Sarah, wife of Abraham.[53] By contrast God favors and blesses the fruits of legitimate marriages. One sees his children grow around his table like young olive-trees:[54] a woman who is delighted to be a mother is looked on with kindness by him whom she has made a father of such lovable children. One teaches them that modesty, frugality, and saving (governed by reason) is the principal part of riches: and, nourished in a home that is good but well regulated, they know how to condemn the vanity that they have never seen in their parents' house.

The law seconds their desires, when it reprimands luxury. The first ones whom it raised up against their dissolute children were fathers and mothers, whom it made hand them over to the magistrate, saying to him: "This our son is rebellious and stubborn, he slighteth hearing our admonitions, he giveth himself to revelling, and to debauchery and banquetings." The penalty for this incorrigible debauchery was "to be stoned: that all Israel hearing it might be afraid, and withdraw from disorder."[55] One did not escape from this penalty by saying: I do no harm to anyone. That is mistaken; and in connection with the disorders which impede or trouble marriages, one must avoid and punish not only the scandal and the injury which is brought to individuals, but also that which is done to the public – which is greater and more serious than is usually thought.

Let us conclude, then, with the wisest of all kings: "In the multitude of the people is the dignity of the king: and in the small number of the people the dishonor of the prince."[56]

[51] Deut. 15:4.   [52] Deut. 23:17.   [53] Gen. 20:17–18.
[54] Ps. 127:3.   [55] Deut. 21:18–21.   [56] Prov. 14:28.

Article II

On counsel

We have already spoken much about this and laid down the principles – above all when we treated the means which a prince should use in order to gain the knowledge which is necessary to him to govern well. But one can further deepen here that which concerns a matter of this importance: and one can bring together under a single point of view the precepts and the examples which Scripture furnishes to us (even some of those which are to be found dispersed throughout this work) – in order that, after establishing the principle, one can see in the same place the application of it, and the detail in its whole extent.

1st Proposition
What ministers or officials are noted near to ancient kings

Under David, Joab commanded the army; Banais had the command of the Cerethi and Phelethi legions – which were like the prince's own guard, and appeared to be detached from the general command of the armies and [to be] under a special commander who answered only to the king; Aduram was charged with taxes or finances; Josaphat was secretary and keeper of the records; Sivs, who is elsewhere called Saraia, was called a scribe, a man of letters next to the prince; Ira was priest to David;[1] Jonathan, the uncle of David, was his counselor, [and was] an intelligent and lettered man; he was with Jahiel, tutor of the children of the king; Achitopel was the counselor of the king, and after him Joida and Abiathan; and Chusai was the king's friend.[2]

One notices next to Solomon some persons who were called literary men [*gens de lettres*]; Banaias commanded the troops. Azarias son of Nathan was at the head of those who attended the king. Zabud was priest, and friend of the king. Ahisar (if it is permitted to translate thus) was chief steward of the house; and Adoniram was charged with finances.[3]

There are also named some great priests, or the leading ones among the priests who then existed, to show that their sacred ministry

---

[1] 2 Kings 8:16–18; 20:23–26.   [2] 1 Par. 27:32–34.   [3] 3 Kings 4:2–6.

gave them a place among public officials, and that under the kings they were involved in the most important matters: witness Zadok, who had so great a part in the business of providing the kingdom with a successor.[4]

The dignity of their priesthood was so eminent, that this splendor made it be said that "the children of David were priests"[5] – though they could not be such, not being of the sacerdotal race, nor of the tribe from which the priests were drawn. But they were given this great name, to show the important part they had in great matters. And this seems to be the same thing that Scripture notices elsewhere: "The sons of David were chief about the king"[6] – that is to say, were the first to bear and to execute his orders.

The care which they took to bring them up well-read, appears in the title of "man of letters," which they gave to Jonathan, their preceptor.

It is also noted under Ozias, that the troops were commanded by Jehiel and Maasias,[7] who were called scribes, doctors, or men of letters – to show that great men did not disdain to join the glory of learning with that of arms.

Those who were called "lettered," were those who were versed in the laws, and who directed the counsels of the prince in accordance with them.

Care for religion revealed itself not only through the part which the great priests had in the public business but also through the office of the king's priest – who seems to have been the one who regulated religious affairs in the house of the king. Such were, as has been seen, Ira under David, and Zabud under Solomon (whose friend he is also called).

This office of friend to the king, which has been seen in the enumeration of those public ministries which were called and characterized by a particular term, is remarkable, and made the king remember that he was not exempted from the common needs and weaknesses of human nature; and that thus, besides his other ministers who were called counselors (because they gave him their advice on public affairs), he had to choose with care a friend – that is to say a depository of his secret cares, and his other most intimate feelings.

The post of secretary and of keeper of public records, seems orig-

---

[4] 3 Kings 1:8,32,44.　　[5] 2 Kings 8:18.
[6] 1 Par. 18:17.　　[7] 2 Par. 26:11.

On counsel

inally to come from Moses, to whom God spoke thus: "Write this for a memorial in a book (the defeat of the Amalecites): for I will destroy the memory of Amalec from under heaven."[8] As if he said: I will that men recollect memorable facts, in order that the government of mortal men, guided by experience and the example of past things, benefit from immortal counsels.

It was by means of these records that men remembered those who had served the state, in order to show gratitude to their families.

One of the wisest maxims of the people of God, was that services rendered to the public should not be forgotten. Thus in the sack of Jericho, this order was published: "Let this city be as an anathema: . . . let only the harlot Rahalb live, she and her whole family: for she hid the messengers that we sent."[9]

When all the inhabitants of Luza were put to the sword, care was taken to save him (together with his whole family) who had shown the passage by which the city had been entered.[10]

The public ordinarily passes for ungrateful: and it was in the interest of the state to purge it of this sin, so that men might be invited to serve well.

No one is ignorant of the way in which Assuerus King of Persia, during an attack of insomnia which was working on him, made himself read the archives, where he found the service of Mordechai (who had saved his life) recorded according to custom; and he was moved by this reading to recognize him through a striking recompense – which was more glorious to the king than to Mordechai himself.[11]

When Darius King of Persia was informed of the conduct of the Jews who had returned to their country, his officials interrogated them in order to render an account to the king, and told him that their old people had responded, touching on the decrees of Cyrus in the first years of his reign. After which they added these words: "Now therefore if it seem good to the king, let men search in the king's library, which is in Babylon, whether it hath been decreed by Cyrus the king, that the house of God in Jerusalem should be rebuilt, and let the king send his pleasure to us concerning this matter."[12] The records were located not at all in Babylon, as had been believed, but in Echatanes:[13] everything was in conformity to the claim of the Jews, and was also authorized by the king.

---

[8] Exod. 17:14. [9] Josh. 6:17. [10] Jth. 1:24–25.
[11] Esther 6. [12] 1 Esdr. 5:7,17. [13] 1 Esdr. 6:1ff.

Such was the usefulness of public records, and of the post established to safeguard them. They preserved the memory of services rendered; they immortalized counsels; and these archives of kings, by offering examples from past centuries, were counsels always ready to tell them the truth, and which could not be flatterers.

For the rest, one does not claim to propose as invariable rules these practices of ancient kingdoms, nor this enumeration of the officials of David and of Solomon; it is enough that they may give ideas to great kings, whose prudence will be shaped according to times and places.

2nd Proposition
By whom the counsels of the kings of Persia were directed

"The king consulted the wise men who were always near his person, and all he did was by their counsel, who knew the laws, and judgments of their forefathers."[14] The first and most intimate [counselors] were the seven chiefs; or, if one wishes to translate thus, the seven dukes or princes of the Persians and the Medes, who saw the king. For the rest, even the lords, saw him not at all!

3rd Proposition
Reflections on the utility of public records, joined with living counsels

The usefulness of public records was stressed in this saying of the wise man: "What is it that hath been? The same thing that shall be. What is it that hath been done? The same thing that shall be done. Nothing under the sun is new, neither is any man able to say: Behold this is new: for it hath already gone before in the ages that were before us."[15] And the great events in human affairs, so to speak, merely renew themselves every day in the great theatre of the world. It seems that one need only consult the past, as a faithful mirror of that which passes under our eyes.

From another side the wise man adds that, whatever records one clings to, one misses certain circumstances which change things. And this makes him say: "There is no remembrance of former things: nor indeed of those things which hereafter are to come."[16] And it is rare

---

[14] Esther 1:13–14.   [15] Eccles. 1:9–10.   [16] Ibid., 11.

On counsel

to find examples which correspond exactly to the events in terms of which one must determine oneself to act.

One must, then, join the histories of past times with the counsel of the wise, who – well instructed in the ancient customs and laws (as has just been said of the ministers of the Persian kings) – know how to make an application of them to the matters that must be regulated in their times.

Such ministers are living records who, always brought to preserve ancient practices, change them only when forced by unforeseen and particular necessities, with a mind to profit simultaneously from the experience of the past and the circumstances of the present. That is why their wise and stable counsels produce laws which have all the firmness and (so to speak) the immobility of which human things are susceptible. "If it please thee, these ministers said to Assuerus, let an edict go out from thy presence, and let it be written according to the laws of the Persians and of the Medes, which must not be altered, and which must be published as inviolable through all the provinces of thy empire."[17]

This was the view of the nation: and kings as much as peoples held as a principle this immutability of public decrees.

The great, who wanted to destroy Daniel, came to say to the king: "O king, hast thou not decreed that every man that should make a request to any of the gods, or men, for thirty days, but to thyself, should be cast into the den of lions? And the king answered them, saying: The word is true according to the decree . . . which it is not lawful to violate."[18]

When he afterwards wanted to find an excuse in Daniel's favor, who had prayed thrice daily facing Jerusalem, some dared to say to him: "Know thou, O king, that the law of the Medes and Persians is, that no decree which the king hath made, may be altered."[19]

This was indeed the law of the country; but even the best things are abused. The first condition of these laws, which had to be viewed as sacred and inviolable, was that they be just: and men saw from the first a manifest impiety in wanting to give the law to God himself, to forbid him to receive the vows of his servants. The King of Persia ought to have known, then, that he was being taken by surprise through this law, as it is expressly marked[20] [in Scripture], and that

[17] Esther 1:19–20.
[18] Dan. 6:12.
[19] Ibid., 7,15.
[20] Dan. 6:6.

this was a cabal of the great against his service, in order to destroy Daniel, the most faithful and the most useful of all his ministers, whose credit inflamed their jealousy.

4th Proposition
The prince must give himself relief

This was the counsel which Jethro gave to Moses, who through a zeal for justice and an enormous charity wanted to do everything by himself. "What is it that thou dost, he said to him, among the people? Why sittest thou alone, and all the people wait from morning until night? . . . Thou art spent with foolish labor, both thou and this people that is with thee; the business is above thy strength, thou alone canst not bear it . . . Reserve the important business to thyself: and choose the wisest and the most God-fearing to judge the people at all times (who will expedite matters as they come up), who will give you a report of what is most important."[21]

Take note of three kinds of business. That which the prince expressly reserves for himself, and of which he takes notice himself. That of less importance, whose sheer bulk overwhelms him, and whose expedition he can leave to his officials. Finally, that concerning which he ordains that he be reported to, either to decide it for himself, or to have it examined with more care. By this means, everything is expedited with order and distinction.

5th Proposition
The wisest are the readiest to take counsel

Moses, nourished from infancy in all the wisdom of the Egyptians, and moreover inspired by God in the most eminent degree of prophecy, not only consulted Jethro, and gave him freedom to reproach him over the immensity of his work as a kind of folly: but also he received his advice in good part, and he carried out point-by-point everything he had counseled. This is what was just indicated.

Have we not already seen, too, with what docility David, too overwhelmed by sadness over the death of his son Absalom, listened to the bitter reproaches of Joab, bowed to his counsel, and entirely changed

---

[21] Exod. 18:14–24.

his conduct? And did not Solomon, the wisest of all kings, ask of God a docile heart, while asking him for wisdom?

6th Proposition
Counsel should be chosen with discretion

"Be in peace with many (to whom you give access near to you), but let one of a thousand be thy counsellor."[22]

7th Proposition
The counselor of the prince must have passed many tests

"What doth he know, that hath not been tried?"[23] He knows nothing; he does not know himself; and how will he disentangle the thoughts of others, which is the subject of the most important deliberations? On the contrary "a man that hath much experience shall think of many things," the wise man continues. He will do nothing lightly, and will not walk in a daze.

This is what the wise man Job is made to say: "Where is wisdom to be found? It is not found in the land of them that live in delights,"[24] and nonchalantly amidst pleasures.

And again, "It is hid from the eyes of all living, and the fowls of the air (the sublime spirits which seem to pierce the skies) know it not. Death (extreme old age) has said: With our ears we have heard the fame thereof."[25] It is by dint of experience, and much suffering, that in the end, you acquire some slight enlightenment.

8th Proposition
Whatever care the prince may have taken to choose and test his counsel, he should not deliver himself over to them

"If thou wouldst get a friend, try him before thou takest him, and do not credit him easily."[26]

The character of a prince who is delivered over makes him be viewed and treated with contempt.

"Herod (Agrippa, King of Judaea), was angry with the Tyrians and the Sidonians. But they with one accord came to him, and having

---
[22] Ecclus. 6:6.   [23] Ecclus. 34:9.   [24] Job 28:12–13.
[25] Ibid., 21–22.   [26] Ecclus. 6:7.

gained Blastus, who was the king's chamberlain, they delivered peace, because their countries were horrified by him. And upon a day appointed, Herod being arrayed in kingly apparel, sat in the judgment seat, and made an oration to them (in a public audience, according to the custom of the time); and the people said: It is the voice of a god, and not of a man."[27]

One sees here a solemn embassy, a public audience with all the apparatus of royalty, the acclamation of the whole people for the prince who believed he had done everything. But men knew the truth of it, which was that the Tyrians had gotten Blastus to work for their interest, which was great in this matter; and perhaps they had corrupted him with their presents. However they may have been, everything was accomplished before the solemn treaty; and if men did honor to the king, everyone knew the truth: and others called themselves (out loud) the true authors of this success.

The Holy Spirit does not disdain to mark [in a word] this character of Herod Agrippa, in order to teach princes who are merely vain the esteem in which they are held, and how they are repaid with a false glory.

9th Proposition
The counsels of young men who are not nourished on public affairs have an unhappy effect, above all in a new reign

After the complaint of Jeroboam, made to Roboam the son and successor of Solomon (at the head of the ten tribes) demanding of him some diminution of the taxes of the king his father, this prince answered them: "Come back in three days. And when the people was gone, he took counsel with the old counsellors of the king, his father, and said to them: What counsel do you give me, that I may answer this people? They said to him: If thou wilt yield to this people today (at the beginning of thy reign), and condescend to them, and grant their petition, and wilt speak gentle words to them, they will be thy servants always. Roboam left the counsel of the old men, which they had given him, and consulted with the young men, that had been brought up with him in pleasures, and stood before him . . . And they said to him:

[27] Acts 12:19–22.

Thus shalt thou speak to this people: My little finger is thicker than the back of my father: my father imposed a heavy yoke upon you, but I will add to your yoke: my father beat you with whips, but I will beat you with scorpions. Roboam followed this counsel when Jeroboam (with all the people) came back to him on the third day, spoke to them harshly, and according to the counsel of the young men. He did not defer to the prayers of the people, because the Lord was turned away from him, to make good his word, which he had spoken in the hand of Ahias the Silonite, touching the division of the kingdom. When the ten tribes had heard this answer, they withdrew, saying to one another: What portion have we in David? Or what inheritance in the son of Isai? Go home to thy dwellings, O Israel: now David look to thy own house."[28]

It was at first a wise precaution on Roboam's part, to take time to seek counsel, and to turn to the experienced ministers who had served under Solomon. But this prince did not think his power and his greatness sufficiently flattered by these moderate counsels. Impetuous and lively youth pleased him better: but his error was extreme. That which the wise old men most advised, was gentle words; but on the contrary the proud and impudent young men – instead of realizing that after advising harsh things they should at least temper them by gentleness of expression – joined insult to injury, and affected to make their speech prouder and more unfortunate than the things themselves. This is what caused all to be lost. The people, who had made their request with some modesty, by asking only a slight diminution of the burden,[29] were pushed to the extreme by the harshness of the threats by which the response was accompanied.

These reckless counselors were not lacking in pretexts. One must, they said, put down at once a people which begins to raise its head, or one will render it more insolent. But they deceived themselves, for want of knowledge of the secret inclination of the ten tribes to create a separate kingdom, and to secede from that of Judah, of which they were jealous. The old counselors – who had seen so often in the times of David the sad effects of this jealousy – wanted to make them visible to Roboam, and could have made him understand them; and well instructed about these dangerous dispositions, they counseled a gentle response. Flattering and hot-headed youth viewed these temporiz-

---

[28] 3 Kings 12:5–16; 2 Par. 10:3–16.
[29] 3 Kings 12:4; 2 Par. 10:4.

ings with contempt, and provoked the jealousy of the ten tribes to the point of making them say, with bitterness and raillery: What interest have we in the greatness of Judah? David, content yourself with your tribe. We want a king drawn from our own.

Power wants to be flattered, and regards accommodation as a weakness. But, beyond this reason, young men who were nourished on pleasures (as the sacred text observes), hoped to find in the king's riches means to sustain their cupidity, and feared that the source would dry up through the diminution of taxes. Thus in flattering the new king, they dreamt of this secret interest.

The character of Roboam aided their error. "Roboam was ignorant, and of a fearful heart, and could not resist the rebels,"[30] as his son Abia was constrained to admit. Ignorant because he did not know the principles of government, nor the art of handling men. Fearful, and by nature one of those who, at first proud and threatening, lose their footing in time of peril – as one saw Roboam doing when he took flight after the first noise. A truly courageous man is capable of moderate counsels; but when he is committed, he sustains himself better.

10th Proposition
One must accommodate men of importance, and not make them discontented

After the death of Saul, when all the world was going over to David, "Abner the son of Ner (who commanded the armies under Saul) took Isboseth the son of Saul, and led him about through the camp, and made him recognized as king by the ten tribes."[31] A single man, through his great credit, accomplished so great a work.

The same Abner, mistreated by Isboseth over a trifling matter, said to this prince: "Am I to be treated with contempt, who alone remained faithful to your father Saul, and made you reign? And you treat me as a dog's head because of a woman? As the Lord liveth, I will set up the throne of David."[32] He did so, and Isboseth was abandoned.

It is not only during weak reigns, and under an Isboseth "who feared Abner, and dared not answer him,"[33] that one had need of

[30] 2 Par. 13:7. [31] 2 Kings 2:8–9.
[32] 2 Kings 3:7–10. [33] Ibid., 11.

such accommodations. We have seen that David treated Joab considerately, and the family of Sarvia, though it was dependent upon him.

Sometimes, too, one must take vigorous resolutions, as Solomon did. Everything depends on knowing the circumstances, and on not always pushing brave men without limit and to the extreme.

11th Proposition
The point of counsel is to devote oneself to disconcerting the enemy, and to destroying what is most solid

Counsels achieve no less than courage during great dangers.

Thus, during the revolt of Absalom, where the salvation of the whole kingdom was at stake, David maintained himself not only through courage, but used his whole prudence,[34] as has already been remarked elsewhere. And to get to the root of the matter, he turned his whole mind to destroying the counsel of Achitopel, in whom all the force of the enemy party was concentrated. In order to oppose him usefully, he sent Chusai, whom he furnished with instructions and necessary aids – giving him Zadok and Abiathar as trustworthy companions to act under him. By this means Chusai got the upper hand over Achitopel, who, seeing himself confounded, despaired of success and killed himself.[35]

The success of Chusai against Achitopel appeared in this: that without attacking his reputation for foresight (too well recognized to be weakened), he contented himself with saying to him: "On this occasion Achitopel has not given good counsel"[36] – which accused him only of a passing fault which arose by accident.

12th Proposition
One must know how to penetrate and dissipate cabals, without giving them time to regroup

Under this heading one should observe everything that happened during the revolt of Adonias son of David – who against David's will wanted to ascend the throne destined for Solomon. This story has been recounted elsewhere in its full extent. Here we note only the following.

[34] 2 Kings 15:31ff.   [35] 2 Kings 17:14,23.   [36] Ibid., 7.

At the end of the life of the king his father, Adonias gave a solemn feast for the royal family and all the great in his cabal.[37] This feast was, for Joab and his faction, a kind of signal for rebellion: but it opened the eyes of the king. He prevented Adonias: and during this feast at which this young prince had hoped to get himself authorized, his ruin was announced to him, together with the coronation of Solomon. At this moment fright spread within the faction; the cabal was dissipated; "each returned to his house." The blow was struck: and the treason vanished together with hope.

Vigilance and the penetration of the faithful ministers of David, who warned this prince in a timely fashion, the firmness of this king, and his orders executed with promptitude, saved the state and achieved this great work without any spilling of blood.

13th Proposition
Counsels raise the courage of the prince

Ezechias, threatened by the King of Assyria, "took counsel with the princes and with the most valiant men."[38] And this concert produced the great events and the generous resolutions which raised up dejected hearts, and brought them to say to Isaiah: "This prince will have thoughts that are worthy of a prince."[39]

The people must feel this effect. And Judith was right to say to Ozias and to the chiefs who were defending Bethulia: "Since you are senators, and the very soul of the people resteth on you, comfort their hearts by your speech."[40]

14th Proposition
Good counsels are often due to a wise counselor

"Joas King of Judah reigned for forty years. He did that which was right before the Lord all the days that Joiada the priest taught him ... And after the death of Joiada, the princes of Judah went in, and worshiped their king: and he was soothed by their services and hearkened to their counsels"[41] – which in the end ruined him.

---

[37] 3 Kings 1:1,5,9,19ff.   [38] 2 Par. 32:3.
[39] Isa. 32:8.   [40] Jth. 8:21.
[41] 4 Kings 12:1–2; 2 Par. 24:1–2; 17–18.

15th Proposition
Goodness is natural to kings: and they have nothing to fear so much as bad counsels

"Bad ministers, said the great king Artaxerxes (in the letter which he addressed to the peoples of the 127 provinces subject to his rule), impose through their deceitful lies on the ears of the princes, who are well-meaning and judge of others by their own nature."[42]

16th Proposition
Wise policy, even that of the Gentiles and of the Romans, is praised by the Holy Spirit

We find these fine characteristics of it in the book of Maccabees.

"First, they had done great things in the land of Spain, and they had brought under their power the mines of silver and of gold, by their counsel and patience."[43] Which leads to this important reflection: That without rushing matters, these wise Romans, bellicose as they were, thought they could advance and secure their conquests still better through counsel and patience, than by force of arms.

The second characteristic of Roman wisdom praised by the Holy Spirit in this divine book, is that their friendship was reliable,[44] and that, not content with insuring the repose of their allies through their protection (which was never lacking), they knew how to enrich and enlarge them – as they did for King Eumenes, by augmenting his kingdom with the provinces which they had conquered. It was this that made their friendship desired by everyone.

The third characteristic is that they gained little by little, first subjecting the neighboring kingdoms, and contenting themselves, with respect to far-away countries, by filling them with their glory, sending their reputation from afar – as the forerunner of their victories.[45]

It is also remarked that, in order to regulate all their thought-processes "and to do things worthy of them, they took counsel every day, without division and without jealousy;"[46] and were attentive only to the fatherland and the common good.

For the rest, during this fine time of the Roman republic, in the

---

[42] Esther 16:5–6. [43] 1 Macc. 8:3. [44] Ibid., 12.
[45] Ibid., 12–13.   [46] Ibid., 15–16.

midst of so much greatness, they kept to the equality and the modesty suitable to a popular state, "without anyone wanting to dominate the citizens; without the purple, without the crown, and with no luxurious titles. Everyone obeyed the annual magistrate"[47] (that is to say the consuls, each of whom had his year), with as much submissiveness and punctuality as would have been seen in the most absolute monarchies.

It remains only to observe that when this fine order changed, the Roman people saw its majesty and its power fall.

Such are the counsels that one can derive from Roman policies, provided that one knows on other grounds how to measure each of their steps by the rule of justice.

17th Proposition
Great wisdom consists in using each according to his talents

"I know that your brother Simon is a man of counsel: give ear to him always, and he shall be a father to you. Judas Maccabeus who is valiant and strong from his youth up: let him be the leader of your army, and he shall manage the war of the people."[48]

It was thus that Mathathias, breathing his last, spoke: and he laid in his family the foundations of royalty, to which the family was destined soon thereafter, over the whole people of Israel.

For the rest Simon was a warrior like Judas, as became clear in what followed. But it was not in the same degree: and the Holy Spirit teaches us to take men through their most eminent qualities.

18th Proposition
One must be careful of the personal qualities and of the hidden interests of those from whom one takes counsel

"Treat not with a man without religion concerning holiness, nor with an unjust man concerning justice, nor with a woman touching her of whom she is jealous. Consult not with a coward concerning war, nor with a merchant about the price of traffic (which he will always make excessive), nor with a buyer about selling, nor with an envious man about giving recompense for services rendered to you by another. Do

---

[47] Ibid., 14,16.   [48] 1 Macc. 2:65–66.

not listen to the hard and pitiless heart concerning generosity and benefits (which he will always want to limit): nor concerning the rules of honorability and virtue to him whose morals are corrupt: nor to the field laborer about the price of daily work: nor with him that worketh by the year of the finishing of the year (which he will want to stretch out and never end): nor with an idle servant of much business."[49] Never summon such men to any counsel whatsoever.

The whole of this wise speech is to reveal the blindness of those who accept interested and corrupt counsels, or even those which are doubtful and suspect, in order to determine themselves in important matters.

19th Proposition
The first quality of a wise counselor, is that he be a man of good will

"Be continually with a holy man, whomsoever thou shalt know to observe the fear of God, whose soul is according to thy own soul"[50] (sensible of your interests and disposed to the same virtue).

"The soul of a holy man (without a mask, who cannot flatter you) discovereth sometimes true things, more than seven watchmen that sit in a high place to watch, to discover everything and report the news to you."[51]

Article III

The prince is reminded of different characters of ministers or counselors: good, mixture of good and bad, and wicked

1st Proposition
One begins with the character of Samuel

I want not so much to stress what is supernatural or prophetic in so great a character, but that which brings him close to us by ordinary paths.

---

[49] Ecclus. 37:12–14. [50] Ibid., 15. [51] Ibid., 18.

Samuel was great and singular in this way: that having for twenty years (and till his old age) judged the people as a sovereign [*en souverain*], he saw himself degraded without complaining. The people came to him to ask for a king. "Behold thou art old, they said to him, and thy sons walk not in thy ways: make us a king, to judge us."[1] Thus they reproached him with his great age, and the discontentment they felt with his sons. What can be harder for a father who, far from being able to hope that his children will succeed to his dignity in compensation for such long and wise governance, must endure being deprived of his rank during his lifetime?

He felt the affront: "The word was displeasing in the eyes of Samuel."[2] But without complaining or murmuring, his recourse was "to come and pray to the Lord, who ordered him to hearken to the voice of the people."[3] And this reduced him to private life.

It remained only for him to submit to the king whom he had established, who was Saul, and to render to him an account of his conduct before the whole people – this people which he had seen receiving his sovereign orders for so many years. "I have always been under your eyes since my youth. Speak of me before the Lord, and before his anointed, whether I have taken any man's ox, or ass: if I have wronged any man, if I have oppressed any man, if I have taken a bribe at any man's hand: . . . and I will restore it to you." They had nothing with which to reproach him. "And he added: The Lord and his anointed shall be witness against you of my innocence,"[4] and that it is not at all for my crimes that you have deposed me.

That was his whole complaint: and, much as he was listened to, he did not entirely abandon his concern for public affairs. One sees the people applying to him at certain important junctures, with the same confidence as if they had not offended him.[5]

Far from making the people dissatisfied with the new king who had been established to his prejudice, he profited from every favorable circumstance to shore up the throne. On the day of a glorious victory of Saul over the Philistines, he gave this wise counsel: "Come and let us go to Galgal, and let us renew the kingdom there. And Saul was recognized before the Lord: and they sacrificed victims; and the joy was great in all Israel."[6]

From this time, he lived as a private person: contenting himself

---

[1] 1 Kings 8:4–5.   [2] Ibid., 6.   [3] Ibid., 7.
[4] 1 Kings 12:3–5.   [5] 1 Kings 11:12.   [6] Ibid., 14–15.

with warning the new king of his duties, conveying the orders of God to him, and announcing his judgments.[7]

Since he saw his counsels treated with contempt, it remained only for him to retire to his house at Ramatha, where day and night he mourned Saul before God, and did not cease to intercede for this ungrateful prince. "How long wilt thou mourn for Saul, whom I have rejected from reigning over Israel?, said the Lord to Samuel. Go consecrate another king."[8] This was David. It seemed that, in compensation for the sovereign empire over the people that he had lost, God wanted to make him the arbiter of kings, and give him the power to establish them.

The house of this dispossessed sovereign became an asylum for David, while Saul was persecuting him. Saul did not respect this asylum, sacred though it was. He sent courier after courier and messenger after messenger, to get hold of David[9] – who was constrained to take flight, to leave his sacred refuge, and soon thereafter the kingdom. And the aid of Samuel was useless to him.

Thus Samuel lived, retired to his house, as a faithful counselor whose advice was viewed with contempt, and who could only pray to God for his king. So fine a retreat left the people of God with an eternal souvenir of a magnanimity which till now has known no rival. He died there full of days, and deserved that "all Israel assembled at Ramatha to bury him, and to mourn for his death in great consternation."[10]

2nd Proposition
The character of Nehemias, the model of good governors

The Jews were rebuilding their Temple, and were beginning to restore Jerusalem under the favorable edicts of the kings of Persia, whose subjects they had become through the conquest of Babylon: but they were crossed by the continual hostilities of the Samaritans, and of their other neighbors, the old enemies of their nation, and even by the ministers of the (Persian) kings, with an invincible stubbornness.[11]

It was in these circumstances that Nehemias was sent by Artaxerxes King of Persia, to be governor of Jerusalem. Ambition did not raise

[7] 1 Kings 15.   [8] 1 Kings 16:1.   [9] 1 Kings 19:18,19ff.
[10] 1 Kings 25:1; 28:3.   [11] Neh. 1–4.

him to this high post, but rather the love of his citizens; and he took advantage of the good graces of the king his master only to have the means of relieving them.

Having left Persia with this thought, he found that Jerusalem – desolated and ruined on every side – was no longer anything more than the corpse of a great city, in which one could see neither forts, nor ramparts, nor gates, nor streets, nor houses.

After having begun to repair these ruins, more by his example than by his orders, the first thing that he did was to hold a great meeting against those who were oppressing their brothers. "What is this?, he said to them: Do you every one exact usury of your brethren? Even while they dream only of setting up their fields and their vineyards, and even of selling their very children to have bread, and to pay tribute to the king? We, as you know, have redeemed according to our ability our brethren the Jews, that were sold to the Gentiles: and will you then sell your brethren, for us to redeem them?"[12] By this speech he confounded all the oppressors of their own brothers, and above all when he added, shaking his lap, as if he had wanted to exhaust himself: "Both I and my brethren, and my servants, have lent money and corn to many: . . . let us forgive the debt that is owing us."[13]

"The former governors that had been before me, and still more their ministers (as is usual) had oppressed the people, who could do no more. But I on the contrary have turned back what was due to the government."[14] He knew that in certain conditions of extreme poverty on the part of those who owe us something, it is a kind of theft to demand of them what is legitimately our due.

"His table was open to magistrates and visiting neighbors. There one saw choice meats in abundance, and a store of divers wines."[15] He needed, in these circumstances, to sustain his dignity – and he won people over through this display.

"Thus I lived, he said, for twelve years. I rebuilt the wall at my expense; no one was useless in my house; and all my servants labored on public works."[16]

There is something else remarkable, and of an exact justice: "I bought no land."[17] It is theft to take advantage of one's authority and of public poverty, in order to buy what one wants at whatever price one deigns to give.

[12] Neh. 5:1,2,3,7,8. [13] Ibid., 10. [14] Ibid., 14–15.
[15] Ibid., 17–18. [16] Ibid., 14,16. [17] Ibid., 16.

What is finest of all, is that he did all of this in the sight of God and his duty alone, and said to him with confidence: "Lord, remember me for good according to all that I have done for this people."[18]

One should not be astonished that he used his authority to bring about an exact observance of the Sabbath, of the ordinances of the law, and all the Levitical and priestly rights.[19]

Let us turn to military virtues, which are so necessary in this great employment.

While the city was being diligently rebuilt, to put it beyond danger, "he divided the citizens of whom half did the building-work while the other half guarded those who labored, and repulsed the enemy by armed might."[20] But in the works themselves, the laborers were ready to take up arms. Everyone was armed, and, as Scripture expresses itself, "with one of their hands they did the work, and with the other they held a sword."[21] And since they were dispersed in various places, the order was so good that everyone knew where to assemble at the first signal.

Since no one could fell Nehemias by arms, they tried to draw him into specious treaties with the enemy.[22] Sanaballat and the other chiefs had won over many magistrates, and surrounded him with their emissaries, who spoke highly of them in his presence. They strove to frighten him by letters which they had circulated, and by false alarms. They tried to make him fear secret machinations against his life, to oblige him to take flight; and they did not cease to propose timid counsels to him, which would have spread terror amongst the people. "Let us consult together secretly, they said, in the Temple, in camera."[23] But he answered with a noble pride which reassured everyone: "Should such a man as I flee? My like fear nothing, and know not how to hide."[24] By so many different devices, they meant to slow him down or divert him, if they could not vanquish him; but he was found to be equally above both surprise and violence.

The basis of so many goods was a solid piety, a perfect disinterestedness, a lively attention to duty, and an intrepid courage.

---

[18] Ibid., 19. [19] Ibid., 13. [20] Neh. 4: 16. [21] Ibid., 17.
[22] Ibid., 6:1–2. [23] Ibid., 10. [24] Ibid., 11.

3rd Proposition
The character of Joab, made up of great virtues and of great vices, under David

David found in his family and in the person of Joab, son of his sister Sarvia,[25] a support for his throne.

From the beginning of his reign, he judged him to be most worthy of the charge of general of his armies. But he wanted him to merit it through some signal service rendered to the state; for it was unworthy of so great a king (and scarcely glorious for Joab) that David should only pay attention to blood-ties and to personal interest. When this prince attacked Jebus, which was afterwards called Jerusalem, and which David destined to be the seat of religion and of the empire, he made this solemn declaration: "Whosoever shall first strike the Jebusites, shall be the head and chief captain (this was the reward for valor which he proposed). And Joab went up first, and was made the general of the armies. But David took the castle of Sion, which is called the city of David, because he established his residence there."[26]

After this fine conquest, "David built the city round about from Mello all round, and Joab (who had had so great a part in the victory) built the rest."[27] Thus he attracted attention in the construction of public works, as in combat, and held next to David the place which history assigns, next to Augustus, to the great Agrippa, his son-in-law.

When David had unfortunately undertaken, in Judah and in Israel, the numbering of the men capable of bearing arms, which brought down the scourge of God on him, Joab, to whom he gave the command, did (as a faithful minister) what he could to turn him from this course, saying to him: "The Lord make his people a hundred times more than they are: but, my lord the king, are they not all thy servants: why doth my lord seek this thing, which may be imputed as a sin to Israel?"[28]

God did not will that Israel, nor her king, place their confidence in the multitude of the combatants — which should be left to multiply by the hand of him who had promised to equal the number of stars in heaven and of grains of sand in the sea.[29]

The king persisted; and Joab obeyed, though with regret. Thus in

---

[25] 1 Par. 2:16. [26] 2 Kings 5:7–8; 1 Par. 11:4–7.
[27] 1 Par. 11:8. [28] 2 Kings 24:2–3; 1 Par. 21:2–3.
[29] 2 Par. 27:23.

Different characters of ministers

about nine months he brought the king the enumeration, which imperfect as it was, showed David several times over that he had fifteen hundred thousand combatants in his power.[30]

"But David's heart struck him, after the people were numbered."[31] He was sensible of his fault; and his vanity was no sooner satisfied than it turned to remorse and compunction – such that he dared not cause the enumeration to be inserted in the royal records.[32]

What good did it do him to see on paper so many thousands of youths ready to fight, when the plague that God sent ravaged the people, and made of them a heap of corpses? Joab had foreseen this misfortune: and one could see in his speech, with all the force that the matter merited, all possible consideration and the most gentle hints.

We have already seen in another place – when David had abandoned himself to grief after the death of Absalom – how Joab made him realize that he was putting all his servants in a state of despair; that they all saw how David would willingly have sacrificed them for Absalom; that the army was already discouraged; and that he was going to draw on himself evils greater than all those he had already endured.[33] This was to speak to his master with all the freedom that the importance of the thing, his zeal and his services inspired in him. He went as far as a kind of hardness, knowing well that grief pushed to the extreme needs to be (as it were) consumed and beaten down by a kind of violence; otherwise it finds ways of sustaining itself by itself, consuming the mind as well as the body with the most mortal of all poisons.

For the rest, he loved the glory of his king. In the important siege of the city and of the fortresses of Rabbath, he had David told: "I have fought against Rabbath, and the city of waters is about to be taken: now therefore gather thou the rest of the people together, and besiege the city and take it, so that the victory will not be ascribed to my name."[34] This was not a characteristic of a facile courtier: David had no need of begged-for honors; and Joab knew when conquests should be completed. Rather this was an action meant to be brilliant, in which it was a matter of avenging on the Ammonites an outrage committed against David's ambassadors; and the circumstances of the times demanded that the glory be given to the prince.

When it was necessary to speak to him about the return of

---

[30] 1 Par. 21:4–6; 2 Kings 24:8–9. [31] 2 Kings 24:10.
[32] 1 Par. 27:24.   [33] 2 Kings 19.   [34] 2 Kings 12:27–28.

Absalom, and to enter into the affairs of the royal family, Joab, who knew well that there are matters in which it is better to act through others than by oneself, handled the king with delicacy: and he used the wise woman of Thecua to move David. But so intelligent a prince soon recognized "the hand of Joab . . . and said to him: I have granted thy request: go therefore and fetch back the boy Absalom. And Joab falling down to the ground upon his face, answered: This day thy servant hath understood, that I have found grace in thy sight: for thou hast fulfilled the request of thy servant."[35] He sensed the goodness of the king on this occasion, which concerned the interest of another, more vividly than the graces (which were infinite) that he had received in person.

I pass over the other characteristics which would make familiar the ability of Joab, and his wise accommodations. But private acts of vengeance and his ambitious jealousies deprived him of so many advantages, and the king of the usefulness of so many services.

We have recounted elsewhere the shameful assassination of Abner, which David could not punish in a man as necessary to the state as Joab – whom he was obliged to vindicate in public.[36]

He even saw himself forced to mark out his post for another: and he chose Amasa,[37] who was worthy of it. But Joab killed him as a traitor. "And his friends said: Behold he that would have been in Joab's stead the companion of David."[38] He placed his glory in making himself redoubtable, a man whom one did not attack with impunity.

In a word, he was one of those who will the good, but who want to accomplish it alone under the king. A dangerous character if ever there was one, since the jealousy of ministers – who are always ready to cross each other, and to sacrifice everything to their ambition – is an inexhaustible source of bad counsels, and is scarcely less prejudicial to good service than rebellion itself.

It was the desire to preserve himself which led him to support the interests of Adonias, against Solomon and against David.

Everyone knows the secret orders that this dying king was obliged to leave to his successor,[39] against a minister who had made himself so necessary that circumstances did not permit him to punish him. It was finally necessary to spill his blood, as he had spilled that of others.

[35] 2 Kings 14:19–22. [36] 2 Kings 3:27ff. [37] 2 Kings 19:13.
[38] 2 Kings 20:9–11. [39] 3 Kings 2:5–6.

Too complacent towards David, he was his accomplice in the death of Uriah – whom this prince made the bearer of orders for his ruin to Joab himself.[40] God punished him through David, whose passion he flattered. It was then more than ever that Joab should have contradicted him, and made kings feel that it is a service to them to stop them from finding executors of their bloody plans.

4th Proposition
Holofernes, under Nabuchodonosor, King of Nineveh and of Assyria

Judith spoke to him in these terms: "For as Nabuchodonosor the king of the earth liveth, and his power liveth which is in thee for chastising of all straying souls: not only men who serve him through thee, but also the beasts of the field obey him. For the industry of thy mind is spoken of among all nations, and it is told through the whole world, that thou only art excellent, and mighty in all his kingdom, and thy discipline is cried up in all provinces."[41]

It is clear through these words, that he was not only a military leader, but also that he had the direction of all matters, and that he had the reputation of making justice reign, and of restraining injuries and acts of violence.

His zeal for the king his master shone from his first words to Judith: "Be of good comfort, and fear not in thy heart: for I have never hurt a man that was willing to serve Nabuchodonosor the king."[42]

Always he spoke reasonably, with dignity. The orders which he gave in war were approved by all the men of his profession; and one finds nothing to fault in his precautions while on the march, nor in his foresight concerning the recruiting and sustenance of his troops.

It is useless to expect religion in ambitious men. "If thy God shall do this for me, he shall also be my God."[43] The god of proud souls is always the one who contents their ambition.

"It was looked upon as shameful among the Assyrians, if a woman mock a man"[44] (in preserving her modesty). Men of war take pride in these unhappy victories, and regard the weaker sex as the certain prey of so brilliant a profession.

Holofernes, possessed by this insensate passion, seemed beside

---

[40] 2 Kings 11:14–17. [41] Jth. 11:5–6. [42] Ibid., 1.
[43] Jth. 11:21. [44] Jth. 12:11.

himself at the sight of the astonishing beauty of Judith: and the grace of his speeches brought about his ruin. Raillery was mixed with them: "What an agreeable conquest, that of a country which has such beautiful women! What could be a worthier object of our fighting?"[45] The blind Assyrian was overjoyed: drunk with love still more than with wine, he dreamt only of satisfying his desires.

Men often think these passions (which, they say, do no harm to anyone) innocent or indifferent in men who command. It was in this way that the affairs of Assyria and of so great a king were undone. Everyone knows the outcome, to the eternal shame of great armies. A woman routed them by a single blow of her weak hand, more easily than a hundred thousand fighters would have done.

If one wanted to recount all the misfortunes, all the disorders, all the problems which history relates to these passions which are judged not to be unworthy of heroes, the recital would be too long: and it is better here to take notice of other types of character.

5th Proposition
Aman, under Assuerus, King of Persia

The story is so celebrated, and the character so well known, that one need touch only on the main themes.

"King Assuerus raised Aman above all the great of the kingdom. And all the king's servants bent their knees, and adored the favorite as the king has commanded, except for Mardochai alone."[46] He was a Jew, and his religion did not permit him an adoration which carried divine honors.

Aman, swollen by this favor, "called together his wife and his friends, and declared to them the greatness of his riches, and the multitude of his children, and how with great glory the king had advanced him."[47] Everything supported his greatness; and nature herself seemed to second the will of the king. And he added, as the pinnacle of his favor: "The queen herself also hath invited no other to the banquet with the king, but me: and tomorrow I shall have this honor. And whereas I have all these things, I think I have nothing, so long as I see Mardochai the Jew who, sitting before the king's gate, does not stir himself at my approach."[48]

---

[45] Jth. 10:18.　　　　　　[46] Esther 3:1–2.
[47] Esther 5:10–11.　　　　[48] Ibid., 12–13.

What flatters the ambitious is the idea of omnipotence, which seems to make gods of them on earth. They cannot see without chagrin any place where this power is lacking – and everything seems to be lacking because of this one spot. The feebler the obstacle to their greatness seems to be, the more they are irritated by their ambition to crush it; and all the rest of their life is troubled.

Unfortunately for this favorite, he had a wife as haughty and as ambitious as himself. "Order a great beam to be prepared, fifty cubits high, that Mardochai may be hanged upon it, and so thou shalt go full of joy with the king to the banquet."[49] A striking and prompt vengeance – to ambitious souls the most delicate of all dishes. "The counsel pleased him, and he commanded a high gibbet to be prepared."

"But he counted it nothing to lay his hands upon Mardochai alone; and he resolved to destroy all the nation of the Jews at once"[50] – be it because he wanted to cover private vengeance with a more general order; be it because he wanted to attack this religion, which inspired Mardochai's refusal; be it because it pleased him to give the world a more striking sign of his power, and because the hanging of a single individual was too little food for his vanity.

The pretext could not have been more specious. "There is a people, he said to the king, dispersed throughout your empire, which troubles the public peace through new laws and ceremonies."[51] (No one would be interested in the preservation of so strange a nation.) They are in different places, he observed (without the power of mutual aid, which makes it easy to oppress them). They are a race disobedient to your orders (whose insolence must be reprimanded), this crafty minister added. One could not present to a king a better-colored political view: necessity and facility ran together. Aman, moreover, knew that often the greatest kings – in the midst of their abundance, and to the detriment of the human race – are not insensible to the enlargement of their treasures; and he added in conclusion: "Decree that they may be destroyed, and I (through the confiscation of their goods) will pay ten thousand talents to thy treasurers."[52]

The king was above the temptation of having the money; but not above that of giving it in order to enrich so agreeable a minister, who

---

[49] Ibid., 14. [50] Esther 3:6.
[51] Ibid., 8. [52] Ibid., 9.

seemed to him so devoted to the interests of the state, and of his person. "As to the money which thou promisest, keep it for thyself; and as to the people, do with them as seemeth good to thee; and he gave his ring to seal the orders."[53]

A happy favorite is full of himself alone. Aman did not imagine that the king could count on services other than his own. Thus, consulted about the honors which the king had destined for Mardochai (who had saved his life), he procured the greatest honors for his enemy, and for himself the most shameful humiliation. Kings are often pleased to save the most distasteful things for their favorites, delighted to show themselves the masters. Aman had to walk on foot before Mardochai, and be the herald of his glory in all the public places.[54] One then saw, and predicted to him, Mardochai's ascendancy over him; and his ruin was approaching.

Finally came the moment of the queen's fatal banquet,[55] of which the favorite had been so proud. Men do not know their destiny. The ambitious are easy to deceive because they themselves aid in the seduction, and because they believe all too easily those who favor them. It was at this banquet, so much desired by Aman, that he received the final blow through the just complaint of this princess. The king opened his eyes to the bloody advice which his minister had given him: he was in horror of it. As the pinnacle of disgrace the king saw Aman at the feet of the queen to beg for her clemency, got it into his head that he was making an attempt on her honor – something that had not the slightest likelihood in Aman's state. But confidence, once injured, carries itself to the most extreme feelings. Aman perished; and, deceived by his own glory, he was himself the architect of his destruction – to the point of having built the gibbet to which he was attached, since it was this that he had prepared for his enemy.

---

[53] Ibid., 10–11.   [54] Esther 6:1ff.   [55] Esther 7:1ff.

Article IV

To help the prince to know men well, one shows him, in a general way, some characters drawn by the Holy Spirit in the books of Wisdom

1st Proposition
Who those are that must be kept from public posts, and even from the court, if it is possible

We have remarked elsewhere that one of the most necessary kinds of knowledge in a prince is that of knowing men. We have facilitated this knowledge for him, by painting in detail some characters who are markedly good or evil. We are now going to draw from the books of Wisdom those general characteristics which make it clear who those persons are who must be kept from public employments and even from courts, if possible.

There are those who find nothing good except what they think, nothing just except what they want: they believe that their mind contains all that may be by way of usefulness or good sense, without listening to anything. It is to these that Solomon said: "Be not wise in thy own conceit."[1] And elsewhere: "A fool receiveth not the words of prudence: unless thou say those things which are in his heart."[2] And finally: "The way of a fool is right in his own eyes: but he that is wise hearkeneth unto counsels."[3]

There is also "the innocent, who believeth every word: but the discreet man (holds to the middle and) considereth his steps."[4] This is the one whom the prudent prince must always follow.

"A perverse man stirreth up quarrels: and one full of words separateth princes,"[5] by saying indiscreetly that which harms as well as that which serves.

"The words of the double tongued are as if they were harmless:

---

[1] Prov. 3:7.   [2] Prov. 18:2.   [3] Prov. 12:15.
[4] Prov. 14:15.   [5] Prov. 16:28.

and they reach even to the inner rank of the bowels."[6] He leaves impressions behind, and makes deep wounds by his lying reports.

"Cast out the scoffer, and contention shall go out with him, and quarrels and reproaches shall cease."[7]

Above all fear the flatterer,[8] who is the scourge of courts and the plague of the human race. "Better are the wounds of a friend (who offends you only by telling the truth) than the deceitful kisses of an enemy,"[9] who hides himself under a fine appearance.

The braggart, "he that boasteth and puffeth himself up, stirreth up quarrels."[10] At each word one feels himself pushed to contradict him.

"He that maketh haste to be rich, shall not be innocent."[11] And elsewhere: "Through poverty many have sinned: and he that maketh to be enriched turneth away his eye."[12] Quickly made fortunes are suspect. The modest competence which one has from his fathers, creates the presumption of a good education.[13]

"He that is impatient, shall suffer damage."[14] Things go from bad to worse at his hands, through haste and hitches.

By contrast "the sluggard willeth and willeth not."[15] He can never determine himself; everything escapes his hands because he either fails to give matters time to ripen or does not know the correct moment. And because he has heard it said that one should not precipitate matters, and that "he that is hasty with his feet shall stumble,"[16] he believes himself wiser (in his slowness) than "seven sages that speak sentences whose words are as many oracles."[17]

To avoid these difficulties, the decision of the wise man is that "there is a time and opportunity for every business."[18] One should neither let it slip away, nor move forward too rapidly, but wait and be watchful always.

Are you always joyful, always satisfied with yourself? You see nothing: human affairs do not afford this perpetual transport. This is what brings Ecclesiastes to say: "The heart of the wise is where there is mourning: and the heart of fools where there is mirth."[19]

"Be not over just: and be not more wise than is necessary, lest thou become stupid,"[20] without life or movement. To be too scrupulous is

---

[6] Prov. 18:8; 26:22.
[7] Prov. 22:10.
[8] Ibid., 10.
[9] Prov. 27:6.
[10] Prov. 28:25.
[11] Ibid., 20.
[12] Ecclus. 27:1.
[13] Ibid., 1.
[14] Prov. 19:19.
[15] Prov. 13:4.
[16] Prov. 19:2.
[17] Prov. 26:16.
[18] Eccles. 8:6.
[19] Eccles. 7:5.
[20] Ibid., 17.

a kind of weakness. To want to guarantee human affairs more than their nature permits is another weakness which makes one fall – not only into lethargy and numbness, but even into despair.

There is an opposite vice: that of daring everything without measure, of being scrupulous of nothing. And the wise man reprimands this soon afterwards: "Do not act like an impious person."[21] Do not maintain yourself in crime, as if there were no law or religion for you.

Those who dream of satisfying everyone and swim uncertainly between two shores, or who turn now towards the one, now towards the other, are those of whom it is written: "A heart that goes two ways (and that wants to deceive everyone) shall not have success."[22] He will never have a faithful friend, nor certain alliance: and he will finally set everyone against him.

It is to such persons that the wise man says: "Winnow not with every wind, and go not every way: for so is every sinner proved by a double tongue."[23] Let your steps be firm: let your conduct be regular: and let certainty be in your words.

"Be not called a whisperer, and be not taken in thy tongue, and confounded."[24] Such are those whose lightness of speech one does not cease to reproach, and who destroy one another.

Those who interfere around the king, who want to make themselves necessary in courts, are taken note of in this sentence: "Desire not to appear wise before the king."[25] Wisdom declares itself only in an appropriate way. Those people who always want to give good counsels, are those of whom it is written: "Every counsellor praises his counsel,"[26] and thereby makes it useless and contemptible.

The avaricious man must be execrated. "He that is evil to himself, to whom will he be good? And he shall not take pleasure in his goods. There is none worse than he that envieth himself, and this is the reward of his wickedness."[27]

Finally the most odious characters are drawn together and pointed out in these words: "Six things there are which the Lord hateth, says the wise man, and the seventh his soul detesteth: Haughty eyes, a lying tongue, hands that shed innocent blood, a heart that deviseth wicked plots, feet that are swift to run into mischief, a deceitful

[21] Ibid., 18. [22] Ecclus. 3:28. [23] Ecclus. 5:11.
[24] Ibid., 16. [25] Ecclus. 7:5. [26] Ecclus. 37:8.
[27] Ecclus. 14:5–6.

witness that uttereth lies, and him that soweth discord among brethren."[28]

2nd Proposition
One offers three counsels of the wise man, against three bad characters

"In nowise speak against the truth, but be ashamed of the lie of thy ignorance."[29] Where is the mortal who is never mistaken? Make a good use of your mistakes, and let them enlighten you for another occasion.

"Be not ashamed to confess thy sins, but submit not thyself to every man for sin"[30] – as do weak men, who despair and lose courage.

"Resist not against the face of the mighty, and do not strike against the stream of the river."[31] The reckless man believes everything possible, and nothing stops him.

Here are three further characters cursed by the wise man.

"Woe to them that are of a double heart . . . who go on the earth two ways,"[32] and make disguise and inconstancy their strong point.

"Woe to them that are fainthearted (who let themselves be defeated by the first blow) and who believe not in God."[33]

"Woe to them that have lost patience,"[34] who fail to pursue a good plan.

3rd Proposition
The character of a false friend

This is the one who must be watched the most. We have already taken note of him; but one cannot point him out too much to the prince in order to distance him from him – since this is the most certain mark of a badly brought up soul with a corrupt heart.

"Every friend will say: I also am his friend," and this is a great joy to him. "But there is a friend that is only a friend in name. Is not this a grief even to death,"[35] when one sees the abuse of so holy a name?

This merely nominal friend "is a friend for his own occasion, and

---

[28] Prov. 6:16–19.
[29] Ecclus. 4:30.
[30] Ibid., 31.
[31] Ibid., 32.
[32] Ecclus. 2:14.
[33] Ibid., 15.
[34] Ibid., 16.
[35] Ecclus. 37:1.

he will not abide in the day of thy trouble"[36] – when you have the greatest need of such help.

"There is a friend a companion at the table."[37] He seeks only his pleasure, and leaves you in adversity.

"To disclose the secrets of a friend, leaveth no hope to an unhappy soul,"[38] who no longer knows whom to trust, and sees no way out of his misery.

"But there is a friend who is still worse. It is he that will disclose hidden hatreds, and what has been said in anger or in a dispute."[39] There is a friend who is superficial and thoughtless, "who looks only for an occasion, a pretext to break with his friend: this is a man worthy of eternal condemnation."[40] A man who lets such a fault appear even once in his life is marked forever, to the eternal horror of human society.

4th Proposition
The true use of friends and of counsel

"Iron sharpeneth iron, so a man sharpeneth the countenance of his friend."[41]

Good counsel does not give intelligence to him who has none: but it excites and awakens him who has it. "One must have good counsel"[42] to be useful. There are even cases in which one must advise himself. One must have a sense of himself, and take certain decisive measures himself, where only weak advice can be given.

The rule given by the wise man concerning friendships is admirable: "Separate thyself from thy enemy (do not give him thy confidence): but take heed of thy friend":[43] do not espouse his passions.

5th Proposition
Friendship must presuppose the fear of God

"A faithful friend is the medicine of life and immortality: and they that fear the Lord, shall find him."[44] The fear of God provides the principle: and good faith is maintained under those eyes which penetrate everything.

[36] Ecclus. 6:8. [37] Ibid., 10. [38] Ecclus. 27:24.
[39] Ecclus. 6:9. [40] Ecclus. 18:1. [41] Prov. 27:17.
[42] Ecclus. 37:8. [43] Ecclus. 6:13. [44] Ibid., 16.

6th Proposition
The character of a statesman

"Counsel in the heart of a man is like deep water: but a wise man will draw it out."[45] One does not reveal him, so deep is his conduct: but he sounds the hearts of others, and one would say that he divines, so certain are his discoveries.

He speaks only appropriately; for "he understandeth time and answer."[46] Isaiah calls him the architect:[47] he makes long-term plans; he follows them; he does not build by chance.[48]

The evenness of his conduct is a sign of his wisdom, and causes him to be viewed as a man who is certain in all his undertakings. "A holy man continueth in wisdom like the sun: but a fool is changed as the moon."[49] The true sage does not change at all: one never finds him defective. Neither humors nor prejudice alter him.

7th Proposition
Piety is sometimes creditable, even next to wicked kings

Eliseus said to the Sunamite: "Hast thou any business, and wilt thou that I speak to the king, or to the chief justice?"[50] The impious Achab himself, who was the king, called him "my father."[51]

"Herod feared John the Baptist, knowing him to be a just and holy man: and kept him in prison, and when he heard him, did many things; and he heard him willingly."[52] At the end, however, one knows the treatment he gave him. And Achab prepared a similar fate for Eliseus: "Let me be cursed by God, said this prince, if the head of Eliseus stand on him this day."[53]

Religion causes fear even in those who do not follow it: but the superstitious terror which is without love makes man weak, timid, defiant, cruel, bloody – everything that passion wills.

8th Proposition
[Royal] favor scarcely lasts two generations

What greater services were there than those of Joseph? He had governed Egypt for eighty years with absolute power, and had had time to

---

[45] Prov. 20:5. [46] Eccles. 8:5. [47] Isa. 3:3.
[48] Ibid., 3. [49] Ecclus. 27:12. [50] 4 Kings 4:13.
[51] 4 Kings 6:21. [52] Mark 6:20. [53] 4 Kings 6:31.

shore himself up: him and his. "In the meantime there arose a new king over Egypt, that knew not Joseph."[54] The prince forgot what the state owed to him – not just its greatness, but its very salvation: and he dreamt only of destroying those whom his predecessors had favored.

9th Proposition
One sees a council of religion surrounding ancient kings

If it were needful to speak here of the prophetic ministry, we have seen Samuel next to Saul, the interpreter of the will of God.[55] Nathan, who reprimanded David for his sin, was concerned with the greatest affairs of state.[56]

But besides this we know a more ordinary ministry, since Ira was called "the priest of David."[57] Zabud was that of Solomon: he was called "the friend of the king"[58] – a certain sign that this prince called him to his privy council, no doubt principally in connection with that which concerned religion and conscience.

In this place one should recall the counsel of the wise: "Be continually with a holy man . . . whose soul is according to thy soul: and who, when thou shalt stumble (secretly) in the dark, will be sorry for thee,"[59] and help you to put things right.

Article v

On the conduct of the prince in his family, and on the care he must have for his health

1st Proposition
The wisdom of the prince seems to govern his family, and to keep it united for the good of the state

We have already observed that "the sons of David were chief about the king"[1] to execute his orders. In the Vulgate they are called

---

[54] Exod. 1:8.   [55] 1 Kings 10; 12; 13; 15; 16.   [56] 3 Kings 1:10,12,23,24.
[57] 2 Kings 20:26.   [58] 3 Kings 4:5.   [59] Ecclus. 37:15–16.
[1] 1 Par. 18:17.

Continuation of helps to royalty

Aularchs – that is to say, princes of the court, to keep it together in the interest of royalty.

To bring about peace in his family, David regulated the succession in favor of Solomon, as God had ordered through the mouth of the prophet Nathan.[2] The rule was to give it to the eldest,[3] if the king did not ordain otherwise. And it is still the custom of Eastern kings.

The indulgence of David, who "would not afflict the spirit of his son Amnon, his first born"[4] – he who had violated his sister Thamar – is recounted in Scripture. He also put up too tranquilly with the undertakings of Absalom, who had become the eldest and who wanted to take over the throne. But God wanted to punish him: and his easiness, followed by so frightful a rebellion, left a terrible example to him and to all kings, who do not know how to make themselves the masters of their families.

Thus – though he had still had an excessive indulgence for Adonias, who was the eldest after Absalom – from the moment he knew that Adonias was abusing [his position] to the point of claiming the kingdom, against his express and declared will, and that he had on his side (against Solomon) his princely brothers, together with most of the great men of the realm, he destroyed the cabal at its birth, by consecrating his son Solomon from his deathbed, and giving peace to the state.[5]

Everyone knows the final orders which he left to the king his son, for the good of religion and of peoples. At this moment God inspired in him that divine Psalm whose title is, "For Solomon," which begins with these fine words: "Give to the king thy judgment, O God, and to the king's son thy justice."[6] The whole work breathes forth peace, abundance, the well-being of the poor relieved by the protection and the justice of the new king, who is to beat down their oppressors. This was the heritage which he left to his son and to his whole people, by promising them a happy reign.

It was long since that the Psalm entitled "For the well-beloved"[7] had been dedicated to Solomon – in which the sons of Core see in their minds the reign of Solomon, where peace flourishes. In it Solomon is exhorted to love "truth, mildness and justice."[8] These were the hopes of David, and it was through them that his reign was to prefigure that of the Messiah – who was the true son of David.

[2] 2 Kings 7:12ff.   [3] 3 Kings 1:5–6; 2:15,22.   [4] 2 Kings 13:21.
[5] 3 Kings 1:6,9ff.   [6] Ps. 71:2.   [7] Ps. 44.   [8] Ibid., 5.

The conduct of the prince in his family

In order to omit nothing, the queen, daughter of Pharaoh, who was destined to be Solomon's wife, is pointed out [in Psalm 44]; and in the name of David these words are addressed to her: "Hearken, O daughter, and see, and incline thy ear: and forget thy people and thy father's house,"[9] royal and brilliant as it is, and espouse the interests of the family which you are entering. You will be recompensed "by the love of the king, who shall greatly desire thy beauty,"[10] and will find you still more beautiful and adorned within than without. It was thus that Israel instructed her queens, like her kings, through the mouth of David.

It was this queen, so perfect and so lovable, in whose name Solomon sang the Canticle of Canticles, and the delights of divine love. This magnificent king treated her according to her merit and according to her birth. He built her a superb palace. Though she knew that according to the custom of those times there were – for the magnificence of the court – threescore queens, and fourscore concubines, and young maidens without number, she felt that she alone had the kings heart. "She was the Sulamite, the perfect one, whom the queens and all the others praised."[11] This queen, without swelling with pride over her advantages, let herself be led by her husband the wise king, and joined with him in spirit by saying: "I will take hold of thee, and bring thee into my mother's house: there thou shalt teach me"[12] through gentle suggestions. And again: "The righteous love thee."[13] One is only worthy to love you who have an upright heart: and to love you is uprightness itself.

Similar instructions had brought Bathsheba, mother of Solomon, to imitate the penitence of David. And it was in this spirit that she spoke to her son in these terms: "What, O my beloved, what, O the beloved of my womb, what, O the beloved of my vows? O my son, give not thy substance to women, and thy riches to destroy kings. Give not to kings, O Lamuel (it was thus that she called Solomon), give not wine to kings: because there is no secret where drunkenness reigneth: and lest they drink and forget judgments, and pervert the cause of the children of the poor."[14] It was after these fine words that she offered the immortal image "of the strong woman, worthy spouse of the senators of the land."[15]

Solomon himself reported these words of his mother, and wished

---

[9] Ibid., 11. [10] Ibid., 12. [11] Cant. 6:7–8. [12] Cant. 8:2.
[13] Cant. 1:3. [14] Prov. 31:2–5. [15] Ibid., 10–23.

to consecrate them in a book inspired by God, with this title at its head: "The words of King Lamuel. The vision wherewith his mother instructed him."[16] One should not, then, be astonished that he so often repeated throughout this book, "hear the instruction of thy father."[17] And elsewhere: "I also was my father's son, tender and as an only son in the sight of my mother. She taught me, and said to me: my son, love wisdom."[18] And elsewhere: "My son, keep the commandments of thy father, and forsake not the law of thy mother."[19] To inspire love of wisdom, Solomon drew together in this divine book the precepts of his father and of his mother – the ones stronger, the others more affectionate and tender, and both together making deep impressions on the heart.

If one needs to go farther back, Job, who was a prince in his country, held his family together. "He had seven sons and three daughters . . . His sons went, and made a feast by houses every one in his day. And sending they called their three sisters to eat and drink with them." The task of Job was "to sanctify them all when their turn had passed, and to offer holocausts for every one of them: for fear, he said, that my children (in their joy) may offend the Lord. So did Job all the days of his life."[20]

Princes, like the others, held on to their children, including their daughters, always ready to sacrifice their lives for the salvation of the country.

The only daughter of Jephtha, sovereign judge of Israel, seeing her father arrive "rending his garments in her sight, spoke to him in this way: My father, if thou hast opened thy mouth to the Lord (through some vow which will be fatal to me), do unto me whatever thou hast promised, since the victory hath been granted to thee, and revenge of thy enemies."[21] She was so well prepared that she gave up her life without costing him so much as a sigh, and left an immortal bereavement to all the daughters of Israel.

Jonathan was tested by the same fate. And while he regretted the loss of his life, he was going to be sacrificed, if the people had not stayed the hand of his father Saul.[22]

[16] Ibid., 1.
[17] Prov. 1:8.
[18] Prov. 4:3–4.
[19] Prov. 6:20.
[20] Job 1:2,4,5.
[21] Judg. 11:35–36.
[22] 1 Kings 14:43–45.

2nd Proposition
What care of his health the prince must take

"Asa fell sick in the nine and thirtieth year of his reign, of a most violent pain in his feet. And yet in his illness he did not seek the Lord, but rather trusted in the skill of physicians. And he slept with his fathers: and he died in the one and fortieth year of his reign."[23]

God has not condemned medicine, whose author he is. "Honor the physician, he says, for the need thou hast of him: for the most High hath created him. For all healing is from God, and he shall receive gifts of the king. The skill of the physician shall lift up his head, and in the sight of great men he shall be praised. The most High hath created medicines out of the earth, and a wise man will not abhor them . . . God hath made them to be known: and the most High hath given knowledge to men, that he may be honored in his wonders."[24] If you find that knowledge advances slowly, and that not enough remedies to vanquish all ills are being invented, you must put that down to the inexhaustible source of infirmity that is with us. The little that is discovered, however, must stimulate our industry.

God wills, then, that men take advantage of medicine and the study of plants, which "shall allay their pains by sweet confections . . . and of these works there shall be no end"[25] – through the new discoveries which experience brings us to make.

What the Lord forbids is putting one's confidence in them, and not in God, who alone blesses remedies, since he has made them and directs their use. "My son, in thy sickness, neglect not thyself, but pray to the Lord, and he shall heal thee. Turn away from sin (whose avenger thy illness is) . . . Make a fat offering, and then give place to the physician. For the Lord created him (and gives him to thee). Let him not depart from thee, for his works are necessary."[26]

Guard well against viewing him with contempt, in the manner of those who – since it is God alone who holds life and health in his hand – disdain his work. "For there is a time when thou wilt need their help,"[27] and you will be astonished at the accomplishments of a bold and industrious hand.

---

[23] 2 Par. 16:12–13.   [24] Ecclus. 38:1–6.
[25] Ibid., 7.   [26] Ibid., 9–12.   [27] Ibid., 13.

Article VI and Last

The disadvantages and temptations which accompany royalty, and the remedies that one can bring to them

1st Proposition
The disadvantages of sovereign power are revealed, together with the temptations that go with great fortune

There is no truth which the Holy Spirit so inculcated in the history of the people of God, than that of the temptations connected to prosperity and to power.

It is written of the holy King Josaphat "that his kingdom being established in Judah and his glory and his riches being at their peak, his heart took courage for the ways of the Lord, and he took away also the high places and the groves,"[1] where the people sacrificed — something that had been vainly attempted by the pious kings who had preceded him.

There one sees the true feeling that power ought to inspire. But all kings do not resemble Josaphat.

"The kingdom of Roboam, son of Solomon, being strengthened (by the return of several of the ten separated tribes and by other happy successes), he forsook the law of the Lord, and all Israel with him."[2]

Amasias, victorious over the Edomites, adored their gods;[3] so much did great success, which augmented his power, corrupt his heart.

Ozias, so great and so religious a king, "puffed up to his ruin (by his great success and his power) neglected his God, and had a mind to burn incense, threatening the priests"[4] whose honor he was usurping.

The holy King Ezechias could not resist the pleasure of spreading out his glory and riches before the ambassador of Babylon, with an ostentation that God condemned through these harsh words of Isaiah: "Behold the days shall come that all that is in thy house . . .

---
[1] 2 Par. 17:5–6. [2] 2 Par. 11:17; 12:1.
[3] 2 Par. 25:14. [4] 2 Par. 26:1,16ff.

shall be carried into Babylon (to whom you have shown everything with so much complacency); nothing shall be left, saith the Lord."[5] Everything went well for this prince, except for "the temptation which came on the occasion of this embassy: and God permitted it to reveal all the things that might be in his heart, and the pride which lay hidden there."[6]

This judgment makes us tremble. God ordains magnificence in courts, as we have already shown: God has a horror of ostentation and extravagance, without forgiving it in his servants. What attention must a pious king not pay to this matter? What deep reflection must not he entertain, concerning the perilous delicacy of the temptations of which we speak?

St. Augustine based himself on these examples, when he said that there is no greater temptation, even for good kings, than that of power: *Quanto altior, tanto periculosior*.[7]

Saul was chosen by God to be king, who never thought of it; and we have seen elsewhere[8] that at the time they were choosing him he remained hidden in his house.[9] And nonetheless he succumbed to the temptation of power – by disobeying the orders of God in sparing Amalec; by offering the sacrifice without waiting for Samuel, perhaps out of a jealous wish to reign as absolute master, to shake off an irksome yoke; and finally by persecuting to the extreme, in all the borders of the kingdom, David, the most faithful of his servants.[10]

What happened to David himself, and with what excess did he not succumb to the temptation of power? Still he did penance, and covered his ignominy with this good example. But God did not will that we should have any certain knowledge of a comparable conversion in Solomon his son, who was at first the wisest of kings, and later on (in his softness) the most corrupt and the most blind. The temptation of power plunged him into these weaknesses. He adored almost as gods the women who had depraved his heart; and the enormous expenditures which he had to make in contenting their ambition and in erecting so many temples to them, threw so good a king into the

---

[5] 4 Kings 20:16–17.
[6] 2 Par. 32:31.
[7] St. Augustine, *Enarrationes in Psalmos* 137, 9.
[8] 1 Kings 10:2,3.
[9] Ibid., 2,3,9,22,23.
[10] 1 Kings 15:8,9,13,14; 13:8,9; 18; 19; 20.

oppressions which gave way, under his son, to the separation of half the kingdom.

Blinded by the temptation of power, Nabuchodonosor made himself a god, and offered only a fiery furnace to those who refused their adorations to his statue.[11] It was he who, seduced by his own greatness, no longer adored any but himself.

"Is not this the great Babylon which I have built by the strength of my power, and in the glory of my excellence?"[12] Babylon, which saw the whole world under her power, said in the aberration of her pride: 'I am, and there is none else besides me." And again: "I am the queen, the eternal mistress of the universe! I shall not sit as a widow, and I shall not know barrenness."[13]

Another king said to himself, more through his feelings and through his works than through his words: "The river is mine, and I made myself . . . I made this great river, which brings me so many riches."[14] This is what proud kings say when, following the example of a Pharaoh of Egypt, they believe themselves the arbiter of their fate, and act as if they were independent of the orders of heaven, which they have forgotten.

As Antiochus, dazzled by his power, which he believed to be limitless, "opened his mouth against heaven: and attacking the most High by his blasphemies, he wanted to wipe out the holy and to extinguish the sacrifice."[15] One sees him seeming, in his own time, to be a man "who believed that he could make the land navigable, and the sea passable on foot."[16] Thus his audacity undertook everything, and he wanted the world to know no law save his orders. He was, however, the slave of a woman, whom he called Antiochis (after his own name), and saw whole nations rebel against him because they were the prey of a shameless woman, to whom the king gave his provinces.[17]

Herod, on an august throne and dressed in royal garments, let himself be flattered (while he was speaking) "by the acclamations of the people, who cried to him: It is the voice of a god, and not of a man. And forthwith an angel of the Lord struck him . . . and being eaten up by worms he gave up the ghost."[18] As if God, whom he forgot, had wanted to say to him, as well as to this other king: "Wilt thou yet say: I

---

[11] Dan. 3:6.
[12] Ibid., 26–27.
[13] Isa. 47:7–8.
[14] Ezek. 29:3,9.
[15] Dan. 7:25; 8:11–12.
[16] 2 Macc. 5:21.
[17] 2 Macc. 4:30.
[18] Acts 12:22–23.

am a god, thou who art a man and not a god, in the hand of them that slay thee?"[19]

See the unhappy effects of the temptation of power: the forgetting of God, the blinding of the heart, the attachment to one's will – from which follow the refinements of pride and of jealousy, and an empire of pleasures that knows no bounds.

So it was from the beginning. And as soon as there were absolute powers, men feared everything from their passions. "Abram said to Sarai his wife: I know thou art a beautiful woman. And that when the Egyptians shall see thee, they will say: She is his wife: and they will kill me, and keep thee. Say therefore that thou art my sister (as she was in a certain sense). Pharaoh was soon told of the beauty of Sarai: and they used Abram well for her sake. And they gave him flocks and slaves in abundance: and his wife was taken into the house of Pharaoh."[20] Just as much came to Abraham under another king, that is to say Abimelech, King of Gerara in Palestine.[21] And one sees that, after the erection of absolute power, there was no further barrier against it – neither hospitality which was not deceptive nor any certain rampart against shamelessness, nor finally any security for human life.

Let us grant, then, in good faith, that there is no temptation to equal that of power, nor anything so difficult as to refuse oneself something, when men accord you everything, and when they dream only of even exciting your desires.

2nd Proposition
What remedies one can bring to the disadvantages just mentioned

There are those who, struck by these inconveniences, look for barriers to royal power. These they propose as something useful, not only to peoples, but even to kings (whose empire is more durable when it is limited).

I need not enter here either into these conditions or into the different constitutions of empires and of monarchies. This would be to stray from my plan. I shall only observe here, firstly: that God, who knew these abuses of sovereign power, did not fail to establish it in the person of Saul, though he knew that he would abuse it as much as any

---

[19] Ezek. 28:9,23.   [20] Gen. 12:11–15.   [21] Gen. 20:11–12.

king. Secondly: that if these inconveniences should limit government to the point that some would want to imagine, one would have to take it away from the judges chosen every year by the people – since the story of Susannah alone would suffice to show the abuse they make of their authority.

Without, then, tormenting onself vainly with looking in human life for helps which involve no inconveniences, and without examining those which men have invented in the setting up of different governments, one must go straight to the most general remedies, and to those which God himself has ordained to kings against the temptation of power – whose source is the following principle.

3rd Proposition
Every empire must be taken to be under another superior empire, which is the empire of God

"Hear, therefore, ye kings, and understand your duty: learn, ye that are the judges of the earth. Give ear, you that rule the people, and that please yourselves in multitudes of nations: for power is given you by the Lord, and strength by the most High, who will examine your works, and search out your thoughts: because being ministers of his kingdom, you have not judged rightly, nor kept the law of justice, nor walked according to the will of God. Horribly and speedily will he appear to you: for a most severe judgment shall be for them that bear rule. For to him that is little, mercy is granted: but the mighty shall be mightily tormented. For God will not except any man's person, neither will he stand in awe of any man's greatness: for he made the little and the great, and he hath equally care of all. But a greater punishment is ready for the more mighty."[22]

Neither reflection nor commentary is needed. Kings, as ministers of God, who administer his empire, are threatened with good reason for any personal unfaithfulness – with a more rigorous justice and with more exquisite torture. And he is truly asleep who does not awaken at the sound of his thunder.

[22] Wisd. 6:2–9.

4th Proposition
Princes should never lose sight of death, where one sees the imprint of the unavoidable empire of God

"I myself also am a mortal man, like all others (it is thus that eternal wisdom makes Solomon speak). I am of the race of him that was first made of the earth, and in the womb of my mother I was fashioned to be flesh (that is to say infirmity itself). In the time of ten months I was compacted in blood, of the seed of men, and the pleasure of sleep concurring (my conception shows only weakness). And being born I drew in the common air, and fell upon the earth, that is made alike, and the first voice which I uttered was crying, as all others do. I was nursed in swaddling clothes, and with great cares. For none of the kings had any other beginning of birth. For all men have one entrance into life, and the like going out."[23]

This is the law established by God for all mortals: he knows how to make all conditions equal thereby. Mortality, which makes itself felt at the beginning and at the end, throws together the prince and the subject: and the fragile distinction between them is too superficial and too fleeting to merit being counted.

5th Proposition
God gives examples on earth: he punishes through pity

"The prophet Nathan said to David: Thou art the guilty man whose condemnation thou hast just pronounced (in the parable of the ewe-lamb). Thus saith the Lord the God of Israel: I anointed thee king over Israel, and I gave thee the house of your lord with all its goods . . . Why therefore hast thou despised the word of the Lord, to do evil in my sight? thou hast killed Uriah the Hethite with the sword, and hast taken his wife to be thy wife, and hast slain him with the sword of the children of Ammon. Therefore the sword shall never depart from thy house, because thou hast despised me. Thus saith the Lord: Behold, I will raise up evil against thee out of thy own house, and I will take thy wives before thy eyes and give them to thy neighbors (your own son), and he shall lie with thy wives in the sight of the sun. For thou didst it secretly: but I will do this thing in the sight of all Israel, and in the

---

[23] Wisd. 7:1–6.

sight of the sun[24] . . . And because thou hast given occasion to the enemies of the Lord to blaspheme, for this thing, the child that is born to thee (and is so dear to thee) shall surely die."[25]

Everything was fulfilled point by point. Absalom afflicted David with all the evils and all the affronts which the prophet had predicted. David, until then always triumphant and the joy of his people, was obliged to take flight on foot with his followers, before his rebel son: and pursued on his flight by hurling stones, he saw himself reduced to suffering the outrages of his enemies – and, what was still more deplorable, to needing the pity of his servants. The avenging sword still pursued him. Tossed from civil war to civil war, he could only reestablish himself by bloody victories, which cost him the blood he held most dear.[26]

There is the example that God made of a king after his own heart, whose glory he wanted to reestablish through penitence.

6th Proposition
Examples of strict punishments: Saul, the first example

"Whom shall I bring up to thee among the dead?", said the witch whom Saul consulted on the eve of a battle. "Bring me up Samuel, this prince answered. What hast thou seen? I saw gods (something august and divine) ascending out of the earth (and coming out of the hollow of a tomb) . . . What form is he of? An old man cometh up, and he is covered with a mantle. Saul understood that it was Samuel, and he bowed himself with his face to the ground, and adored."[27] It may have been Samuel himself – God permitting it thus to confound Saul through his own desires – or only the image of him. "And Samuel said to Saul: Why hast thou disturbed my rest, that I should be brought up? . . . Why asketh thou me, seeing the Lord has departed from thee, and has gone over to thy rival, for thy disobedience? . . . God will deliver Israel to the Philistines. Tomorrow thou and thy sons shall be with me (among the dead): and the Philistines will cut the army of Israel to pieces."[28]

At this short and terrible judgment, the heart of Saul was struck with terror.[29] The next day the Philistines made a horrible carnage of the whole army, as it had been said: Jonathan and the children of Saul

[24] 2 Kings 12:7–12.   [25] Ibid., 14.   [26] 2 Kings 15; 16; 18; 20.
[27] 1 Kings 28:11ff.   [28] Ibid., 15–19.   [29] Ibid., 15–19.

who fought at his side perished there. This king, as unfortunate as he was impious, killed himself in despair, so as not to fall into the hands of his enemies, and thus passed from temporal to eternal death.[30]

7th Proposition
Second example: Belshazzar King of Babylon

"Belshazzar the king made a great feast ... And being now drunk he commanded that they should bring the vessels of gold and silver which Nabuchodonosor his father had brought away out of the Temple in Jerusalem (as if the wine would have been better and the profanation could have added a new taste). And the king and his nobles and his wives and his concubines drank in them. They drank wine, and praised their gods of gold, and of silver, of brass, of iron and of wood, and of stone. In the same hour there appeared fingers (in the air), as it were of the hand of a man, writing over against the candlestick upon the surface of the wall of the banqueting hall. And the king beheld the joints of the hand that wrote; then was the king's countenance changed, and his thoughts troubled him: and the joints of his loins were loosed, and his knees struck one against the other. And the king cried out: the whole court was frightened; they called in the wise men"[31] (as was the custom).

But none of the wise men could read the writing. They brought in Daniel, as a man who understood the mind of the gods. And this faithful interpreter gave this answer: "King, the most High God raised up Nabuchodonosor, thy father: in his time he did all that he willed on earth. But when his heart was lifted up, and his spirit hardened into pride, he was struck down, and his glory was taken away. His reason was taken from him, and, deposed from his throne, he was ranged with the beasts, eating grass like an ox and wet with the dew of heaven: till he knew that the most High ruled in the kingdom of men, and that he will set over it whomever it shall please him. Thou also his son, O Belshazzar, hast not humbled thy heart, whereas thou knewest all these things; but thou hast profaned the sacred vessels of his Temple, and hast praised thy gods of wood and of metal. Wherefore he hath sent the part of the hand (that appeared in the air) which hath written this that is set down. And this is the writing that is

---

[30] 1 Kings 31:1–4.   [31] Dan. 5:1–7.

written: *Mane*: God hath numbered thy kingdom, and hath finished it. *Thecel*: thou art weighed in the balance, and art found wanting. *Phares*: thy kingdom is divided, and is given to the Medes and Persians."[32]

"The same night Belshazzar was slain, and Darius the Mede was placed on his throne."[33]

8th Proposition
Third example: Antiochus (called the Illustrious), King of Syria

"Antiochus was going through the higher countries of greater Asia: and he heard of the riches of Elymias in Persia, and of its temple, where Alexander, son of Philip King of Macedon, that reigned first in Greece, had left the rich spoil of many vanquished kingdoms. And he approached the city, which he wanted to take by surprise; and beaten by his enemies, he took shameful flight."[34]

"Plunged into deep sadness, he learned at Ecbatana, one of the capitals of his kingdom, of the defeat of his generals (Nicanor and Lysias), whom he had left in Judaea to subjugate it. And swelling with anger he thought to revenge upon the Jews the injury done by them that had put him to flight, threatening to make Jerusalem (in his pride) a common burying-place of the Jews."[35]

While he was breathing out nothing but fire and blood against the Jews, pursued by divine vengeance, he hastened the course of his chariots, and in overturning received some rude blows. The news which reached him, blow by blow, of the ill-success of his plans in Judaea, frightened and troubled him. From the excess of melancholy into which he had been thrown by his mistaken hopes, he fell sick: his sadness renewed itself in a long languor, and he felt himself failing. In the midst of his threatening speeches, God struck him with a hidden wound which caused him intolerable torments. "And indeed very justly, seeing he had tormented the bowels of others . . . he that seemed to command even the waves of the sea, and believed himself above the stars, was carried in a litter, bearing witness to the manifest power of God in himself. So that worms swarmed out of the body of this man . . . The army could not suffer the smell, which became intolerable even to him."[36]

[32] Ibid., 18–28. [33] Ibid., 30–31. [34] 1 Macc. 6:1–4.
[35] 2 Macc. 9:1–4. [36] Ibid., 6–10.

"And he called for all his friends, and said to them: Sleep is gone from my eyes, and I am fallen away, and my heart is cast down for anxiety . . . But now I remember the evils that I have done in Jerusalem, and the unjust pillage of so many riches, and so I have no rest. And behold I perish with great grief in a strange land."[37]

Thus he began to wake up, as from a deep sleep; and in the continual increase of his evils, came back to knowledge of himself: "It is just, he cried, to be subject to God, and that a mortal man should not equal himself to God. Then this wicked man prayed to the Lord, of whom he was not like to obtain mercy. He claimed to make Jerusalem free, which had been the object of his hate. He promised to make the Jews equal with the Athenians – whom he earlier wanted to make a prey to be devoured by the birds and wild beasts. He spoke only of the fine presents which he would give to the holy Temple, and promised to become a Jew, and to go from city to city, and declare the power of God."[38] But he did not receive the pity which he wanted to buy (rather than bend), nor any fruit from a conversion which God (who reads hearts) knew to be deceitful and forced.

"Thus the murderer and blasphemer, being grievously struck, as himself had treated others, died a miserable death in a strange country among the mountains."[39]

It is enough to have reported these sad examples: and we shall be silent about the infinite number of them that remains.

9th Proposition
The prince must respect the human race, and revere the judgment of posterity

While the prince sees himself as the greatest object on earth from the standpoint of the human race, he must revere its opinion, and see in each of the men who look at him an unavoidable witness of his actions and of his conduct.

Above all he must respect the judgment of posterity, which renders the supreme accounting of the conduct of kings. The name of Jeroboam will walk eternally with this infamous notation: "Jeroboam who sinned, and made Israel sin."[40]

The praise of David will always bear this restriction: "Except for

---

[37] 1 Macc. 6:10–13. [38] 2 Macc. 9:11–17.
[39] Ibid., 28. [40] 4 Kings 14:24; 15:9.

the matter of Uriah the Hethite."[41] For David, again, his glory was restored through his remittance: but the penitence of Solomon not being known, he will remain (after so many praises given him by Ecclesiasticus) with this blemish adhering to his name: "O wise one, thou didst bow thyself to women . . . Thou hast stained thy glory, and defiled thy seed; and thy folly hath made thy kingdom to be divided."[42] Nothing wiped out this sin.

And if one wants to take Ecclesiastes as a work expressing the penitence of Solomon, let us at least profit from this admission: "I have surveyed all things with my mind, all the occupations of human life: to know the wickedness of the fool, and the error of the imprudent; and the fruit of my experiences is to have found a woman more bitter than death."[43]

10th Proposition
The prince must respect the future regrets of his conscience

How many times, his heart pierced by compunction, did David not say to himself: Uriah was known as one of the strong men of Israel and as one of the most faithful to his king; nonetheless I deprived him of his honor and his life: "O Lord, deliver me from his blood"[44] (which persecutes me)! The wound which I caused him to receive through the arrows of the Ammonites, while he was fighting in the front ranks in my service, is always open before my eyes: "and my sin is always against me."[45] What would he not have done to deliver himself from this bloody reproach?

May the fear of a similar feeling stay bloody hands, and prevent the deep wound which is made in hearts by the victory of base and shameful passions.

11th Proposition
A reflection which a pious prince should undertake, following the examples which God makes of the greatest kings

Who could tell me, if I were rebellious against the voice of God, that his justice would not place me among that number of unfortunates

---

[41] 3 Kings 15:5. [42] Ecclus. 47:21–23. [43] Eccles. 7:26–27.
[44] Ps. 50:16. [45] Ibid., 5.

whom he uses as an example to others? Does God fear my power? And what mortal is hidden from [divine justice]?

But perhaps it is only against villains that he will exercise his vengeance? No: he blamed David for the numbering of the people, by which this prince seemed only to derive confidence in his forces: and without any other mercy than giving him the option of his torment, he ordered him to choose between famine, war, and the plague.[46] We have just seen Ezechias spread out his riches before the Babylonians, which after all was only ostentation; and nonetheless the Lord told him in punishment through the mouth of his prophet Isaiah: "All these riches of so many kings shall be carried into Babylon; and thy sons shall be eunuchs in the palace of its kings."[47]

It is of the most pious kings that God demands a more complete detachment from their greatness. It is on them that he most harshly avenges the confidence they place in their power, and their attachment to their riches. What will he not do under the new alliance, following the example and the doctrine of the Son of God descended from heaven, to destroy all human greatness?

12th Proposition
Particular reflection on the state of Christianity

Here one must remember the foundation of the whole of Christian doctrine, and the first beatitude that Jesus Christ offers to man, established through these words: "Blessed are the poor in spirit: for theirs is the kingdom of heaven."[48] He expressly does not say: Blessed are the poor: as if, indeed, one cannot be saved if one has a great fortune. But he says: Blessed are the poor in spirit, that is to say, blessed are they who know how to detach themselves from their riches – to deposit themselves before God through a true humility. The kingdom of heaven is bought at this price: and without this despoiling within, the kings of the earth will have no part in the true kingdom, which without doubt is that of heaven.

Nothing suited Jesus Christ so much as to begin, with this saying, the first sermon in which he wanted (so to speak) to offer the plan of his doctrine. Jesus Christ is an humiliated God, a king descended from his throne, who willed to be born poor, of a poor mother, in

---

[46] 2 Kings 24:10–13.   [47] 4 Kings 20:17–18.   [48] Matt. 5:3.

whom he inspired the love of poverty and low birth, as soon as he chose her as his mother. "God, she said, hath regarded the humility and the lowness of his handmaid."[49] It was not only the virtue of this admirable mother that God chose for his son, but also the lowness of her condition. That is why she adds soon after: "He hath scattered the proud in the conceit of their heart: he hath put down the mighty from their seat, and hath exalted the humble: he hath filled the hungry (those who are in need and poverty) with good things, and the rich he hath sent away empty."[50]

The divine mother explains in these few words the whole plan of the Savior. A king such as Jesus Christ, who willed to keep nothing of the external greatness of the many kings who were his ancestors, could propose nothing else in coming into this world than to pull down the powers before his eyes, and to raise up the humble to the highest places in his kingdom.

13th Proposition
One recounts the effort of a pious king to suppress all the feelings that greatness inspires

"Lord, said David, my heart is not exalted: nor are my eyes lofty. Neither have I walked in great matters, nor in wonderful things above me. (I have fought ambitious thoughts: and I have not let myself be possessed by the spirit of greatness and power.) If I was not humbly minded, but exalted my soul (Lord, look on me not). As a child that is weaned is towards his mother, so has my soul been cut off (from the sweetness of human glory, in order to be capable of more solid and substantial nourishment). Let Israel (the true Israel of God, that is to say the Christian) hope in the Lord, from henceforth now and for ever."[51] Let there be no other feeling, neither in the past nor in the present.

This is the life of every Christian, and of kings as well as the others: for they must, like the others, be truly poor in spirit and of heart; and, as St. Augustine said, "they must prefer to the kingdom in which they are alone, that in which they do not fear to have equals."[52]

David, filled with the spirit of the New Testament – under which he already lived through his faith – collected all of these great senti-

[49] Luke 1:48.
[50] Ibid., 51–53.
[51] Ps. 130.
[52] St. Augustine, *De civitate Dei* I, v, xxiv.

ments in one of the smallest of his Psalms: and he offers it to pious kings as sustenance and as discipline.

14th Proposition
Every day, from the morning, the king (under God) must make himself attentive to all his duties

"Give ear, O Lord, to my words, understand my cry. Hearken to the voice of my prayer, O my King and my God. For to thee will I pray: O Lord, in the morning thou shalt hear my voice. In the morning I will stand before thee, and will see: because thou art not a God that willest iniquity. Neither shall the wicked dwell near thee: nor shall the unjust abide before thy eyes. Thou hatest all the workers of iniquity: thou wilt destroy all that speak a lie. The bloody and the deceitful man the Lord will abhor. But as for me in the multitude of thy mercy, I will come into thy house; I will worship towards thy holy Temple, in thy fear. Conduct me, O Lord, in thy justice: because of my enemies, direct my way in thy sight. For there is no truth in their mouth: their heart is vain. Their throat is an open sepulchre (engulf the innocent). They dealt deceitfully with their tongues (through flattering words). Judge them, O God: let them fall from their devices: according to the multitude of their wickednesses cast them out: for they have provoked thee, O Lord. But let all them be glad that hope in thee: they shall rejoice for ever, and thou shalt dwell in them. And all they that love thy name shall glory in thee: for thou wilt bless the just. O Lord, thou hast crowned us, as with a shield of thy good will."[53]

One sees David, so great a king, beginning in the morning (and in the moment when the mind is the most clear and one's thoughts are the most free and pure) to place himself in God's presence, to enter into his temple, to make his adoration and his prayers while thinking of his duties, on the basis of this immutable foundation – that God is a God who hates iniquity (which obliged this prince to suppress it in himself and in others). It is thus that one renews himself every day, and that one avoids forgetting God, which is the greatest of all evils.

---

[53] Ps. 5.

15th and last proposition
The exemplary life of a prince in his private capacity, and the resolutions he must make

"Mercy and judgment I will sing to thee, O Lord: I will sing, and I will understand in the unspotted way, when thou shalt come to me. I walked in the innocence of my heart, in the midst of my house; I did not set before my eyes any unjust thing: I hated the workers of iniquities. The perverse heart did not cleave to me; and the malignant, that turned aside from me, I would not know. The man that in private detracted his neighbor, him did I persecute. With him that had a proud eye, and an unsatiable heart, I would not eat (as a friend). My eyes were upon the faithful of the earth, to sit with me: the man that walked in the perfect way, he served me. He that worketh pride shall not dwell in the midst of my house: he that speaketh unjust things did not prosper before my eyes (my zeal was lighted from morning against the impious). In the morning I put to death all the wicked of the land (I planned their destruction): that I might cut off all the workers of iniquity from the city of the Lord."[54]

It was thus that David spoke as a king zealous for religion and for justice: and by his example he taught kings which counselors, which ministers, which friends and which enemies they ought to have. What a sight, to see the most gentle and the most clement of all princes, from the morning on, in the midst of the spiritual carnage of the enemies of God, when he saw them scandalous and incorrigible! But what a pleasure to consider, in that admirable Psalm, his innocence, his moderation, his integrity, and his justice; [to consider] who he let near him, and whom he kept away; [to consider] his watchfulness over himself, and his zeal against the wicked.

With all these precautions, he fell, and with a terrible fall; so great is human weakness; so dangerous is the temptation of power. How much more exposed are those who are always outside themselves, and who never retire into their conscience! That is the great remedy to temptation of which we speak; and I cannot finish this work better, than by placing in the hands of pious kings the beautiful Psalms of David.

---

[54] Ps. 100.

Conclusion

In what the true happiness of kings consists

Let us learn from St. Augustine, speaking to the Christian emperors, and in their persons to all the princes and all the kings of the earth. This is the fruit and the summary of this discourse.

"When we describe certain Christian emperors as happy, it is not because they enjoyed long reigns; or because they died a peaceful death, leaving the throne to their sons; nor is it because they subdued their country's enemies, or had the power to forestall insurrections by enemies in their own land and to suppress such insurrections if they arose. All these, and other similar rewards or consolations in this life of trouble (which God gives either to make them feel his liberality, or to use as consolation for their miseries) were granted to some of the worshipers of demons, as their due; and yet those pagan rulers have no connection with the Kingdom of God, to which those Christian rulers belong. Their good fortune was due to the mercy of God; for it was God's intention that those who believe in him should not demand such blessings from him as if they represented the highest good. We Christians call rulers happy, if they rule with justice; if amid the voices of exalted praise and the reverent salutations of excessive humility, they are not inflated with pride, but remember that they are but men; if they put their power at the service of God's majesty, to extend his worship far and wide; if they fear God, love him, and worship him; if, more than their earthly kingdom, they love that realm where they do not fear to share the kingship; if they are slow to punish, but ready to pardon; if they take vengeance on wrong because of the necessity to direct and protect the state, and not to satisfy their personal animosity; if they grant pardon not to allow impunity to wrong-doing but in the hope of amendment of the wrong-doer; if, when they are obliged to take severe decisions, as must often happen, they compensate this with the gentleness of their mercy and the generosity of their benefits; if they restrain their self-indulgent appetites all the more because they are more free to gratify them, and prefer to have command over their lower desires than over any number of subject peoples; and if they do all this not for a burning desire for empty glory, but for the love of eternal blessedness; and if they do not fail to offer to their true God, as a sacrifice for their sins, the oblation of humility, compassion, and prayer. It is Christian emperors of this kind whom we call happy; happy in hope, during this present life, and to be happy in reality hereafter, when what we wait for will have come to pass."[55]

---

[55] St. Augustine, *De civitate Dei* I, v, xxiv. The entire conclusion was added to Bossuet's MS by his nephew, the Abbé Bossuet, at the time of publication in 1709. For details see *Les Dernières Années de Bossuet: Journal de Ledieu* [secretary to Bossuet], ed. C. Urbain and E. Levesque (Paris: Desclée de Brouwer, 1928), Vol. I, appendix II, "La *Politique* et la lettre à Innocent XI" (pp. 380ff.).

Index

Abimelech, 338-39
Abraham, xliv, lxi, 14, 42-43, 199, 225, 245, 288, 296-97
Absalom, rebellion against King David, 308-11, 331-32
absolutism, not to be confused with arbitrariness, 263ff.
Achab, 130-31, 254, 265ff.
Adonias, son of King David, 342-43, 367-68
Allemans, Armand Joubert de Lau, Marquis d', Bossuet's letter to, xxviff.
Aman, 94-95, 330ff.
Ambrose, St., kings subject to law, 83-85, 182-83, 284
Antiochus, King of Syria, 1, 73-74, 187ff., 402-403
Aquinas, King of Syria, 1, 73-74, 187ff., 402-403
Aquinas, St. Thomas, does not "privilege" Scripture over philosophy, xvi, xix-xx
Aristotle, Bossuet views his moral theory as "uncertain," xvii; on kingship and tyranny, 68
Arnauld, Antoine, praises Bossuet's *Histoire universelle*, xxiii

Augustine, St., *De civitate Dei* cited, 409-10; his stress on charity diminished by Bossuet, 27; on conquest, 301; on importance of good will in *De Trinitate*, 99; presented by Bossuet as advocate of passive obedience, xxxviii; presented by Bossuet as unequivocal monarchist, xlvi-xlvii, 161, 177; treaties with barbarians valid, 194

Babylon, 247-48
Bayle, Pierre, criticizes uncritical acceptance of Scripture, lxvff.; subordinates Abraham and King David to "equity" and "natural light," lxvff.
Belshazzar, 1, 134, 401-402
Bossuet, Jacques-Bénigne, antirationalism of, xviff., xxiv; *Cinquième avertissement aux Protestants*, xxxvii, xliff., lv; *Conférence avec M. Claude*, xxxix; criticizes Hobbes' social contract theory, lviiff.; criticizes Jurieu's theory of popular sovereignty, xl, lviiiff.; criticizes

411

Index

Bossuet (cont.)
Malebranche's rejection of divine "particular Providence," xxiff.; *Défense de la tradition et des pères*, xxxii; God rules world through *Providence particulière*, xxvff., xxxviff., 250ff.; *Histoire des variations, des églises protestantes*, xxxiv, xxxix; *Histoire universelle*, xvii–xix, xxviii, xxxiv–xxxv, xlii, lxvii; life of, xiii–xv; *Oraison funèbre d'Anne de Gonzague*, xx, xxix; *Oraison funèbre de Nicolas Cornet*, 13 n. 2; *Oraison funèbre de Michel Le Tellier*, liii–liv; *Oraison funèbre de Marie-Thérèse d'Autriche*, xxv–xxvi; Scripture as "perfect," xviii; *Traité du libre arbitre*, xxxvi–xxxviii; treatment of divine-right monarchy, xliff., 57ff., 160ff.; *see also* Louis XIV; monarchy

Buchanan, attacked by Bossuet as defender of regicide, lxiii

Calvin, Jean, criticized by Bossuet, xiv

charity, Augustine's theory of Christian charity versus Jewish law, xxxiii–xxxiv; Bossuet subordinates charity to monarchy and to patriotism, xxx, xxxii, xlvii; Leibniz on justice as "charity of the wise," lxvi–lxvii; St. Paul on charity as first of Christian virtues, xxx

Charlemagne, as respecter of Church's rights, lv, 209, 232–33

Christ, as giver of "new law," xxxii; as king, royally descended from David, xxxivff., xlv, 33; as supporter of passive obedience to established authority, 2, 31ff.; "render to Caesar," xlv, lii, 32, 176, 354; sacrificed by Pontius Pilate, 91–92

Cicero, *De natura deorum*, 193n. 8

civil society, defined by Bossuet, 8ff.

Constantine, Emperor, liii

Cornet, Nicolas, mentor of Bossuet, xiii

coronation-rites of kings of France (*Cérémonial français*), 240ff.

Cromwell, Oliver, viewed as advocate of regicide and popular sovereignty, lxiii

Daniel, sacrificed through weakness of Darius, 90–91, 361–62

Dante, *De monarchia*, lv–lvi

David, King of Israel, as model of kingship, xlvii, lvi, 2, 163ff., 349ff., 357ff., 389ff.; did not act against Saul despite persecution, 59, 172–73, 184ff.; did not pursue his rights violently, 304–307; good judge of men, 119–21, 135–36; his goodness, 77ff.; not permitted to build Temple because of "bloody hands," lvi, 50, 224, 320–21; on importance of David's goodness to the poor, 67; punished for enumerating the Jews, lxviii; repented of his crimes, 73ff., 100–101, 107ff., 255, 395, 399–400, 403–406; treaty-violators harshly punished by him, 341

Index

Descartes, René, Cartesian "method of doubt" decried by Bossuet, xx, xxvii
Diocletian, 140
Douay Bible, lxxiv–lxxv

Esther, Queen, 94–95, 380ff.

Fénelon, François de Salignac de la Mothe de, on quietism and disinterested love of God, xiv
Fronde, Bossuet's fears about, xxix

Gallicanism, Bossuet's defense of, liv–lv
Gerson, Chancellor, *De justitia*, 273
Guyon, Jeanne Marie Bouvier de la Motte, Mme de, xviii

Hegel, G.W.F., on "truth of monarchy," xviii
Herod, King, feared "kingship" of Christ, xlviii, 147, 220-21, 230
Hobbes, Thomas, "covenant" in Bossuet and Hobbes, lxiff.; defender of monarchy through will and consent, lxiff.; *Leviathan*, lxiff.; *Liberty, Necessity and Chance*, lxii
Homer, viewed as monarchist in *Iliad*, xlviii, 46

Innocent XI, Pope, Bossuet's 1679 letter to, xix
Isaiah, on bloody conquerors, 300–301
Israel, Bossuet on Israel as "most just polity that ever was," xix; as "throne of God," 41

Jansenism, xii-xiv

Jeremiah, 89, 171, 197
Jeroboam, 200–201, 244, 403
Jerome, St., lxxiv, 83–84
Joab, 376ff.
Job, as benevolent prince, 66–67, 78–79, 144–45
John the Baptist, 175, 221
Johnson, Dr. Samuel, lxxiv
Josaphat, King of Israel, 111, 122–23, 130–31, 231–32, 299, 316–17, 394
Joshua, as "royal" successor to Moses, 18, 92–93, 315; defender of sanctity of oaths, 242–43
Jude, St., 202
Judith, and Holofernes, 318–19, 379ff.
Julian, "the Apostate," passively obeyed by persecuted Christians, lv, 180
Jurieu, Pierre, as defender of popular sovereignty and social contract, xiv, lvii; *Babylonian Captivity*, lviiff.
just war, motives of, 287ff.
justice, the true nature of a king, 261ff.; must be resolute, 275

Kant, Immanuel, on Cromwell, lxiii
Kelly, George Armstrong, his qualities, xi; as interpreter of Bossuet and Hobbes in *Mortal Politics*, lxi–lxii

Lamartine, on Bossuet as obliging courtier, liv
law, defined by Bossuet, 19ff., 268ff.; of divine origin, 22ff.
Leibniz, G. W., as critic of Bossuet's Scripturalism in *Mars Christianissimus*, lxvi–lxvii; on

Index

Leibniz (cont.)
  justice as "charity of the wise," xxxiii, lxvi
Locke, John, his contractarianism, lxiii
Louis IX, St., xxvi, 258
Louis XIV, as greatest of all kings, liii; as "most just of all kings," 1; as new Constantine–Theodosius following revocation of Edict of Nantes, lii–liv
Luther, Martin, as bad interpreter of Scripture, xiv, xxxix

Maccabees, as great patriots, 29–30, 369ff.; their rebellion divinely authorized but not a precedent for later revolutions, xxxvii–xxxviii, 108–109, 186ff.
Malebranche, Nicolas, argues that Scripture is "full of anthropologies," xxiiff.; rejects divine *Providence particulière* in favor of "Cartesian" general laws, xxiff, lxiv
Milton, John, attacked by Bossuet as advocate of regicide, lxiii
monarchy, absolute but not arbitrary, l–li, 81ff.; divinely ordained beginning with Moses, xlvi, 1–2; hereditary form best, 49ff.; majesty and its adjuncts, 160ff.; monarchy as defender of true religion, 191ff.; monarchy as natural, 46–47; monarchy as paternal, 62ff.; monarchy as "subject to reason," 103ff.
Montesquieu, Charles Secondat, Baron de, *Considerations on the Greatness and Decline of the Romans*, xxviii; *Lettres persanes*, 1
Moses, as establisher of tribunals, 272ff.; as first "king" of Israel, xliv, 278; as founder of perfect politics, 2, 315; as public person without personal satisfaction, 64, 69–70, 181

Nabuchodonosor, 252, 294–95, 396
Nantes, Edict of, Bossuet justifies revocation of, liii–liv
Nehemias, 13, 67–69, 93–94, 228–29, 328, 373ff.

Oakeshott, Michael, on "will and artifice" in Hobbes, lvii

Pascal, Blaise, "God of Abraham, not of philosophers," xx
Paul, St., Acts of the Apostles, 192–94, 211–12; Bossuet views as advocate of passive obedience, xxxv, 58–59; 1 Corinthians, xxix–xxx; Hebrews, 239; Romans, 57–58, 173–74, 345; 1 and 2 Timothy, xviii, 197, 235
Pilate, Pontius, as feeble and unjust ruler, xlviiiff., 91–92, 99
Plato, *Crito* viewed by Bossuet as defense of non-resistance, li–liii; *Republic*, xv–xvi

republicanism, Bossuet's aversion to, xlii–xliii, xlvii–xlviii, 45–46
Roboam, inflexibility led to division of Israel, xxxiv, 97–98, 106–107, 312–14, 351–53, 364ff.
Roman republic, virtues of, 369–70

Index

Rousseau, Jean-Jacques, *La Nouvelle Héloïse*, lxviii

Samson, 323–24
Samuel, faithful to Saul despite crimes, 177–78, 371ff.; loyal to Jews despite ingratitude, 371ff.; viewed by Bossuet as "sovereign judge," xlii–xliv, 59, 371ff.
Saul, King of Israel, good beginning ruined through jealousy of David, 70–72, 149ff., 230, 333–35, 395; his dangerous superstition, 156–57, 400–401
Scripture, as "a perfect book," xxxv; as source of political principles, 1–2
Shklar, Judith, on Bossuet as "Judaizing Calvinist," xi
Simon, Richard, Bossuet criticizes his "Spinozist" reading of Scripture, xiv, xxxix–xl
social contract, defended by Hobbes and Jurieu, lviiff.; rejected by Bossuet, lviiff.

Socrates, as defender of passive obedience in *Crito*, li–lii
Solomon, King of Israel, as magnificent without ostentation, 166, 346ff.; as peaceable builder of Temple, 223, 320–21, 346; as pre-figuration of Christ, lvi; as theorist of "common law of monarchies," xli; "wisest of all kings," xx, 390ff.

Tertullian, on Christian obedience to Roman power in *Apologeticus*, 34–36, 60–61
Themistocles, 12
Titus, ruins the Jews, xxxivff.
Trent, Council of, 236
Truchet, Jacques, on Bossuet's privileging Old Testament over New, xxx–xxxi; on Bossuet's Scripturalism, xvi

war, rules for conduct of, 287ff.

Cambridge Texts in the History of Political Thought
Titles published in the series thus far

Aristotle *The Politics* (edited by Stephen Everson)
Bakunin *Statism and Anarchy* (edited by Marshall Shatz)
Bentham *A Fragment on Government* (introduction by Ross Harrison)
Bossuet *Politics drawn from the Very Words of Holy Scripture* (edited by Patrick Riley)
Cicero *On Duties* (edited by M. T. Griffin and E. M. Atkins)
Constant *Political Writings* (edited by Biancamaria Fontana)
Filmer *Patriarcha and other writings* (edited by Johann P. Sommerville)
Hobbes *Leviathan* (edited by Richard Tuck)
Hooker *Of the Laws of Ecclesiastical Polity* (edited by A. S. McGrade)
John of Salisbury *Policraticus* (edited by Cary Nederman)
Kant *Political Writings* (edited by H. S. Reiss and H. B. Nisbet)
Leibniz *Political Writings* (edited by Patrick Riley)
Locke *Two Treatises of Government* (edited by Peter Laslett)
Machiavelli *The Prince* (edited by Quentin Skinner and Russell Price)
J. S. Mill *On Liberty* with *The Subjection of Woman* and *Chapters on Socialism* (edited by Stefan Collini)
Milton *Political Writings* (edited by Martin Dzelzainis)
Montesquieu *The Spirit of the Laws* (edited by Anne M. Cohler, Basia Carolyn Miller and Harold Samuel Stone)
More *Utopia* (edited by George M. Logan and Robert M. Adams)
Paine *Political Writings* (edited by Bruce Kuklick)